SISTERS OF FORTUNE

Princess Louise: Queen Victoria's Unconventional Daughter
Kleinwort Benson: the History of Two Families in Banking

SISTERS OF FORTUNE

Marianne, Bess, Louisa and Emily Caton

1788–1874

Jehanne Wake

Chatto & Windus
LONDON

Published by Chatto & Windus 2010

2 4 6 8 10 9 7 5 3

Copyright © Jehanne Wake 2010

Jehanne Wake has asserted her right under the Copyright, Designs
and Patents Act 1988 to be identified as the author of this work

First published in Great Britain in 2010 by
Chatto & Windus
Random House, 20 Vauxhall Bridge Road,
London SW1V 2SA

www.rbooks.co.uk

Addresses for companies within The Random House Group Limited can be found at:
www.randomhouse.co.uk/offices.htm

The Random House Group Limited Reg. No. 954009

A CIP catalogue record for this book is available from the British Library

ISBN 9780701173081

The Random House Group Limited supports The Forest Stewardship
Council (FSC), the leading international forest certification organisation. All our titles
that are printed on Greenpeace approved FSC certified paper carry the FSC logo. Our
paper procurement policy can be found at www.rbooks.co.uk/environment

Mixed Sources
Product group from well-managed
forests and other controlled sources
www.fsc.org Cert no. TT-COC-2139
© 1996 Forest Stewardship Council
FSC

Typeset in Goudy by Palimpsest Book Production Limited,
Grangemouth, Stirlingshire

Printed and bound in Great Britain by
Clays Ltd, St Ives plc

To Katie and David

Contents

PART ONE   NORTH AMERICA 1770–1816

PART TWO   FAMILIAR STRANGERS 1816–24

PART THREE   ANGLO-AMERICAN WIVES 1824–34

PART FOUR   HEIRESSES 1834–74

List of Illustrations

Colour Plates

Black and White Plates

Text Illustrations

NOTE: The author and publishers have made every effort to contact the owners of works reproduced: we apologise for any omissions, and would be grateful for further information.

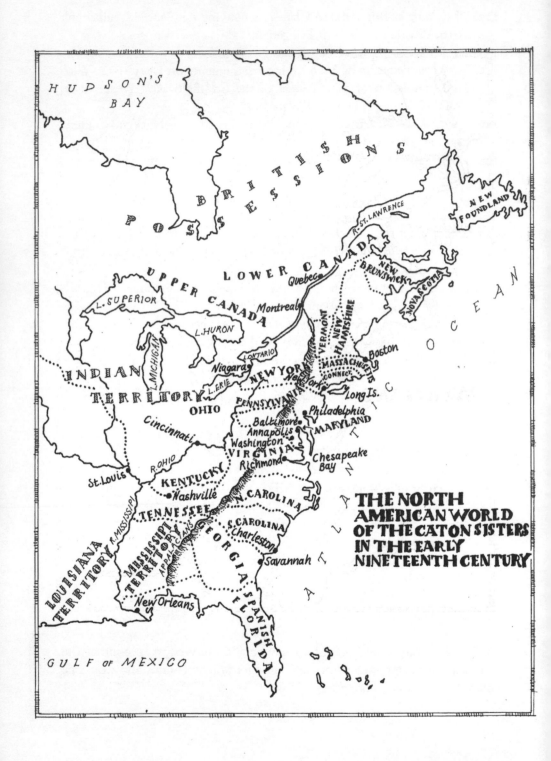

THE NORTH
AMERICAN WORLD
OF THE CATON SISTERS
IN THE EARLY
NINETEENTH CENTURY

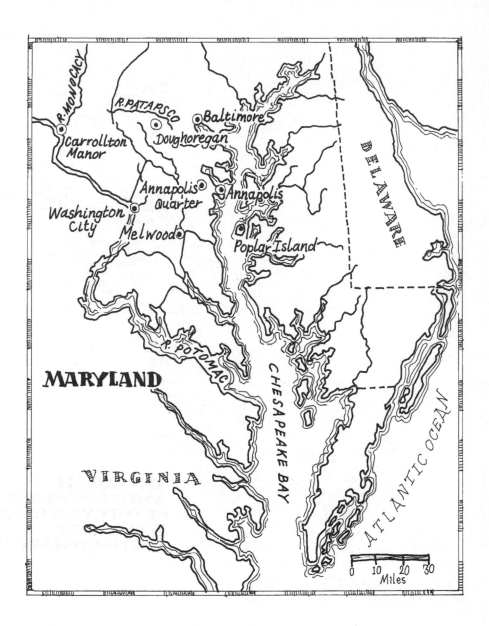

R.MONOCACY

R.PATAPSCO

Baltimore

Doughoregan

Carrollton
Manor

DELAWARE

Annapolis
Quarter

Annapolis

Washington
City

Melwood

Poplar Island

R. POTOMAC

MARYLAND

CHESAPEAKE BAY

ATLANTIC OCEAN

VIRGINIA

0   10   20   30
Miles

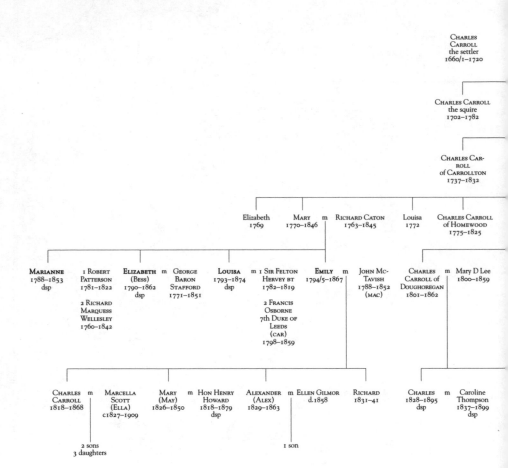

CHARLES
CARROLL
the settler
1660/1–1720

CHARLES CARROLL
the squire
1702–1782

CHARLES CAR-
ROLL
of CARROLLTON
1737–1832

Elizabeth
1769

MARY   m   RICHARD CATON
1770–1846   1763–1845

Louisa
1772

CHARLES CARROLL
of HOMEWOOD
1775–1825

MARIANNE
1788–1853
dsp

1 ROBERT
PATTERSON
1781–1822

2 RICHARD
MARQUESS
WELLESLEY
1760–1842

ELIZABETH
(BESS)
1790–1862
dsp

m   GEORGE
BARON
STAFFORD
1771–1851

LOUISA
1793–1874
dsp

m 1 SIR FELTON
HERVEY BT
1782–1819

2 FRANCIS
OSBORNE
7th DUKE OF
LEEDS
(CAR)
1798–1859

EMILY   m
1794/5–1867

JOHN MC-
TAVISH
1788–1852
(MAC)

CHARLES   m   Mary D Lee
CARROLL of   1800–1859
DOUGHOREGAN
1801–1862

CHARLES
CARROLL
1818–1868

m   MARCELLA
SCOTT
(ELLA)
c1827–1909

MARY
(MAY)
1826–1850

m   HON HENRY
HOWARD
1818–1879
dsp

ALEXANDER
(ALEX)
1829–1863

m ELLEN GILMOR
d.1858

RICHARD
1831–41

CHARLES
1828–1895
dsp

m   Caroline
Thompson
1837–1899
dsp

2 sons
3 daughters

1 son

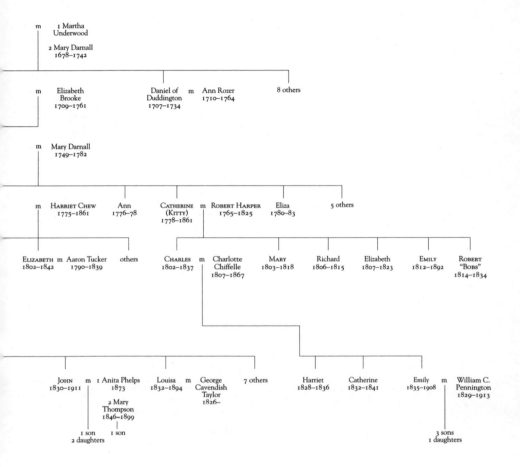

m   1 Martha
     Underwood

2 Mary Darnall
1678–1742

m   Elizabeth   Daniel of   m   Ann Rozer   8 others
     Brooke   Duddington   1710–1764
     1709–1761   1707–1734

m   Mary Darnall
     1749–1782

m   HARRIET CHEW   Ann   CATHERINE   m   ROBERT HARPER   Eliza   5 others
     1775–1861   1776–78   (KITTY)   1765–1825   1780–83
                                     1778–1861

ELIZABETH m Aaron Tucker   others   CHARLES   m   Charlotte   MARY   Richard   Elizabeth   EMILY   ROBERT
1802–1842   1790–1839   1802–1837   Chiffelle   1803–1818   1806–1815   1807–1823   1812–1892   "BOBS"
                                                     1807–1867   1814–1834

JOHN   m 1 Anita Phelps   Louisa   m   George   7 others   Harriet   Catherine   Emily   m   William C.
1830–1911   1873   1832–1894   Cavendish   1828–1836   1832–1841   1835–1908   Pennington
                                          Taylor   1829–1913
           2 Mary   1826–
           Thompson
           1846–1899

   1 son   1 son   3 sons
2 daughters   1 daughters

Prologue

On a wet June afternoon in 1816 a capacious carriage-and-four bowled along the leafy western highway, paused briefly at the Hyde Park toll gate, and entered London. Driving past Apsley House, the coachman turned the horses into Piccadilly and pulled up outside the bow windows of the Pulteney Hotel. Two drenched footmen clambered down from the rumble seat at the back and opened the carriage doors, whereupon three ladies and a gentleman were handed out and greeted by a respectful hotel manager. The beautiful American Caton sisters Marianne, Bess and Louisa, with their escort, Marianne's husband Robert Patterson, had safely completed their long journey from Maryland in North America.

The arrival of the sisters passed unnoticed as the fashionable world was engrossed in the gaieties of the Season. Yet, within a week of arriving in Town, the unknown Caton sisters were transformed from 'insignificant' foreigners into society favourites. Marianne, in particular, had a remarkable effect upon the susceptibilities of Regency high society. The nation's hero, the Duke of Wellington, whose good looks and military fame conquered many female hearts, was so overcome by her charm that 'he fell violently in love with her'. To be seen with or singled out by the Duke endowed any woman with social prestige; 'his conversation conferred distinction, his wish was law'. London soon echoed with her name and she became the latest Regency celebrity. At the crowded routs and balls everyone wanted to gaze upon Marianne, 'who is making the greatest sensation in all fashionable circles', the American attaché declared. 'It's impossible to describe the effect produced by her entrance.' Everywhere she went, comments were whispered: 'How beautiful!' 'How charming,' 'And her sisters, how pretty, how amiable!' – followed by the two questions of overriding importance: 'Who are they?' and 'What is their fortune?'[1]

These were the two questions that I also asked as I sat in the archives of ING Barings Bank in London seven years ago. My interest was in moneyed women in the nineteenth century and the long-held assumption that 'they cannot understand investments' and had no interest in finance and the stock market. I was reading through a collection of letters concerning women clients when I came across a letter written by an E. Caton. It was extraordinary. Her voice was so vivid and beguiling, so intelligent and authoritative – on the subject of investments and speculations, no less. Then I heard it again when, using words familiar today as the jargon of the global financial markets, she advised a female friend to buy bonds as 'if peace continues the fives will rise above a hundred & one wd now get very nearly 5 & ½ pr Ct interest buying at 92'. She was writing not in the early twenty-first century but in the early nineteenth-century. I was intrigued. Who was she and how did she come to be active in the Regency stock market?[2]

I discovered references to her and her sisters in two books published in America before the First World War, *Dames and Daughters of the Young Republic* by Geraldine Brooks and *Romantic Days in the Early Republic* by Mary C. Crawford. They had also been written about in Britain in 1916: *A Painter of Dreams, and Other Biographical Studies* by A. M. W. Stirling contains a chapter about 'the dazzling triumph of the three American Graces' who were 'favourites of destiny'. There is no echo in any of these books, however, of the voice I heard in The Barings Archive. To catch it again I followed the trail of the sisters' letters back to Maryland.

Marianne, Bess, Louisa and Emily belonged to one of the first families of America. They were the granddaughters of Charles Carroll of Carrollton, a rich landowner and planter who was a Signer of the Declaration of Independence, along with such famous founding fathers as Washington, Adams, Jefferson and Madison. At the time of the 50th anniversary of the Declaration in 1826, Carroll of Carrollton was the sole survivor of the 56 Signers, and sons, towns and counties throughout America were named in his honour. The four sisters passed their early life with their grandfather, and Emily most of her adult life as well, so that they grew up with impeccable connections and, living near the new capital, Washington City, socialised with the elite families of the early Republic.

Born in the years after the American Revolution, the sisters were, nevertheless, aristocrats in republican America. After the Revolution, there were no titles of nobility, no English laws of entail and primogeniture and no *de jure* aristocracy as in Britain. Instead, as one Philadelphian pointed out in 1821, there was a *de facto* aristocracy and 'the power thus enjoyed by blood, riches, and by learning is as extensively exercised'. Their grandfather perceived himself to be an aristocrat and, as the term in America continued to convey an ideal of social distinction, wealth and refinement, so were his granddaughters.[3]

They were heiresses of American independence in more ways than one. Washington told a fellow gentleman planter in 1790 that Carroll of Carrollton was 'the most moneyed man' he knew; indeed, the Carroll estates were still said to be the largest in the union in 1816. He was generous to his granddaughters, providing them with ample funds and dowries so that they had an independence which most women could only aspire to before the Married Women's Property acts (started state by state from 1839 in the USA and in 1870 in Great Britain). They were also co-heirs with their cousins of the vast Carroll estates and each was left an independent fortune.[4]

Yet the sisters conducted their lives in a manner quite at odds with traditional accounts of early nineteenth-century heiresses. They actively managed their fortunes, speculated on the stock market and made informed investment decisions. As part of an Anglo-American network of female investors, they used their contacts in high society to find out the latest political and financial news at balls and routs. They show that women on both sides of the Atlantic were not always segregated from the male-driven world of money. Their female circle thought and conversed about money and participated in the public realm of finance and politics, not as some extraordinary activity but as part of daily life – in the same way rich men did. Where they differed was in having first, to protect their fortunes from predatory male hands through trusts, and second, to keep investments if married in the name of a single or widowed sister or female friend.

The sisters' effect upon the fashionable world was not so surprising; they were, after all, heiresses – a pre-eminent attribute in English society. They have been called Dollar Princesses because three married English peers, though two earlier such unions occurred in 1783 and 1789 and the transatlantic exchange of American wealth for British titles would not become commonplace until the late nineteenth century. Nevertheless, as the diarist Thomas Raikes noted: 'It is a singular instance of three sisters, foreigners, and of a nation hitherto little known in our aristocratical circles, allying themselves to such distinguished families in England.' They differed, though, in crucial respects from the later Dollar Princesses, such as Consuela Vanderbilt. In the first place they were Old Money, patricians of a landowning family long settled in Maryland and, unlike the rich of the later Gilded Age, they abided by the Carroll family maxim: avoid 'shew of any Sort'. In the second place, far from being the pawns of a scheming mother, forced into loveless marriages to satisfy social ambition, all the sisters fell in love and decided to marry independently of their parents, a state of affairs at odds with prevailing mores of parental authority on both sides of the Atlantic. The Caton sisters were far too independent-minded to be married off against their wishes; Bess announced firmly that she had no intention of marrying except for love while Emily married a comparative stranger. Their story is, in part, about the exhilarating freedom of being independent and deciding whom to love in a world where women were usually unable to choose. And it is also about the blindness of love and having to live with the consequences.[5]

The sisters' family letters form the backbone of this book. The waters of the Atlantic had been closed to tourists during the long Napoleonic wars and when Marianne, Bess and Louisa arrived in England, they were thought remarkable for not being 'wild savages'. Their letters home offer a unique view of fashionable society, which swept them into a glittering world from which most other Americans were excluded. They reveal the patronising, if not hostile, British view of Americans and provide illuminating material about Anglo-American relations in that era. The sisters' affection for each other remained strong throughout the long years of exile and unhappiness, their devotion acting as an amulet against British condescension and the envy of their own compatriots.

The story of the four Caton sisters – Marianne gentle and beautiful, Bess indecisive and independent, Louisa fashionable and businesslike, and Emily practical and domestic – begins in the 1770s in colonial America when their grandfather risked a family fortune by becoming an American revolutionary, and ends in 1874 in Victorian Britain when Louisa's fortune sustained one of the Dukedoms of England. Restricted as they were by law and convention, their attempts to participate in the male-dominated worlds of politics and finance and to make their own decisions ran against the grain of their time and are still relevant today.

PART I
North America 1770–1816

It is of the utmost importance, that the women should be well instructed in the principles of liberty in a republic.

Maxims for Republics, 1787

Persons of discernment perceive nothing of higher importance to a nation, than the Education, the Habits, and the Amusements of the Fair Sex.

Lady and Gentleman's Pocket Magazine, 1796

I

A Revolutionary Heritage

It is likely that all four sisters were born at Carroll House in Annapolis, the capital of the southern state of Maryland, on the east coast of North America. It was their mother's favourite house and Marianne, the eldest, was born here on 18 August 1788. 'My darling, precious MaryAnne' was, their affectionate mother believed, always 'more of a saint than anyone I know'. Neither the birth in 1790 of Elizabeth, called Bess by her sisters, nor the arrival of Louisa in 1793 nor Emily in about 1795/6 displaced her central and steadying influence. Where her siblings could be opinionated and rash, she was discreet and measured; where they could be flighty and foolish, she remained serene and sensible. Yet her humility and intelligence made them cherish her – 'my beloved', 'my angelic one' they would croon.[1]

The girls were Anglo-American, their father Richard Caton being English and their mother Mary Carroll an American, but their young lives were shaped entirely by her family, the Carrolls. Unlike most children born in Annapolis at the end of the eighteenth century, the sisters were fifth-generation Marylanders. The room at Carroll House that spoke most of the past to them was the family's private chapel, resonant with the whisperings and confidences of their ancestors. There they were baptised Catholics by their grandfather's cousin, the Reverend John Carroll, consecrated in 1789 as the first Catholic bishop in the United States.

The sisters' faith and revolutionary inheritance were of paramount influence upon their identity, character and upbringing. It was primarily for religious reasons that their family had settled in the English colony of Maryland, founded in 1632. Their earlier history lay in Ireland – Carroll forebears were ancient Irish chiefs of the Gaelic clan of O'Carroll, descended from Cearbhaill, a ninth-century king of Eile, and the princes of Ely O'Carroll (Eile Ur Chearbhaill), an area that today encompasses South Offally and North Tipperary.[2]

The sisters' great-great-grandfather Charles Carroll the Settler, an 'urbane and erudite young man' received the commission of Attorney-General of Maryland in 1688 and sailed for Chesapeake Bay just before the Glorious

Revolution that brought William and Mary to the throne and led to the slaughter of many Irish Catholics. From '"Sivilite" or Civility', the leading chief of the Susquehannocks, and six other 'Kings and rulers of the Five Nations', Carroll the Settler purchased 'a lycense to take up his Tract of Land in the ffork of the Patowmeck and Monockesey' rivers. This land would become the family's most productive estate, Carrollton Manor, and would later be inherited by the sisters and their cousins.[3]

The Bay and its waterways abounded in fish and waterfowl; the forests were rich in game and berries; the cleared land yielded wonderful harvests of corn and apple and, most importantly, tobacco. Chesapeake tobacco plantations became the jewels of England's trade empire, enabling gentlemen planters such as the Carrolls to become exceedingly rich. Carroll the Settler added to his fortune and influence by marrying two rich wives in succession, first a landed widow and then the fifteen-year-old Mary Darnall, daughter of Maryland's most powerful Catholic as cousin and agent of Lord Baltimore, the colony's Proprietor. Although religious liberty vanished after the Protestant majority staged a political and religious coup against Lord Baltimore's government, when the Settler died on 1 July 1720 he owned nearly 48,000 acres, with warrants for another 20,000 acres. This was the largest personal estate ever probated in Maryland, valued at up to £30,000.[4]

It was inherited by his son, the sisters' great-grandfather – also called Charles, as all the subsequent eldest Carroll sons were. In contrast to the Settler, he was known as the Squire and was the builder of Carroll House (1723–30). His house still stands on a peninsula commanding 'a delightful prospect' across Carroll's Creek, now Spa Creek, which meanders among wooded islets to join the fast-flowing waters of Severn River, and away to the undulating hills of the eastern shore of Chesapeake Bay. Throughout most of the eighteenth century, Annapolis was Maryland's premier port. Ships loaded with iron from the Baltimore Company, the profitable iron-works that the Carrolls financed in 1731, passed through on their way to English markets, from which they returned carrying tea, sugar, wines and other goods. Tall square-riggers lay in the Creek, waiting to carry the hogsheads of Carroll tobacco on consignment to England and bring back the latest fashionable items.

Annapolis was 'one of the most sparkling communities of British America', accommodating the British Provincial Governor, his officials and court, and lawyers pleading in the colonial court. While the legislature was in session, all the plantocracy – wealthy Maryland and Virginian plantation families – came for the winter season. The end of the eight years' French and Indian Wars, in 1763, brought unprecedented prosperity, seen in the fine brick mansions, garden squares and cobbled lanes winding down to the waterfront. These are much the same today as when the Carroll women

Carroll House, Annapolis, Maryland. Detail from a lithograph of Annapolis by Sachse, Baltimore. The family lived here during the winter season, November to May.

stepped away 'in such a mincing gait in shoes of many colours with formidable points at the toes and high tottering heels delicately cut in wood'.[5]

The Squire's only son, the sisters' grandfather, was called Charley when young. He became the most formative influence in their lives; they lived for most of the year with him, were guided by his judgement and taste and loved him dearly. Born in 1737, Charley began an educational odyssey when, aged ten, he started at the Jesuit College of St Omer in Flanders before taking a degree at the Collège Louis-le-Grand in Paris. Legal studies took him to England in 1759. Four years later, while studying law at the Middle Temple, he was painted by Joshua Reynolds. The arresting portrait shows an assured young man with what Marianne would describe as, 'that look at once intelligent and expressive' in his fine grey eyes. His return home in 1764 was celebrated by the Squire with a handsome gift: 'not only 40,000 pounds but the whole of my Father's estate is at my disposal,' Charley informed a friend on 15 September 1765, 'we are and we like to continue, on the best terms, never a Father & Son were on better.' To distinguish himself from his father and cousins, Charley took the name of the most productive plantation, the 12,000 acre Carrollton Manor estate, and always signed himself Charles Carroll of Carrollton.[6]

In 1768 he married his second cousin Molly Darnall, who had grown up in the care of the Squire, after her father ran through the family fortune, leaving her abandoned mother penniless. This Carroll wedding established romantic love as the basis for future family marriages. When Carroll of Carrolton declared of Molly: 'I prefer her thus unprovided to all the women

I have ever seen', he was overriding the normal criteria of fortune and rank in favour of personal attraction. The memory of the Darnall women's powerlessness and destitution also led Carroll of Carrollton to take a most unusual step. Determined that the women of his family would never have to suffer a similar fate, he settled independent fortunes upon his daughters and granddaughters. These would be legally protected to ensure that the Caton sisters held their wealth free from the control of, and watertight against possible attempts to gain access by, their husbands and male relations.[7]

The young married couple improved their house and ordered items from London such as two carved and gilded pier glasses – 'of a solid kind, it has been found by experience that slight carving will neither endure the extremes of heat or cold nor the rough treatment of negro servants', books 'of the best Editions' for their library and an expensive carriage. Two pleasure pavilions were built at either side of the terraced gardens, projecting from the sea wall out over the water, and the sisters loved to sit here and sketch and gossip in the late spring sunshine. They learned, however, always to avoid 'shew', for it was considered to be the epitome of vulgarity. 'Enjoy yr Fortune, keep an hospitable table,' the Squire encouraged Molly and Charley in 1772. 'But lay out as little money as Possible,' he ordained, in 'shew of any Sort'. Hospitality, though, was essential for their rank and the more generous the better in the mind of the South. The Carroll family always kept an excellent table, offering such delicacies as truffles and chocolates as well as the finest imported champagne and wines.[8]

Carroll House was thus well equipped to receive the fashionable world. The Season's rituals hardly changed from their grandmother Molly's day in the 1770s to their own in the 1800s. It began with Race Week in the late autumn, much enjoyed by their grandfather who was a keen rider and a breeder, having brought two mares back with him from England. He joined the Maryland Jockey Club in 1772, entering his chestnut stallion Marius in the two-mile heats the following year. As the Annapolis racecourse was judged 'the best in the country' it attracted racegoers from neighbouring colonies who also enjoyed the whirl of routs, balls and plays. One of the plantocracy who regularly attended and socialised with the Carrolls was George Washington. '27. Dined at Mr Carroll's and went to the ball' Washington laconically recorded in his diary in 1771. Molly shone at such gatherings and her sociability and ease in company were undoubted assets to Charley as he assumed a more public role in Maryland, a role that was to become dramatically prominent during the American Revolution.[9]

One of Marianne's most treasured memories was of being taken to see the place where her grandfather burned the tobacco, rather than let it fall into the hands of the English. She valued her revolutionary heritage, she said,

'more than she would the proudest heraldry'. The War of Independence
'with all its dangers' was 'deeply riveted' in her grandfather's recollection;
as a family friend confirmed, 'often have I heard him tell, with an eye
flashing with enthusiasm, of the destitute state of the country, of the want
of troops, of discipline, of ammunition, of everything, when the first Congress
declared the Colonies independent.'[10]

As Catholics the Carrolls were political outcasts, barred from even paltry
office and intermittently threatened with compulsory land seizure by jealous
petty officials of such 'Malice that they would not only deprive us of our
Property but our lives', according to the Squire. Less than 10 per cent of
the population in Maryland were Catholics but ten of the largest twenty
fortunes belonged to the long-settled Catholic gentry, a statistic resented
by the Protestant majority. How then did Carroll of Carrollton become a
welcomed member of the Protestant revolutionary leadership?[11]

During the agitation leading up to the American Revolution, local newspapers shaped as well as reflected public thought, acting as a medium for
political exchange. The *Maryland Gazette* publicised the British Governor
Eden's peremptory proclamation of an increase in the rate of fees charged
for government services but also published the vociferous opposition to this
'robbery'. With elections scheduled for spring 1773, a January issue published
a defence of Eden's proclamation by an official, Daniel Dulany, as 'Second
Citizen'. On 4 February someone using the pseudonym 'First Citizen' struck
back in a stinging, erudite letter declaring that the fees were a tax in all
but name: as such, they could be regulated only by the general assembly
not the Governor, whose action was therefore arbitrary and invalid. The
public adopted 'First Citizen' as a people's hero, a rallying point for anti-
British government sentiment, and political support quickly followed after
a congratulatory address to 'First Citizen' from two representatives of the
lower house of the colony's Assembly. The celebrity made anonymity impossible to retain. 'I did not write for reputation,' Charley Carroll declared,
'but to instruct my countrymen, & to apprise them of the pernicious designs
of Government.' He gathered supporters in a new political group, the
Popular Party. Although Dulany's party tried to rouse anti-Catholic hostility,
at the Assembly elections in May 1773 the Popular Party won control of
the lower house. Yet, as penal laws against Catholics still existed, Charley
was the only leading member ineligible for the Assembly.[12]

The year of 1774 proved a watershed for colonial America. In May, the
British Parliament imposed military rule on the colony of Massachusetts
and closed the port of Boston until it paid for the destroyed East India tea.
Anti-British meetings were convened throughout the colonies. 'All America
is in a flame!' exclaimed William Eddis, a British office-holder, on 28 May
1774. In Maryland the politicians overthrew Governor Eden and his officials.

Future elections would thus fall outside English law and not be subject to penal restrictions on Catholics. Carroll of Carrollton was elected to the Assembly and was appointed a member of the Anne Arundel County and Annapolis Committee of Correspondence, formed to join other colonies in opposing new British taxes. He was a committed Patriot, affirming on 7 September 1774 'I will either endeavour to defend the Liberties of my country, or die with them: this I am convinced is the sentiment of every true & generous American.'

After a British garrison in Boston, in searching for arms caches, opened fire on a group of 'Minute Men' (volunteer farmers) in Lexington and then Concord in April 1775, civil war appeared inevitable. Nicholas Cresswell, an Englishman travelling through Maryland that spring, found 'the people arming and training in every place. They are all liberty mad.' Carroll was trying to raise a militia in Annapolis as volunteers from each colony joined General Washington's new Continental Army (the Patriot or pro-Independence army) based in Cambridge, Massachusetts, and that autumn Generals Arnold and Montgomery began the first offensive of the Revolutionary War, to try to cut off British troops in Canada and take Quebec.[13]

In February 1776 the Second Continental Congress appointed Carroll of Carrollton to join Benjamin Franklin, a Philadelphia delegate, Samuel Chase, a Maryland colleague, and his cousin John Carroll on a diplomatic mission to Montreal to persuade British Canadians to support the American cause. Although the mission failed, Charley's reputation was enhanced and he was elected on 4 July to represent Maryland at the Second Continental Congress, the first Catholic ever to serve as a member of congress. Then, on 2 August 1776, he was present for the initial signing of the Declaration of Independence.

None of the signatories were aware that by this act they had stepped into posterity's spotlight as America's revolutionary elite although they knew that taking-up arms against their king, George III, was a treasonable offence. When John Hancock, President of the Continental Congress, pronounced, 'There must be no pulling different ways We must all hang together', Franklin reportedly replied, 'Yes, we must, indeed, all hang together, or most assuredly we shall all hang separately.' They were preoccupied with creating a confederation of states out of the thirteen former colonies and with fighting a war. Carroll was on the Board of War and Ordnance, wrestling with the task of helping Washington organise a novice rebel force capable of defeating the experienced British army. He later told Marianne that 'it was not my wish or design to strip England of her influence & powers, which hereafter might be useful to us & to others, but to rid the colonies from a church establishment, and to separate them for ever from England and its

Congress voting for Independence July 1776 by Edward Savage. The two figures seated in the foreground with their backs turned are, on the left, Benjamin Franklin and, on the right, Charles Carroll of Carrollton.

government unacquainted with our habits and manners and from distance of situation incapable of ruling justly & fairly.'[14]

The American Revolution was also a central event for Molly and their daughter Mary, the sisters' mother. Mary grew up in the disruption of nearly eight years' of civil war, with Loyalist (pro the British Crown) fighting Patriot (pro American Independence) and families torn apart supporting opposing sides. In March 1775, when Mary was five, the Carroll male line was secured by the birth of Charles Carroll Jr 'the finest Boy in the World' their relieved mother declared. She was pregnant again when, early the following year, she and her infants fled Annapolis after reports arrived of the blockade of Chesapeake Bay by British men-of-war. In the event the British never bothered with Carroll House on their numerous raids along the Bay, preferring to damage another Carroll property, the 1000-acre Poplar Island to the south.[15]

Carroll's wartime duties kept him from home for extended periods. From Philadelphia or York came requests to 'kiss little Poll for me & tell her to mind her book & to be a good girl.' Mary was a merry child 'of a sweet & lively temper' with thick dark curly hair, large dark eyes and later a 'wondrous' charm of manner. She would always hold first place in her father's heart. 'I really miss you,' he would write fifty years' later. 'I have met with severe trials, but were I to lose you, it would be the severest of all I have felt.'[16]

As the war turned against them Carroll worked closely with Washington to obtain extra supplies and funding. His fluent French proved useful as well. France had been secretly supplying arms and money to the Patriots since May 1776, hoping to avenge its defeat by Britain in the Seven Years War, and French officers were now openly joining the Continental Army. The Marquis de Lafayette, smitten with the concept of American liberty, was only nineteen when he travelled to America to offer his services to his hero General Washington in 1777 and he thereafter worked tirelessly to obtain France's support. In February 1778 Louis XVI signed a military treaty of alliance and a commercial treaty. When Spain in 1779 and the Dutch in 1780 joined France, Britain was outnumbered at sea and her entire empire was menaced as French forces struck at India and the West Indies.

The war work of their grandmother Molly was important in nurturing a female devotion to the public good, that 'germ of virtue' extolled by Thomas Jefferson, that would be inculcated in republican women of the sisters' generation. Ten years earlier women had to offer profuse apologies if they so much as mentioned politics. Yet, as the colonies rebelled, women were not only talking about politics – 'As we cannot be indifferent,' pointed out a group of North Carolina women, 'on any occasion that appears nearly to affect the peace and happiness of our country' – but being forward with their opinions. Carroll's letters home about politics and war were, he told his father the Squire, 'for Molly as well as you, for I find she is become a politician & has given me a good acct of the proceedings in & about Annapolis.'

The first women's national fund-raising campaign in American history began in 1780 in Philadelphia, when Esther De Berdt Reed published a broadside *The Sentiments of an American Woman*. She asked women to renounce 'vain ornaments' and donate the money, otherwise spent on fashionable clothing and hairdressing, to those 'valiant defenders of America' the Patriot troops. Networks of ladies could canvass door-to-door to collect subscriptions. Any man who truly understood the soldiers' desperate needs, Reed wrote, could only 'applaud our efforts for the relief of the armies which defend our lives, our possessions, our liberty'.

The response was immediate. By 5 July the drive was underway in Maryland. Molly became a county Treasuress and set about the 'unfeminine' task of publicly collecting money, organising the rota of collections and keeping records of the contributions to be sent to Martha Washington. 'Of all the absurdities the Ladies going about for money,' sneered some female friends, for 'people were obliged to give them something to get rid of them'. John Hanson, a Maryland delegate whose wife had been canvassed, wrote hoping 'Mrs Carroll will Succeed to the Utmost of her Wishes in the laudable Business she is at present engaged in.' This she certainly did. *The Maryland Gazette* announced on 14 July that her county alone had subscribed more than $16,000 in paper and specie (coin money) sums. Washington insisted the money be used to provide soldiers with decent shirts and, after over two thousand had been delivered by December, he assured the ladies' committee that their 'love of country is blended with those softer domestic virtues'. [17]

At the end of March 1781, the Carrolls were at Carroll House when they learned that British ships had once again visited their Poplar Island estate. Yet Maryland, often threatened with attack and sandwiched between battle-torn Pennsylvania and Virginia, miraculously saw neither battle nor occupation. Elsewhere in the South, British forces had become aggressively destructive in their slow advance northwards. As the war entered its sixth year the overstretched, undernourished Americans were becoming desperate. 'We are at the end of our tether,' Washington admitted that spring, 'now or never our deliverance must come.'[18]

Early on 30 March 1781, four French regiments of about 1200 Continental Light Infantrymen were camped in the fields on the other side of Carroll's Creek. A space had been cleared for an altar and, as Mass was celebrated, the family could hear the chant of a thanksgiving *Te Deum*. Later that morning, the tall, thin figure of Major-General the Marquis de Lafayette escorted by his officers called to pay his respects to Monsieur and Madame Carroll and attend Mass in the Carroll chapel. Resplendent in fresh white and green uniforms, gold epaulettes and buttons glinting, the elegant, heroic Frenchmen bowed their way into the hearts of female company in Annapolis, just as they had in Philadelphia and Newport. ''Tis all marquesses, counts &c,' agreed Mrs Ogle, a friend of the Carrolls. 'The divine Marquis de Lafayette is in town, and is quite the thing. We abound in French officers – But the Marquis – so diffident, so polite, in short everything that is clever.' [19]

Lafayette had returned from Paris the previous year with the promise of further French support and, in May 1780, 6,500 soldiers commanded by the Comte de Rochambeau had sailed from France. This was the deliverance for which Washington and patriot America had waited. Lafayette's halt in Annapolis almost a year later was short, though he dined at Carroll House on 4 April before breaking camp to join the small Army of the South in Virginia. When they received reports on 15 August 1781 of the French fleet's imminent arrival in Chesapeake Bay, Rochambeau and Washington dashed southwards to join the attack on Lord Cornwallis's army trapped at Yorktown. After five days of fierce bombardment Cornwallis surrendered. At a cost of over 25,000 military deaths, the American struggle for independence was over. On 19 October 1781,

Washington's ADC rode like the devil to carry the signed Articles of Capitulation to the Continental Congress up in Philadelphia. On 20 October, Carroll of Carrollton, ever the 'First Citizen', announced the news to the public in Annapolis. As Thomas Paine had hoped, 'the birth day of a new world' was at hand.[20]

2

Miss Carroll's Choice

Amid celebrations following the British surrender, Molly Carroll fell ill. She turned to opium and was soon addicted, a common condition when doctors treated most illnesses with heavy doses of the drug. But death, when it came that spring, took the strongest first. The Squire celebrated his eightieth birthday at Carroll House in early April 1782. Standing on the porch one day, he lost his balance and fell headfirst down the steps. Unable to speak again, the Squire died within the hour. Molly was profoundly shocked and her own illness worsened. Eleven days later, on 10 June, after begging 'her Women, who were crying about her not to grieve but pray for her', she too died.[1]

With the deaths of her mother and grandfather, twelve-year-old Mary's emotional security was vested in her father Charles Carroll of Carrollton: her link with the past, comforter of the present and enabler of the future. In April 1783, after the peace treaty was negotiated in Paris and the British relinquishment of New York effected, Congress issued a proclamation ending all hostilities. As the Annapolis bells rang out in celebration, the State House was turned into a candlelit ballroom and a 'grand dinner' was held on Squire Carroll's Point, as it was known locally, in the grounds of Carroll House. 'A whole ox to be roasted, & I can't tell how many sheep & calves, besides a world of other things', Mary Dulany informed her absent son on 23 April. 'Liquor in proportion. The whole to conclude with illuminations & squibs, etc.' Their 'First Citizen' greeted the townsfolk of Annapolis, his eldest daughter Mary, Miss Carroll of Carrollton standing beside him to dispense Chesapeake hospitality.[2]

Eight months later Mary again stood beside her father in one of the most famous scenes in American history. With the coming of peace, General Washington could unbuckle his sword at last. 'Gentlemen, you must permit me,' he had said as he put on spectacles to read a letter to officers contemplating insurrection. 'I have not only grown gray but almost blind in service to my country.' En route to retirement at Mount Vernon,

he visited Annapolis to resign his commission from Congress, which had
moved there from Philadelphia and was in session. Annapolis was *en fête*
during three days of public celebration preceding his formal resignation,
held at the State House on 23 December 1783.

This historic ceremony is commemorated in one of John Turnbull's
four Revolutionary War paintings encircling the Rotunda of the Capitol
in Washington DC. In *George Washington Resigning His Commission*, Carroll
of Carrollton, as President of the Senate, stands with his arm on the
empty presidential chair; in front of him to his left, are placed Mary, aged
thirteen, and her younger sister Kitty aged five, neither of whom is well-
painted, Mary was older, taller and dark-haired. Their presence was an
honour, as they are the only two children seen on the floor of the Senate
Chamber. Above their heads, clustered round Martha Washington in the
ladies' gallery, are the wives of members of Congress and prominent
Annapolis ladies; women of the new Republic were welcomed to hear
debates in the American seat of government. 'The General seemed so much
affected himself that everybody felt for him', Molly's close friend Mary
Ridout reported. 'He addressed Congress in a short speech, but very affecting.
Many tears were shed.'[3]

By 1787 a momentum had built up for constitutional change. Washington
was pulled out of retirement to be elected president of the Constitutional
Convention held in Philadelphia that May. The Founding Fathers, as they
came to be known, replaced the inadequate Articles of Confederation of
1781 with a new written constitution that limited the authority of self-
interested state legislatures and created a federal government for the
American nation. Elected the first US Senator for Maryland in 1788, Carroll
of Carrollton attended the First Congress in New York at which, in February
1789, the Electoral College chose George Washington as the first President
of the United States of America.

The social tone for New York's brief reign as the capital of America
was set by Sarah Jay, wife of the Secretary of Foreign Affairs. In the
absence of an American equivalent to social bibles like *Burke's Peerage*
and the *Almanach de Gotha*, she composed a special list of eligible people
– precursor of the New York Blue Book, the '400' and the Social Register.
Her list was remarkable for 'there was not a single New Yorker with a
million dollars – such a prodigy being reserved for Maryland with its
Charles Carroll and Philadelphia with its William Bingham'. Mary, who
was described in the New York press as 'a vivacious beauty' and 'a favourite'
of both the Washingtons, accompanied her father to the Inauguration
and the levees, Drawing Rooms and dinners held at the first Republican
'court'. By then, however, she was no longer Miss Carroll of Carrollton.[4]

*

The sisters loved the story of their mother's spirited independence and their grandfather's sensible love, and a heady mix of romantic love and independent choice would reappear with variations in their own lives. Mary's father had assumed that she would make a good Catholic marriage with a planter from their large Maryland cousinhood. Such a ready-made suitor presented himself in the summer of 1785, when she was fourteen and her brother Charles Carroll Jr, following Carroll tradition, set off to study at the English Jesuit College in Liège. To mark the occasion, their father commissioned a conversation piece of his son's departure. Not in the picture but of great importance was a cousin, Daniel Carroll of Duddington. Deprived of a European education because of the War, he decided to go with Charles Jr. Before sailing, Daniel declared his love for Mary. He was already an intimate of the family, Kitty called him 'cousin long-legs'.[5]

Mary, however, preferred a much less eligible pair of legs: those belonging to the tall, fine-looking figure of Richard Caton. Although in 1786 she was the belle of her first Annapolis season with many suitors, at sixteen she had fallen in love and had no wish to wait for either the return of her cousin or more offers of marriage. Although the revolution, with its opposition to patriarchy, had taken America much further than Britain down the road of female freedom to choose a husband, the family was aghast.

The republican belief that young people could achieve their independence from parental interference, as the American colonies had done from Britain, and choose a partner on the basis *only* of love, not fortune, was well-publicised and becoming accepted. American magazines excoriated 'parents . . . who are daily offering up the honor and happiness of their children at the shrine of interests and ambition.' This was of especial importance to rich women, heiresses whose marital fate had customarily been decided through a process of barter in the market place of society with little consideration for personal feelings. Mary also adored novels, especially tales of thwarted love and handsome heroes. Her father tried to warn her of the dangers of 'lolling on the bed reading romances' – he worried that 'a person much addicted to novel-reading seldom reads with pleasure or profit other books.' Now that Mary had a tall dark stranger of her own to fight for, such stories strengthened her resolve.

Her family had always taken a somewhat idiosyncratic approach to matrimony. Their independent fortunes had been accompanied by an unusual freedom of choice. Selecting a marriage partner 'to force a child's inclination' was 'the highest cruelty a father can be guilty of', Carroll of Carrollton wrote in 1763. He realised if his attempt at dissuasion failed, he must accept his daughter's choice with grace, although if she had wanted to rebel against everything her family stood for, Mary could not have chosen a better way than by marrying Richard Caton. He had neither means nor position; he was in debt and, worst of all, he was an English Protestant.[6]

The Caton family was originally French, having held the manor of Caton in north-east Lancashire since 1066. Richard, however, was born in 1763 in the booming port of Liverpool where his father Joseph Caton was a slave trader and captained his own ship *The Great Tom of Lincoln*. At least two of his other ships were engaged in the Africa slave trade and he probably had shares in others as a customary way of spreading the risk in Liverpool mercantile circles. Richard was twenty in 1783 and an apprentice merchant when the *Williamson's Advertiser* reported that: 'The Mercantile World is in a hurry and bustle unknown at any former time,' owing to the huge demand for English goods in America, where cargoes were expected to sell 'at an immense profit'. As merchants scrambled to charter ships, Richard joined them, using £500 from his father, 'in order to establish or promote his interest in business', to take a shipment of wine and other goods to Baltimore in Maryland.

At some point, however, he contracted debts, by speculation or gaming. This proved an obstacle to his prospective marriage with Miss Carroll of Carrollton. But Mary remained resolute. When a family friend passed on her father's question, 'ask her if her lover gets into jail who will get him out?' Mary, raising her hands heavenwards, exclaimed theatrically, 'These hands shall take him out.' Out of affection, rather than appreciation of her dramatic skills, her father eventually consented to her engagement. There were compensations to this *mésalliance*: he could settle her nearby and live intimately with his future grandchildren. He did stipulate that, before the couple could marry, Caton had to 'extricate himself from some debts' and 'get into a business sufficient to maintain himself and a family'. On 13 March 1787, breaking the news of his daughter's match to Daniel, he admitted that 'I do sincerely wish that she had placed her affections elsewhere, but I do not think I am at liberty to control her choice.'

Caton had nothing to bring to his marriage on 25 November 1787 except a precarious financial situation and a handsome face. His family was not personally known to the Carrolls. And so it would remain. Not surprisingly, though the sisters loved their father and bore his name, they thought of themselves foremost and forever after as Carrolls. In the mind of the Chesapeake gentry he was seen as a shadowy figure without family ties – an adventurer, who had seized one of their marital prizes, and landed in a family whose name and financial resources could further his speculations.[7]

Mary Carroll, the sisters' mother. Drawn from an original picture by R. E. Pine, around the time of her marriage in 1787. Richard Caton, the sisters' father, after Gilbert Stuart.

Although the wealth of the Carroll family remained under the control of Carroll of Carrollton, and was preserved chiefly – according to the English law of primogeniture – for his heir, Charles Jr, it was also used to maintain the family estates and to provide substantial dowries for the Carroll daughters. From the day of their marriages each of his three children received an average of £10,000 a year in gifts and annuities. In addition, he gave each of them their own townhouses and large country establishments while welcoming them and their families for as long as they wished to stay at his own houses, as the aristocracy did in England.

Part of Mary Carroll's marriage settlement included a small 1,000 acre estate situated on part of the 30,000 acres of Carroll land near the small town of Baltimore, an area still known as Catonsville. Her father built a new house here for her which was named 'Castle Thunder' although the plain late eighteenth-century stucco building bore little resemblance to a castle. Mary, however, shared the Carroll fondness for Voltaire, especially *Candide* in which Castle Thunder is an 'earthly paradise' of calm and unquestioning optimism. The Voltairean association proved all too prescient. Caton's varying business operations shared one characteristic: an unvarying optimism about their outcome.

In the event Mary Carroll Caton hardly lived there, preferring to stay in Annapolis, the centre of Maryland social life: like her mother Molly, she loved a party. She could continue to live with her father as much as possible, a situation they found mutually agreeable. And when her daughters were born, their names reflected the consequence of the Carroll family. The first child was baptised MaryAnne in memory of Molly and Anne 'Nancy' Darnall, while the second, Bess, bore her great-grandmother's name Elizabeth.[8]

3
Plantation Girls

The Maryland plantocracy set off for their country seats as soon as the state legislature adjourned for the summer. 'Whe-ew-ew – by George this is a Toaster,' exclaimed an English diplomat, unaccustomed to the temperature. 'A pint of American summer would thaw all Europe in ten minutes.' Summers in the city were uncomfortable and hazardous. 'I am apprehensive this excessive heat will generate pestilential fevers in our large cities', Carroll of Carrollton gave as a reason for not going to Philadelphia in July, when outbreaks of malaria, typhus and yellow fever were more frequent. He presented his children with their own plantations to safeguard health as much as for occupation.[1]

The sisters, though, mostly passed their summers and autumns at Doughoregen Manor, in the Elk Ridge Hundred in Anne Arundel County (now Howard County), the plantation designated by the Settler as the chief Carroll seat in the New World. Every year, usually on the last day of May, they set off from Annapolis on the thirty-two-mile journey north and did not return until the winter season began in November.

Starting out in the cooler air of early evening, escorted by their grandfather and father riding ahead, the sisters with their mother and nanny settled back against the cushions of morocco leather in the largest family carriage. They were attended by four black postilions in green Carroll livery, while waggons trundled behind containing servants and provisions. Over the previous two days the housekeeper and the bulk of the house servants had travelled ahead by wagon and boat, with the plate, linens and a prodigious amount of luggage and supplies, including the two barrels holding 125 gallons of port wine, and five barrels of whisky for the harvest.

Leaving behind Annapolis, like other American towns but a speck of civilisation flicked onto the wild country covering the long eastern seaboard, the sisters were jolted along bumpy tracks of mud and loam, over craggy hills covered with cedar and pine, fording rivers and creeks, and swaying through forests of oak, tulip and hickory. They travelled on into the night, often under stars and moon brilliant against the deep shade of the forests, the still night air intermittently pierced by the scream of bitterns, the wailing cry of the whippoorwills and the howl of wolves.

The sublime scenery of the wilderness was already exciting the interest of European artists and poets but it was the flora and fauna, rather than the prospects, which were appreciated in the girls' childhood. They learnt about natural history from their father, an amateur scientist and geologist. Visitors to the Manor included scientific explorers, botanical collectors and travellers hastening to discover and classify the abundant flora, fauna and minerals. Many would publish accounts of their travels, copies of which lay in the Carroll libraries and at the Library Company of Baltimore founded by their father, amongst others, in 1796. Natural history had become so fashionable on both sides of the Atlantic that works on the subject were bestsellers; in France, the Comte de Buffon's *Histoire naturelle* (1749–1789) had a greater vogue than Voltaire's writings. Pehr Kalm, the Swedish naturalist, found so many plants and trees he could not name, he wrote in *Travels into North America*, that he 'was seized with terror at the thought of ranging so many new and unknown parts of natural history'.

The America the girls knew was a minuscule part of a vast uncharted continent. In the 1790s, Florida was a Spanish colony which none of their family had visited; nor had they been to Louisiana, a vast territory that stretched northwards to British Canada and also belonged to Spain. Most of the southern states did not exist as separate entities; Kentucky, Tennessee and Ohio were still subsumed into Virginia. In their childhood, Indian tribes roamed over land which would later become the states of the Deep South while all the western regions beyond the Allegheny range of mountains bordering Maryland, remained imagined territory, known through books and travellers' tales to be full of bison and deer, buffalo and antelope, towering waterfalls and unbroken forests.[2]

Emerging from the forests west of Baltimore, the Carroll carriage entered the cultivated rolling country of northern Maryland. Some hours later, Carroll land was reached: planted near the road was the weather-beaten old stone marked with the inscription 'Here Stand the Beginning Trees of Doughoregan, Push Pin and the Girl's Portion'. Shortly after four o'clock, they swung through the gates of the 13,500-acre estate, past a small village of neat brick-and-wood houses, along an avenue leading through wooded parkland and, via a large court, to the house. Standing on the crest of a high ridge of ground offering the prospect of a landscape rolling away to distant hills, the solid walls of the early Georgian manor house had been built to bear with fortitude the extremes of a climate annually producing intense heat, heavy snowfalls and lashing downpours with hailstones 'the size of hen's eggs'.

Doughoregan Manor, 'the most English house in America' and the chief Carroll plantation. The sisters lived with their grandfather here during the summer and autumn months.

Not surprisingly, the Manor (as the family called it) barely acknowledged the image traditionally associated with a southern plantation mansion. Its unpretentious hipped roof, entrance porch, tall thin chimneys and numerous mullioned windows had little in common with the white Doric columns supporting the portico and wide verandahs of the ante-bellum mansion. This latter building, which would appear later in the Deep South states and more arrestingly in the South of popular imagination, was then a mere upstart in the plantation world.

Scarlett O'Hara's legendary Tara in *Gone with the Wind*, the apogee of this later plantation tradition, smouldering amid the rubble of burnt cotton-fields, symbol of all that the South would lose in the American Civil War (1861–4), was over a century away from the sisters' Doughoregan, rich in wheat and tobacco, 'The very air scented by wood-smoke and the fragrance of that sweet smelling tobacco'. Their South was rooted in the slaveholding, manorial aristocracy of colonial Maryland, Virginia and South Carolina. Nonetheless, the lineage and fine breeding of the Old South are conveyed in *Gone with the Wind* by Melanie's aunt Pittypat, struggling to maintain standards of southern hospitality in wartime, who triumphantly produces a bottle of her father's fine Madeira, declaring 'He got it from his uncle Admiral William Hamilton who married Jessica Carroll of Carrollton, his second cousin once removed!'

The girls' grandfather would walk off with his spaniel Flora to the stone bathing house, about half a mile from the house, where he plunged headfirst into the five-foot deep bath. In this early example of an indoor swimming pool, deeper than the plunging pools later found in England, the water was 'cold as ice', fed by a spring, cool and invigorating in hot weather. He bathed early every morning, a practice suspected by visitors as the cause, for one there had to be, of his longevity. The English diplomat Henry Addington recorded, 'I frequently met him walking back at five o'clock at a swinging pace, on which occasions he used to triumph over me as indolent and lazy compared to himself.'

Mary Carroll Caton, with her body maid, was usually in the bathing house by six. On her return to the house a larger, noisier group set out. As toddlers, Marianne and Bess were put into a pair of panniers slung either side of a pony's back, escorted by their nurse and two maids, and led by a black groom to the bathing house. There, amid squeals and whimpers, barking dogs and laughter the children were taken into the cold water by their maids until they learnt to copy their pet spaniels and splash about on their own.[3]

Their education reflected their grandfather's ideas of a sound upbringing. At the Manor after morning bathing everyone went riding. Once they had learnt to ride and had graduated to reins they rode twice a day. 'In the cool of the evening three ponies were brought out for the children, who had been anticipating their evening ride all day with great glee', wrote Adam Hodgson, a Liverpool friend of their father's; either their grandfather or father would ride with them, leading the ponies with long reins. Their earliest ambition was to be able to ride out with their grandfather over the plantation, and horsemanship was an essential skill for any plantation girl; like learning letters, it threw open the universe and encouraged a spirit of independence.

It also gave them a sense of what one cousin called 'our earth'. Writing of her childhood on another Carroll plantation, Clynmalira, she felt 'It was not only the house but all that it overlooked that was loved – the distant sky line toward the south, the hills coming round toward the north, the way the shadows fell across the lawn at moonlight, the large sense of home, boundless home, *our earth*'. The sheer joy in the physical experience of land was an intense one for many of the family, especially marked in the Squire, their uncle Carroll and Louisa. The nurture of the Manor into a productive, experimental plantation had been the Squire's life work and given him enormous satisfaction. 'I took a tour this Morning to Jacobs, the Folly & by the Pool Meadow, all my Fields smiled on me', he had written to Charley in 1772. The girls rode out frequently to visit the ten farms on the plantation, especially to the home quarter [farm] nearby, to understand the rhythm of the agricultural year, the duties and responsibilities of land ownership, the management of people and the way

Doughoregan operated within the Carroll enterprise that sustained the family in such wealth.*

They absorbed one other precept from their grandfather, in whom it had been inculcated by his own father the Squire: the importance of being independent. Although the goal of self-sufficiency was clearly not unique to him, disciplined habits of consumption and expense set the family apart from other members of the Chesapeake gentry. The Carrolls were careful to consolidate their wealth, improve their estates and forswear debt through attentive husbandry. 'Who is so happy as an independent man? and who more independent than a private gentleman possessed of a clear estate, and moderate in his desires?' declared Carroll of Carrollton. He took care to instil in his granddaughters diligent habits of keeping daily accounts for, as he pointed out, 'if you will not habituate yourself to keeping an account of small sums you will assuredly neglect large ones' (a lesson they were less likely to learn from their father, whose finances were precarious).[4]

Binding all this were the teachings of their religion with its emphasis upon personal humility and accountability, a sympathy for all peoples, and a belief that all were equal in God's, if not southern, eyes. At seven o'clock every morning the chapel bell pealed for prayers, and the family slipped across to the chapel, built in 1735 as one of the symmetrical dependencies flanking either side of the house. Visitors, servants and slaves joined them at will, though Protestant Richard Caton never attended. Usually, and especially on feast days, slaves trooped up the avenue from their quarters for Mass. After prayers, the family's resident priest heard the girls' catechism before they walked back to the Manor for breakfast.

The children sat at a low separate table with their nurse and later with their governess, Miss Woodbridge; once they had demonstrated a proper ease in company, a place was allowed at the main table. Breakfast was Marianne's favourite meal. Besides chocolate, tea and coffee, there were hot breads and pancakes: Maryland biscuits, egg ponc, cookies (Indian corn pancakes rather like oatmeal biscuits), hot rye loaf, johnnycake (a bread made of corn, milk and eggs), as well as ham, bacon and hominy. Years later, when Marianne had a new cook, Bess sent her the exact receipt for Doughoregan hominy (ground maize used as a cereal, rather like semolina, and eaten boiled with water or milk) so she could enjoy a good Manor breakfast far from home.

During the rest of the morning, from about nine till twelve, the girls studied a range of subjects, starting when young with French, arithmetic,

---

* An idea of comparable land ownership: Lord Baltimore, proprietor of Maryland, 7 million acres; George Washington's Mount Vernon 8,000 acres; John Tayloe of Mount Airey 11,700 acres; the Ridgelys at Hampton about 24,000 acres; and Carroll of Carrollton over 90,000 acres.

deportment, reading, singing and dancing. The schoolroom lay on the first
floor above the chapel. Plantation children's education was, generally, a
sporadic affair, dependent upon the availability of itinerant tutors of vari-
able standard. In contrast, the sisters received a regular, rigorous education
owing to the presence both of their grandfather and a resident priest who
doubled as a tutor, to the excellent library and to the family's interest in
learning. Their grandfather took an especial interest in their French, his
command of the language remaining fluent. He never allowed the diversion of company to interrupt French conversation with his granddaughters;
indeed, illustrious visitors provided a captive audience for his infant prodi-
gies. The sisters and their cousins performed a French song or two 'Grandpapa
beating out the time with an encouraging forefinger'.[5]

The convenient situation of the Manor for American statesmen and
foreign diplomats travelling from the South to Philadelphia and New York
or from the North to Washington City produced a flow of guests, as welcome
at Doughoregen as at Jefferson's Monticello and Washington's Mount Vernon
in Virginia. In the plantation tradition the Manor was 'open as an inn and
rich as a castle'. The sisters' grandfather revelled in domesticity, having
missed so much of home life himself, and at Doughoregen he was able to
combine domestic, political and plantation life. But no matter how distinguished his guests – whether President and 'Lady' Washington on their way
to Mount Vernon, Jefferson come to discuss the site of a new capital city,
or the new British and French Ministers and their families to stay for ten
days – the girls' routine remained unchanged. Marianne and Bess rode out,
learned Latin, sang French songs and sat listening to the talk of their family
and the guests.

The essayist Josiah Quincy, who stayed at the Manor and knew Marianne,
believed that 'The fashionable ladies of the South had received the education of political thought and discussion to a degree unknown among their
sisters of the North'. He related how a friend, commenting on a young lady
who had completed a costly education at a fashionable school in New York,
told him: 'She can read bad French novels, and play a few tunes on the
piano but, upon my word, she does not know whether she is living in a
monarchy or a republic', and Quincy declared: 'The sneer would never have
applied to the corresponding class at the South. These ladies were conver-
sant with political theories, and held definite political opinions.' Politics
was in the familial air breathed at the Manor, an indivisible part of the
sisters' schoolroom world.[6]

There was, however, nothing in the way of formal entertainment for
guests as there was at Carroll House. Visitors remarked on the extraordinary, to them, informality and simplicity of life. Stratford Canning, later
Lord de Redcliffe, posted to America as a young diplomat, spent 'the most

enjoyable days of 1821' at the Manor and wrote home that Mr Carroll 'lives in a simple manner, more so, perhaps, in some respects than we should think consistent with the enjoyment of a handsome fortune'. The house gleamed with beeswax polish but not 'splendour which certainly never is thought about', Henry Gilpin, a friend of the sisters' cousin, noticed. Along with family portraits and the well-thumbed leather-bound volumes in the library, were to be found faded Turkey rugs, worked footstools covered in dog hairs, mahogany side chairs chewed by dogs, old silk brocade curtains in one room and 'fine new curtains of the gayest colours' in another. There were, he reported, 'sofas & chairs, covered with glorious old cushions, and so deep that you cannot sit, but must really lie back in them' juxtaposed with a 'singular medley of old and modern furniture'. Old English plate and Sèvres and Spode dinner services were produced to dine off but never in 'costly Piles'.[7]

In good plantation tradition, the informality extended to the bedrooms. Although the Manor could boast up to fifty beds for guests, it lacked anything like that many bedrooms. Diplomatic immunity could not be invoked to escape the bedtime mêlée, as the British chargé d'affaires learned. 'As the manor was generally full of company all the summer, it was frequently expedient to stow close, many garçons being on those occasions packed in one room, and many virgins in another.' Nineteen gentlemen in two bedrooms and eleven ladies in two others were not uncommon and then there were also the personal servants to accommodate, many of whom slept on the floor of the bedchamber or outside the doors. The girls, and their cousins piled into Aunt Kitty's bed, their mother had Mrs Decatur and two Miss Chases in her bedroom, and an uncle and a couple of his friends tucked themselves into the absent chaplain's room; their cousin Charles Harper could recall years afterwards his terror as a boy at having to sleep in the chapel when no bedroom space was available elsewhere.

None of these customs deterred visitors or caused offence. On the contrary invitations were avidly sought, the Manor providing a glimpse of country-house life almost unique in America. English diplomats were eager to obtain letters of introduction and, in spite of certain transatlantic differences, feel a little closer to home. 'It was', said one of them, 'the most English household in America.' Yet it was also more informal than country-house life in England. At the Manor 'everybody seems to catch in ten minutes all the freedom & ease of the place', Gilpin noticed. Guests could amuse themselves as they pleased: card tables in one room; harp, guitar and songs in another – with none of that insistent playing to have to sit through; people eating in the dining room while in one of the drawing rooms there was chattering in corners.

However hot the day, there always seemed to be a breeze stirring through the wide hall where, in front of open doors leading to the gardens, on a large table from midday onwards a generous bowl of iced punch stood alongside fresh lemonade, toddy, applejack and wine cakes. In the heat of the day, 94 degrees in the shade was not unusual, as Gilpin recalled, 'with heaps of newpapers, new novels &c You may loll on the sofa & read them, & nobody expects you to rise, even ladies, unless inclined' until they rose to prepare for the most important meal of the day, dining at three and remaining in the dining room two or three hours.[8]

After Marianne and Bess returned from riding in the early evening they would join their mother and guests either in a drive to the vineyard or a walk through the gardens. The Squire had battled for ten years to establish a *premier cru*, sending for two *vignerons* from France to improve the quality of the wine. To no avail; the climate and American grapes defeated him, though the output of Carroll *vin ordinaire* increased. In place of a superior vintage he bequeathed to his descendants a beautiful vineyard of about four acres, where the grapevines were planted alternately with hollyhocks and amaranths. It was a favourite outing.

The 'magnificent' gardens were equally popular. From the open doors leading onto the western terrace and the drawing-room windows above, the warm summer air, heavy with the scent of roses and white jessamine, floated into the house. Along the walkways shaded by chestnut trees, fragrance and colour were provided by an old-fashioned flower garden. Frances Trollope, the Englishwoman whose later critical account of her travels would enrage Americans, gushed over Maryland and its flowers and shrubs: 'No description can give an idea of the Variety, the profusion, the luxuriance of them.' Beautiful wild roses, which bore no relation to the pale ephemeral blossoms of English bramble hedges, carried a rich, delicate scent and were larger than any English single rose. Louisa, who later had several rose gardens to manage, thought there were 'no roses like Doughoregan ones'; they clambered over porches and windows, threaded through trees and over the old southern wall; roses of every hue, all sifting down their petals onto the smooth green lawns.[9]

The charm of these summer walks was enriched by the clouds of brightly coloured butterflies 'like gossamer bouquets of flying blossoms'. And there was an inexhaustible profusion of fruit. 'We children went to the garden and ate fruit at all times of the day,' their cousin remembered, 'and when cherries were ripe we were as much in the trees as the robins and blackbirds.' The Carroll orchards produced 22–23,000 gallons of cider annually, mostly consumed on the plantations, and an abundance of pears, peaches, cherries, currants, gooseberries and strawberries. A fruit supper of peaches, pears, cantaloupe and watermelon – but only after it had been a week in the ice house – would be served before bed.

Later, in the cooler air of evening, Marianne and Bess and their body maids liked to look out at the glittering stars or watch the sparks of fireflies 'their glancing light, now here, now there; now seen, now gone'. Down below, the murmur of the gentlemen sitting talking on the porch, floated up towards them: travels on the Continent, news from France, a tour in Indian country. And before bed they received their grandfather's benediction, words repeated in his letters: 'God bless and prepare you for a better world'.[10]

As often as not, Marianne and Bess shared a bed and a bedroom with their bodymaids, Anny and Polly. Mistress and maid were inseparable companions. Anny belonged to Marianne as Polly did to Bess. Among the family portraits hanging in the dining room was one of a set of Carroll/Darnall children, painted by Kuhn around 1710. *Henry Darnall as a Child* shows a black boy standing just behind his younger master Henry, aged about seven, who owned him. It was a custom in early Maryland for great planters to present their children with a slave as a playmate who would become a trusted personal servant in maturity. This custom was perpetuated in the Carroll family. Carroll of Carrollton presented each of his granddaughters in turn with such a playmate of their own.[11] The Manor was inhabited not only by white indentured servants but also by black and mulato slaves. Only a very few Chesapeake planters owned as many slaves (then about 625 at Doughoregan alone) on such extensive estates. As the Carroll house slaves were usually members of the same family, it is likely that when Anny and Polly were about six, their mothers brought them to be 'trained up' as good maids for the sisters. At first Anny would have followed her mother about, helping her, running errands and 'just playing around', and gradually being absorbed into the ways of the household. Anny could then join the nursery to become Marianne's body maid, 'her little keeper' as Cicely, a maid from Georgia, called it. Nanny Mahony, the old Carroll nurse, was in overall charge and directed several other girls who performed specific duties. One laid the morning fire, brought up and carried down bath water and washed the children. Another swept the floors and dusted, and came and went all day long with baskets of linen, ruffled petticoats and dresses of the finest lawn.

Anny, however, only looked after Marianne: dressed her, fanned her when she was hot and fidgety, kept the flies off her face, and was also her playmate and friend. A young Virginian plantation boy described his childhood friends as 'two negro boys of about the same age, my satellites and companions, partners in any mischief and with whom I cheerfully divided any good fortune which came to me in the way of cakes, fruit or other edibles.' Harriet Benton, a black Georgian, spoke of the games she played with the other plantation children, 'hide and seek and stealing bases. I thought of us all white and black as belonging to one family.'

The rich plautocracy, such as the Carrolls and Calverts, tended to distinguish between slaves who were house servants and those who were field workers, those who were skilled artisans and those who were labourers. Rosalie Calvert differentiated between the field hands and the house servants on her Riversdale plantation, always referring to household slaves as 'servants'. That the Carrolls distinguished between their servants and their workers is evident from a letter the Squire wrote when once irked by Charley's criticism: 'You will have it that my People are not well fed, it is true they do not live so well as our House Negroes, But full as well as any Plantation Negroes & think I Can safely say no Man in Maryland Can shew in proportion to Our Number, Such likely well looking Slaves.'

House servants were part of 'our family' rather than 'our People' and, as one southerner Josey King realised, 'these little girls have been brought up under our care and we love them, not as servants, but as something nearer.' Eleanor Baker, a northerner, could not understand such feelings: 'I look with perfect wonder at the indulgence & patience of southern housewives. The ladies take as much care of their slaves as if they were children & I am quite shocked to see the familiar way in which many of them are treated.' Fanny Kemble, the English actress who married a plantation and then became a fervent abolitionist, was another woman who could not understand how almost every planter's wife and daughter had 'one or more little pet blacks sleeping like puppy-dogs in their very bed-chamber', who were slaves.[12]

As children, Marianne and Bess and Anny and Polly lived in ignorance of the legal and financial aspect of their relations – that Marianne and Bess had rights of ownership and that Anny and Polly were capital assets – partly because they were infants and partly because by the 1790s the term 'slave' was rarely used in family letters about black house servants. While this might seem purely euphemistic expediency – even in the Civil War years children claim they grew up in ignorance: 'we had never heard the word "slave",' Letitia M. Burwell, a Virginian plantation girl asserted – it is true that Marianne and her sisters spoke of Miss Nelly or Miss Ruthy, the head sempstress and under-housekeeper, or of 'the servants' in their letters.

Mary Carroll Caton, trying to explain the nuances of the subject to Fanny Kemble in 1833, likened it to Highland estates in Scotland. 'Being born upon the land, there exists among [us] something of the old spirit of clanship,' she said, '& "our house", "our family" are the terms by which they [the house servants] designate their owners.' She had no hesitation in telling Fanny that the black servants on the Carroll estates 'she found the best & most faithful servants in the world'. Fanny, not unnaturally for a woman who would later write in her Journal 'I am going [to Georgia] prejudiced against slavery, for I am an Englishwoman, in whom the absence of such a prejudice would be disgraceful', remained sceptical, confining herself to the comment 'Mrs – [Caton] amused me much'. Henry Addington, however, thought the Doughoregan servants 'lived in clover, and seemed to do pretty much as they pleased, at least the house-slaves, for the whole internal administration is conducted by serfs. They ruled the roost completely, from the butler to the scullion'.[13]

The Carroll slaves, both house and field, found one advantage in being owned by Marianne and Bess's family. The sisters' grandfather, unlike many other planters in America, could afford to keep most of his slave families together. It was usual for plantation owners, especially indebted ones, to sell slaves and move them around, so that most blacks experienced forcible separation from their immediate families at some stage, if not often, in their lives, with all its ensuing heartbreak. In her speech at the National Women's Right Convention at Akeron, Ohio, in 1851, the black abolitionist Sojourner Truth would tell white women of the common experience of black women and children forcibly deprived of maternal love. She was related as saying: 'I have borne thirteen children and seen most of 'em sold into slavery, and when I cried out with my mother's grief, none but Jesus heard me . . .'. Former slaves who later recounted their life stories viewed the separation of mothers and children as the major crime of slavery.

Anny and Polly, in contrast, lived with their mothers and were surrounded by their family, generations of whom served the Carrolls. At Riggs Quarter, there was a large network of families; as listed in a 1774 inventory, nearly half of all the slaves were kinsfolk, whose members were either direct descendants or in-laws of one slave Fanny, who herself had belonged to the Settler. This network had enlarged through the marriage of children and grandchildren with those of other original slaves. Similarly, at Annapolis Quarter in 1774 thirteen out of seventeen slaves were descended from Iron Works Lucy. As it was Carroll policy to keep families together, during the Revolutionary War, the Poplar Island slaves were all evacuated to the Manor, even though it put an additional strain on resources at a time when the other Carroll plantations were short-staffed. It was this sense of family and stability that Mary Carroll Caton would later try to convey to Fanny Kemble.[14]

Nonetheless, even in regulated plantation households, order was maintained in ways a later age condemned. The sisters, however protected as young girls, must have been aware of the whippings and lashings carried out in the name of discipline. 'Little Nan has been whipt about Mrs Morcton's shifts, she confessed she stole them & said she gave them to Moll', was the sentence passed by the Squire for misbehaviour in 1772. The sisters' grandfather had this advice to give their uncle in 1808: 'Let me recommend to you never to strike a servant in anger'; this did not herald leniency for, he continued, 'when your negroes commit a fault deserving punishment, and to not be overlooked, take them to Homewood have them stript and tied up and make Ben . . . give them 25 lashes'. It was important to 'correct but seldom but when you do correct, let not the correction be a trifling one'.

Punishments were not restricted to black servants. White ones were treated as harshly: 'Harry shall have a good flogging and a Collar this Evening.' Part of the girls' early training included learning to assume the mantle of command and responsibility, dispensing orders, care and discipline when they became plantation mistresses. Although the beneficiaries of Independence, they were equally the beneficiaries of Slavery.[15]

'If there be an object truly ridiculous in nature, it is an American patriot signing resolutions of independence with the one hand, and with the other brandishing a whip over his affrighted slaves', Thomas Day, the English author, wrote. Not that this situation was accepted with equanimity by all plantation society. Carroll of Carrollton had been appointed to a Senate committee to consider a bill for the abolition of slavery in the first session of the First Congress in New York and had recommended to the House that the issue was 'such as to require peculiar investigation and the most serious attention of the legislature' and should go to a joint committee of both Houses. Pressure of business meant it was referred to the next session, and thereafter never considered. He believed that the constitution was 'the very wisest political document that man had ever produced' and he anticipated but one possibility of its disruption – the slavery question. Thomas Jefferson, likewise a plantation Signer, who, throughout his life, wrestled with the predicament of all southern slave owners, intimated there seemed no solution to the slavery issue, writing in 1820: 'But, as it is, we have the wolf by the ears, and we can neither hold him, nor safely let him go.' The spectre of slave revolt – the 'wolf' tearing free – had, he knew when he wrote these words, already materialised to confront Chesapeake plantocracy families at the time of the French Revolution.[16]

4

French Influences

On 10 July 1793, when Marianne was almost five, black messengers from Baltimore brought news so alarming as to disturb the Manor's absorption in harvest-time. Thousands of slaves had risen up and taken vengeance on their owners in the French Caribbean colony of Saint-Domingue (today the Republic of Haiti). At that very moment, lying anchored off Baltimore at Fells Point, was a flotilla of ships and schooners bulging with 619 white, black and mulatto passengers who, as the *Maryland Gazette* reported, had managed to escape 'the dreadful carnage and shocking massacre of the Whites by a savage enemy'. Marianne's father, who had business interests in the Caribbean, set off for Baltimore. At the Exchange he learned that 'The Distresses of those unhappy People have not been exaggerated' and that 'a great exertion of humanity' and funds were required to provide aid for them and, furthermore, for those still sailing up the Chesapeake to Baltimore.[1]

The fate of these émigrés and of Saint-Domingue was of considerable economic concern to Baltimore, and to Europe. According to one historian, the progress of Saint-Domingue from 1783 to 1789 was 'one of the most astonishing phenomena in the history of imperialism'. Its exports were one-third more than those of all the British West Indies in 1788; besides two-fifths of the world's sugar, the colony produced over half of the world's coffee. Although Baltimore merchants were thunderstruck by the scale of the massacre, they were by no means surprised. Flickers of agitation had already been kindled throughout the Caribbean by the revolution in France. Smouldering Saint-Domingue had needed little stoking to produce its own fiery rebellion from a discontented population where over 450,000 slaves – replenished *every year* by 40,000 manacled slaves from Africa – and some 28,000 mulattos were ruled by about 40,000 whites who, Mirabeau declared, slept '*au pied de Vésuve*'. [2]

Initial reactions to the French Revolution were overwhelmingly favourable in America. Lafayette sent Washington the key to the Bastille and in Baltimore bunting and illuminations appeared everywhere. Americans were flattered by the abolition of the nobility and titles in France in July 1790.

In the Senate Chamber, Carroll of Carrollton had declared: 'How fatal to our fame as lovers of liberty, would it have been had we adopted the shackles of servility which enlightened nations are now rejecting with detestation.' Although he felt 'a particular attachment' to France, by the following year even this lover of liberty had become uneasy at the violent fanaticism confirmed by the stream of newly-arrived French émigrés.[3]

Marianne and Bess were now brought into closer contact with Baltimore, French Catholic and émigrés society. Their grandfather could recall the time when Baltimore was a village of only seven houses – he knew because the Carrolls had owned the land upon which it was developed. By the time the Saint-Domingue refugees arrived, Baltimore was well-established as the entrepôt of a large trading network linking the American States with the West Indies and Europe in 'a double V-shaped trade'. Soaring foreign demand for wheat had encouraged production in the Monocacy River valley where the Carrollton estate was a major producer; and trails were cut through the wilderness to connect the rich granary of this hinterland with the nearest port, at Baltimore. The value of exports of wheat, flour and iron rose from $1.7 million in 1792 to over $10 million by 1799.

Not surprisingly the town oozed prosperity. The more prominent the merchants, the more civic responsibility they were expected to assume and the more largesse they were expected to dispense – just as their mercantile counterparts did in Amsterdam, Bristol, Bordeaux and Hamburg. Thus Caton, already a director of the first Bank of Maryland founded in 1790, would be as forthcoming as the greater merchants with pledges in the crisis and nearly $11,000 to help the refugees was raised in two days.[4]

After the outbreak of war between England and France in 1793, Washington, who had been re-elected with John Adams as Vice-President, was able to withstand the lobbying of Hamilton and Jefferson in favour of Britain and France respectively, and proclaim America's neutrality. This opened the United States to a flow of political refugees from both countries. And in Maryland, they came to Baltimore 'humming with trade', rather than to Annapolis, sagging under the collapse of the tobacco market in 1793. Still the seat of government and the state legal centre Annapolis, like a grande dame sedately upholding tradition, regarded the brash antics of upstart Baltimore with distaste.

Marianne and her sisters continued to winter at Carroll House though, increasingly, they would visit Baltimore. On 24 July a concert was held there in honour of Marie Antoinette, attended by many prominent citizens with their children, who would later form part of Marianne's circle of close friends. The horror felt at Louis XVI's execution heightened the emotional response to the image of his poor Queen, somehow embodied at the concert in the young figure of the émigré performer Mademoiselle Buron, announced to be formerly 'Singer to the Queen of France'. The arrival of the Saint-Dominguans doubled the Catholic population of Baltimore, a situation that drew forth some of the dying gasps of colonial bigotry against Catholic 'foreigners' in the *Maryland Journal*. But in replying to an official letter on behalf of the Catholics of America from five eminent Catholics including Charles Carroll of Carrollton, President Washington acknowledged the claims of Catholic citizens to equality and freedom of worship, adding 'I hope to see America among the foremost Nations in examples of justice and liberality.' The Caton sisters were thus the first of their family to enjoy a Catholic upbringing in Maryland free from religious persecution.[5]

One of the young priests in the flotilla from Le Cap was the Abbé Georges de Pérrigny, a *royaliste* doctor of the Sorbonne, accompanied by his sister Madame Le Pelletier and, in August, he started his duties as Chaplain and tutor to the family. In addition to French, he taught Marianne Latin as part of her religious education. Shortly afterwards, she acquired a new playmate. Breakfast was interrupted one morning by the arrival of three children: Victoire, Honoré Pierre and five-year-old Emile Morancy. After their father and uncles were massacred in Saint-Domingue, their black nurse had saved them. Honoré Pierre never forgot 'the terror and agony of the flight, the hurried drive through the blood-stained streets to the ships which took them away' to America. They gradually became integrated into Carroll family life; Marianne and Emile were the same age and became friends, Marianne speaking more French and Emile learning English.[6]

A year later, shortly after Marianne's sixth birthday, two more escapees arrived. Her uncle Charles Jr, aged nineteen, and her aunt Kitty, aged sixteen, had long been expected from England. Marianne's mother and grandfather waited in an agony of uncertainty for over a month before learning that the British ship had been captured by a French privateer. Luckily, the privateer fell in with an American vessel, *Pallas* and compelled its captain to take passengers and crew on board, a relieved Carroll reported on 8 October 1794 'and for 30 guineas landed them in Boston'.

Now Marianne had a new uncle and aunt to know. Like her Carroll great-aunts in 1723, Kitty had been sent to the Convent of the Holy Sepulchre at Liège and, as Austrian and French armies fought, escaped with the nuns to England, where her brother was studying. They both regaled the family with stories of their travels and Kitty sketched the latest fashions in clothes and hairstyles. The adventures of such an uncle and aunt evoked a new, different European world.[7]

*

One place in America did, however, offer the cultural, intellectual, commercial and social life of a cosmopolitan city: Philadelphia. The capital and leading region of the nation, during the 1790s it was in effect a microcosm of Europe. The largest American city, with a population of 70,000 compared with Baltimore's 13,000, Philadelphia was also 'one continued scene of Parties upon parties, balls and entertainments equal to any European city', according to Abigail Adams.[8]

'There is room for everyone in America', the influential French writer St Jean de Crèvecoeur had promised and French exiles of all political persuasions crowded into a French quarter full of French shops brimming with the latest Parisian fashions. At the famous playhouses in the mid-1790s, at the beginning and end of the play, Federalists led by Adams and Hamilton, supported by the Carroll family, would call on the orchestra to play 'Yankee Doodle' or 'Hail to the Chief'; at the same time their political opponents, the Democratic-Republicans led by Jefferson and Madison, would sing out the Ça ira, the song of the French Revolution.* The contest became part of the evening's spectacle and, in 1795, Ça ira prevailed.[9]

The winter season of 1796 was notable for the gaieties occasioned first by the departure of a president. Washington was retiring from office at the end of his second term, an event marked by numerous farewell balls and dinners. A second excitement was the arrival of a French prince. The eldest son of the powerful Duc d' Orléans (called Philippe-Égalité in the revolution and eventually executed), Louis Philippe, Duc de Chartres, had come to America and had obtained the release from a Marseilles prison of his two younger brothers. He awaited their arrival, living in lodgings over a barber shop in the French quarter. He was well received in Philadelphian society, which in the 1790s revolved around the delightful figure of Mrs William Bingham, whose daughters would become close friends of Marianne and Bess. When he sought permission to propose to her second daughter Maria Bingham, he was refused. 'Should you ever be restored to your hereditary position, you will be too great a match for her,' her father explained, and 'if not, she is too great a match for you.' When the Prince was reunited with his younger brothers, the trio of Égalités set out on the long journey to the Spanish territory of New Orleans. They stayed with the Carroll family in Maryland and, when illness prolonged their visit for some weeks at Carroll House, Marianne came to know them. Many years' later, she would receive a warm reception from Louis-Philippe in Europe. [10]

---

* Hearing the disastrous news of American humiliation at Valley Forge whilst in Paris, Franklin exclaimed 'This is indeed bad news, but ça ira, ça ira, it will all come right in the end.' The phrase was used in the French revolutionary song Ça ira, predecessor of the Marseillaise, as an anthem of the French Republic.

It was also in Philadelphia that the sisters' uncle Charles Carroll Jr planned to wed Harriet Chew in the summer of 1800. At twenty-five Carroll Jr was an accomplished, warm-hearted man but without the rigour of mind of his father. The marriage was delayed by religious difficulties as Harriet's family were Protestants and since the dangerous fever season was nearing, their mother decided that Marianne and Bess must remain at the Manor with their grandfather. Also absent from the ceremony were the Washingtons. The death of George Washington, on 14 December 1799, was marked by the first proclaimed period of public national mourning in the Republic's history. An immense crowd assembled in the capital to hear an oration pronounced over the bier by the Virginian General Henry Lee, in which he spoke of Washington as 'First in war, first in peace and first in the hearts of his countrymen'.

Marianne and Bess were at Carroll House when the tidings came of his death. On a December day they accompanied their mother and aunt to the State House where they watched their grandfather and John Howard of Belvedere read the Address to the House. Tears streamed down their cheeks as they read the eulogy: these brave men of revolutionary renown felt no loss of dignity in showing emotion for such a man. Throughout the House, men, women and girls wept silently. Sixteen years previously, Mary and Kitty Carroll had stood on the floor of the House, and Martha Washington and the ladies had been up in the gallery, watching General Washington resign his commission. Now, in the more formal days of the early Republic, Marianne and Bess stood beside their mother and aunt in the gallery, listening to Carroll of Carrollton's speech. It was the end of an era. And the first year of the new century would bring upheavals in all their lives.[11]

5

Republican Girls

On a spring day in 1800, Anna Maria Thornton, wife of the designer of the Capitol, wrote in her Washington journal: 'Mr. Law called – No news but of failures – many of the principal houses in Baltimore have stopped & some in Philadelphia.' With the ports of Europe closed by blockade during the French-British war (the Napoleonic wars), first Britain then Holland and Germany slid into depression, credits were suspended and prices were plummeting everywhere. Richard Caton's small firm only just managed to survive after his bills were protested in London.

Although the outlook for American trade remained 'goloomy' with schooners, worth $7,000 a few months previously, fetching only $2,500, Robert Oliver, a friend and leading Baltimore merchant, retained confidence in Caton's financial stability, writing to his London bankers, 'I consider Mr. Caton a very worthy and honorable Man.' His firm Robert Oliver & Brothers [Olivers] duly renewed one of Caton's bills. By July, however, business was wretched and, in August, Caton's hopes of making a good profit on a West Indian trade were disappointed: his Leghorn cargo sold very low at St Thomas's.[1]

The political outlook was also bleak. Taking shelter in a poor cottage during a thunderstorm that autumn, the sisters' grandfather pondered upon the receding chances of retaining his public position and on the general precariousness of life; such reflections, he afterwards told the family, 'enable us to bear the Frowns & rubs of Fortune with resignation and fortitude . . . [and] remain firm and unbroken in the midst of adverse storms'. In December, he lost his Maryland seat in the Democratic-Republican rout of the Federalists in the elections.* Jefferson's defeat of President Adams deepened 'party hatreds' and the ideological rifts that had arisen between Revolutionary colleagues. 'Men who have been intimate all their lives', Jefferson noted, 'cross the street to avoid meeting, and turn their heads

* The Democratic-Republican Party formed by Jefferson and Madison opposed a strong central government and a national bank and supported states' rights. The Federalist Party formed by Alexander Hamilton believed in a strong federal (national) government, the assumption of states' debts from the Revolution, creating a national debt and a national bank.

another way, lest they should be obliged to touch hats.' He believed Federalists, as enemies of 'pure republicanism', would restore a monarchy floating upon a sea of aristocratic corruption. Federalists, in turn, were convinced that his Republican presidency heralded a reign of Jacobin terror. 'Murder, robbery, rape, adultery, and incest' would not only be practised but taught, the Federalist *Connecticut Courant* warned its readers. The Caton sisters were Federalists and considered Jefferson to be, in their grandfather's words, a 'shortsighted man blinded by his passions', with a marked 'antipathy for England, too much inclined to favour the view of Napoleon agst that country, the bulwark of this and the Independence of Europe'.[2]

Their father's mercantile cares, meanwhile, were growing heavier. In 1802, he had to reveal to the family that he was 'overtaken by ruin'. Olivers thought Caton had been 'too speculative'. The firm lost no time in requesting Kirwans, on 16 April 1802, to secure any surplus in Caton's account for them 'without letting him or any person know that we wrote to you to that effect – it may perhaps be necessary to lay an Attachment [a legal seizure] and if possible do it privately'. The reason for this kid-glove treatment lay in the assumption that Carroll would come to the aid of his bankrupt son-in-law and save the Carroll Caton family from ruin. But would he?

He was profoundly shocked by Caton's failure for the large sum of £40,000 [£2.85 million today]. To dishonour, it added dependence. Marianne, at thirteen, already knew that Grandpapa Carroll would not countenance extravagace. While he would outfit her and Bess, provide $1,000 for a fine pearl necklace for aunt Kitty and give all of them millinery accounts, he taught them always to proportion expenditure to income. Where possible, 'every trifle which can be saved decently ought to be saved', for, he explained, 'a prudent economy is one of the foundations of Independence, & consequently of happiness'. Their father's bankruptcy went against the grain of everything they were being taught.[3]

Indebtedness had also been the reason for their grandfather's initial opposition to aunt Kitty's marriage to Robert G. Harper in May 1801, a match which otherwise had much to recommend it. Harper, the son of a successful cabinet-maker, had attended the College of New Jersey (later Princeton), been admitted to the Bar, became a prominent congressman in 1795 and would serve as chairman of the House Ways and Means committee. He was a persuasive speaker and, as his prospects were excellent and his legal practice successful, Carroll of Carrollton finally agreed to the match on the assurance that Harper would be able to meet all the debts he had incurred through unsuccessful land speculations, 'the fever of that age'.

Then, as now, he cared deeply about his daughters' happiness. 'A woman's consequence depends so much on the respectability of her Husband', wrote Martha Washington's granddaughter Nelly Parke Custis Lewis. Caton's bankruptcy would disgrace Mary Carroll Caton and ruin the eligibility of the Caton daughters. America still upheld the English common law of coverture which meant that, as a married woman, their mother's personal property belonged to their father and would be assessed to meet his debts; the income derived from her capital estate also went to him – though the land did not, as it was held for her by trustees under her marriage settlement, devised under the law of equity. Thus, in order to prevent any of her property being seized by their father's creditors and the courts, their grandfather had to act swiftly. If he decided not to help Caton but to confine himself to ensuring that their mother kept her own home, under Maryland law, the girls' father would be arrested and incarcerated in a debtors' prison.

Their grandfather's solution was to buy from the liquidating bank all the property standing in Caton's name. Aware that Caton would need some sort of income, he allowed him to become the paid manager, on the stipulation that he must submit regular accounts and that any profits would be used to support the family. Thus the sisters' father exchanged his independent mercantile hat for a dependent agent's one, a Carroll employee paid on commission.

The sisters were with their grandfather and mother at Carroll House in January 1803 when the Carroll agent brought more distressing news. He warned that their father was about to 'be arrested & sent to gaol on the judgᵗ obtained against him' for not meeting a call on his US government bonds. Caton had hoped in vain that funds owed to him in Lima, Peru would arrive to meet the $16,000 due on the bonds. Again their grandfather saved them by coming to an arrangement with their father's creditors whereby he would pay them the equivalent of an agent's annual salary: $3,000 [now about £48,000] every year until such times as Caton was able to discharge all his debts.[4]

During these two difficult years, Louisa and Emily, then a nine- and a seven-year-old were considered too young to be made aware of their father's misfortune. Their grandfather was therefore disconcerted to be told that Emily had suddenly said, 'Alas my dear Papa what bad doings there are in this world!' She had picked up a sense of their troubles, perhaps from overhearing her elder sisters or the servants' chatter. 'I hope my dear Emily that you will never experience any very severe trials during this life,' her grandfather wrote, 'but you must expect to meet with crosses and some affliction which I hope you will have virtue enough to bear with resignation to the will of God.'

From a distance, their lives appeared unchanged; their father lived as a gentleman retired from business, and of service to his father-in-law. To the world closer to home, to extended family and friends, the Baltimore mercantile community and Chesapeake planter society, the situation was known to be somewhat different – and judgements were made accordingly. As a result of the bankruptcy, their grandfather directed their lives more closely and they grew up holding few illusions about their intelligent, likeable but unfortunate father. As Bess remarked, on one of the many occasions when he failed to keep to business arrangements: 'I well know how uncertain all his movements are & how apt he is to procrastinate.'[5]

When a character in the graduation play at Greenfield Academy playfully asked: 'Really now what do you think of these times? Everybody is going to school, do you think they gets any good by it?' the 'Everybody' referred not to those traditional scholars, boys, but to girls. This was remarkable because in America, as in England, female education throughout most of the eighteenth century had been a haphazard pastime for even the upper-class girl. She might be taught to read and spell but it was considered far more advantageous to prepare her for her future decorative role in society so that deportment, embroidery and music were taught by a governess and dancing and drawing by visiting masters either at home or, from mid-century, offered at fee-paying 'adventure schools' of uneven quality. [6]

In the decades following the Revolution, however, there was a dramatic change. Marianne and her sisters were of the generation of well-to-do young women who benefited hugely from the public debates about female education, which intensified in the 1790s and early 1800s. In England, Catherine Macauley's *Letters on Female Education* (1790), Maria Edgeworth's *Letters to Literary Ladies* (1795) and Hannah More's *Strictures on the Modern System of Female Education* (1799) pleaded for women's education. In America, the most influential publications were the English import, Mary Wollstonecraft's *The Vindication of the Rights of Women* (1792) even though it was denigrated in both countries due to its author's reputation and radical ideas; Massachusetts essayist Judith Sargent Murray's *On the Equality of the Sexes* (1790) and *The Gleaner* (1798); and the anonymous *The Female Advocate Written by a Lady* (1801), which urged better education for girls to encourage their self-respect and remove sexual inequality.

The interest in the subject led to 'the age of the academies'. Starting in 1790, at least 350 female academies were established in the United States before 1860. When the Napoleonic Wars prevented Marianne from receiving a French education, her parents were able to give her a decent American one. In the autumn of 1802, Marianne travelled to Philadelphia, home to some of the foremost academies in the country. She enrolled at Green Hill Young Ladies Academy, which followed the curriculum laid down by the Young Ladies Academy of Philadelphia, founded in 1787. Marianne could study geography, history, mathematics, science and the 'system of the Universe', besides the traditional feminine accomplishments of reading, spelling, music and dancing, drawing and French.

Marianne's grandfather, however, reminded her, on 2 February 1803, that 'the fleeting pleasures of this world leave a dreadful void in that heart which feels not the blessedness of virtue. – Do you wish for happiness? be virtuous. – Do you wish to gain the love & esteem of those, whose affection & esteem will render you estimable in your own eyes? be virtuous.' Such was the power of virtue that 'Even the vicious secretly venerate' it, he assured her. 'The most wicked of celestial spirits was awed' by it:

> . . . abash'd the Devil stood,
> And felt how awful goodness is, and saw
> Virtue in *her* shape how lovely.

'Virtue, you see my child,' he continued, 'in the opinion of the poet acquired *grace invincible* from *beauty & youth*: nay he has personified virtue as *female*, plainly intimating it shall ever be the attendant of your sex.' Marianne was, he knew, familiar with Milton's *Paradise Lost*.[7]

In advising Marianne to be virtuous, her grandfather was also showing how she could best serve her country as a republican girl. Benjamin Rush, physician, Signer and supporter of female education, had declared in 1778, 'Virtue, Virtue alone is the basis of a republic', for it was the virtuous citizen who, by adhering to the highest moral standards, would ensure the stability of the new republic. Virtue was not demanded of women as citizens – for they had been granted no rights of citizenship – but as fit companions for republican men, guarantors of masculine virtue. Young ladies like Marianne were assured in the periodicals of the day that, for instance, '*society* is interested in your goodness – you polish our manners – correct our vices – and inspire our hearts with a love of virtue'. By being a moral force, they could transform 'manners into mores, into the moral foundation of the society'. Young women thus had the power 'to make our young men, not in empty words, but in deed, and truth, republicans'. And by doing so, their continued influence would banish from America, one widely printed commencement ovation proclaimed in 1795, 'those crimes and corruptions, which have never yet failed of giving rise to tyranny or anarchy. While you thus keep a country virtuous, you maintain its independence'.[8]

If these young women were to assume such a crucial role in the nation's life, the theorists reasoned, they would need to be better educated than their mothers had been. Then, they could make 'the *American people* in general *an* EXAMPLE *of* HONOUR *and* VIRTUE to the rest of the World.' Marianne's grandfather, however, took a more personal view of her education: 'it enlightens the understanding and mends the heart,' he explained to her, adding 'but yours, my dear Mary[Anne], does not need mending, you possess a very good heart & good sense; the latter only wants cultivation.' He believed that both she and Bess possessed 'good understandings,' and that 'occupation, study & reflection are only required to polish them and to gain those acquirements most suitable to young ladies'.

The bravest amongst Marianne and Bess's generation, women such as Lucretia Mott and the Grimke sisters, would later be at the forefront of enlightened womanhood fighting for abolitionism and equal rights. As Marianne was told by her grandfather, 'I treat you not as a child but as a rationale being capable of judging correctly, and desirous of acting rightly.' In his letters to her after the bankruptcy of her father he deliberately emphasised the importance of virtuous behaviour and piety, talismans to ward off the evil eye of her father's failure as much as national precepts for republican girls.[9]

Marianne's departure for boarding school concerned her family because she was an asthmatic: her ill health was chronic. Since childhood she had been seized by sudden fits of suffocation, so severe she seemed on the point of dying. Propped upright by a mound of pillows, at the onset of an asthmatic attack her frail body, held by her bodymaids, nurse or mother, would tense with spasm as she gasped for air and then lapsed into momentary relaxation in their arms before the agonising fight for breath began again.

Asthma was then categorised as a constriction of the airways to the lungs – it would not be until the 1960s that it was identified as an inflammatory disease. Marianne's treatment combined the national panaceas of calomel, bleeding and opium, with myrtle and mustard seed poultices. Calomel, however, is toxic and was often deadly in the long term, especially for women. A tasteless powder of mercury and hydrochloric acid, it was not diluted by other medicine to lessen the cumulative effect of mercury poisoning, as was customary in England because it could make women barren or miscarry. Marianne's general health deteriorated under a constant regimen of purging, bleeding, calomel, and opium, the most effective sedative available. With the help of her mother, her old nurse and the family priest, Marianne learnt to calm herself through a combination of breathing exercises and of concentrating her mind upon a favourite prayer or psalm, even a saying from one of her grandfather's books. 'I find the Pensées soothes me', she wrote of the little book of Pascal that she kept with her red leather-bound missal always at hand. The Irish writer Maria Edgeworth assumed that Marianne's calmness came from trying too hard to be English, her manner 'too composed – *compassée* rather more than appears quite natural – as if studiously *formed* on English manner'. She had no notion of either Marianne's asthmatic condition nor that a well-bred American lady must, as Aaron Burr advised his daughter Theodosia, 'always be calm and serene, and never to hurry'.[10]

Fortunately Marianne's sisters were healthy and robust. Bess, bound in age and closeness to her elder sister, nevertheless chose not to follow her to boarding school in Philadelphia. Bess lacked Marianne's disarming beauty but her features were still attractive. Her grandfather, always the soundest in his evaluation of character, considered that she possessed 'an excellent understanding & a good heart'. She was affectionate and generous – speaking 'with delight' of how Louisa was 'thought very pretty', and of Marianne's 'great beauty'.

Bess was slower in reading and music than Marianne. 'I'm sorry my little Betsy can't apply', her grandfather had commented when she was seven, not from lack of intellect but from lack of effort. She easily grasped the subjects she liked but could not be bothered with those she disliked so, as the least musical of the sisterhood, she never practised regularly, to her musical mother's chagrin. Languages, however, were another matter. In 1805 when Bess was fifteen she decided that her written French was not fluent enough and obtained her mother's permission to board with Madame Le Pelletier, who had established a small, select school in Baltimore. Although many émigrés had returned to France, in the first decade of the nineteenth century Baltimore still contained a sizeable émigré community so that Bess and her sisters continued to have French dancing masters and dressmakers and confess their sins to French émigré priests.[11]

In childhood, Louisa and Emily were always paired off and rarely separated. 'How was poor Louisa when you left Annapolis?' their grandfather asked their uncle Harper. 'She must be somewhat desolate without Emily'. She and Emily were such a mischievous pair that, before they started at Mrs Keets' school in Annapolis, their grandfather warned them about their behaviour. 'I hope you & yr sister will conduct yourselves with great propriety when you go to school in Annapolis', he wrote to Louisa on 19 September 1803, 'if you do not apply & improve yourselves I shall send you both back to your Mama!' She proved to be a model student and was awarded a gilt ten-pointed star medal not just for good conduct but, the engraving stated, also for 'Genius Rewarded', a tribute immodest Louisa would doubtless have considered quite justified.

When she was only four her grandfather had noticed how well she applied herself to a task. She was determined to keep up with her two elder sisters, and pushed herself to do as well as she imagined they did. She was also the most methodical of the sisterhood, a decisive, organised young lady, full of confidence, and apt to be bossy, especially with Emily. Her grandfather teased her by telling her that her little cousin Charles Harper 'does not like contradiction; in this respect he resembles a little cousin of his – I believe you can guess whom I mean.'[12]

Like her mother and Marianne, Louisa was dark-eyed and dark-haired; her small head was perched upon a swan-like neck around which she later would drape ropes of exquisitely cut diamonds, and her slender figure was like her elder sister's, except that where Marianne was willowy and fragile, Louisa was petite and lusty. She was the most emotional of the sisters, veering from elated exaggeration one moment to level-headed consideration another. When she was excited or making a plan, her cheeks flushed, her eyes flashed as, making up for a lack of inches with a charge of energy, she galvanised those around her into action. She and Emily, like their elder sisters, were taught by their grandfather to keep daily accounts from an early age, a habit they always maintained, both becoming proficient managers of financial affairs.

Although they were always close, Louisa and Emily were physically and temperamentally quite unalike. Emily, a lisping waif-like child born in 1795/6, grew into a more solidly built young girl. Of average height, she was the plainest sister but with her mother's charm of manner and bearing that enabled her to appear more attractive than her features warranted. She had inherited the small slightly upturned Carroll eyes of her great-grandfather and her great-aunts. In temperament she was as placid as Louisa was volatile, and had none of Louisa's sense of adventure, much preferring home life to jaunting about. She was not much interested in studying and had to be chivvied by her grandfather. 'I perceive by your writing that your fingers are yet unsteady', he wrote in 1802 when she was about seven, advising her that 'more practice, attention & pains will soon improve your hand writing'.[13]

During their childhood the regular family journeys between Carroll House and the Manor became triangular, to include Brooklandwood, their plantation conveniently situated between the Manor and uncle Carroll Jr at Homewood. Frequent visits were also made to their aunt Kitty and uncle Harper at Gay Street in Baltimore and at Oakland plantation, four miles from Brooklandwood. Moving between family houses, and paying social visits, was so routine that the girls always called Sunday the 'journeying day of the family', which originated from Sunday being the day the priest travelled to say Mass in the Carroll chapels, and the day they travelled there, too, if necessary.[14]

Their father Richard Caton had started building Brooklandwood for their mother in 1793. Their grandfather had bought an initial 303 acres in 1788 for Mary as an alternative to Castle Thunder and over the years he increased the plantation so that in 1812 it comprised 1,400 acres, including a tract not calculated to attract by its name: 'Part of Addition to Poor Jamaica Man's Plague' but which, nonetheless, covered good, high land. The plantation

Brookland Wood

Brooklandwood, the Caton plantation in Baltimore County. It was bought for Mary
and her family to escape from the summer 'fever season' in Annapolis and Baltimore.

overlooked the lush Green Spring Valley, now the site of the National Point
to Point course where one of America's most exciting steeplechase races is
run in April. The Catons built it to escape the summer heat of town and
chose a hill-top site with cool breezes and magnificent views. From the two
descending semi-circular terraces of the south front, the lawns and meadows
fell away to the broad valley floor on which farm buildings were clustered;
away beyond them stretched open fields leading to the wooded Suter hills.
Through this landscape of rolling hills meandered numerous streams, tribu-
taries of the Big Gunpowder and Little Gunpowder Falls nearby.[15]

  Caton described Brooklandwood as 'an elegant house' and it conformed to
the idea of a Southern plantation mansion with its wide colonnaded portico
entrance, and spacious high-ceilinged rooms, including a large saloon, a library
and fourteen bedrooms. (It is today St Paul's School.) Beyond the mansion
lay a bathing house, an ice house and the dairy, a favourite childhood haunt
for Emily and her cousins. Dairies in the Chesapeake were often ornamental
as well as functional buildings. The Harper dairy at Oakland designed by
Latrobe, architect of the Capitol, was built in the form of an ancient temple,
embellished with oak leaves and flowers over an Ionic portico of four columns,
and judged 'the prettiest building' by family friend Robert Gilmor; it survives
in the Baltimore Museum of Art.

Louisa's favourite childhood haunt, the stables at Brooklandwood.

A Carroll cousin remembered how at nearby Clymnalira's dairy, the 'walled-in dairy spring held a speckled trout that we liked to watch dart in and out of his hiding place. Then there was a crayfish or two lumbering about.' Delighted children loved to see 'the pans lifted out of the water troughs and the thick yellow cream roll up on the skimmer. Everything that went on at the dairy was of interest – the curd draining on pointed bags from trees, the crocks and pans boiling over their own oven, the wooden paddles turning in the wooden churns', and, last of all, to end their visit with a tiny pat of butter and a cup of fresh creamy milk to drink. [16]

Louisa's favourite haunt, however, was the stable block. In those days, women rode everywhere: to church, to hounds, to balls and to pay visits. For Louisa this was a blissful, exhilarating occupation. On learning that Marianne's asthma would sometimes preclude riding, Louisa aged nine sobbed, as if the world was ending, that she must pray to God all day never to make her stop riding. As she grew up Brooklandwood was perfect for Louisa as it was situated in some of the best fox-hunting country in America. The Valley, later home to the exclusive Green Spring Valley Hunt – equivalent to such English hunts as the Beaufort, Quorn and Althorp & Pytchley – had no organised hunt in Louisa's day as landowners kept their own packs of hounds and hunted with their family and friends whenever they pleased. Louisa could hunt with her grandfather at the

Manor and used his hounds elsewhere. Although he had bred racehorses and laid out a racecourse at Carrollton, his political career had left him with less time for the turf and he confined himself to hunting and field sports. He did, however, provide horses for all his grandchildren.

Fox hunting in America was never limited by area so that a thirty-mile gallop through three counties, from the Chesapeake to the Atlantic, was by no means unusual, broken by stops at hospitable manor houses on the way. During the hunting season, Doughoregan and Brooklandwood kept the traditional open house to receive returning riders. Louisa became a superb, daring horsewoman, like many of her southern female contemporaries. Visitors were impressed by the self-reliance of these Chesapeake plantation girls. The French traveller Ferdinand Bayard observed how 'the women, riding very beautiful Virginia horses, would challenge each other to a race', and he explained their independence, an unusual phenomenon in France, as owing to the fact that 'Since they often travel by horseback, often ride down steep mountains, cross rivers and since in their earliest years they are exposed to all the mettle of very fast horses, they are skilful and fearless riders'.[17]

6

The Patterson Connection

In the summer of 1804 shortly before her sixteenth birthday, Marianne left school. She was, her grandfather noted with satisfaction, possessed 'of a good understanding'. Her asthma attacks had been less frequent of late and, slender and graceful, she was strikingly lovely and danced with elegance. She looked forward to the excitement of her entry into society.

The Carroll agent Greatham was at home with bills of lading and of exchange for bulk amounts of plantation crops, tools and cloth but he was quite at sea with the polite, neatly dressed émigrés who besieged his office clutching accounts for embroidery, lace, dressmaking and dancing lessons *pour Madame Catin*. He floundered amidst the scrappy indecipherable receipts for a bandeau here, a chemisette there, several plumes, ribbons and garlands, six pairs of dancing shoes and one exquisite merino shawl which cost more than the cloth to make one hundred plantation shirts; all of which he was under instructions from Mr Carroll to settle.

Marianne's grandfather had not quite grasped the extent of a debutante's requirements. 'All expensive ornaments I object to; a neat simplicity in dress best becomes a young lady just entering into the world', he had directed Marianne, stressing that her own qualities were far more important, for 'sweetness of manners, great modesty, affability tempered with dignity, playfulness without levity are the most attractive ornaments of a young lady; these she may call her own; they are the ornaments of mind, which will be permanent; those of the person will fade, and tho' in youth they may be aided by dress, in which taste may be displayed, yet their chief merit must be ascribed to the milliner & manufacturer.' Much as she always respected his advice, it was no doubt with relief that she learned he would leave the selection of her debut clothes to her mother.[1]

Carroll of Carrollton himself continued to wear the eighteenth-century attire which had characterised the republican courts of Washington and Adams: silk waistcoats, knee-buckled breeches, silk stockings, and square-toed boots, his hair long, powdered and tied behind in a queue. As in revolutionary and then Napoleonic France, dress in republican America was invested with political significance. In 1804, his costume was associated with

Federalist politics and sound, old-fashioned Georgian Britain. He belonged to a world in which the typical entertainment amongst conservative circles was not, in Henry Adams' inimitable depiction, 'the light feminine triviality which France introduced into an amusement-loving world, but the serious dinner of Sir Robert Walpole and Lord North, where gout and plethora waited behind the chairs'; one in which 'every Republican must dress like a Frenchman, and every Federalist like a subject of King George.'[2]

In assembly rooms throughout the principal towns of the Atlantic seaboard states, dignified dowagers curtsied resolutely in their court dresses of stiff buckram and brocade, feeling 'scandalized at the exhibition of low-cut dresses and French draperies' displayed by the young ingénues of Marianne's coterie. As the older generation turned their backs, rampant Gallomania seized the younger generation, defiantly adopting the daring new style of dress or, to be more accurate, undress. In women's fashions, it was the era of the 'merveilleuse' who wore a narrow dress characterised by a light fabric artfully draped for decency. This originated from a British undergarment, the chemise, adapted by French couturiers who bared the arms, lowered the neckline, raised the waist and shortened the skirt. It was made fashionable by Madame Fortunée Hamelin, who caused a sensation walking through the Tuileries gardens in Paris wearing only 'a sizeable gauze veil'.

In America the merveilleuse soon became the fashion, but it was adapted to be less revealing and indecent for young women. Thus Marianne would wear flesh coloured pantaloons and a matching underskirt, raise the neckline to cover her chest and drape a flimsy scarf or shawl over the top of her chemise. Despite belonging to Federalist families, when Marianne and her girlfriends appeared in society for the first time in 1804, they replaced the traditional court dress of elaborate hoops, ruffles and powdered wigs with the new French fashions: the simple clinging high-waisted gowns and unpowdered curls popular in fashionable republican circles. In doing so they were deemed to be making not just a stylistic statement but also a political one.

While this might seem to attach too much weight to the flimsy clothes of girls who just wanted to have fun, it was otherwise understood in the inflamed political atmosphere of the times. Marianne's gauzy gown and her young dancing partner's cropped locks à la Brutus indicated solidarity with Jefferson's pro-French Republican America rather than Adams's pro-British Federalist America. Although government attitudes and public opinion had both cooled towards Bonaparte's France, Empress Josephine's French Empire furniture nonetheless became a craze in America. In 1804, Angelica Schuyler Church, daughter of General Philip Schuyler and sister-in-law of Alexander Hamilton, (all friends of Marianne's family) and the most fashionable hostess in New York, made it *comme il faut* to receive while reclining upon her beautiful boat-shaped gilded bed, forerunner of the chaise-longue.[3]

During the winter season of 1804/1805 when Marianne was making her debut, a rival *merveilleuse* from Baltimore was holding American society in thrall. Betsy Patterson was the early Republic's first female celebrity. Famous for her beauty, her clothes, her marriage, her wit and her independence, from her early days as a belle in Baltimore, she provoked admiration even from her foes. Marianne was an ingénue when she met vivacious Betsy, three years her senior and a star in the social firmament, and she happily responded to the guidance of such an experienced socialite.

Before her debut, Marianne had only a passing acquaintance with Betsy's family, the Pattersons, as they belonged not to the Chesapeake plantocracy but to the Baltimore mercantile community. The burgher respectability of Betsy's father, William Patterson, belied an adventurous profiteering past. In 1776, aged fourteen, Patterson had arrived in Philadelphia from the north of Ireland. At the outbreak of the American Revolution he invested everything he owned in a stake in ships bound for France, aiming to return with scarce 'Powder and Arms'; a venture profitable enough to send Patterson into clandestine arms dealing. Rich at twenty-six, he married into a Baltimore mercantile family, and founded the firm of William Patterson & Sons, settling his eleven children in a town house in South Street. Betsy was his eldest daughter, and at her core, glittering like the diamonds she wore in Washington City, lay the steel of ambition.

In July 1803, Betsy had met Napoleon's youngest brother Lieutenant Jerome Bonaparte of the French Navy who had landed in Virginia ostensibly en route to France from Sainte-Domingue. He was utterly bewitched by her and the couple were soon engaged. Despite disapproval from her father and an ominous silence from Napoleon, they married on Christmas Eve. The ceremony was conducted by Bishop Carroll, and Betsy's father took the precaution of drawing up a firm marriage contract. It was the gossip of the season. And when President Jefferson refused to escort Mrs Merry, wife of the British Minister, into dinner but a week later gave precedence to Betsy Bonaparte, it signalled the pro-French sympathies of the US Government to the British Minister, who thereafter boycotted official invitations.[4]

Betsy was 'proud of her position, and only thinks about enjoying all the glory which it gives her,' observed Pichon the French Consul-General. The glory of her position was by no means what first struck people who met her that winter. 'We hear strange reports of Madame Bonaparte's dress on public occasions,' Marianne's grandfather wrote to his son on 14 February 1804. 'I ought rather say, *of her no dress*, for if the reports are not much exaggerated, she goes to public assemblies nearly naked, or so thinly covered that all her charms are exposed, and little left to the imagination.' Although Betsy was insouciant about men ogling her, it would be harder to remain in society if her costume upset women. Catharine Mitchill, wife of the Federalist Senator Dr Samuel Mitchill, noticed that the 'state of nudity in which she appeared attracted the Gentlemen, for I saw several of them take a look at her bubbies'. Betsy's immodesty so horrified her Smith aunts that she had to 'promise to have more clothes on'. Betsy merely draped a gauzy scarf around her much admired bare shoulders but otherwise made no attempt to change her *merveilleuse* 'undress'.

The Washington ladies were less concerned with Betsy herself, whose marriage and rank allowed her some leeway, than with her influence upon other susceptible minds. The effect could corrupt girls newly in society, such as Marianne, for whom, it was argued, 'such fashions are astonishingly bewitching & will gradually progress, &', Congressman Simeon Baldwin suggested, 'we may well reflect on what we shall be when fashion shall remove all barriers from the chastity of women.' Marianne was captivated by Betsy, whose cousin Mary Smith, daughter of General Samuel Smith, was one of her close friends, and a strong element of hero-worship pervaded their friendship. Marianne passed on that the English papers 'Say you are the most *lovely* woman in the world,' and pleaded, when Betsy was abroad, 'if you can spare the time', to send 'the fashions for all ages', as 'I have great confidence in your taste, & judgment. Write to me, I beg you, your letters are charming.'[5]

The other person who happily deferred to Betsy was her husband. When Napoleon's verdict finally reached America in August it was evident that William Patterson's mercantile caution was no match for the wrath of an Emperor. Napoleon's meteoric rise to power had culminated on 18 May 1804 with his proclamation as Emperor of all the French. But Napoleon only rewarded those who pleased him and he instructed his Minister to tell Jerome that 'he would treat with cold indifference those who dared to act independently of him'. Jerome was in trouble. 'If he comes alone, I shall forgive the error of a moment and the fault of youth,' Napoleon ordained but, if he brought Betsy with him, 'she shall not put a foot on the territory of France'. Betsy, however, was not at all frightened and was certain that the Emperor's cold resolve would melt before her beauty.[6]

She and Jerome sailed on the ship *Erin* and arrived in Lisbon in April 1805: she was now six months pregnant. But Napoleon had declared their marriage null and any offspring of it illegitimate. As for 'Miss Patterson', his most polite term for Betsy, she was a mere piece of jetsam easily discarded; if she evaded his order to be sent home and went to Bordeaux or Paris she would be taken forcibly to Amsterdam and put on board the first American vessel. Jerome left her to meet Napoleon in Turin and Betsy finally sailed for Amsterdam but was refused entry to the port. For the first time, she broke down. [7]

Fortunately, her brother Robert Patterson was waiting onshore. He alerted the American Consul whose official enquiry enabled the *Erin* to put to sea and make for the nearest country not in France's imperial pocket – and in May 1805 the only choice was the England of Pitt and George III. The British newspapers had already reported her story. When the *Erin* party came ashore on 20 May, the crowds assembled to see her were so immense that 'it was with the greatest difficulty she could get as far as the carriage' waiting to take her to the Inn. And far from shrinking at such attention Betsy was like a flower suddenly come into bloom in the hothouse of adulation. She was back at the centre of attention. In Camberwell, in the countryside south of London, in the middle of war between France and England and in the presence of witnesses, as at a royal birth, Napoleon's nephew was born on 7 July.

Her absent husband might assure her that October, '*Sois tranquille, ton mari ne t'abandonnera jamais*', yet that was what he had, in effect, already done. Jerome's only advice was that she return to America. In November, overwhelmed by 'insupportable disappointment', she sailed with her baby 'Bo' and brother Robert for home.[8]

In America Betsy became even more famous, cast in the role of the virtuous abandoned wife returning to the Republic to protect her young son from the corrupting influences of Europe, a symbol of republican motherhood – an interpretation entirely at odds with the truth. Betsy would later describe her return as the time 'the Emperor hurled me back on what I hated most on earth – my Baltimore obscurity'. During the winter season of 1806, young belles and beaux clustered about her, as she was escorted by her handsome brother Robert around town.[9]

Robert Patterson was a personable young man, aged twenty-five and in possession of independent means as well as a partnership in the successful family firm. He also carried the sophistication of a two years' stay in Paris and London. Taller than average, he wore his curly dark hair short and unpowdered and his pantaloons tight fitting down to his leather top-boots; his white cravat was immaculate and his top coat cut away to a mathematical point behind. Paul de Maupertiers, the acting American consul in Rotterdam, who had seen a good deal of him in Paris, thought highly of him, describing him as 'a charming young man'.

Robert was undoubtedly one of the beaux of that season, the aura of Betsy's celebrity lending him glamour, even though from the Chesapeake gentry's vantage point he did not own a plantation. This did not discourage

him from wooing Marianne, passing an inordinate amount of time in
Annapolis. He had to press his suit assiduously in the teeth of other devoted
rivals – and there were a number – although Mary Carroll Caton thought
Robert would never do for her seventeen-year-old daughter, he was 'so cold
a lover' that Marianne could have 'nothing to say to him'. Against these
odds, Robert prevailed over his rivals and discussions between the two families began in earnest in February.

After the marriage settlement was negotiated, the wedding took place
on 1 May 1806. Just as he had married Catholic Jerome to Presbyterian
Betsy, so Bishop Carroll married Catholic Marianne to Presbyterian Robert.
It was a situation he lamented. He treated her and her sisters as his 'very
dear relations' and honorary granddaughters and was concerned that
Marianne's attachment to her religion would be diminished. To an old
family friend, he confided that it was only to be expected given that her
'uncle, mother and aunt have all formed connections, as you know, out of
the Church. I endeavour while I live to save the children but cannot hope
much from my weak endeavours.'[10]

Mary Carroll Caton, too, lamented privately; her precious daughter was
not marrying a plantation but the son of a republican mercantile family
whose fortune was based upon risky operations like Caton's rather than the
solid wealth of land. She had to accept, however, that the marriage was
Marianne's own choice. Besides which, if she agreed that 'the business of
a mother's life is to marry her daughters' she could console herself with the
thought that she still had three more daughters to marry.

7

Debutantes

Bess was almost sixteen when she attained the rank of Miss Caton, the senior unmarried daughter of the family. In spite of her elevation, Bess could never quite elude society's perception of her as merely one of the Caton sisters, cast for ever in a supporting role to their eldest sister. Moreover, it was Marianne with her breathtaking beauty and serene disposition, rather than Louisa or Emily, with whom Bess was compared. And where Marianne was thought 'a remarkably . . . handsome woman, and elegant in her manners', by one English acquaintance, Bess was judged 'not handsome, and far from elegant'. Bess never minded, though, and she did possess attractive features. Her deep grey eyes were quick and bright, gleaming with intelligence, and the hint of a smile around her mouth conveyed a sense that she knew how to listen as much as to talk. Tall and slim with brown hair and her mother's slightly pointed nose, she was light and fluid in movement, admired for 'her *undulating* grace' and already held to be a good conversationalist.

Of all the sisters, she wrote the most interesting letters but she never dated them and her handwriting bore witness to the speed of her thoughts, words tumbling over each other so quickly that, as her grandfather pointed out, they were almost impossible to disentangle: 'Your letters my dear child were they ever so long & written in a hand even worse than yours would never appear too long to me; their contents, their style and good sense amply compensate the punishment of deciphering them.' Bess was to be the chronicler of the sisterhood and although her sisters might tease her, their own handwriting was not much easier to read.

On 16 June another chronicler of the family, Bishop John Carroll, related that he was expecting the newly weds in Philadelphia in a few days. As part of their marriage tour and to remove Marianne from the severe heat that exacerbated her asthma, they were travelling to the cooler climate of upstate New York. Bess and aunt Kitty Harper accompanied them and afterwards the party met Richard Caton and Robert Harper in New York City. On their return to Maryland, Marianne and Robert moved into their own house in Baltimore, and Bess consequently became better acquainted with his brothers and sisters who lived nearby. Through them she was introduced to Eliza Anderson, Betsy's companion on the *Erin* voyage, whose influence upon her would be considerable.[1]

Eliza and her widowed father Dr John Crawford, a former surgeon to the East India Company, had settled in Baltimore in 1796, when she was sixteen, on the recommendation of an uncle who had made a fortune in the China trade. She married a merchant kinsman, Henry Anderson but in 1801 his business failed and he fled his creditors, abandoning her and their baby daughter. She turned to writing to make a living. Women in Bess and Marianne's circle ensured an adequate provision of the latest 'good reads' by forming book clubs. 'You know how books travel in this country (much to the detriment of their covers), but it is an excellent idea', Rosalie Calvert, a Belgian heiress married to a Maryland planter, explained to her brother on 10 December 1808. 'The expense of a complete library would be too great, so everyone purchases several new volumes each year, and they are loaned around and their merits discussed.' There was one novel these Maryland women wanted to read: 'Have you read *Corinne*, by Madame Staël-Holstein, an extremely interesting new romance?' Rosalie asked while Bess recommended it to her grandfather as 'a wonderful book'. One of the books Eliza Anderson passed around her Baltimore friends was *A Vindication of the Rights of Women* which continued to be widely read in America, though only brave women applauded its ideas in public.[2]

When Bess became her friend, Eliza Anderson was associate-editor of the *Companion and Weekly Miscellany*, a journal first published in 1804. Two years later she became the editor of its short-lived successor *The Observer*, under the nom de plume 'Beatrice Ironside'. Her writing attracted the *Federal Gazette*'s criticism of the 'fierce Fury who edits *The Observer*'. To Bess, however, Eliza Anderson was a gate-keeper to an unrealised intellectual world. When Bess was at Marianne's in Baltimore, she would go round with Polly to see Eliza at Dr Crawford's house in Hanover Street, a house 'bursting with books'.

It was quite unlike any of the Carroll Caton houses. 'This house is miserably out of sorts', Benjamin Latrobe, the architect, would tell his wife when he stayed there in 1812. 'Dr. Crawford's library is black with smoke, and covered with dust, cumbered with papers, and choked with books, bookcases and desks.' Eliza was translating a popular French novel, Sophie Cottin's *Claire d'Albe* which was published as *Dangerous Friendship, or the letters of Clara d'Albe* in 1807. Not surprisingly, Bess thought her the 'most intelligent & interesting friend'. Eliza considered that Bess 'had more heart and more head than all the rest of the family' and that her good brain was wasted on being a southern belle shining in society.

Around 1807 Eliza Anderson met Maximilien Godefroy, a French émigré who found employment in Baltimore as a drawing master. A talented, self-taught architect, he was helped by Latrobe to gain his first commission, the construction of St Mary's Chapel, upon which he was working when Eliza was translating his book, and they fell in love. The opportunity for a delicious scandal presented itself for, however charming this cultured, clever Frenchman, Mrs Anderson was a married woman. 'As for what the Town says of me, and much I hear they say, I care not,' she declared as she made a plan to divorce her errant husband and marry Godefroy. Yet this was no easy matter as she had to give proof of infidelity and, as she recognised, infidelity 'is not an affair to which men usually call witnesses'. Bess had been privy to these tribulations and the happy denouement of this complicated love affair influenced her own attitude to marriage. Eliza recalled Bess saying that 'until she loved some one as enthusiastically as I did Maxime she never would marry at all'. Although Eliza teased her about it, Bess just laughed and said that 'she would only marry for love alone'.[3]

Despite Bess's popularity, after two seasons she remained unmarried. This puzzled her family for she was always surrounded by eligible beaux at the balls and assemblies. And, as Eliza Anderson Godefroy said of her, 'perhaps no woman breathing ever had more offers' of marriage. John Penn, of the famous Pennsylvanian family, was so 'mighty smitten' with her that he proposed; so did the rich, eligible Philadelphian John Powel; while the devoted Count Jules de Menon, beloved by her family, proposed again and again. Much to her mother's despair, Bess rejected all her suitors. Apart from the Count, not one of them was a Catholic. But Bess never showed any inclination to become a religious. This was not true, though, of all her sisters.[4]

After Louisa left Mrs Keets' Academy in 1807, aged thirteen, she attended a new school for Catholic girls through the recommendation of Bishop Carroll. The founder of the school, Elizabeth Seton, was a widow with five children when she was received into the Catholic Church; her conversion was bitterly opposed by her Anglican family in New York. The school on Paca Street in Baltimore (later designated a national historic shrine to commemorate 'Saint Elizabeth' as she became) was a little 'neat, delightful mansion . . . in the new French style of folding windows and recesses'. The surrounding orchards, garden, cows and dogs added to its delight and when the doors and windows were open in fine weather, the sound of the altar bells from neighbouring St Mary's chapel could be heard. Louisa joined the other nine girls in prayers, reciting the Rosary together and assisting at daily Mass; otherwise the studies pursued included the usual subjects of a ladies academy as well as 'Christian Doctrine', which Mother Seton 'impressed deeply on their minds'.[5]

So deeply was Louisa's mind impressed that she decided to become a nun. While her father had been perfectly happy for his children to be brought up in their mother's faith, the thought of his lovely, vivacious fifteen-year-old daughter shrouded in a habit and hidden away from life was unbearable. Distressed and irate, he immediately accused Mother Seton and Father Du Bourg, from neighbouring St Mary's School for Catholic Boys, of persuading Louisa to join the American Sisters of Charity. He was so 'profuse with indecorous epithets' that Father Du Bourg complained to Robert Harper, on 8 April 1809, 'his displeasure might have been more moderate, even had I been the instigator of that business'. Du Bourg declared: 'Now, sir, I protest that she never spoke or wrote to me on that subject before Tuesday evening last, when she did it standing outside of our Chapel door, and then it was a general talk all over the city.'

Cousin John Carroll, now the archbishop, was delighted to report to his sisters on 20 April, that Louisa was 'resolved on renouncing the world altogether and joining the virtuous Mrs Seton', who was going to establish a

Elizabeth Seton by Charles Saint Memin, 'un émigré français', in 1796.

girls' boarding school at Emmitsburg in western Maryland. Louisa wanted to be one of the pious young ladies trained by Mother Seton 'to the duties of a perfect life' in the Sisterhood, particularly 'to aid the poor by their work and industry' and to nurse the sick. The archbishop was all too aware of the family's opposition.[6]

Louisa poured out her heart to Mother Seton, who was elated that 'one of the most elegant and highest girls in Baltimore' wanted to join her community and was even 'refusing matches to unite herself to Our Lord'. Her rejection of several suitors including Mr Clark, a rich Catholic of New Orleans, who had proposed before she was sixteen, had elicited her grandfather's comment, 'Notwithstanding we all thought Louisa would have accepted the address of Mr Clark, and her former conduct warranted this opinion, she refused him yesterday. I think she stands in the way of her own happiness and will hereafter repent of her silly conduct.' Louisa instead spoke in 'the most forcible terms' of her vocation, confiding how she had been teased by some of the family about taking the veil.

The family generally considered her too young to make such an irrevocable decision. Although Louisa was 'very ardent in her wishes and obstinate

Louisa's love of jewellery was evident from a young age.

in her notions', after delicate negotiations between her and the Harpers, she finally agreed to wait until at least August before joining the sister-hood. In the meantime, she was packed off with Bess to stay with the archbishop's sister Mary Carroll Young in Washington City. If her parents hoped that a change of scene would effect a change of heart, their wishes were fulfilled. She returned home full of her amusements and, as her mother assured the archbishop, 'speaks with rapture and gratitude of her entertain-ments at Washington'. Although Louisa did not renounce the veil without a struggle – the archbishop divulged that 'she has, as her Mother says, been sick *indeed*' since she returned – there was no more talk, in public at least, of becoming a nun. This episode made Caton exceedingly uneasy about his daughters' continued friendship with Mrs Seton. There was little he could do about it.

Emily did not inspire the same devotion as Louisa. When, aged fourteen, she left Mrs Keets, she was thought a frivolous, idle girl. 'Her family are truly unhappy about her,' Mrs Seton confided to Juliana Scott in March 1809, 'but what can be expected from a warm heart and lively imagination, nourished only by romances.' After Louisa and Father Du Bourg took her in hand, though, she turned more to her religion, reading the first two volumes of Butler's *Lives of the Saints* and volume one of the *Devout Christian*. 'Dear Soul! how pious and generous she is!' thought Du Bourg when he saw her running a large Sunday school at Annapolis.[7]

8

In Washington City

All three sisters were trying in their different ways to work out what direction their lives should take but it was all too easy to be diverted by the amusements of Washington City. Bess had already become so absorbed in politics that she missed no chance to improve her knowledge of domestic and foreign events. Bess 'is learning Spanish, & is as lazy & good for nothing as ever', said Emily. Bess wanted to read Spanish newspaper reports of the war Britain and Spain were fighting against France (the Peninsular War 1808–1814). She liked nothing better than a good political discussion with her grandfather and uncle Harper. When the latter was away pleading an important legal case in the Supreme Court, she instructed him to write with '*some news*' about 'the general opinion' in Washington City. She loved it when, getting into his 'talkative mood', he discoursed upon all manner of political issues with her.

Whenever the opportunity came to go to Washington City she seized it. Family letters are sprinkled with references to the length of Bess's visits and her enjoyment of the capital. Her interest was by no means unusual at this time of nation-building, though some American women carried their interest to extremes. Betsy Bonaparte's Aunt Spear never allowed herself to be deflected from attending every session of Congress. Her exasperated brother-in-law, William Patterson, left her a legacy in his will on condition that she give up her Congressional attendance altogether.[1]

Since its inception as the new capital in 1800 disparaging comments about Washington City had become common currency among both American politicians and foreign diplomats. The place, like the *merveilleuse*, was in a state of 'undress', bare of basic necessities as well as adornments. Bereft of ancient buildings, of embassies, palaces or churches, and without paved streets, roads or bridges, Washington City consisted of unfinished buildings, the President's House and the Capitol. And along the track linking them lumbered 'The Royal George', an old-fashioned four-horse stage coach, which the architect Benjamin Latrobe remembered 'either rattled with members of Congress from Georgetown in a halo of dust, or pitched like a ship in a seaway among the holes and ruts' of what is better

Pennsylvania Avenue, Washington City, as the sisters' knew it. Watercolour, attributed to Benjamin Latrobe, 1811.

known today as stately Pennsylvania Avenue. The ornate gilded coach, containing the Spanish Minister His Excellency the Marqués de Casa Urujo in full court dress, stood no chance in the 'mass of mud' and yellow clay and rolled over in defeat. The Minister's reaction was echoed in a politer form by a French diplomat, 'Mon Dieu! what have I done to reside in such a city?'

Politicians exiled from the elegancies of New York, Philadelphia and Boston were no more reticent; Ebenezer Mattoon, New Hampshire congressman, writing 'If I wished to punish a culprit, I would send him to do penance in this place, oblige him to walk about this city, city do I call it? This swamp – this lonesome dreary swamp, secluded from every delightful or pleasing thing – except the *name* of the place, which to be sure I reverence.' This was still, in essence, the capital city that the sisters found a decade later.[2]

Bess, Louisa and Emily noticed little of this. They loved Washington City. It might have appeared to political veterans like a stage with an inadequate set and props but to young women it offered the opportunity to participate in a unique thespian experience, in which everyone could appear in crowd scenes full of action and dialogue on a national stage. This was a most unusual role for women in the early nineteenth century, and for the Caton *ingénues* launching into adulthood it was exhilarating.

They were usually escorted there by their uncle Harper, whose political as well as legal interests frequently required his presence in the city, and they stayed with cousins, such as the Youngs and the Carrolls of Rock Creek and of Bellevue, or with their mother's good friends the Decaturs. To the core of resident wives and families of the government, and diplomats with their visitors, was added the local gentry living in Georgetown and the surrounding Maryland and Virginian plantations, all of whom enjoyed the entertainments held to coincide with the sitting of Congress and the Supreme Court.

Women were visible everywhere in the city in a way in which they would not have been elsewhere in America. This was the result partly of being away from home and without customary domestic ties but mostly of having an unprecedented access to public spaces and finding there was no loss of propriety in mingling freely with gentlemen in public. Thus, of the annual Washington Jockey Club races – the Washington equivalent of Ascot, when the whole of Congress emptied for three days – a visitor wrote: 'You must not be astonished at hearing that a number of beautiful females were present, sitting exposed on the tops and boxes of carriages, and in other conspicuous seats.' Furthermore, women in Washington City did not remain seated in mixed company and passively wait to be 'noticed' on male whim. 'The women here are taking a station in society which is not known elsewhere', noted a resident, Margaret Bayard Smith. 'The consequence is that ladies and gentlemen stand and walk about the rooms in mingled groups, which certainly produces more ease, freedom and equality than in those rooms where the ladies sit and wait for the gentlemen to approach and converse.'[3]

By the time Bess, Louisa and Emily were frequenting Washington City, the person who did most to mix the social and political, to open up new worlds for women and to create a milieu peculiar to the capital of the Republic was Dolley Madison, wife of their Democratic-Republican President James Madison, who had succeeded Jefferson in 1809. Although the British Minister Francis Jackson famously described her at first sight as 'fat and forty but not fair' Dolley Madison possessed presence, style and kindness and extended a sympathetic welcome to young people.

The sisters, in common with most young ladies, found it easy to talk to her as they had an interest in common: the latest fashions and shopping. Dolley, a prized customer everywhere, was an early promoter of 'retail therapy': she shopped for herself, for Jefferson's daughters, for her sisters and nieces, for anyone who asked her, for America – she simply adored shopping. Having discarded the Quaker dress of her youth, she enjoyed being well dressed. While turbans, feathers and gold-leaf hairbands were interchangeable, her gold and enamel snuff box was permanent. She used it as an effective ice-breaker, and handing it round also gave her time to think how to react and to observe her guests. 'You are aware that she [Dolley] snuffs; but in her hands, the snuff-box seems only a gracious implement with which to charm', Washington resident Sarah Gales Seaton decided. And Dolley charmed everyone with her warm-heartedness and enjoyment of life. Scholarly senator Dr Samuel Mitchill found 'Her smile, her conversation, and her manners are so engaging,' that he deemed her 'a QUEEN OF HEARTS,' or Queen Dolla lolla, as she was irreverently called by Rosalie Calvert, the 'most accomplished hostess' in the city. [4]

She was also putting a stylish stamp on American public life, a stamp that provided the sisters and their female friends with access to the political world, and the opportunity to learn about the use of information, of lobbying, and to gain a political education; skills the sisters would later put to excellent use. Yet the very existence of a Baltimore booklet *The Female Friend* (1800) reveals the disquiet this could occasion. 'A female politician is only less disgusting than a female infidel,' it declares, whereas 'a female patriot is what Hannah More was and what every American woman should study to be.'[5]

Women of the early Republic were, nevertheless, not only riveted by politics – 'Here we talk of practically nothing else – men, women and children' Rosalie Calvert informed her father in Europe – but were also acting with 'a conscious political intent', as one historian has lucidly shown, and were busy influencing and politicking in their own style all over the city. Dolley Madison set about renovating the neglected President's House to create not just a national symbol for all Americans but also spaces for them to have access to the daily business of politics. In providing formal entertaining rooms, she combined Republican simplicity with Federalist tradition in fine furniture, looking glasses and pictures which, at a time of deep division between the two political parties, reassured both while also impressing European visitors and diplomats. Thus in the formal oval drawing room she and Latrobe employed a classical Greek theme in chairs carved with US insignia on the back, looking glasses and rich red velvet curtains. Latrobe explained the Greek theme: 'Greece was free; in Greece every citizen felt himself an important part of his republic.'

The sisters attended Dolley's Wednesday evenings, known as drawing-rooms, at which they could mingle freely in mixed company, something they had never been able to do before in public. In the most formal of settings the sisters were in close proximity to 'all those whom fashion, fame, beauty, wealth and talent have rendered celebrated'. They were free to listen, to come and go, breaking into one group, leaving another, to utter opinions about issues of the day, to talk politics, to flirt and to make new friends, even though they were young unmarried women.

Through Dolley Madison's regular attendance at congressional debates and Supreme Court hearings, women were encouraged to follow suit; indeed she organised parties of ladies, inviting young friends of nieces and grandchildren to accompany her party to the Capitol. In 1811, Louisa was invited to accompany Dolley and Phoebe Morris to hear a Senate debate at the Capitol, and she and Bess went daily with uncle Harper to the Supreme Court hearings.

Their presence created no stir. The floors of the House and the Senate, the legislative antechambers and the Supreme Court were noisy and crammed with visitors and residents who chatted and laughed while members played and responded to the ladies in the galleries. A German visitor called the Senate 'the finest drawing-room in Washington', comparing it to a European opera house in its capacity to entice young ladies who wished to 'exhibit their attractions'. As issues of national importance were debated on the floor below, the audience debated the merits of the argument in the gallery above. In warmer months, members tied oranges and other pieces of fruit in handkerchiefs with notes to identify the recipients and then extended the bundle attached to a long pole up to the ladies in the galleries for refreshment.[6]

To the attractions of politics were added those of flirtations in a city where men outnumbered women. Augustus Foster, the new British Minister and formerly Merry's chargé d'affaires, decided Washington during the season was 'one of the most marrying places of the whole continent'. The city was a 'whirl of activity' for the girls. A friend of aunt Harper's told her they 'were much admired' in Washington, which he thought full of 'so much good society' that 'one might dine out every day for 6 months, & see different faces, & characters, every day.' It seemed that society here was worthy of a capital city anywhere in Europe.[7]

In the spring of 1811, Bess and Marianne had the chance of comparing it with a European capital. Robert had to travel to Lisbon on business and Marianne, still suffering acutely from asthma, was to accompany him, as the long sea voyage was considered a medical treatment in itself. Although their stay in Lisbon would be short, Bess could not resist the opportunity of foreign travel. Their passage was rough; Marianne, exhausted by seasickness, was unable to get on deck until the coast of Portugal was sighted. Once in Lisbon, however, her health was 'better than it had been for years'. They enjoyed attending the theatre and the opera, where they heard the famous Catalani sing on the King's birthday, and visiting the palaces, which Bess described as enchanted abodes 'the ceilings so lofty as to be almost obscure, painted superbly with historical pieces . . . mirrors in every direction & the Gardens, statues &c, beyond everything delightful'.

But this cultural picnic was overshadowed by warfare. The supremacy of

Napoleon's armies in the Peninsular War was being shaken in Portugal by the British under the command of Wellington. The carnage on both sides from battles fought near Lisbon in May was appalling. When Wellington visited the Albuera battlefield on 21 May, where 4,000 out of 10,000 Allies and 7,000 out of 24,000 French were lost, he came upon one regiment 'literally lying dead in their ranks as they had stood'. Marianne and Bess visited the sick and wounded in the British army hospital in Lisbon in early June and found, Bess wrote home, 'the windows filled with beautiful flowers – the mangled bodies covered with neat white muslins whilst their faces are partly concealed by caps as white as themselves'.

The sisters were living in a war zone. There was 'a constant arrival of fresh troops from England – & the sick & wounded from the armies – french Prisoners &c – the continual firing of cannon, drums, trumpets &c' – the deprivation of sleep and feeling afraid 'without well knowing why', Bess explained to her anxious mother. They left Lisbon on 25 June and by mid-August were at home. Relieved to have exchanged the 'misery & filth' of war-torn Lisbon for clean, tranquil Washington City, they prepared for the winter with renewed gusto.[8]

9

The War of 1812

Everyday life in Washington City during the season of 1812 was so compelling for Bess and Louisa that they could hardly bear to tear themselves away. Everyone was riveted by the debates in Congress on 'warlike' resolutions and, in particular, by the Speaker Henry Clay – the 'star' of the debates – and John C. Calhoun, leaders of the Democratic-Republican 'War Hawks' who were calling for war against England.

Their father, however, began to fret at their long absence: Bess had been away three months and Louisa nearly two. 'Give my love to the Girls,' he requested Harper on 22 February 1812, 'and tell them I am anxious to see them at home in that I think they have been long enough in the vortex of pleasure.' As the clamour for war grew more insistent uncle Harper took them back to Baltimore on 14 March.[1]

Throughout their childhood America had been teetering on the edge of conflict. As the United States was caught in the cross-fire of the economic warfare between England and France during the Napoleonic wars, there had been immense provocation to American neutrality (the right theoretically to trade with all nations). The French torched American ships or used privateers to seize American merchantmen and sold the cargo. The English insisted by Orders in Council upon a blockade, effectively closing American trade with Europe and the West Indies, the right to search neutral vessels at sea, and continued to impress about 3,800 American sailors into the Royal Navy. Yet both Jefferson and Madison had, in fact, done their best to avoid war, agreeing with Washington's farewell warning not to become embroiled in foreign quarrels.

By 1812, however, the chalice of American neutrality was being wrested from the Founding Fathers by the rising generation of politicians, many elected to Congress from the West and the South in 1810. These new men were interested neither in British nor French influence but in American nationalism and expansion. To build a continental empire across to the Pacific Ocean, they needed to clear the west, north and Florida of Indian tribes whose resistance was supposedly being equipped by the British. And, most important of all, they wanted to conquer British Canada. When Britain refused to revoke the Orders in Council, the choice was war or submission. 'We are going to fight', said Andrew Jackson, another rising star, 'for the re-establishment of our national character, misunderstood and vilified at home and abroad.' On 18 June 1812, in response to the majority of votes in Congress, President Madison formally declared war against Britain.

The British Minister Foster left Washington on 25 June, driving off in a chariot and four to pay his respects to the Calverts at Riversdale and then to stay with his compatriot Caton at Brooklandwood before heading north for Halifax in British Canada. There need never, it transpired, have been a war. After the British Prime Minister, Spencer Perceval, was assassinated in May, his successor Lord Liverpool had not formed a government until 8 June. On the point of sailing from Halifax in August, Foster received a despatch suspending the Orders in Council: the main *casus belli* had been revoked four days before the United States declared war. As the President had assured Foster that 'were the objectionable Orders in Council revoked, hostilities would be suspended,' Foster immediately requested an armistice. It was, declared the US government, now too late.[2]

From the outset the sisters were aware of the dangers of this Anglo-American war. They were born and bred Americans, yet their English father was now an enemy alien and could be killed. Furthermore, they and their family remained Federalists, although Marianne's husband and all his family were Democratic-Republicans. Yet the strategic complexities of war against British Canada soon dented convictions of easy victory. It was no small matter to be a Federalist then, as the family discovered when personal safety and freedom of expression were already being threatened by mob rule in Baltimore.

On 20 June their local Federalist newspaper the *Federal Republican* had published an editorial opposing the war. Yet Baltimore's maritime trade was eager to profit from such a war. In July, 'a number of privateers were fitting out', observed George Little, who shipped on one, and 'the most intense excitement prevailed throughout the city'. After printing further critical articles, the paper's proprietor-publisher Alexander C. Hanson (a close friend of the family) and his supporters were savagely beaten on 27 July by a large anti-Federalist mob. 'Last night and this morning, our city, has been again under mob-government, the most disgraceful that ever visited any city except Paris in the commencement of the French revolution,' reported the *Lancaster Journal*.

When Hanson, determined to uphold the freedom of the press, returned with some supporters to Baltimore, their lives were so endangered they were taken to the city jail. Throughout the following day, 1 August, the mob raged worse than ever, leaving the city trembling 'in a state of unutterable tumult and horror'. The local militia was out-numbered and 'the men were dragged out of their cell and badly beaten, stabbed, and tarred and feathered'.[3]

That same August day, Carroll of Carrollton, riding from Brooklandwood, met his daughter-in-law's distressed sister Peggy Chew Howard escaping from Belvedere. As known Federalists, the Carrolls and Howards feared for their safety in Baltimore and Caton must needs lie very low, or risk lynching by the mob. Carroll set about arranging his affairs in case first, his family could no longer continue to live in Maryland safely; and second, no one would be allowed to speak their minds – and 'to take what newspapers they please' he fumed to his son. Tensions remained high in Baltimore – and there was not, as yet, even a sighting of the enemy.[4]

Such fighting as there was occurred far away in British Canada or out on the high seas but reports of battles took months to arrive. One early naval victory was won on 25 October off the coast of Africa by their family friend Stephen Decatur USN commanding USS *United States*. At the end of December the sisters attended the ball held in Decatur's honour at the Navy House Yard. An immense company assembled there in high spirits, and Louisa was in her element. She was always especially partial to a beau in dress uniform, once telling Mother Seton's daughter Anna Seton, 'You don't know the enchantment of cockades and epaulets.' The belles, all wearing coloured dresses rather than ingénues' white, coquetted with officers gleaming in gold buttoned blue coats, white pantaloons and waistcoats.[5]

It was not until the spring of 1813 that the war became a military under-taking in Maryland. As the British blockade of the Chesapeake intensified, the spur for action was provided by the sight of Admiral Sir George Cockburn's fleet sweeping along the Bay to take position at the mouth of the Patapsco River on 16 April 1813. On the alarm gun being sounded in Baltimore early that morning nearly 4,000 barely-trained recruits rode to the assembly point prepared to defend their city. On 24 April, however, Cockburn sailed away without firing a shot. He was waiting for the arrival of reinforcements: the timing of which would depend upon defeating France. In1813, England's military resources were largely concentrated in Spain where Wellington defeated the French at Vittoria in June; her diplomatic ones were in the hands of the Foreign Secretary Lord Castlereagh who that month formalised an alliance with Prussia and Russia. These two events were crucial in the fight to defeat Napoleon. This was England's main objec-tive. The war with America was an annoyance, and a distraction. America had started this war and, shrugged England, must bear the consequences. The attack on Baltimore was only postponed.

It moved nearer on 31 October 1813 when the sisters were at the Manor. 'Your servant Sam delivered your letter while we were at dinner', their grandfather answered their uncle Carroll, and 'the foreign intelligence it imparted was more acceptable than the most luxurious dessert could have been.' The British Allies (Russia, Prussia and Austria) had won a decisive victory at the battle of Leipzig on 18 October and Napoleon, 'Perfidy person-ified' or 'PP' as he was called in the family, was on the retreat. Meanwhile, Wellington in Spain had driven the French and the King of Spain, Joseph Bonaparte, out of the country and, once Pamplona fell, was preparing to cross the frontier into France. As more details appeared in the Baltimore *Federal Gazette* and were read eagerly at the Manor, the family prayed: 'God send that the disturber of the world may meet with his deserved fate & punishment.'[6]

In Canada, the American army was being repulsed by the British. Dolley Madison did her best to keep up morale in Washington City and held a splendid traditional New Year's Day reception. Robert Patterson escorted the sisters to the President's House, crowded with well-wishers hopeful of peace in 1814. Dolley presided as a queenly symbol of unity, dressed in a satin robe trimmed 'elaborately with ermine', a trademark turban of white velvet decorated with ostrich plumes and a jewelled cres-cent, and a gold chain and clasps around her waist and wrists; as Sarah Gales Seaton pronounced: 'Her Majesty's appearance was truly regal.' The Winter Queen's image was somewhat marred by the unseasonably warm weather and a crush in the Oval Drawing Room. It became as overheated as a hot-house with unfortunate consequences for some of the *merveilleuses*. Anna Maria Seaton was amused by the sight of 'the rouge which some of our fashionables had laid on with unsparing hand, and which, assimilating with the pearl-powder, dust and perspiration, made them altogether unlovely to soul and to eye'.[7]

After the victorious entry of the European Allies into Paris on 31 March, which led to Napoleon's abdication and exile to Elba, and Wellington's victory at the battle of Toulouse on 10 April, the US Congress began to ponder the destination of the large number of British troops and ships suddenly available for redeployment. In early August an enemy squadron entered the Bay. As the Chesapeake waited, the sun scorching the roofs of houses emptying in preparation for enemy attack, reports confirmed that a British armada of fifty ships, commanded by Vice-Admiral Sir Alexander Cochrane and carrying between 3,000 and 7,000 troops, was sailing majes-tically but swiftly up the Bay. The British fleet moved into the Patuxent River. On 19 August some 4,500 troops under the command of Major-General Robert Ross landed at Benedict, about thirty-five miles south-east of Washington City. The following day at four o'clock, bugles sounded across the fields. The British army, at the leisurely pace necessitated by the excruciating heat, marched northwards towards Washington City. On 23 August it bivouacked at Melwood, south of the village of Bladensburg.

Although the family had expected Robert or uncle Harper to be the first to meet the enemy, Bess and Louisa apparently had the honour. They were staying with aunt Digges at Melwood plantation when a group of British officers called to pay their respects and courteously request a meal. The British officers were bidden by the butler to dine while Mrs Digges waited with the girls in the drawing room. When the officers asked for her to preside over the meal and the young ladies to join the company, she politely declined, declaring they could neither eat nor drink with enemies of their country. The officers, it is said, drank a toast to the health of their valiant and patriotic hostess.[8]

On the same day, while another valiant and patriotic lady sat in the President's House guarding the Cabinet Papers, British troops easily swept aside American resistance at Bladensburg and entered Washington. Colonel Charles Carroll of Belle Vue had meanwhile been trying to persuade Dolley Madison to leave. 'Our kind friend Mr Carroll has come to hasten my departure', she scribbled in a journal letter to her sister, 'and is in a very bad humour with me because I insist on waiting until the large portrait of General Washington is secured, and it requires to be unscrewed from the wall.' With Carroll of Bellevue urging her to hurry, she saw the picture safely removed and then thrust into the surprised hands of two visiting New Yorkers, Jacob Barker and Robert De Peyster, for safe keeping. In this manner, was the famous Stuart portrait of Washington saved. Only then did Carroll of Belle Vue get her into the carriage and on the road out of the City. She had hurriedly ended her letter with the words, 'When I shall see or write you, or where I shall be tomorrow I cannot tell.'[9]

The British order was given to burn all the public buildings but leave private property intact. 'You never saw a drawing room so brilliantly lighted as the whole city was that night,' related Mary Hunter. 'Few thought of going to bed – they spent the night gazing on the fires and lamenting the disgrace of the city.' By ten that night the fires could be seen as far away as Doughoregan Manor. A providential downpour doused the flames the next day; a hurricane later on inflicted damage upon private property untouched by the British. This was of little consolation to those returning after the British withdrawal on 26 August. 'The poor Capitol!' sighed Margaret Bayard Smith, and the President's House with just cracked and blackened walls and mounds of ashes.[10]

Although the British forces had left Washington City they were not quite done with the Chesapeake. On 12 September the battle of Baltimore began at Patapsco Neck. Marylanders were once again mystified as the British refrained from pressing their advantage while Cockburn's fleet unsuccessfully bombarded Fort McHenry on the other side of Baltimore. This inspired Francis Scott Key to write a poem 'Defense of Fort McHenry' which became known as 'The Star-Spangled Banner' (adopted as the US national anthem in 1931). Unable to land troops at Fort McHenry, where the crafty Baltimoreans had placed scuppered hulks to block the harbour, British land forces rejoined Cochrane's fleet and the armada sailed down Chesapeake Bay for Bermuda. The Chesapeake campaign, considered unfinished business in England, was viewed somewhat differently in America. Despite the continued existence of Canada as British, Americans believed they had completely vanquished the British.[11]

At eight o'clock on Saturday evening, 11 February 1815, two gentlemen disembarked from a British sloop of war just docked at the Battery in New York City. The elder man was Anthony St John Baker, Secretary of the British Legation. The younger man was Henry Carroll – Emily's cousin and beau – private secretary to Henry Clay and a Secretary to the American commissioners in Ghent. Each had the care of a copy of the Treaty of Ghent which had been signed on 24 December officially bringing the War of 1812 to an end; Baker's copy to be ratified by the US government and Carroll's for the President to learn the final terms.

While the English diplomat lingered, the American secretary wasted no time in leaving. He drove out by post-chaise-and-four at noon on Sunday, pounded through Philadelphia just twelve hours later and some time between five and six o'clock on Tuesday evening, a record time for the journey, entered Washington City. As he reached Capitol Hill, the ruins clear in the moonlight, and drove along the avenue deep in mud and puddles, he was surprised to hear shouts and cheers in the darkness. The previous evening an express from Baltimore had brought rumours of his arrival but people feared they had been started by speculators in stocks. After the coachman answered 'Henry Carroll' to the inquiry 'Who passes?' a crowd of boys and men ran out to follow the carriage to Secretary of State James Monroe's house. He came out to accompany Carroll to deliver the precious document into the President's hands.

The Madisons were living in temporary but luxurious quarters at Octagon House. When Henry Carroll was announced he knew he was the bearer of good tidings but he could not know their significance for the future of the Union. As he travelled south, a delegation, sent by a convention of pro-secessionist New England states at Hartford, Connecticut, had also set out to demand amendments to the Constitution. Peace, however, would largely remove the grounds for grievance and the Yankee demands were dropped.

When the President told Dolley that peace had come, she called out 'Peace!' and the house bell was rung in honour. Her young cousin Sallie

Henry Carroll, Emily's beau
and cousin. Anonymous
painting.

Coles stood at the head of the stairs and echoed the joyous tidings and
then went to the head of the basement stairs and called down Peace!,
Peace! to the servants, who also took up the cry. The house was then illuminated as a sign of celebration so that in a short time friends and
government colleagues thronged in to celebrate.[12]

Henry Carroll was the toast of Washington society, treated as warmly as
if he had brought about the peace himself. The belles flirted around him
during that season of 1815, known by everyone as 'the peace winter'; but
Henry could not be diverted from his true love, Emily. He had received
permission from Caton to write to her and upon his return he resumed his
courtship, which was welcomed by Emily and both their families.

Emily and Henry had in common their family and their faith. He
belonged to the Carrolls of Duddington, solid landowning Catholic gentry;
his uncle ('Cousin Longlegs') had wanted to marry Emily's mother. Henry
was brought up at Belle Vue, the 1,000-acre estate near Hagerstown which
his father Colonel Charles Carroll had purchased, and at another Belle
Vue (his father liked the name), a large house in Georgetown, better

known today as Dunbarton House. A squire and director of the capital's first bank, Carroll of Belle Vue was a prominent Washingtonian. Henry was his eldest son and, at one stage, he had become extremely devout, even considering the priesthood. After a successful assignment at Ghent, at the age of twenty-three Henry was, Mary Carroll Caton knew, a personable young man of ample means, impeccable lineage and on course for a diplomatic career. She looked with satisfaction on the expected match and the idea of having two daughters married.[13]

The peace treaty of Ghent threw open the gates of London and Paris that had been barred to Americans, not just by the War of 1812 but also by the Anglo–French Wars. From Brussels Lady Caroline Capel wrote to her mother in London: 'We heard yesterday from Ghent that Peace with America was signed. What à Blessing to be at Peace with all the World!' After enduring twenty-five years of terror and destruction stemming from the French Revolution, Europe revelled in peace, relaxed in the knowledge that Napoleon had abdicated and was safely confined to the isle of Elba.

Marianne knew that no one had been more desperate than Betsy Bonaparte to get a glimpse of Europe. 'O my God, what have I not suffered in that cruel exile from every pleasure and every comfort,' Betsy had wailed. Napoleon had foiled her first attempt to see France but now she was free at last to escape from 'the stagnation of life' in America. In 1807, when it became evident that Jerome had permanently abandoned her, she had accepted an annuity from Napoleon, who had given Jerome the throne of Westphalia (a territory carved out of parts of defeated Germanic states). Two years later Jerome had bigamously – in the eyes of the Church and America – married Princess Catherine, daughter of the King of Württemberg. In 1810 Jerome offered to settle the duchy of Smalkalden and 200,000 francs a year [£466,000] upon Betsy on condition she lived in the backwater of Smalkalden and sent their son Bo to France. Westphalia was 'indeed a large kingdom,' she retorted, 'but not quite large enough to hold *two Queens*.'[14]

She was, however, forced to postpone her journey. Her mother died and then, on 28 February 1815, Napoleon escaped from Elba. Marching rapidly through France, he took possession of Paris on 20 March and was installed once more as Emperor of the French. Betsy then had to wait until Wellington's final victory at Waterloo removed Napoleon once again. As soon as accounts of his defeat reached Baltimore, she obtained a divorce from Jerome by a special Act of Maryland and then entrusted the care of Bo, aged ten, to her father and Marianne, his godmother. In July 1815, she sailed for the Old World.

Marianne was now drawn more closely into her sister-in-law's concerns. She promised to let Betsy know 'every particular' and to ensure that Bo was back at school for the new term on 15 August. Marianne knew the misery and insecurity Betsy concealed. In some eyes Betsy remained the female victim incarnate, the young beauty powerless in the face of male weakness (Jerome), tyranny (Napoleon) and authority (William Patterson).[15]

She had, however, gone to Europe against the advice and wishes of her family who 'very much disapproved' of the way she had dispensed with the usual proprieties solely to satisfy her own whim. After discovering that 'people of fashion never live in boarding-houses,' she had ditched her travelling companions, far too bourgeois for her liking, and moved into a rented house. Her independent stance was incomprehensible to her conventional family and to genteel society everywhere. While Robert thought Betsy's behaviour selfish and unladylike, Marianne continued to be loyal and supportive. She admired Betsy's courage and empathised with her desire to live a little and find happiness, even though Betsy was resorting to methods Marianne herself would never contemplate.

Betsy, however, was now in financial straits. Napoleon's exile to St Helena had ended her annuity and she was entirely dependent upon the allowance of $3,000 a year from her father. This would meet her needs in Maryland but not her expenses in Europe. 'I hate, I abhor America. I can never exist there & yet how can I live here on my Pittance?' she cried to Marianne. 'I sincerely sympathise with you for your want of cash,' Marianne responded on 15 November, 'it is at all times a dreadful want, but in E[urope] the temptations and expenses must make it indispensable'. Moved by her plight, Marianne pleaded with her stern father-in-law to help his daughter. William Patterson rebuffed her. Then she turned to her own soft-hearted mother who understood that Betsy wanted to find a husband of high rank and position in Europe but, as Marianne reported to Betsy before Christmas 1815, 'he will not give you the money – that is he refused Mama.'

Betsy knew her unyielding father did not like to be disobeyed. All she asked him was not to disabuse people of the idea that she was an heiress. As she wrote from London, 'The power of riches here is great, and your money, I assure you, would, if you say nothing more about me or your not liking my absence, be of great use to me.' Besides, she cheekily added, 'I am sure you cannot object to my having the honour of it, provided you keep the substance.' And in this she was right – Europeans did, indeed, as the sisters would find, respect the power of riches.[16]

Emily's Canadian Adventure

While Betsy was sailing to Europe in the summer of 1815, Emily was re-covering from a long bout of bilious fever which had left her exceedingly 'pulled down'. Her doctors diagnosed palpitations of the heart due to disease, not to Henry. She must avoid the heat and the fever season. Fortuitously, her grandfather decided that his Canadian investments warranted personal attention and, as he had not been there since the Revolutionary War, he would send Caton as his emissary. Emily could accompany her father and since she would like Louisa with her, and their mother would be happier if they were in the care of Bess, it was settled they must all go.[1]

The excited party set off on their three-month excursion on 8 July, travelling by coach-and-four to New York City from where they sailed along the Hudson River to Albany, a town bustling with trappers and backwoodsmen. After visiting their grandpapa's old friends the Schuylers, the Caton party travelled on into northern frontier country. This vast swathe of land, forming an undefined boundary with British North America, was the country of the Indians and the Dutch but also of Scottish and English colonists, military men settled into husbandry after the French–Indian wars (1756-63), and of the French, who had settled there or invested in land.

Despite the influx of settlers, the fertile valleys of the Genesee, the Mohawk and the Hudson, nestling at the feet of the Great Lakes and stretching from the Hudson River across to Niagara in the west, were largely wilderness. In the clearings of primeval Mohawk forest, Chateaubriand had wandered from tree to tree in 1791, saying, 'Here there are no more roads, no more towns, no monarchies, no republics, no presidents, no kings, no human beings,' and had suddenly come upon a score of 'savages painted like sorcerers'. They were dancing a quadrille to a violin played by a little Frenchman with powdered locks and muslin ruffles, whom the Indians paid as a dancing master in return for beaver pelts and bear hams.[2]

The girls' father and uncle Harper had invested in Genesee Valley land, borrowing from their wives' fortunes. Caton wished to see the properties, which Emily and her sisters would inherit; one of the parcels of land later formed part of the city of Rochester. After leaving the Genesee, the Catons travelled across the Lakes and along the St Lawrence River to Quebec, home of the largest Catholic community in North America.

Solicitous Archbishop Carroll, never without hopes for these 'very dear relations', had informed the Bishop of Quebec of their visit. It was the first time that Louisa and Emily had ever been in a Catholic city and through the obliging Bishop, the sisters visited the Hôtel-Dieu founded by Augustinian nuns in 1639, as well as several convents and the Ursuline school for Catholic girls. After the spiritual life of Catholic Quebec they encountered the secular world of Montreal. A fortified city, its turrets and steeples glittering with tin, Montreal remained a garrison for the British army. The Champs de Mar resounded with the music of fife and drum and the tread of regiments on parade.[3]

Fashionable Montreal society, however, was led not by the wives of commanding officers but by those of fur barons. International trade was the life blood of this island in the St Lawrence River; commerce in the pelts of beaver, fox, musquash, marten, lynx and otter (some 78 per cent of the Canadian fur trade) made the great fortunes of the partners of the North West Company [NWC]. The Montreal-based partners formed the British colony's first commercial company, in contrast to their fur rivals at Hudson's Bay who were managed from London. And unlike their notoriously mean American rival John Jacob Astor, the buccaneering, independent-minded Nor'Westers were generous with their wealth and hospitality, liberally dispensed at their exclusive Beaver Club.

While their father met the NWC partners to discuss their grandfather's investments, Bess, Louisa and Emily were entertained by their wives and daughters. The girls were much admired. Among their new acquaintances were two young beaux, John and Alexander McTavish, who were also on the point of leaving for the Mohawk Valley where they had Fraser relations, so arrangements were made to meet again. The sisters left Canada in August 'with regret & attachment'.[4] They nonetheless looked forward to their stay just north of Albany at Ballston Springs, then the most fashionable resort in America. The mountains, wooded hills, innumerable waterfalls and rivers of the Adirondacks could not hope to hold the notice of visitors so preoccupied with costume and promenades. Although their grandfather believed that the girls would enjoy a gentle programme of 'the waters, change of air, & exercise & relaxation' he must have forgotten the cares and regimen of a fashionable spa. They were staying at Sans Souci, the largest and best hotel in Ballston, built in 1803 to the designs of a French émigré architect and ideally situated – near to the springs yet with space for a piazza and a ballroom. From the time the bell rang for breakfast at eight o'clock the routine of idleness accounted for almost every moment.

Bess, Louisa and Emily had been at Ballston only a few days and were promenading in the piazza when they saw approaching them the McTavish brothers from Montreal. Many were the exclamations at their meeting again, and at Ballston of all places, quite as if it had never been thought of in Montreal. The Mr McTavishes, 'looking exceedingly pleased', Bess told Marianne, promptly engaged them for a drive after which Louisa and Emily undertook to take them down to the springs. An invitation by their father to join them in the dining room quickly followed and it was not long before the brothers had been absorbed into their circle. Spa life was unusual in that 'ceremony is thrown off and you are acquainted very soon', twenty-year-old Eliza Southgate explained to her mother. While Bess and Louisa went rambling, driving, and riding, Emily, semi-convalescent and more retiring, preferred to stay with her father, who talked at length about Canadian affairs with the elder McTavish. At the end of such talk John McTavish would, naturally, offer to escort Miss Emily into the dining room or down to the springs, and engage her for a dance at the ball – should the exertion not be detrimental to her recovery.

Such were the faltering notes with which Emily and John began the first movement of their courtship. 'The chat of the tea table', as Caton described the spa's matronly gossip, was, like the purr of a replete cat, full of satisfaction at an imminent proposal. At nine o'clock on a clear September morning, however, the sisters were handed into a travelling carriage, the step put up, and they were whirled rapidly southwards to Albany. Emily took away no offer of marriage; and she left Ballston and John McTavish behind without the power to do anything to alter the situation. In certain areas of her life, an American girl's independence remained circumscribed. Discussing marriage with a cousin, Eliza Southgate spoke of 'the inequality of privilege between the sexes' which existed for women when it came to choosing a husband, for 'true we have the liberty of refusing those we don't like, but not of selecting those we do'.

Emily returned home on 1 October 1815 in improved health. According to their father 'the girls have benefitted much by their journey, so far as muscular strength, and ruddy faces have title to benefit.' As Emily was expected to marry Henry Carroll, the talk at home centred upon Bess and Louisa's beaux and whether 'they had any offers'. On this subject their father was quite unable to enlighten their mother.[5]

On 19 February 1816, Richard Caton sat in the library at Brooklandwood writing to Robert Harper, then in Washington City as the newly elected senator for Maryland. After giving Harper news of his family, Caton casually wrote: 'Mr McTavish is the bearer of this – he is from Montreal.' What startled Harper were Caton's next words announcing that this McTavish

was 'an *acquaintance* of Emily's, and likely to be more'. Harper was confounded; he knew Henry Carroll was in the city, and indeed he was helping
him obtain another diplomatic post on the understanding that he and Emily
would then marry. Yet here was Caton asking on behalf of McTavish: 'Shew
him what civilities you can. He will go to the Drawing Room if an opportunity offers; Mrs Decatur can probably take him & if not; do you have
the goodness in person or by proxy', and ending coolly 'Adieu it is late'
without any further explanation.[6]

Emily was delighted that 'Mac', as she began to call him *à deux*, had
come, swathed in furs, riding from the frozen wilderness to claim her.
Showing the same stubborn disregard for opposition to her marriage as her
mother had done, shy, placid Emily, usually content to follow in the wake
of her sisters' beauty and force of personality, was now strengthened in
resolve by her love for John McTavish to accept his proposal and jilt cousin
Henry Carroll. Amid the flurry of letters, notes, pleadings, tears and grief
that flowed from her decision, Emily stood resolute. Despite his welcome
of McTavish, her father pleaded Henry's cause; but he tried in vain. Emily
was spared painful discussions with Henry's parents as they had already
settled in upstate New York; and his reaction had the effect of making her
appear almost justified in jilting him.[7]

He was so distraught at losing Emily that he refused to return her letters
and, furthermore, threatened to publish them. These were not the actions
of a gentleman; a lady's reputation would be irretrievably damaged by being
brought in such a manner before the public. Although she had persuaded
her father there was nothing compromising in the letters, there was enough
of what he called 'loving' to cause uneasiness. The Catons therefore asked
uncle Harper to help avert a family scandal. 'Every honorable feeling requires
his surrender of them.' Emily, distressed beyond measure, wrote: 'indeed
uncle it pains me to confess that the honorable feelings of Henry Carroll
were only in my imagination – he must either be unacquainted with the
customs of the world or act from the impulse of revenge – which he cannot
gratify without blasting his own reputation – no one will blame me if he
is contemptible enough to shew my letters.' Through the mediation of
Harper and Archbishop Neale, and her undertaking never to say anything
that might injure him and 'certainly never speak of Mrs Somerville' with
whom he was said to be entangled, Henry Carroll agreed to return the
letters.

As his true character emerged, she felt relief: 'his conduct has been so
degrading, that I congratulate myself upon my escape'. She was now sure
that John McTavish was superior to Henry in every way: 'Mac at least
pretends to nothing he does not possess' in the way of honour and character, she declared. Her family, not unnaturally, possessed less confidence

in McTavish's eligibility; with the exception of her father none of them had been acquainted with him before his arrival in Maryland. Who, asked her grandfather, was Mr McTavish?[8]

The Carroll family enquired discreetly from the Schuylers in upstate New York. As the family lawyers began to negotiate the settlements, Emily's family learnt that he was neither extremely rich nor necessitous, having about £4,400 a year (an NWC clerk earned £100 a year), expectations from the McTavish family and excellent prospects as a partner in the Montreal firm McTavish, McGillivrays & Co and its London branch. As they came to know him, they discovered a personable young man with a fund of stories and 'a charming sense of humour' and agreed with Harper's opinion that 'He seems to be a very amiable excellent man.'[9]

Much of what McTavish told the family about himself concerned the two areas of the world he knew best, namely the north of Scotland and the Canadian wilderness. The Highlands had been popularised in the United States and, indeed, in the Carroll Caton family by the publication of Scott's *Waverley* (1814) and *Guy Mannering* (1815). The Quincy sisters reported that the editor of the *Edinburgh Review* had been treated like royalty in Boston, such was the interest generated in all things Scottish by these books. The Waverley novels, featuring the '45' Rebellion and 'Bonnie' Prince Charles Edward, the Young Pretender, were made even more enthralling for Emily and her sisters by John McTavish's family history.[10]

John was a Highland Scot, born and bred in the wide, wooded valley of Stratherrick, lying along the eastern bank of Loch Ness, on land held by the Lords of Lovat, chiefs of Clan Fraser. It was to Stratherrick that the Young Pretender had fled from the carnage of the battle of Culloden on 16 April 1746 to meet the elderly fourteenth Lord Lovat, who advised him to make for France. Lovat was beheaded at the Tower in 1747 and it was at Stratherrick ten years later that John's Jacobite grandfather McTavish of Garthbeg, who had fought at Culloden, answered the call of the new clan chief, Lovat's son Simon Fraser. As part of Pitt the Elder's policy of conciliation with the great Highland Jacobite families, Fraser had been granted letters of service to raise the 78th Regiment (Fraser's Highlanders) for employment in the French–Indian Wars in British North America.[11]

Although Lieutenant McTavish of Garthbeg returned home after the war ended in 1763, he had forged the first significant link with the country in which his family would make its fortune. The McTavishes had long been tacksmen. Of this gentry class, Dr Johnson in 1785 explained 'Next in dignity to the Laird is the Tacksman' or chief tenant. Yet McTavish of Garthbeg's sons Alexander, John's father, and Simon, his uncle, could no longer retain 'a dignity of independence' as tacksmen. Under a draconian

Hanoverian onslaught on the clan system, tacksmen became merely tenants facing an often 'precipitate and injurious rise in rents'.

This promoted an 'epidemical fury of immigration', as Dr Johnson called it, to North America. Boswell, travelling with Johnson, found himself learning a new dance on Skye: 'We performed, with much activity, a dance which, I suppose, the emigration from Skye has occasioned. They call it *America*. Each of the couples, after the common *involutions* and *evolutions*, successively whirls round in a circle, till all are in motion; and the dance seems intended to show how emigration catches, till a whole neighbourhood is set afloat.'[12]

The first McTavish to catch the contagion was John's aunt Elizabeth. On her marriage to a kinsman Hugh Fraser, they emigrated with her thirteen-year-old brother Simon McTavish to the Mohawk Valley. It was this Simon McTavish, a young man who loved 'good wine, good oysters and pretty girls', who would make a fortune in the fur trade, forming the NWC in Montreal in 1779. 'McTavish is entirely unequalled here in acuteness and reach of thought', observed a rival in 1804, when the NWC controlled more than three quarters of the subcontinent's fur trade. [13]

This, in effect, was the 'family' business that John, born in 1787, had entered. After graduating from King's College, Aberdeen [now Aberdeen University], he started around 1810 in London before joining the Montreal office and his tales of the Nor'Westers and the Canadian wilderness were coloured by his own experiences. Every young clerk, aspiring to be a partner, left his comfortable leather seat in the Montreal counting house to earn his fur spurs by passing at least one winter at one of the hundred or so NWC trading outposts. These were strung for over 3,000 miles along the rivers in *le pays d'en haut*, the wilderness north and west of Lake Superior on which, at the mouth of the Kaministika River, the company had built their large headquarters at Fort William. This was Canada's first inland metropolis, capable of housing 2,000–3,000 people within its stockaded walls.

Every May, as soon as the rivers thawed, crowds of Montrealers travelled out to Lachine, a village some miles upstream from the St Lawrence Rapids to celebrate the start of the fur trading season and to watch relays of canoes set off for the interior on the six-to-eight-week journey to Fort William. All the partners, including junior ones like John, gathered for a farewell luncheon. Gloriously inebriated fur traders proposed the Gaelic toast to departed friends with a proliferation of Highland speeches until by 'six or seven o'clock', recalled one young army officer, 'I had in common with many of the others, fallen from my seat'.

The French Canadian voyagers were equally drunk, paddling the canoes, loaded with kegs of liquor and packs of goods, to convey the partners with their servants and luggage to the annual meeting with the wintering partners and traders, who brought back the valuable beaver pelts and other furs purchased from the Indians. Over the ensuing four weeks the partners negotiated profits, contracts, strategy and exploration while clerks arranged the exchange of pelts, to be sold in London fur auctions, for the Montreal goods they would use to barter with the Indians for next year's supply. The fort's pivotal function as the crossroads of the NWC enabled the company to export the huge quantities of beaver pelts required to meet the insatiable European demand. These were used not for coats but to manufacture the fine felt that supplied men with their black hats.[14]

These hats, in effect, funded the NWC's most enduring legacy: the vast territories that would create the nation of Canada. The explorers and cartographers who saved western Canada from being swallowed up by the United States, were all NWC fur traders. When Jefferson sent Lewis and Clark to find a route to the Pacific in 1804–6, the NWC had already found are. In 1793 Alexander MacKenzie, a partner, became the first man to cross the North West Passage of the Rockies and reach the Pacific Ocean. John met this great explorer in Montreal in 1810 and would later work with him in London. In an 1805 expedition, another partner Simon Fraser discovered the Fraser River and New Caledonia, which became British Columbia. And, in the war of 1812, the NWC captured Astoria, Astor's trading post on the Oregon coast.

William McGillivray, the senior partner, was so pleased at gaining a base on the Pacific that John, who had been in line for promotion, was forthwith made a full partner in the Company on a 1/36 share and a partner-director of both the Montreal and London firms. From 1800 to 1815 Nor'Wester partners had earned net profits estimated at £1.85 million, so John could expect to earn a heap of money. On the strength of this exponential leap in his financial worth and earnings he was in a position to propose to Emily in 1816.[15]

Family Troubles

'I think sometimes of how many hours of sickness and suffering I passed,' Louisa wrote of the spring of 1816, when she endured several long bouts of bilious fever (malaria) which left her in a 'frail and wasting' condition. Marianne could not visit her because she too was ill. Her asthma attacks and severe headaches were more frequent and their severity also made it difficult for her to look after Betsy's son Bo in the holidays. This was especially poignant as her care of him was some consolation for the children she did not have.[1]

After ten years' of marriage, such an event, however much desired, was not considered likely. In the hundreds of surviving family letters, many pages are sprinkled with news and gossip about the women's 'hopes', about lyings-in, breast-feeding and wet-nurses, and about babies' illnesses and deaths; all of these topics were discussed by both the men and women of the family. The girls' grandfather, for instance, was a firm advocate of breast-feeding and hoped that Harriet would be able to suckle her baby or that Kitty's painful breast would not affect her milk. And as infants played on the floor – 'Bob is cutting papers at my feet', wrote Marianne – or demanded attention from a cradle – 'I have not time to say more, I hear my child's voice', Kitty Harper hurriedly ended a note – the women wrote letters. Yet no word remains about Marianne's or Robert's infertility and the effect upon their marriage. No 'hopes' are expressed concerning her, and she never mentioned the subject. Her headaches and asthma were probably exacerbated by the strain of suppression and disappointment.[2]

Marianne still enjoyed her extended family life. Her uncle Charles Carroll Jr was kind and hospitable, possessing both 'an urbanity' and the houses with which to entertain his nieces and introduce them into the best society. Young, attractive and cultured, he and Harriet Carroll were one of America's 'golden couples'. As the Homewood plantation had contained only a small farmhouse, Carroll of Carrollton had given them a new and furnished mansion. Built to Charles Jr's own design, Homewood House stands amidst the lawns and dells of what has become The John's Hopkins University and is one of the finest examples of early American architecture to survive, a 'pure Federal masterpiece', listed as a National Historic Landmark.

Marianne and her sisters grew up with the 'gaiety and social distinction' of Homewood, dancing at the fashionable balls given by aunt Carroll or seated for dinners in the acquamarine dining room, its windows festooned in silk and muslin, the light of candles reflected on the pier looking-glasses, the chandeliers and tall candelabras. The elegance was offset by the prac-tical covering of a baize cloth beneath the Chippendale chairs and table to protect the carpet from children's crumbs and the sprinklings of less fastidious diners.[3]

By the second decade of the nineteenth century, however, the social life of Homewood had been snuffed out. Uncle Carroll was wrestling with alco-holism. The sisters, like the rest of the family, were reluctant to visit. More often than not aunt Harriet would be confined 'indisposed' to her bedchamber or would flee with the children to Belvedere while uncle Carroll, in aunt Harper's words, raged like 'a perfect Madman'. The family tried everything but his drinking binges grew more frequent and he started beating Harriet. By 1816, Caton related, 'Many in their great tenderness for him, wish him to leave the country, to die in a ditch, or a madhouse, but his father will not consent, and Charles prays that it may never be allowed, altho' he himself should appear to ask it.' One day he unexpectedly called to see Louisa, confined to bed at Brooklandwood, and there met a visiting priest, who persuaded him to go to confession. 'It was the work of provi-dence,' decided Emily, 'religion alone can save him.'[4]

When it did not save him, Carroll of Carrollton arranged for Harriet and her four daughters in live in Philadelphia and gave her an annuity of $4,500 [£60,000] a year. He would educate their only son, young Charles Carroll now aged fifteen, and Carroll Jr would remain at Homewood with pin money of $1,500 a year. The impact of their uncle's suffering upon Louisa and Emily was such that neither of them ever drank any alcohol. Louisa's abhorrence of drunkenness caused her to dismiss a footman summarily when, for the first time after years of service, he appeared to be tipsy.[5]

The key to Carroll Jr's torment, as he called it, lay in having to fulfil the expectations of a long-living father who was constantly carping about how he spent his income – most of it went upon improving the Homewood estate and his in-hand Folly Farm. By contrast he appeared blind to the large sums of Carroll money that his sons-in-law Caton (who was insol-vent) and Harper (whose large debts had been cleared) were using for speculations. When Carroll Jr complained, Kitty Harper could not under-stand what he meant – she had no idea that Harper borrowed money against the security of her fortune or that, in 1807, he used her profits from the sale of Baltimore Company land to pay interest on the large debts from his land speculations. Mary Caton was likewise ignorant of Caton's latest speculative venture – until it, too, failed in June 1814. 'Caton has gone bankrupt for a second time and in a manner so dishonourable that he is generally scorned', Rosalie Calvert informed her father.[6]

Marianne, Bess, Louisa and Emily thus had examples within their family of different approaches to the management of inherited wealth. They could choose between financial knowledge or ignorance, independence and control of money or dependence and vulnerability to mismanagement. In choosing the route of fiscal rectitude and control of their own money, they followed their grandfather's course, avoiding debt with as much fervour as they avoided spirits. Although Bess would later insist that she was the most capable money manager of the four and Emily would 'tut tut' about her sisters' lavish way of life, all four were unusually competent with money.

After their father's second bankruptcy, their mother feared that this time his financial disgrace would destroy the Caton family's reputation and, in particular, her daughters' marriage prospects; to suffer from one family bankruptcy might be regarded as a misfortune, to suffer from two was, if not carelessness, undoubtedly a stigma. Her father was, as ever, able to allay Mary's concerns, making a fresh division of the Carrollton Manor estate to increase his granddaughters' fortunes. He conveyed one-third of it to their mother to be divided equally among them, thereby giving each of them over 1,000 acres to add to their separate fortunes. 'I hope the different divisions of the Carrollton estate may be productive of the good effects mentioned in your letter,' he advised their mother on 12 June 1814, '& among others be the means of marrying your daughters well; independent of expected fortunes, their good qualities merit husbands of character & dispositions to render the married state happy.'[7]

12

Mad About Europe

In 1816 the sisters had to meet heavy expenses, not only on account of Emily's marriage. Marianne's health deteriorated so much the doctors feared she might not survive another year in the extreme, energy-sapping Maryland climate. Her grandfather wanted her husband to take her to Lisbon or England for a year but Robert Patterson was disinclined. The family doctor, however, thought 'a Voyage and change of climate absolutely necessary' to the recovery of Marianne and also for Louisa's health and recommended the Cheltenham waters. Bess quickly set about convincing the Pattersons that they must follow doctors' orders.[1]

Bess was in excellent health and spirits, vital and busy. Apart from helping to look after her ailing sisters, sharing shopping expeditions with Emily and reporting back all the political news from Washington City, she was in the whirl of yet another proposal. Bess was unruffled by offers of marriage and, to her mother's chagrin, regarded suitors as accessories to be changed at whim. The Patterson family liked to think she had designs on Joseph, one of Robert's younger brothers, but although she liked to flirt with him she and Louisa felt one Patterson in the family was quite enough.

This time, though, she was taking a proposal seriously. Her suitor John Howard was eminently eligible – Mary Carroll Caton would at last see one of her daughters marrying a plantation. The marriage negotiations, however, were proving difficult. One impediment might have been religion since the Howards were Protestants, but there was another one: money. 'Robert thinks [John] will succeed if the Colonel [Howard] will come down with 150,000 – this is a sine qua non that will not be abandoned & will prove a rock to the young hearts,' Edward Patterson told Betsy. Bess was so relaxed about the delay, her mother thought a change of heart imminent. The real reason was that Bess just did not want to miss a trip to Europe with her sisters; once their health had improved, as the doctors agreed it would, they would have fun together. As marriage was considered the most important event in a girl's life, no one outside the family and her 'very devoted' suitor could understand her. Edward Patterson, who did not like Bess ('if ever a lady was overrated this Miss certainly is'), put it another way: 'the great ambition of this lady is to dazzle the courts of Europe with her charms & accomplishments, there she can be estimated & there she must & will go.' He was confusing the Elizabeths: it was his sister Betsy who wanted to conquer Europe, Bess merely to enjoy it.[2]

Soon there was so much talk about Europe that Emily, who had her own adventure to plan, grew quite tired of hearing about it: 'I think they are all mad about Europe, & they will return sadly disappointed', she sniffed to uncle Harper. While Robert Patterson prevaricated, their mother decided that an effective inducement was a tract of land – for Robert relished his link with a large landowning family. And Marianne, so conveniently, had one to hand. In addition to the Tuscarora farm of about six hundred acres, she had received 650 acres in the redivision of the Carrollton Manor estate. To secure her estate, uncle Harper stipulated by deed that she could give her husband Robert only a life interest in up to half of her share of Carrollton Manor. She could thus offer him some land and raise $25,000 [£301,000] against her estate to meet their European expenses. Uncle Harper also arranged for Bess's and Louisa's expenses to be covered by a bond drawn on their fortune. The ruse was successful. 'The Ladies remain resolutely determined on the expedition – And I have consented,' Robert finally told Harper in March. Friends were astonished. 'You will perhaps be surprised to find Robert & his attendant Graces in Paris before long', Eliza Godefroy wrote to Betsy at the end of March, 'by what means Maryanne has contrived to change his character or rather to make him sacrifice all his tastes & prejudices to *caper* with her & her Sisters about Europe is an enigma to which I have no key'.[3]

Throughout the spring, the four sisters were engrossed in their respective plans. Emily had not appreciated that she was marrying a foreign company as well as a man, an unusual state of affairs in her circle. Maryland weddings were informal, flexible occasions dependent for timing upon settlements and licences and, in the case of Catholics, the availability of a priest; it was the wedding tour not the ceremony that involved formal entertainments. And Emily had a perfect plan. She would have a May wedding, bid farewell to her sisters – if they ever left for Europe – and after visiting relations in Maryland, she and John would go on a northern tour accompanied by the Harpers, ending in Montreal with the Highland celebrations planned by the McTavish family.

Meanwhile, Bess followed her usual winter routine while Congress was in session and accompanied uncle Harper to Washington. In 1816, public buildings remained desolate and defaced. Newly arrived Congressman Thomas Hubbard of New York described Capitol Hill as resembling 'the picture of the ruins of Palmyra more than the heart of the great city'. The rest of the city, though, seemed 'to have risen, like the phoenix from the flames', and Marianne told Betsy that 'since the burning of Washington every thing has taken a wonderful start, houses erecting in every direction, and all the property much appreciated'. What had also changed was the acceptance of Washington as the capital of the United States. Once Congress had decided, amid fierce debate, against relocation, and had voted federal funds to rebuild all the public buildings, Washington City was fixed permanently and was, for the first time, accepted by both Republicans and Federalists. Furthermore, peace brought on an unprecedented outburst of national feeling in which the regeneration of the city was seen as the focus of a new national pride. The United States was an independent power on the international stage and Washington City its symbolic centre.[4]

When Bess went back with Emily for another visit that March, the city exuded confidence and prosperity; it was the beginning of what became known in America as 'the era of good feeling'. Yet change was also in the air as James Madison, the last of the revolutionary leaders to hold office, entered the final year of his presidency. The Madisons had been the leading couple for sixteen years and Dolley's presidential parties were still the social attraction that no one wanted to miss. 'Such a crowd I never was in. It took us ten minutes to push and shove ourselves through the dining-room', declared one guest. Dolley, resplendent in yellow satin embroidered with butterflies and white feathers nodding in her turban, welcomed everyone with a smile and friendly remark as she stood next to her more reserved husband. With their departure the flavour of Washington life would alter in a manner few then expected. The warmth, accessibility and intellectual rigour that distinguished the makeshift capital under Jefferson and Madison would be lost.[5]

There was, though, another attraction to the season that year. For the first time since the outbreak of war in 1812 a full complement of European diplomats had returned to add a dash of sophistication and display. The ladies of Washington saw little to interest them in either the Portuguese Minister Abbé Correa, a scholar with scientific interests, or the Spanish Minister Don Luis de Onis, who was known to dislike dancing. The new French and British Ministers and their wives were, however, of prodigious interest. And Bess was eager to become acquainted with them.

Her family already knew the new French Minister, Jean Guillaume Hyde de Neuville, though not as a diplomat. He and his wife had been among the flood of *royalistes* to flee France during the Terror, living eventually in New York where Madame had opened a school for young ladies. The Carroll family was delighted to receive them again at the Manor and the de Neuvilles were delighted to provide some introductions for the girls to take to Paris. They proved a popular addition to Washington society and his costume excited admiration from younger Americans. After attending a drawing room, Margaret Bayard Smith's niece wrote of 'Blue coats cover'd with gold embroidery. The collar and back literally cover'd with wreaths of fleurs de lys with white underclothes and large chapeaux with feathers' and, she exclaimed, this was not even court dress! Rosalie Calvert, a more discerning witness, found the French couple 'most gracious. They have more visitors & give more dances than anyone else in Washington.' Their graciousness and *sang-froid* were somewhat tested in Washington society. As the British Minister's wife wrote in her journal: 'Came away about 1/3 after eleven & left the most disgraceful scene I ever saw going on – the men most of them drunk & running at the champaine & Madeira which they drank like savages.'[6]

When the arrival of the new British Minister, the Honourable Charles Bagot, and his wife was delayed in December 1815, rumours had swept through the capital. Marianne reported to Betsy: 'The Democrats had us all in fear and trembling at his [Bagot's] detention, expecting another War, when the mystery was removed in the christening of a Baby.' The Bagots and baby finally arrived on 18 March 1816 and the following day, in a note to uncle Harper in Washington, Emily passed on a message from Bess: 'you must tell her all about Mr & Mrs Bagot, particularly the latter, as she is the niece of Lord Wellington. She wishes to know if she is pretty, how she dresses & c.' Before the week was out Bess was able to see for herself.[7]

Given the history of relations between America and Britain, Bagot's diplomatic instructions from Lord Castlereagh could be encompassed in one word: conciliation. Bagot was to be firm in negotiating some of the issues unresolved by the Treaty of Ghent but he was to further friendly relations with America. In this he was supported by Mary Bagot, whose approachable manner and attractive, stylish appearance charmed everyone. The Bagots wished to remove any lingering anti-British feeling, which Bagot described to a close friend, Lord Binning, as 'the food upon which the great, and I am sorry to say, the predominant [Republican] party in the country is nourished'.

After Bagot presented his credentials to the President, he and his wife sallied forth to attend Dolley Madison's drawing room on 27 March. That evening Mary Bagot brought her mother Mrs Wellesley-Pole up-to-date with events. 'There has been such a pother here about precedence & rules of etiquette at this *Court* ever since Charles's arrival as would make you laugh if you like ourselves had come out here thinking such things of no consequence amongst the American republicans.' She assured her mother, 'we minded our p's & q's far more than if we had been at one of the P[rince] R[egent]'s scrambles' in London. Although she had found the party hard going, her fellow guests would not have guessed from the consummate ease with which she managed her introduction to Washington society.[8]

Bess gushed along with everyone else, telling Louisa, who was still confined to bed that they had seen the Bagots at the drawing room, that Mary Bagot was most elegantly dressed and 'most amiable'; that they had left cards the next day; that they were dining with the Decaturs to meet the Bagots and that they were all making a party to go to the Navy Yard to see the ruined buildings. Over the ensuing weeks, invitations were issued to the Carroll and Caton houses, in response to letters introducing the new British Minister.

As several generations of their family had been educated in England and France, the sisters understood that their reception there would be determined by the quality rather than quantity of letters. The most important items on any travelling agenda were, first, the letters of credit to provide foreign exchange facilities. These, and any other financial requirements, would be met by a combination of the Carroll agent in London, William Murdoch, the Liverpool partners of their own bankers in Baltimore, Alexander & James Brown & Co; and Baring Brothers of London who acted for their grandfather. As the elder Bingham daughter Anne had married Alexander Baring and resided in England, the sisters had social as well as banking connections with Barings. Second in importance were the letters of introduction, the *sine qua non* of social enjoyment for any traveller in a foreign land. These were vital in England, where the proprieties were strictly observed, as one German nobleman confirmed from London: 'in this country nothing is to be done with respectable families without an introduction, even if you were a prince.' It was as true of well-bred American families; none of the great and good calling for the first time at the Manor, for instance, did so without letters of introduction.[9]

No sooner had the Bagots heard of the sisters' travel plans than they offered, indeed insisted as their dearest wish, to supply them with letters. And what effusive letters they were, exceeding by far all the sisters' expectations. To what did the sisters owe their good fortune? They were, after all, relative strangers and the Bagots did not produce similar letters for other American travellers. But they were 'charmed beyond measure' by Marianne and Bess and their family who were the nearest to kindred spirits they found in America; it was the contrast between them and most other Americans that made such an impact.

Charles and Mary Bagot belonged to the British aristocracy and their families were prominent in political circles. Bagot believed, as he told Binning, that he was better liked than any of his predecessors owing to 'never indulging in any of the sarcasms' expected from Englishmen. Mary Bagot succeeded by being the epitome of a fine lady and a virtuous wife. Washington society, though, had no idea of Mary Bagot's soubriquet in London, where she was known as 'The Fair Penitent' after Nicholas Rowe's tragedy of that name. Her love affair with Captain Arthur Upton had been the scandal of the 1810 season. 'At the Opera I noticed that Mrs Bagot had drawn the curtains of her box so that no one could see who was seated there', the Persian Envoy recorded in his journal. 'When the Colonel [*sic*] arrived, they left together. I do not approve! They seem to be madly in love.' The Wellesley-Poles intervened to put a stop to the flagrant affair and despatched Mary to cool her heels in the country.

Bagot, unusually in that era, had stuck by his wife, though Lady Harriet Leveson Gower heard he would be cut by men in town as 'his conduct is looked upon as so weak and humiliating'. Yet society neither cut him nor consigned Mary to oblivion, largely owing to the support of her family and perhaps to her own attitude. Far from hiding herself away as a woman disgraced, Mary displayed great effrontery – 'rouged to the eyes', talking incessantly and flirting with all the men. Americans would have found this account difficult to equate with the circumspect, lightly rouged wife of the British Minister in 1816.[10]

In contrast to their public utterances, the Bagots' letters to their family and closest friends reveal what a shock American society was to them. Mary Bagot found that she was expected to entertain and meet numerous frontiersmen 'many of whom came in boots & perfectly undone & with dirty hands & dirty linen,' their hair matted and unwashed, chewing tobacco and spitting everywhere – a type she had never met in the fields, let alone the polite society, of England. She tried to give Ralph Sneyd, a relation, an idea of the young ladies and their conversation: '"Lark" (as Miss Worthington says) "we are so free & easy here *Mam*! when you gets in our way – if you will *Mam* but lay aside form & step in sociably to us, we have such merriments. You'll laugh your heart out *Mam*."' Indeed, as Mary Bagot mimicked them to him, 'you don't know what you lose by livin' in England! You wou'd find so much "hospitality" here – "such nice junkettings", such "*handsome* Peach Brandy."' Charles Bagot told the family he 'once heard Mary say rather hastily to one of her guests "My dear Mrs S-, what can you be doing?" The salad bowl had been offered to the lady in question, and her arm was embedded in it up to her elbow. "Oh," came the reply. "Only rollicking for an onion, my lady."'[11]

Although she tried to make light of it, Mary found the constant trivial chatter heavy going and her determination to be pleased sometimes 'an agonizing effort'. She was used to conversation that flowed around the tables of a London dinner; the sort of evening which could be found at the Carroll Catons. Marianne and Bess, lovely, cultured intelligent gentlewomen, were far removed from the 'unreasonable, ill-bred' Americans that the Bagots generally met. Marianne had finally been able to leave her room and pay a visit to the capital. In April 1816, Mary Crowninshield wrote to her mother, discussing the sisters after they had left. 'It is so disagreeable to part with those we like, – for certainly they were as fine, elegant women as I ever knew – so amiable and agreeable. They dressed elegantly had the most superb ornaments I have seen here, – one comb cost two hundred dollars, – amethyst set and necklace, earrings and bracelets etc etc to match . . . They are very rich.' It is no wonder that Mary Bagot took refuge in the society of the sisters and their family; at the Manor she could enjoy country house life with good books and dinners and wide ranging conversation. It was the nearest to home and friendship that the Bagots found in America and they wished to reciprocate by offering the sisters some English hospitality when they, too, would be far from home.[12]

After Dolley Madison heard about the forthcoming trip she also offered to help. The President had just appointed Albert Gallatin as Minister to France and, as the families knew each other, it would be most agreeable for them to sail together. Dolley wrote to Hannah Gallatin on 20 April and the sisters delighted in the plan to sail in early June after Emily's marriage. But Robert suddenly decided that they must leave within four weeks, forcing everyone to rush. Their grandfather wrote frequently to remind their mother to give him good notice of their sailing date 'tho taking leave of such near & dear connections must be painful to me & them'. He was conscious that he might never see them again, given his age of seventy-nine, and prayed that Marianne and Louisa would recover their health. Remembering his own days as a young man in London he hoped 'that dissipation & late hours may not counteract the benefit proposed to be derived from the Cheltenham waters'.[13]

As the date of their departure drew nearer, though dependent as ever upon wind, tide and cargo, the date of Emily's wedding drew further away, dependent, as it seemed to her, upon the NWC's whim. William McGillivray, who was also a cousin, would permit John to cut short his attendance at Fort William but not to miss the meeting altogether, as John would lose corporate credibility if he was seen to be dallying elsewhere at such a critical period in the fortunes of the NWC.

The sisters were disappointed to find that they would miss Emily's wedding and not be together in the early days of her marriage. Still, there were compensations; they heard about the amusements of London from Mary Bagot and of Paris from Betsy, who had written to Marianne that it was enchanting and she only wished she had spent her life there. She had been treated with the utmost distinction at the Duke of Wellington's ball and, she declared, 'it was the happiest moment' in her life. Betsy did not yet know that Marianne and Robert were to join her in Europe (letters took at least two months to reach the Continent); that Marianne had left her mother *in loco parentis* to Bo; or that Marianne and her sisters had been given an entrée to society which, added to their wealth and beauty, could give them a position far superior to hers. Ever fickle, the fashionable world in Europe might agree with the Bagots and be 'charmed beyond measure' by the Caton sisters, or it might take its cue from acerbic Betsy Bonaparte. On 27 May the three sisters escorted by Robert and accompanied by a retinue of servants and a mountain of baggage set sail for England, that familiar, long-imagined, yet foreign land.[14]

PART II
Familiar Strangers 1816–24

*They were familiar strangers as it were, and people at once so initiated
and so detached could only be Americans.*

Henry James, *Lady Barberina*

13

In London Society

When Marianne, Bess and Louisa landed in Liverpool on 22 June 1816 they were so debilitated by seasickness that they could only collapse into the comfortable beds of the Adelphi Hotel where they remained closeted for days. By the time they recovered and were eager to explore the city, Robert, always hale at sea, had already completed his business and insisted on leaving immediately for London. As Bess confided, 'Robert is an impatient traveller.' They hardly saw their friend Washington Irving, who was living there to help his brother in business, and had to leave their curiosity unsatisfied about the English Catons, their father's three married sisters who lived nearby. Consoling themselves with Mary Bagot's advice that they must arrive in London well before the prorogation of Parliament, signalling the end of the season, they set off.

Instead of the harshness of a Maryland summer, with fierce heat, dust and scorched earth, they met with the softness of an English summer with light rain, freshening air and the 'grassy balm' of fertile meadows. The wet weather revived them, where it dismayed everyone else. Jane Austen, in the process of finishing *Persuasion*, gave a taste of that summer when she wrote, 'Oh! it rains again! it beats against the window.' The rain obliged her to turn back on drives and walks, 'but not soon enough to avoid a Pelter all the way home'. On meeting a local farmer: 'I talked of it's being bad weather for the Hay – & he returned me the comfort of it's being much the worse for the Wheat.'[1]

Unlike the sodden crops, Marianne bloomed in the moist cooler air, which kept her free from asthma. Having expected to be confined to her rooms at the Pulteney Hotel, she found herself unexpectedly well and able to participate in the gaieties of London. Louisa, too, began to recover her former energy and to enter into everything with a renewed *joie de vivre* that delighted her sisters.

Princess Lieven, wife of the Russian Ambassador, a leader of Regency society and a Lady Patroness of Almack's, the most exclusive Assembly Rooms in London, pronounced that London in July was boring: 'All the mothers and all the daughters fret themselves, wear themselves out, make themselves thin. The roses in their cheeks fade, and the suitors do not appear.' The Caton sisters, fast regaining the roses in their cheeks, were exhilarated by their arrival in the largest city in the world. England during the Regency was enjoying an era of civilised living and vulgar excess; its double standards were clearly delineated by the extraordinary personage of George the Prince Regent, heir of his mad father George III and now regent, leader of the *ton* and all that was fashionable in the western world.[2]

The sisters knew that first they had to participate in the 'card-and-call' ritual by which ladies regulated social life in Britain and America. The preliminary steps in this dance of acquaintance were the same, as was their purpose, namely to join a new social world, to announce arrivals and departures and to vet strangers and unfamiliar connections. It was, during the season, a time-consuming daily performance of steps and turns as cards were left and returned, leading into calls and then the final turn of invitations issued. Marianne Hudson wryly noted:

'A thousand cards a–day at doors to leave,
And, in return, a thousand cards receive,
Is the one great employment of all women of fashion.'

Shortly after two o'clock on 28 June, Marianne and Bess stepped into the costly carriage which, at their insistence and expense, Robert had hired through the Pulteney Hotel. The cost of keeping a family carriage and horses in London was estimated by *The Traveller's Oracle* eleven years later in 1827, at a minimum of £400 [£30,000] a year but 'Jobbing' (long-term hire) was cheaper, costing the sisters around £350 a year. Heeding the advice of their grandfather about the importance attached to a handsome equipage, they had a better idea of what was expected than Robert; a handsome equipage was not deemed as necessary for social happiness in Camberwell, as in St James's. 'How the man who drives his close carriage looks down upon him who only drives his barouche or phaeton; how both contemn the poor occupier of a gig', wrote William Howitt.[3]

Marianne and Bess knew what they were about when the resplendent coachman pulled at the leader reins, the two liveried footmen jumped up and stood on the back of the carriage and, to the accompaniment of a jingle of harness and clattering of hooves, they started out to announce their arrival to London society. They drove first to Savile Row where one of the footmen, having knocked at the door of No. 3, ascertained that Mrs Wellesley-Pole was out. Marianne sent in her card, two of Robert's, and a budget of letters from the Bagots. Bess also sent in her card, later explaining to aunt Harper how 'you must send your card with the name of the Hotel you are in at the corner'. Their friend Richard

Rush, who would succeed Adams as American Minister the following year, was clearly not as *au fait*. At a party at the Duchess of Cumberland's a gentleman approached Rush saying: 'I am going to bring a bill into Parliament, making it indictable in any stranger, whether ambassador from a republic, kingdom, or popedom, ever to leave his card without his address upon it: how do you do, Mr Rush, how do you do? I've been trying to find you everywhere – I'm Lord Erskine.'

From Savile Row, Marianne and Bess sent in cards and letters to a host of Mary Bagot's Wellesley family connections: to the Dowager Lady Mornington (her grandmother), Lady Anne Culling Smith and the Duchess of Wellington (her aunts), Lady Salisbury (her father's cousin) and Lady Jersey (her sister's sister-in-law), known as the 'Queen of Society' or 'Queen Willis's' for her prominent role in society and at Almack's. At each house one of the well-trained Pulteney footmen produced the requisite London knock, rapping out a great knock, then several smaller ones in quick succession and then a final flouish 'as on a drum, with an art, and an air, and a delicacy of touch, which denote the quality, the rank, and the fortune of his master', as another American visitor Louis Simond described it.[4]

The Prince Regent,
engraving after
Sir Thomas Lawrence.

Once they had finished leaving cards, etiquette demanded they wait for cards to be left on them before they made their calls and, in return, hopefully received invitations. While they had to wait passively for social life to come to them, they shopped. And nowhere else in the world was shopping such a vocation for those with money and leisure than in Regency London. The Prince Regent, a style leader in this area of life, too, was a compulsive shopper. From the day in 1783 when he had taken his seat in the House of Lords as a young Prince of Wales, tottering into the Chamber on pink, heeled shoes to match the pink satin lining of a suit of black velvet, covered in pink and gold spangled embroidery, it was clear that being fashionable was important. By 1816, his body swollen with obesity and gout, the Prince Regent was trussed in corsets under his still flamboyant costume, like a huge lame old bird of once glorious plumage.

The dandies and bucks who daily paraded along St James's Street, visiting their clubs (White's, Brooks's and Boodle's), their tailors, perfumers, hatters and boot-makers, had long regarded Beau Brummell's immaculate, simple but exquisitely tailored, expensive clothes as the *ne plus ultra* of style. There were no female equivalents to either the Prince Regent or Beau Brummell in London. Paris with its clinging *directoire* gowns had defined a style that still set the fashion for women in London. Where London excelled, though, was in the tailored riding dress for ladies and, after their first ride in Hyde Park, both Louisa and Bess felt they had to have new English riding habits to look their best.

Just around the corner from their hotel was Bond Street, the most fashionable street for women. Accompanied by a pair of footmen, the sisters strolled along, joining in the daily promenade, seeing smart Londoners and thereby discovering the latest fashions. As she walked about, Louisa began to jot down items of interest in black notebooks, the size of her palm. It became a lifetime habit. Into them, written or sketched in pencil, went doodles of hairstyles and fashions, names of shops, a scrap of material she liked, instructions for a dye, a recipe for a cordial, a setting for a tiara she admired, directions to a dressmaker in Paris, the cost of Mechlin lace, several possible designs for livery buttons and quantities for an order of plate. From these snippets Louisa organised the business of her life. In the late morning, when she and her sisters saw the dressmakers and milliners, who arrived at the hotel to receive orders, some of her designs and ideas would be used for a new dress or hat. When the bill arrived, she would always pay promptly, writing 'Paid' with the date and a consecutive number so that she could refer to the bill from a list she made in a companion book. She kept to these habits, leaving boxes of little books and neatly packed paid bills as evidence of a life of considerable consumption whose expenses she efficiently controlled.

By the time the sisters were ready to go out after completing their orders and fittings, some time after noon, Bond Street would be full of coaches and barouches, the pavements crowded with ladies as well as the corinthians and exquisites, sporting their eyeglasses. One of the best places to see fashionable women was at Hookham's circulating library, which specialised in novels and where copies of the anonymous novel of the year, *Guy Mannering*, and Jane Austen's *Emma*, published the previous year, could be found. As well as several artists' studios (Thomas Lawrence, the celebrated portrait painter had his studio at No. 24), jewellers such as Phillips, and the most expensive tailor in London, Weston's, perfumers, linen-drapers, milliners, dressmakers and corsetiers spilled over into the surrounding alleys and side streets. Americans were surprised to find so many shops hugger-mugger with mansions in Mayfair. Rush, for instance, expected 'buildings more by themselves, denoting the richest people in the richest city in Europe', in the way the houses of the rich stood in America. Instead he saw 'haberdashers's shops, poulterers' shops, the leaden stalls of the fishmongers, and the slaughtering blocks of the butchers, in the near vicinity of a nobleman's mansion and a king's palace'.[5]

Although Americans were most struck by the size of London, 'its inconceivable immensity', the Caton sisters gained little idea of the geographical layout mainly because on this visit they did not venture further than Town, as the West End of London was called. They were most struck by the noise of London and the paradoxical feeling of being in a familiar yet unknown country, at the centre of fashionable life yet in the midst of so many strangers. The Pulteney Hotel, for which the highest prices in London were extracted from guests, was all that was most comfortable but there was no rest to be had there. At first, the sisters took a suite of rooms arranged with their bedchambers at the back overlooking the mews. Over the cobblestones from about half past six o'clock every morning came the dust carts with their bells and the dustmen with their chants of 'Dust-ho!'; then came the porter-house carts rattling with pewter-pots; then the milk carts; and then the vegetable sellers: so that 'the succession of cries, each in a different tune, so numerous' which mixed with the stables housed there and stirring for the day, meant that there was an unholy noise throughout the morning. This cacophony was not well received by women who had only gone to bed at three o'clock in the morning.

Next they moved to a suite at the front of the hotel, looking out onto Piccadilly. From about midnight the night mail and stagecoaches from the west passed by; until about five o'clock in the morning, there was 'a rushing sound' like Niagara Falls, as a steady flow of carriages drove up and down Piccadilly taking their occupants to and from routs and balls and gaming

clubs; and should there be one half-hour's quiet, it was sure to be punc-
tured by the watchman's call reporting on the state of the weather. Deciding,
as Bess wrote, that 'the monotonous roll of carriages distracts less than the
cries of women selling vegetables & c in the mews behind', the sisters
remained at the front. They resolved to stay elsewhere upon their return
from Cheltenham. In comparison, American cities were havens of peace
and much more conducive to a good night's sleep.[6]

They found the theatres no quieter, even during the performances. 'You
never saw such crowds,' exclaimed Bess after their first visit to the King's
Theatre at the Haymarket on 29 June. They were thrilled by the virtuoso
display of some 3,300 people arrayed in dazzling orders and jewels, and
astounded at the way Londoners expended as much energy upon social-
ising as the performers were upon the stage trying to make themselves heard.
The women nodded, smiled and teased their fans, gossiping and flirting
with the men coming in and out of their boxes while others called up from
the pit. One Regency wit was reputed to have declared that the trouble
with the opera was that they sang so loud one could never hear oneself
talk. Amongst such animated, chattering, stylish crowds, it was hard for
American visitors to differentiate between the *beau monde* and the *demi-
monde*. The theatres and Hyde Park were the only places these two female
worlds overlapped, observing each other from a distance but never meeting.
One American exclaiming over the 'extraordinary beauty' of an elegantly
dressed young lady was told by his London companion, 'Ah, yes, but she
is *not* a lady!'

It was the people, the well-dressed multitudes, that impressed the
sisters; such streams of people that to Nathaniel Hawthorne 'it always
seems there like the Fourth of July, or Election day'. Yet the scale of
humanity offered a sense of a cultured society and community moulded
over the ages which was still quite undeveloped in America. It was the
people and London life that Charles Bagot most missed. 'I would now
give my little finger to be dining at the – [in London]. Tell Watt to go
& dine with Desbrowe and then play a couple of rubbers at Boodles with
Egerton', he told his sister Louisa Sneyd, 'and do you put on a pot of
rouge and slap to Lady Harcourt's.'[7]

Marianne, Bess and Louisa, however, expected to wait some time before
they, too, were putting on the rouge and slap to sally forth to a rout or
ball. They had been warned by fellow Americans that it would take some
weeks before they would be noticed, if at all, by Londoners. 'The Letters
we brought have not procured many useful or agreeable acquaintances,'
observed Louis Simond after a month in London, 'some of them have not
been followed by the slightest act of politeness.'

Yet, after finding their cards on her return from a country visit,

Mrs Wellesley-Pole came the very next day, such was her eagerness to meet them. Marianne was at the Pulteney when Mrs Wellesley-Pole was announced and the two women spent a good hour together, much longer than the usual time etiquette allotted to a first visit. They discussed the Bagots and Washington life, and then turned to the sisters' plans. Catherine Wellesley-Pole had by this time ascertained what she had come to the Pulteney to verify: that Marianne would not cause her any embarrassment, for one never quite knew what to expect from random strangers. In the process of this sociable interview she also realised, as Mary Bagot had written so effusively, that Marianne was indeed a well-bred, charming woman of great beauty, who would be a positive asset to introduce into Society.

By the time the two women parted, Marianne had arranged to drive out with Mrs Wellesley-Pole and her second daughter Emily, Lady Fitzroy Somerset, in Hyde Park the following afternoon; to order hooped dresses from the best court dressmaker for the next of Queen Charlotte's Drawing Rooms, where she and her sisters must be presented; to attend various routs (the equivalent of a drinks party) including Lady Jersey's on 8 July; and, most particularly, that Mrs Wellesley-Pole would obtain vouchers for them to attend the next Almack's to be held in two days' time.[8]

The weekly subscription balls held at Almack's Assembly Rooms in King Street, St James's, were described by one *habitué*, Count Gronow, as 'the Seventh Heaven of the Fashionable World'. Almack's was the most exclusive, unique ladies' club in the Regency world and entry was in the gift of seven formidable *grandes dames* known as Lady Patronesses; in 1816 these were Ladies Jersey, Cowper, Castlereagh and Sefton, Mrs Drummond Burrell, Madame (later Princess) Lieven and Princess Esterhazy. They wielded enormous power through their strict control of admission vouchers – 'half London is running about from Ly Jersey to Mme Lieven to beg for a cast of tickets' affirmed the Hon. Charles Percy. Almack's was, indeed, a word known to cause sleepless nights to the match-making Mama and her daughters. 'I have tried every one of the Lady patronesses and not one single ticket could we obtain – I am quite sorry for your Sisters,' lamented Lady Louisa Hardy to her married daughter in 1816, 'the Balls [are] so very good, quantities of Men &c.' Exclusion was social death but as 'three-fourths of the nobility knocked in vain for admission', those deemed the 'insignificants' and the '*inconnues*', which included nearly all foreigners, had no hope of entry.

It was, thus, most convenient that Marianne had already left cards with a Lady Patroness, Lady Jersey; Mrs Wellesley-Pole would not lose a moment before writing to request vouchers, and they were to accompany her there, of course. And to complete their social happiness she invited them to dine before going to Almack's and to meet her brother-in-law the Duke of Wellington, who was arriving that very day in London. Such an invitation was quite remarkable for, as Prince Pückler-Muskau explained in a letter home, English grandees were liberal with their invitations to foreign visitors for routs and soirées 'for the sake of filling their rooms' but the most signal honour to be conferred upon even a most distinguished foreigner was an invitation to dinner: 'an honour only to be obtained by long acquaintance, or by very powerful letters of introduction'.[9]

On Wednesday 3 July they dined at the Wellesley-Poles. It was their first London dinner party, an occasion when their social credentials commanded the interest of the assembled company and a *faux pas* would lead to oblivion. Many, native and foreign, blushed and blurted their way through the conversational gambits thrown into the ring of company: the subjects that summer ran from Camelford House (rented by newly married Princess Charlotte of Wales), to the new sovereign (a freshly minted coin), from the Algerines (Algerians had massacred fishermen under British protection) to the Dandy affair (Beau Brummell had been obliged by gaming debts at Watier's, dubbed 'the Dandy club', to retire to France) and the Louvre business (looted art controversy in Paris), to *Glenarvon* (Caroline Lamb's novel about Byron) and the Byron scandal (he separated from his wife). Then there was the confusing British proclivity for bandying nicknames about: the cotton weaver (Robert Peel, MP), Silence (the talkative Lady Jersey), Cupid (Lord Palmerston), Calantha (Lady Caroline Lamb, after her heroine in *Glenarvon*) amongst many others.

Furthermore, a host or hostess could be driven by boredom to humiliate guests so as to enliven the evening or at least try their patience as Lady Holland was apt to do. On one occasion she repeatedly dropped her napkin and cutlery beside the young dandy Count d'Orsay, who repeatedly returned them until, finally, he called one of the footman behind him. 'Put my couvert on the floor,' he said, 'I will finish my dinner there; it will be so much more convenient to my Lady Holland.' George Ticknor, an American visitor, found that London society 'will not tolerate any one who cannot contribute his fair share to the common stock of entertainment'. At even the well-disposed Wellesley-Poles', the Caton sisters were, like stall holders, displaying their wares to discerning customers.[10]

They treated it just as any dinner party at home. The talk turned to the latest news from Paris, of the French king, how the Duke would decide the Louvre business, and with Bess asking about the return from exile of Mme de Staël whom she longed to meet; to hunting, when Louisa discussed which county had the best fox-hunting; to the new Joe Manton gun; to French opera and theatre – Marianne had heard about Mrs Siddons's recent performance for Princess Charlotte; to the Walter Scott poem on Waterloo, and much more.

The evening was memorable for being the first time they met the Duke of Wellington. The great soldier had been Bess's hero since her visit to Lisbon. She and Grandpapa Carroll had followed in the English newspapers his campaigns in Portugal and Spain so that the names of Salamanca and Vittoria meant more to them than to many Americans. Since then Wellington had beaten the French in the Peninsula and at Waterloo and, as Lady Charlotte Williams Wynne wrote, 'Everybody is wild with admiration of our wonderful hero.' The lionised duke was 'treated almost as a sovereign prince' in London where 'his conversation conferred distinction' upon any woman singled out by him. And here was Bess meeting him, not at a crowded rout where conversation was difficult but at a more intimate family party where they could converse. She thought it heavenly.[11]

It was fortunate that they met at a family dinner. One of his friends Lady Shelley wrote after first meeting him: 'The Duke's manner is formal, and, at a first introduction, very imposing. He seldom speaks until he is well acquainted.' On that July evening though, he appeared as he did with old friends, 'gay, frank and ready to converse'. Pleased to be released briefly from the cares of the Occupation of France and to be in England, amongst the Wellesley-Pole family to whom he was much attached, and interested to meet Mary Bagot's Americans, he was in good humour, displaying what the Whig wit Samuel Rogers called his 'great gaiety of mind' when his 'laugh is most easily excited, and it is very loud and long, like the whoop of the whooping cough often repeated'.[12]

Arthur Wellington was an attractive man. He stood five feet ten inches tall and, at forty-six, retained the lean, lithe, upright figure of a man of action. He was the third of five notable brothers: Richard, Marquess Wellesley, former Governor-General of India and Foreign Secretary; William Wellesley-Pole, current Master of the Mint; Dr Gerald Wellesley, Dean of St Paul's; and Sir Henry Wellesley, Ambassador at Vienna. A Wellesley grandson, later seeing four of them bury a fifth, remarked on 'those old brothers with their Wellesley faces so like each other'. Arthur and Richard had compelling, some said piercing, eyes, black-lashed with thick black eyebrows – what the Irish call 'blue eyes put in with dirty fingers'. Arthur's other distinguishing features were an aquiline nose and prominent chin beloved by caricaturists, and cropped dark brown hair, now fashionable but which he had always worn short and unpowdered even when queues and powder were required dress in the army – at any rate it enabled him to appear different from his two clever elder brothers and two equally promising younger ones.[13]

The feature in his character which many found most distinguished was simplicity, in the sense of being unpretentious. After meeting him that evening, Bess wrote to her grandfather of 'his unaffected simplicity of manner', and to uncle Harper of the Duke's modesty. The latter was an endearing trait. At a grand banquet at Wanstead House given by Mary Bagot's brother for some hundred people, royal dukes, the Wellesley family and the great of society, the Prince Regent proposed Wellington's health in a very neat speech. Rising to reply the Duke took his time, hesitated and at last began: 'I want words to express –' The Prince Regent promptly interposed: 'My dear fellow, we know your *actions* and we will excuse your *words*, so sit down.' This he did with the delight of a schoolboy who had been given an unexpected holiday.

He was not, for all this simplicity, a man lacking polish for he possessed the elegant manners expected in high society; rather, he liked to present himself as ordinary, as consciously unheroic even when laden with honours. People ascribed this 'simplicity' to Wellington in contrast first to Napoleon's behaviour and second to their expectations of a hero as a man who would display a semi-regal haughtiness. This explains the adulation over his manner as much as his achievement – why he was considered such a gentleman, which he was, and so delightful and so kind – when in fact he could be brusque and cutting and, when tried, demonstrate that characteristic Wellesley impatience, arrogance and explosive temper.[14]

Dining at the Wellesley-Poles', however, he was all that was delightful. Bess gushed to her grandfather that 'his affability is charming & his kind-ness' prodigious. While Bess particularly noticed the Duke, she was particularly noticed by his brother. 'Mr and Mrs Patterson and the two Miss Catons dined with us', William Wellesley-Pole wrote to Charles Bagot on 5 July. 'We like the ladies very much particularly the eldest Miss Caton, we reckon her and Mrs Patterson handsome – and the former particularly agreeable.' But the Duke did not notice Bess as much as he noticed Marianne.

After dinner the whole party went to Almack's for the Wednesday ball. To the sisters' surprise, Almack's was not nearly as elegantly arranged as the Assembly Rooms at Annapolis. Prince Pückler-Muskau thought it highly overrated: 'a large bare room with a bad floor, and ropes around it . . . two or three naked rooms at the side, in which were served the most wretched refreshments – In a word, a sort of inn-entertainment.' His jaundiced view no doubt reflected lack of success at snaring an heiress, which was the purpose of his visit to London. Almack's was the perfect rendezvous, as the whole point of the place was to match-make and confer social distinction; no one came for the fine furniture and delicious suppers, which they could find at home.

The Wellesley-Pole party made quite a sensation as they entered and were warmly greeted by Lady Jersey herself. Prince Pückler-Muskau thought

her: 'one of the handsomest and most distinguished women in England'.
Her father Lord Westmorland and her sister-in-law Lady Burghersh, the
youngest Wellesley-Pole daughter, had dined with the sisters. Everyone
turned to look at them. Marianne's beauty excited the admiration of the
gentlemen and many a glass was put up to gaze upon her lovely face and
striking figure before moving on to Bess and Louisa. As the sisters were
taken round by Lady Jersey and Mrs Wellesley-Pole to be introduced, the
chatter began and there were many exclamations when it was known that
they had come from dining at Savile Row with the Duke of Wellington.
Their prestige soared on that snippet alone.

Their first Almack's passed in a swirl of dancing, introductions and
conversation; they each waltzed with the Duke, joining the couples
revolving, gliding and twirling around the ballroom. Marianne had to
conserve her breath and energy and the Duke was delighted to walk
about with her during the evening. His attentions to the beautiful
American were of as much interest to the rest of the company as if they
had been directed at themselves. After passing the evening talking to
the Duke at a party, Lady Shelley acknowledged in her diary that 'it
promotes the *agréements* of London life' and above all 'it excites attention
from others'. Certainly by the time the sisters left Almack's at a little
before three in the morning, they were already thought of as the most
fashionable women in London; their names waiting on everyone's lips
to be released into society during the calls and visits of the day.[15]

Consequently, over the ensuing fortnight, they became the darlings of
society, 'greatly admired and caressed by people of the highest rank in
England', their uncle Harper reported to his eldest daughter Mary, who had
just been sent to school in Poitiers. Catherine Wellesley-Pole chaperoned
the sisters everywhere, selecting the best invitations amongst the myriad
they were receiving. She treated them like her three American daughters
and grew genuinely fond of them. Bess thought her not only very elegant
but also 'one of the best-hearted women in the world'. On 6 July she
presented them to the unpredictable Prince Regent at Savile Row. The
discerning but susceptible prince's marvelling comment about Marianne,
'Is it possible there can exist so beautiful a woman?', was not entirely unexpected. He was most attentive to her, and then called up Lord Fife to
be introduced to her with the less pleasing words: 'See the specimen that
America has sent us', though he followed it up with invitations to his ball
on 12 July and a visit to the Pavilion at Brighton.[16]

On 10 July at Lady Jersey's popular rout, they learned what it was to be
nearly squeezed to death. Where 200 people at Dolley Madison's drawing
rooms were a squeeze, 2,000 could be experienced at a London rout. Some
dozen were held every night from 10 until 4 o'clock in the morning during

the season, when the crowds of guests found 'no conversation, no cards, no music; only elbowing, turning, winding and being pressed and pushed from room to room' until they could escape down the stairs to the hall. Once there they experienced an even longer wait for carriages: more time was passed with the footmen than upstairs with their hosts.

At one rout such were the cries of alarm that even Wellington could not provide sufficient reassurance; he called out to the ladies below that there was not the slightest danger, but 'the pressure was so great that many of them fainted'. The sisters managed to survive Lady Jersey's rout without his protection, as he had joined his wife and their two sons at Cheltenham to take the waters on 7 July. They next met him on 12 July at the Prince Regent's magnificent fête at Carlton House. Before then they had attended a Drawing Room to be presented to Queen Charlotte and, attired in the court dress of hoops, train, white ostrich feathers and diamonds, they believed they had stepped back into their grandmother Molly's day. It was somewhat of a relief to dress again in the formal Regency costume of white satin woven with gold and headdresses of feathers and diamonds for the Carlton House ball.

'Nothing could have been more beautiful', declared Louisa in a letter home. 'The Queen, all the Royal Dukes and the Princesses were there and we were all presented *again*.' They had arrived at ten o'clock and Bess described the suite of rooms they made their way through as vast, full of mirrors, chandeliers and hundreds of paintings; all 'beyond everything delightful' but she felt at a loss amidst such grandeur. It was the only time she would be overawed in England. It was also the first occasion they were separated at supper from the Wellesley-Poles and the Duke, who sat with the Royalties in the Gothic Octagonal Conservatory. The sisters joined a throng of some 2,000, and supped at half past one in an enormous marquee. Despite the numbers, everything proceeded smoothly with 'no crowding, hurry or bustle in waiting', hot dishes hot, delicious champagne iced, excellent music and delighted guests. The Prince Regent, as always, threw the best parties, 'a perfection of taste' as one guest described them. With dawn breaking, the guests rose from the supper table and the roll of carriages began.[17]

'What a dissipated life the great in London lead!' Carroll of Carrollton wrote after reading the sisters' accounts. He wondered though, 'what time they have for reflection? the nights consumed in a variety of entertainments & amusements, and a large portion of the day in bed'. Philosophical reflection, however, rarely formed part of the amusements of a first London season. Bess and Louisa were entirely absorbed by the people who, their grandfather observed to Marianne, 'by your description are most agreeable & fascinating'. He and their parents were apprehensive that 'dissipation &

late nights' would counteract any benefits of the voyage and injure their health. Yet it was gratifying, the sisters felt, to be so well received, to have not a moment to reflect except to consider dress and the next entertainment, and most of all to luxuriate in the novelty of being in London where, as American women, they were themselves a novelty.[18]

14

Anglo-American Differences

England, in 1816, was barely acquainted with republican American women. Although Washington Irving noted 'This place swarms with Americans', he was referring to American men, in particular the merchants, shippers and commercial travellers who had business in Liverpool, the chief port for the revitalised America trade and for Atlantic sailings. In common with all American visitors, businessmen were reluctant to bring their women-folk to England, partly from a wish to spare them the discomforts, if not dangers, of an Atlantic crossing, and partly to avoid the heavy expense.

With the development of their own schools and colleges, it was no longer either necessary or of social consequence for the southern plantocracy to educate their children at Eton or Westminster, at Oxford or Cambridge. Potential young leaders, likewise, saw little advantage in attending the Inns of Court, as America developed its own law, and its courts cited English precedents less; indeed, that very year, the Supreme Court affirmed in *United States* v *Coolidge* that common law had no standing before the federal courts.

Nor was there a large American expatriate colony in London. Many Loyalist exiles had long since either settled in British Canada or become re-assimilated into their British families. Of those who remained, many suffered pangs of homesickness for America: they liked to gather in the Maryland Coffee-house and the New England Coffee-house in Threadneedle Street to hear American gossip. Hankering after some home produce, Jonathan Sewell, a Loyalist whose father had been Attorney-General of Massachussetts, asked a friend there: 'Cannot . . . you send me two or three barrels of Newtown pippins, large and sound, a few of our American walnuts commonly called *shagbacks*, and a few cranberries?' There were also some American artists, headed by the President of the Royal Academy and long-term exile, Sir Benjamin West, whose house in Newman Street had long been far more of a centre for Americans in London than their small Legation. Apart from these and a smattering of mercantile families, the remaining American residents consisted of the wives of Englishmen, such as Marianne's friends Mary Smith Mansfield and Anne Bingham Baring.[1]

Marianne, Bess and Louisa thus joined an extremely select group of

American women in England. This lent them added interest in British eyes: with their well-bred elegance of manner, they acted almost as unofficial envoys, providing evidence that another type of American existed. Otherwise, Britons continued to assume that Americans were, in Irving's words, 'a motley race of beings – some seem as if just from the woods', ill-mannered and 'downright unsophisticated'. The sisters needed to keep their diplomatic wits about them, to mind their 'ps and qs' as Mary Bagot put it. Although America and Britain were officially at peace, they were un-officially at war, engaged in what John Quincy Adams called 'the warfare of the mind'.[2]

Tides of nationalist enthusiasm were running high on both sides of the Atlantic, bringing to each shore the invective of travellers, using pen and periodical to deliver their cargo of criticism of politics and manners. In Britain the sisters found that at a personal level the people were friendly and gracious: 'nothing can be more kind and attentive than the English are to us', Marianne assured Betsy. At a national level, though, they were suspicious and condescending: 'In this country, unhappily, we look upon the Americans as the lees [dregs] of society', ran one *Times* leader; while the author Robert Southey thought Americans tended to 'level down everything to the dead flat of vulgar influence'.

The undercurrent of animosity had undoubtedly grown stronger after the War of 1812 and the defeat of Napoleon. Britons could not forget that when America's shipping (roughly 900 ships between 1807 and 1812) was captured by both Britain and France, she declared war on Britain but not on France; nor could they forget America's attempt to annex Canada at a time when Britain was already engaged in the herculean task of trying to defeat France. Fed by the steady drip of hostile comment, latent prejudices became more explicit.[3] The conservative *Quarterly Review*, for instance, had devoted a major article in its first issue in 1809 to the lack of culture in the United States and thereafter released a flow of anti-Americanism, which rose to a torrent in 1814. In a review of an anti-British pamphlet *Inchiquin, the Jesuit's Letters*, which presented 'a favourable view' of America, the critic took a hatchet to America's political institutions, morals and prominent citizens; even Franklin was deemed 'half plagiarist and nearly half imbecile'. With relief, the *Quarterly* declared that all talk of Anglo-American friendship was dead. Britain had taken up position in the 'warfare of the mind'.

While the sisters were at sea in June 1816, several articles were published in America reviving the controversy over the *Quarterly*'s review. Americans pronounced it to be 'the most laboured, revolting libel'. Both the *Quarterly Review* and the other leading British periodical the *Edinburgh Review* were widely circulated in America, doubtless to the surprise of their British readership, which had been led to believe most Americans were illiterate. The sisters were familiar with both periodicals as copies were regularly sent from Britain to their grandfather, who liked to discuss the latest articles with the family. While the bellicose tone had been tolerated both as a product of the War of 1812 and as identifying certain 'home truths' about America shared by the Federalist anglophile Carroll household, the aggressive barbs in peacetime had become distasteful. Bess, in particular, had not expected to find the ignorance of Americans and blanket acceptance of their disparagement by the press, so universal in England. Everyone they met in society had read or knew of the latest articles in the *Reviews*. British expectations of Americans were so low that they were almost in wonderment at the superior qualities of the Caton sisters.[4]

Their unusually enthusiastic reception owed much at first to their excellent introductions and the attentions of the Duke but, thereafter, it depended upon novelty, beauty and fortune. English high society in the Regency had a penchant for novelty. In announcing the arrival of a new French ambassador, who had somehow already annoyed the British, Princess Lieven was prepared to bet that he would still be fêted. 'I know the English well enough to have discovered that any new arrival, with a certain reputation and a certain polish, is sure to begin by winning their hearts', she assured Prince Metternich. 'To last, you have to have merit; but, at the beginning, it is immaterial. The Englishman is the most inquisitive creature in the world and the most given to staring.' He liked nothing better than something new. In 1810 it had been the Persian Ambassador Abdul Hassan, resplendent in flowing robes and turbans of silk and brocade and sporting a unique thick black beard. In 1815, a little Russian girl reciting verses was the latest fad at Almack's.[5]

Marianne's appearance endeared her to everyone. 'Tall, lithe and extremely graceful, her figure was perfect and her face one of the handsomest I have ever seen', is how John Latrobe's rhapsody on Marianne begins. With 'large and wondrous eyes of deep hazel, with hair that corresponded, every feature regular, and a mouth, the sweetness of whose expression was unequalled, with teeth faultless in form and colour, and, with her head set on her sloping shoulders, as head was never set before, Mrs Robert Patterson's beauty was a thing not to be forgotten'. Latrobe, the eldest son of the architect Benjamin Latrobe and a protégé of Robert Harper, became a lawyer, prominent citizen and friend of the family. Such was the power of Marianne's beauty that, after hearing her talk about religion, he said he was in more danger of converting to Catholicism than he otherwise had any thought of doing. The *beau monde* of London was equally in thrall and she drew gasps of admiration from men and women, some of whom even stood on chairs so as to catch sight of her face.

She possessed in addition a remarkable sweetness, noted by acquaintances and more remote members of her family – 'a better person does not live', a stepson-in-law, Edward Hatherton, later wrote. 'Anger, and ill-humour and prejudice seem quite foreign to her nature', he had 'never known any kind of more Christian purity'. There was a strong likeness between the sisters but although Bess and Louisa were very attractive they could not match her 'perfection of great beauty'. There was, however, one distinction that they did share with her, one that made them famous in London: the pre-eminent attraction of possessing a fortune.[6]

In 1816, Britain was struggling to retain its footing as the most prosperous nation in the western world. Visitors marvelled at the healthy faces and tidy, clean clothes of labouring people and 'the solids and substantials of England' in comparison with war-torn Europe. Yet by the time of the sisters' arrival, rents and prices were tumbling and country banks calling in their money, some stopping payment, as the vast wartime purchasing machine of government abruptly ceased to operate and wheat prices dropped from 120 shillings a quarter in 1813 to 53 shillings 6 pence in 1816. Thousands of soldiers and sailors were discharged to fend for themselves without money or pension. On the very day the sisters first dined in Savile Row, the *Morning Chronicle* reported that in the previous week not a single entry for export or import had been made at the usually bustling London Custom House, an unprecedented event. Trade was at a standstill.[7]

The rich, and especially the supposedly rich, found themselves slipping further into debt without any ready money. This state of affairs did not appear to concern them unduly, or make them modify their style of living. The sisters, like other American visitors, were doubtless unaware of the true financial position of many of the grandees in whose London houses they were being so pleasantly entertained. Fashionable life continued in the manner to which it was accustomed because everyone simply turned, without a thought about repayment, to the bankers, moneylenders and tradesmen when they needed to borrow money.

There is nothing more paradoxical about the Regency era than the attitude it displayed towards money. The dun, the tipstaff, the bailiff and the debtors' prison menaced the humble and the grand alike. 'The deep insolvent' in Charles Lamb's phrase, started from the pinnacle of society with the Prince Regent and his brothers, who were unusual in that, from time to time, they could call upon Parliament to pay off their debts. There was no stigma attached to living in debt, it was simply a way of life. Rawdon Crawley's attitude to money in *Vanity Fair* captured the spirit of the age: 'He lived comfortably on credit. He had a large capital of debts, which, laid out judiciously, will carry a man along for many years, and on which certain men about town contrive to live a hundred times better than even men with ready money can do.' Even the richest noblemen lived in debt. The sixth Duke of Devonshire, for example, inherited the enormous income of over £100,000 [£5.5 million] a year in 1811 – a rich man of fashion's income was about £5,000 [£295,000] a year in 1816 – and had mortgages and borrowed money totalling £593,000 in 1814.[8]

Those who did not have his vast resources, in desperation turned out servants – 10,000 livery servants were said to be out of place by 1816. They consigned pictures to be sold in such numbers that prices in the art market plummeted – a Claude that fetched 1,000 guineas in 1813 went for £70 in 1816. They closed up their London houses and retreated early to the country. When all else failed and no fresh funds could be borrowed from loyal friends they fled to France, like Beau Brummell. While the sisters were in London, the playwright and politician Sheridan died 'a deep insolvent' on 7 July 1816. Yet all was forgotten at his public funeral when he was taken in state to Westminster Abbey attended by two royal dukes and a throng of distinguished people. Such contradictions were inherent in Regency England.

Rich Englishwomen seemed more circumspect about money, largely eschewing turf and gaming debts, perhaps as a reaction against their mothers' predilections; they were better able to manage it, like Lady Cowper writing about some Parisian shopping in 1816, 'I know, my dearest Mamma, that you would not like me to get into debt.' Yet they, too, had no compunction about running up large bills and leaving them unpaid for years.[9]

Marianne, Bess and Louisa held attitudes to money quite at odds with the prevailing mores of England. In America, living in debt with unpaid bills was not fashionable then. It was thought wrong; no one who could afford otherwise did so and the weight of social disapproval ensured that people tried to clear their debts. Bankruptcy was regarded with a certain indulgence in England, as if it was just a matter of bad luck, and did not entail automatic social or business ostracism.

The difference between the British and American rich lay not just in their use of credit and attitude to debts but also in the scale of their entertainments and establishments. The Carrolls of Maryland were large, rich gentry landowners but they did not live on the scale of the rich English. They lived simply, almost frugally, and conserved their wealth, and yet were considered to live like grandees by Americans. Similarly, the sisters were heiresses but whilst Marianne had a town house in Baltimore and a plantation at Tuscarora with servants and field slaves, she ran them with less ostentation and expense than would be acceptable in England. In comparison with most rich women in London, though, the sisters' incomes were not bolstered by living on credit. They were worth exactly what their capital and income yielded.

Remarkably quickly after their arrival Bess and Louisa were known to be fashionable unmarried girls with a fortune who must therefore want husbands. And, at a time when the income from landed estates was reducing, match-making mothers cooed over their amiability and charming manners and showered them with invitations. Their own mother grew anxious about the effect of such an 'overblown' reception upon their reputations. Writing about the girls to Robert Harper away in New York, she begged: 'pray do not speak of them but to *contradict* the exaggerated tales you will no doubt hear – calculated merely to make them ridiculous & if they reach England or Mrs Bagot, may injure them.' Their grandfather confined himself to drawing their attention to the publicity. 'I understand', he wrote to Marianne, 'that the marked civilities & attentions you have met with from the Prince Regent and Duke of Wellington, and other great People & distinguished persons have been noticed in the public prints as well as in private letters.' He knew that he need say no more to be understood perfectly.[10]

Americans in England, especially the diplomats, were nonplussed by their reception. On the one hand it was flattering and promoted good relations; on the other the contrast between it and their own was stark. The American Legation in London then consisted of the Minister, John Quincy Adams, his two young secretaries and a small office in Craven Street. The US government believed a republic had no need to lavish funds upon appearances, and it paid a measly salary to its representatives in the Old World. So as not to bankrupt themselves, Adams and his wife Louisa first lived in Ealing, then a village in the countryside, and could never indulge in diplomatic largesse for, regardless of republicanism, there were certain appearances, such as expensive carriages and liveries, which they had to maintain. Although always provided with the entrée to society and royalty, most diplomats beneath ambassadorial level were deemed insignificant. Adams, with merely the rank of an American Minister, had to remind Wellington of their previous introductions, the Duke had so obviously forgotten him. 'This is one of the many incidents,' sighed Adams, 'from which I can perceive how very small a space my person, or my station, occupies in the notice of these persons, and at these places.'[11]

The Caton sisters, though, were occupying a very large space, too large and prominent for comfort. They continued to be lionised by Society. 'These distinctions they owe to their charm of manner, grace of comportment and cultivation of mind and not to their beauty,' uncle Harper decided, 'for there are many handsome women but very few who can be compared to them in other & much more attractive accomplishments.' At first, Marianne was 'much pleased at having received every kindness and attention, which is so gratifying to strangers', but now she was beginning to feel overwhelmed and fatigued. She was not pleased to have her name mentioned in the prints, and nor was Robert, and she was uncomfortable with the fawning

compliments paid by people with whom they were barely acquainted. She
and Bess felt 'tossed about' and satiated and thought Louisa was becoming
quite giddy, emulating the quizzing ladies of society and affecting a Priscilla
Burghersh drawl. Her elder sisters reined her in sharply and decided it was
high time they escaped from 'all this splendid confusion' and forthwith left
for Cheltenham – the purpose of their visit, as they took care to remind
Louisa.[12]

Cheltenham, though, was reputed to be 'the merriest sick-resort on earth'.
A contemporary guidebook confirmed its distinction, listing innumerable
aristocratic visitors for that year ranging from three duchesses to seventy
Ladies. While drinking the waters there, Jane Austen revealed that 'the
Duchess of Orléans, the paper says, drinks at my Pump'. Marianne had not
met the Duchess before but she had met the Duke when, as Louis Philippe,
he lived in Philadelphia. He was staying at Cheltenham for three months
and the sisters for two, so there was ample time to vary the spa routine
with reminiscences and enquiries about American friends.

Bess and Louisa discovered that drinking the waters at Cheltenham was
a serious business. The invalids, Dr Granville instructed, were to take the
daily promenade to the Pump Room at eight o'clock; meals were to be
meagre, breakfast to consist of one cup of tea, coffee or chocolate and white
bread with no butter, and only beer to be drunk at dinner; before the
contents of four pint tumblers of water could be drunk between eight and
ten in the morning, the teeth must be cleaned with a brush and some
proper tincture such as burnt bread or sage leaves. Thereafter, the spa guests
were given liberty to amuse themselves. Marianne's doctor had suggested
Cheltenham because its saline springs were particularly effective in treating
liver complaints, so she and Louisa began the strict regimen straight away.

Bess and Robert, being in good health, simply signed their names in the
subscription book; had they neglected to do so, they would have been
consigned to the social gloom of Nobodies. Then, so that they could send
in cards, they scanned the last pages to discover the names of other visitors. After that they proceeded along the main street. Here the *beau monde*
strolled up and down, seeming, Johanna Schopenhauer recorded in her
travel diary, 'rather bored. In twos and threes the ladies, with many a yawn,
wander slowly from one shop to another while the gentlemen try to while
away time by riding, drinking and reading newspapers.'

Bess was far from bored. Cheltenham boasted seven subscription libraries,
and everyone frequented Williams' British and Foreign Library which also
had tickets for the evening balls, concerts, benefit occasions and relief funds.
There she could read the latest novels, newspapers, journals and pamphlets
or, having paid a 2s. 6d. weekly subscription, take a selection to read at
home of those she did not wish to purchase. The subscription library was

where everyone gathered to gossip and discover the latest news and arrivals. 'What bliss' was how Johanna Schopenhauer described it. 'There one always meets company, exchanges a few politenesses with acquaintants, staring at strangers who stare back at one.'[13]

And the sisters again met the Duke of Wellington, who was drinking the waters for a bilious complaint. When he had joined the Duchess there on the night of 7 July, crowds surrounded his house, got into the garden and knocked at the door desiring him to show himself, which he refused to do. And so it continued throughout his stay, with crowds constantly following him and, according to Charlton Wollaston, 'the little Duchess nearly trampled on in their eagerness to get a sight of him'.

The little Duchess had hoped to have her husband more to herself but, with the crowds on the one hand and the American party on the other, she had as usual to share him with the world. She noted happily, never-theless, that he had more time for his two sons, who accompanied him on his walks. He also escorted Marianne and Louisa to drink the waters every morning and then afterwards on the morning promenade along to the library to meet Bess and Robert. They passed most days together, Marianne driving out with the Duchess, who spoke incessantly of Wellington to her, while Louisa and Bess went riding with him and Robert, and they all attended the balls and concerts or dined at nearby Berkeley Castle. It was not surprising that Cheltenham gossip should concern itself with the Duke and the beautiful Mrs Patterson and that, in a smaller place than London, she felt herself to be constantly observed.

By the time the Duke left for London on 1 August en route for France, another of his friends Harriet Arbuthnot had heard that he was 'really wonderfully improved by Cheltenham, and got a brown, healthy colour, and seems to have got his head and stomach quite right'. He was not only invigorated by his holiday but also by the plans he had made with the sisters to receive them later that winter in Paris and at the country house he was renting near his army headquarters at Cambrai.[14]

From Cheltenham Marianne answered Betsy's latest enquiry about their arrival in Paris. Betsy expected them at the beginning of September, hoping they would either help her to obtain fresh funds, or pay for Bo to travel from America, so she could remain in France. 'Dear paris, how I adore you,' she had written to her cousin John Smith who, she knew, would pass on her views to Marianne and Robert. 'All I *want* for happiness is a larger income & my Child to live here for ever.' She was enjoying the intoxi-cating homage of social success. Her letters glow with the pleasure of being fêted at the balls, soirées and dinners, which, she made sure to relate, left her without a spare moment. Mary Berry met her at Madame Récamier's salon and thought her 'pretty, without grace, and not at all shy'. As the notable victim *souffrante* of Napoleon, Betsy was welcomed by the Bourbon *royalistes*; the King even wished to see her at court. Betsy, though, as her friend, the Irish writer Lady Morgan, wrote, 'was not of the *pâte* out of which victims and martyrs are made. She held her difficult position with a scornful courage.'

Betsy hoped that Marianne and Robert would witness her triumph and report home the details of her success. Marianne, however, had to disappoint her. Instead of leaving for Paris on 15 September they would be going to stay first at Holkham and then at Apethorpe in the middle of October so they would not be able to see her before the middle of November. Marianne affirmed that 'London is delightful, the people most hospitable, and the Society charming. I like Cheltenham but London has made me a little fastidious.'

She mentioned that the Duke was 'very pleasing and affable; he left us yesterday on his way to Paris', because she knew Betsy would have heard they were together in Cheltenham. When Marianne wrote that their friends the Mansfields were coming to see her, Betsy sneered 'they are in *no* society'. Betsy had no time for those who could not help her whereas Marianne cherished old friends – she was learning to be a little more guarded about what she said to her indiscreet, caustic and unpredictable sister-in-law.[15]

On 15 September, when the Caton party drove through a triumphal arch and along the seven miles of approach to Holkham Hall in Norfolk they were following a route taken in homage by many Americans. In the way that Americans sought Washington at Mount Vernon and Lafayette at La Grange, they also sought Coke at Holkham, regarding him as a keeper of the flame of American Independence. Thomas Coke was a Whig and, by supporting the colonists against the government and the King's party in the 1770–80s, the Whigs were seen as enemies of their king and country. In 1782, after George III had consistently evaded acknowledgement of the colonies' independence, Coke brought forward the successful motion in the House that the Independence of America should be recognised. He was then called upon by his party to present the Address to the King and he arrived unceremoniously dressed before His Majesty. A knight of the shire, as Coke was, had the right to wear his spurs in the House and to attend court 'in his boots' – that is, his country clothes – but no one ever did, it was not court etiquette. Coke, however, wished to make a point. To the horror of the court, he appeared as an English country gentleman in long-tailed coat, broad-brimmed hat and light leather breeches fitted into top boots with spurs. He is depicted in the clothes he wore on this historic occasion in Gainsborough's portrait of him, which still hangs in the saloon at Holkham.

It was understandable that Americans revered him, especially after a remark he made at a Holkham sheep-shearing became known. 'Every night during the American War,' he said, 'did I drink the health of General Washington as the greatest man on earth.' Americans also admired Coke, as indeed did Britons, as an influential agronomist. Coke admitted often that 'the peaceful pursuit of agriculture has always been much more my happiness than the turbulence of politics', and it is as an agriculturist that he is widely remembered. At the time of his marriage in 1775 this must have seemed unlikely. On hearing that his bride was going down to Norfolk, old Lady Townshend, a county neighbour, remarked: 'Then, my dear, all you will see will be one blade of grass, and two rabbits fighting for that!'

Coke, then a twenty-two-year-old gentleman with no practical experience of farming, proceeded to change, literally, the face of Norfolk. By the time the sisters visited Holkham, forty years later, the barren waste and primitive farming had been transformed into a model estate. He exchanged ideas with local farmers at sheep-shearings, or 'Coke's clippings', as they were known locally, which became the greatest annual event in rural England. 'Accounts of the Holkham sheep-shearing are extensively circulated by the public journals in the United States', mentioned one of his correspondents. Andrew Oliver, later introduced by the Catons, was one who found the journey there worthwhile. General Devereux, a mutual friend, wrote to Coke: 'Mr Oliver has enlarged and improved his system of farming since his return, no doubt to imitate your great example, so that he is now considered the *Coke of Maryland*.'[16]

It was, however, Coke himself and his Palladian house that most excited the sisters. 'We are at present at the Country seat of Mr Coke surrounded by splendid elegance', wrote Bess to cousin Mary Harper:

> the walls are entirely covered with sattins and velvets, besides a number of the finest pictures, and statues, twelve footmen in the smartest liveries attend us at table, where everything is served on silver in the richest manner. What is better than all this the excellent Master of the House now treats us as old Friends & makes us perfectly at ease in his House.

Thomas Coke was now sixty-two and had been a widower for sixteen years. He loved company, and with his youngest daughter Elizabeth as his hostess, offered generous hospitality to a large number of people, only wishing 'his house were as large again, so that he might accomodate more'. His son-in-law described him as 'a very handsome man', who 'has an unrivalled charm of manner, combined with a simplicity of mind and character which are infinitely attractive'.[17]

Coke was enchanted with his three lovely Americans and begged them to stay all autumn at Holkham. They found, as Marianne described, a charming party there: Lord and Lady Cholmondeley, Lord Gwydr, the Marquis of Bath 'with half a score of younger brothers, Sir Williams & Rt Honbles without number'. The whole party then decamped to neighbouring Houghton, the Cholmondeley seat, for two days – perhaps just to vary the view for, as Marianne scribbled, the routine was much the same at both houses:

> After dinner a play was performed, then some dancing, left supper table at three in the morning, all met the next day at breakfast at one o'clock, drove around the Park in open carriages; I went with the noble Marquis in his Barouche and four shining blacks; dine at seven, and spend the evening in the most agreeable society

– and then back to Holkham. One of the many 'Honbles' there was Captain Spencer to whom Marianne gave an account 'as never was heard before of the Bagots' popularity and influence in America'. After he returned to Althorp, Robert Spencer told a mutual friend William Lyttelton, who helpfully passed it on to Bagot. Spencer added some more gossip about 'the Yankeys' which naturally was also passed on: 'Coke made much – too much of them, and was, as usual, very ridiculous with the *young ladies*. The male Yankee called Spencer Spencer immediately, and talked of Westmorland and Bathurst *tout court*, and was altogether very coarse, but neither brutal nor sulky nor intentionally uncivil. The women were much better behaved.'

There were, however, a few surprises for American visitors. It was customary after dinner for everyone to repair for prayers to the chapel where family and guests sat in the upper gallery. On their first evening, the Caton party was invited to attend. The sisters, used to daily devotions, had adopted a 'free-and-easy' approach to worship, in that they did not mind the how and where as long as they *could* pray, and immediately accepted. Patterson, however, responded with gravity, 'I thank you – I thank you; but I pray, devoutly and sincerely, *once* a week!' The Holkham ladies concluded that he preferred to worship with a clear head on Sunday morning than be hoisted up unceremoniously by the two footmen employed to help to their feet those who were too drunk to rise from their knees.[18]

15

'We are all for Americans very well'

By this time the sisters had received the long-awaited news from home of Emily's marriage. As the provisional dates for the wedding kept changing, the Harpers had set off at the beginning of July without her. She was determined, however, to meet them on her honeymoon tour in New York City in September. John, still in Montreal, took the canoe from Lachine to Fort William as usual. After only a week he took leave of his fellow partners, returned to Montreal and rushed south to be wed. Having fleetingly seen the Harpers in Vermont, he arrived in record time at Doughoregan Manor. Emily's relieved grandfather was at last able to send a horse to Baltimore to bring the priest M. Maréchal to marry Emily and John at 7 o'clock on the evening of 16 August.

'Your letter my beloved uncle altho' addressed to Emily Caton was opened with equal delight by Emily McTavish', was how Emily announced the event to the Harpers from the Manor on 2 September. 'I can scarcely believe that I am married – but when I bid adieu to this dear old house . . . I shall no longer doubt it.' She and John set off on a leisurely journey to New York on 15 September. Their arrival and meeting with the Harpers were marred, however, by a summons for John to return with all speed to Montreal. Emily was understandably upset about not being able to pass more than two days with the Harpers, her last link with home. She was harried to finish her shopping, flustered by another change of plan and distressed at taking such abrupt leave of the Harpers; the manner of her arrival in Montreal did little to reconcile her to her new Canadian home.[1]

Although she was 'most tenderly treated' by all John's extended family her welcome and introduction to Montreal society as Mrs John McTavish was neither what she had been led to expect nor, it seemed once again, what had been planned. The entertainments were muted affairs, more like wakes than the joyous exuberant Highland celebrations John had described. Moreover, John himself had little time to party as he immediately passed long hours closeted with colleagues in business he told her she would not understand. While she was kept busy settling the housekeeping at their town house in rue St Antoine, she was alone with the servants for most of the time; it was, oh, so different from home; home, where she was never alone but in the company of family, friends and servants she had known all her life – how she missed them all.

It would have been otherwise if her sisters had been with her; they would soon have known everyone and in no time at all would have learned everything important about Montreal society. Emily, a shy and conventional young woman bereft of her family's support, could only follow and adhere to the etiquette of a newcomer in a polite provincial society in which ladies diverted themselves with talk about the mundane. And so fashions, a little music, pew owners at St Gabriel's Presbyterian Church – the fashionable Montreal church where most NWC families including the McTavishes worshipped – the weather, the approaching garrison balls, the styles of a new sleigh were discussed at length but, in a town so dependent upon the North West Company, the ladies showed no inclination to refer in the slightest way to its concerns.[2]

It was some time, therefore, before Emily was able to find out, mostly from her own family connections, that for a number of years the NWC had been engaged in a commercial war of attrition with a revitalised Hudson's Bay Company [HBC] and Lord Selkirk's Red River Colony; a war which, over the last few years, had degenerated into real guerrilla warfare with traders trapping each other rather than the animals. While Emily had heard tell of the savage life of the American frontier she was unprepared to find it in Canada as part of the NWC's everyday business. Yet snipers prowled the river banks, canoes were ambushed and cargoes stolen. The fur wars were the Canadian equivalent of the American wild west, and murder, ambush and kidnapping became part of conducting business. 'From the arsenal of war were drawn raids, the levelling of each other's trading posts, incitation of the Indians and half-breeds to open fighting; and secret stabbing and shooting in the shadows of the forest', Frederick Merck, the fur historian, wrote of this period.

Although these skirmishes were far removed from Montreal, they were thrust into the consciousness of drawing-room society. Troubles came upon the house of McTavish, McGillivray & Co and its NWC subsidiary in the frail person of consumptive Lord Selkirk, whose 'lungs and soul were on fire'. Through his marriage in 1807, he pre-empted the NWC bid and bought a majority shareholding in the Hudson's Bay Company. Selkirk had no interest in the fur trade – 'It is a business which I hate from the bottom of my heart', he had told Lady Selkirk – but it was a means to realise a long-cherished colonisation scheme. He therefore persuaded the HBC to grant him land for a colony for displaced crofters on the Red River in Canada, which he would finance. The HBC was unusually generous: for a nominal 10 shillings it had given him a present of 74,240,000 acres, a land empire four times the size of Scotland.

The HBC committee was 'a mere machine in the hands of Lord Selkirk', confirmed Simon McGillivray of the NWC's London office. It would take time and much expense to make Selkirk abandon the project, 'yet *he must be driven to abandon it*, for his success would strike at the very existence of the [fur] trade'. The NWC then tried to negotiate with Selkirk and to effect a compromise plan with HBC but to no avail. The Red River Colony went ahead. And it did strike at the very existence of the NWC for several good reasons. The huge valleys were filled with buffalo herds, the chief source of buffalo-based pemmican, the dry food used to feed locals, *voyageurs* and trappers; the colony lay between Fort William and the Rockies and contained many of the NWC's most important trading forts and supply routes; and it provided the HBC with an entry into the Athabasca Country, the NWC's most lucrative fur preserve.[3]

To Selkirk, though, his 300 crofters were more important than the thousands dependent for their livelihood upon the fur trade. When the indigent Indians and Métis defended their land and livelihood against the intruding crofters and the HBC, violence erupted. On 12 August, with a large posse of hired mercenaries Selkirk rode to Fort William and arrested William McGillivray and the remaining partners. John escaped arrest only because he had left to marry Emily. Selkirk charged the partners with treason and accessory to murder and sent them under guard to Montreal. Of fourteen of John's closest colleagues, only McGillivray and four others reached a Montreal prison; nine were somehow drowned during the journey. John passed long hours in the office because he was one of the few surviving Montreal partners at liberty. Selkirk's actions were the trigger on the gun of the HBC whose subsequent attacks on NWC trade produced a ferocious escalation in the fur wars.

Emily, sitting in comfort in Montreal, had no idea that the career and fortunes of her new husband were being so severely threatened. She shared Selkirk's prejudice over the fur trade and the more she saw of Montreal, the more she was persuaded that neither offered the future that John ought to have. It was not the start to married life that she could have expected, and she missed her sisters: 'I long to see them once more – heaven only knows when I shall again embrace them.'[4]

Her sisters were in the throes of another country-house visit. In October they left Norfolk and went into Northamptonshire, where they passed three weeks at Lord Westmorland's seat, Apethorpe. Bess wrote of their host as 'a nobleman who has treated us with much attention', and Apethorpe as a place 'where I have no doubt we shall be much amused' though it was very cold. They were in good hunting country and once Louisa had shown her mettle and skill, she was well mounted and had some good runs. Fox-hunting had been transformed into a national sport in the eighteenth century by Hugo Meynell of Quorndon Hall, whose reputation had made Leicestershire famous as fox-hunting country. Meynell was the first master to attempt to breed fast hounds; faster hounds, and more fences with the Enclosure Acts, required better-bred horses, and Meynell's preference for thoroughbreds saw their introduction into the hunting field. With well-bred hunters, riders to hounds learned to gallop at their fences and felt the exhilaration of a fast, long, hard ride.

It was a very different experience to hunting in Maryland where there were few fences and a great deal of wooded forested country. Robert, however, wished to hunt in Meynell country and went for a few days into Leicestershire. John Quincy Adams afterwards met Lord Westmorland in London, who told him that Patterson had gone to a Leicestershire fox-hunting party 'which was quite a new and extraordinary scene' to him. His experience was such as not to encourage a novice, for Westmorland gave Adams 'a ludicrous account of his having supplied Patterson an old broken-down hunter to mount, and of Patterson's inability to manage him'. Lord Westmorland said of the sisters that 'they had made themselves universally beloved by every one who had become acquainted with them'.[5]

They returned to Holkham in November, though only for two weeks as they were expected at Brighton, after which they would make their way to France. Thomas Coke was desolate. He had hoped they would remain with him throughout the winter and now it was unlikely that he would see them again before their departure from Liverpool the following May. He immediately asked his friend William Roscoe to look after them in Liverpool. 'There is the most beautiful and lovely woman in my house,' he wrote with some emotion about Marianne, 'she is so extremely amiable and natural in her manners as to engage the admiration of everybody. She is an ornament to her sex, and has a claim to every attention that can be shown to her in this country. I shall ever lament the day she leaves us.' He had fallen quite in love with her.

Many others were inspired with love for her that winter. Charles Percy, brother of Henry Percy, told Ralph Sneyd about 'the temptation of pretty Patterson', and again from Brighton on 18 December of how *The Morning Post* had informed the world that he was laying himself at the feet of 'ma belle Americaine, who is a *really pretty* Woman & well received at the Pavillion'. Thomas Coke was not so light-hearted about his love and began to correspond with Bess, writing to enquire about Marianne's well-being. His letters became more frequent after he learned that she had caught a heavy cold and was unwell for the first time since her arrival in England.[6]

The Court at Brighton à la Chinese. This caricature by George Cruikshank, 1816, captures the atmosphere of exotic luxury which so discomfited the Duke of Wellington.

'Who do you think is among the number of our most attentive acquaintances?' Bess asked uncle Harper from Brighton on 17 December. 'The terrible Cockburn, whose very name has scared away sleep from us so often at Annapolis.' Admiral Sir George Cockburn was the 'bogeyman' who had commanded the Chesapeake Bay expeditions. Bess told how they met at the Pavilion and were soon deep in discussion about the war. The Prince Regent, seeing them talking so earnestly, came up to them and said laughingly, 'Why, Cockburn, that Lady used to sleep with a little Bundle under her head to be ready to run away from you – you'll frighten her to death!'

Cockburn, unexpectedly faced with the well-informed probes of an attractive sceptical young woman, had been manfully trying to palliate his conduct in America. He confirmed that Baltimore had been destined for destruction, and that he was eager to march straight from Washington City the day after it was burnt and order their ships to await them near Baltimore, but, as Bess reiterated, 'Thank heavens! his advice was rejected, for I fear we could not have assembled our forces in time to check him.' The Prince Regent diplomatically steered their conversation away by bidding Cockburn to talk of Napoleon. Cockburn, former commander of the Cape Station which included St Helena, told them that Napoleon had become the execration of the island from his tyrannical temper, and had shown himself to be a 'completely selfish & cold hearted Being'. Bess was in her element talking to 'some of the interesting people' she met at the Pavilion, where they now passed their evenings.[7]

Owing largely to the Prince Regent's patronage, Brighton had succeeded Bath as the fashionable winter watering-place with, in place of a pump room, the prince's domed Pavilion. 'It was indeed a masterpiece of bad taste', decided Countess de Boigne, daughter of the French Ambassador, who stayed there in 1816–17 but Lady Cowper was more magnanimous: 'all the gold and glitter and bright colours makes it look like an enchanted palace.' It looked far more like something else to Wellington: 'Devil take me, I think I must have got into bad company.' As Princess Lieven told Metternich, 'One spends the evening half-lying down on cushions; the lights are dazzling; there are perfumes, music, liqueurs.' In spite of the atmosphere of the seraglio, Bess and Louisa were quite safe. Of the interesting people there, none of them were single men 'so that we run no risk of breaking our hearts for love – as it cannot exist without some hope', Bess wrote home. The 'delightful' Duke passed one night at the Pavilion on a brief visit to England, Bess writing to Emily that he had 'the eyes of an angel, so bright & clear' and he promised to make their time in Paris pass agreeably.

The Prince Regent was a most attentive host. During the sisters' visit he was 'all graciousness and goodness' and there were balls and concerts innumerable. On 2 January 1817 they dined in a large party which included the royal Dukes of York and Clarence, Lord Liverpool the Prime Minister and Lord Castlereagh the Foreign Secretary and, if they read the *Morning Chronicle*, they would have seen themselves listed under the heading 'the invited nobility'. Their names featured more prominently in reports of the magnificent ball held there on 10 January to celebrate Princess Charlotte's birthday. The sisters performed several quadrilles 'danced in a manner to rivet the attention of His Royal Highness the Prince Regent and his illustrious visitors'. The dancing was so enjoyable that, unusually, few bothered to sit down to the two o'clock supper, and it continued until five o'clock in the morning. The ball ended, *The Times* noted, 'in the true *Old English style*, with the deservedly popular dance of *Sir Roger de Coverley*, led off by the Duke of Clarence and Miss L. Caton'.[8]

At these entertainments and those they had attended in London, the novelty of being American women in England was brought home to the sisters by countless incidents. Bess was complimented by one gentleman upon her 'excellent English'. Another comment was repeated so often about them that it became a favourite saying in the family: 'they are all for Americans very well'. Whenever they used the phrase 'We are all very well' in their letters home, they were referring amusedly to the English prejudice. Some Americans were equally prejudiced. Their fourteen-year-old cousin Charles Harper, full of republican ardour, disapproved of all European society and was not pleased to hear that their cousin Charles Carroll was going to be educated in France. 'I think it absolutely wrong to send one's sons from a free country like this, to a country governed by a King: because when they come home, they are full of "His Majesty," "His Lordship" and "Her Ladyship" etc, which sounds very badly in the ears of an American.' He did not know when he wrote these words that he would be accompanying his cousin to receive a French education. France also beckoned for Marianne, Bess and Louisa, though Bess admitted, 'I am not half tired of England yet.'[9]

16

Dancing in Paris

'We spend our time very agreeably in Paris which is the most splendid city I ever saw', wrote Bess to Mary Harper on 5 March 1817. 'The Duke of Wellington is all kindness and attention to us. I have just returned from riding with him – he mounted me on his fine horse Copenhagen which he rode during all the battle of Waterloo.' The Duke was proving the most constant of friends. Bess thought that on the whole the English were rather lazy about friendships. Good introductions, though necessary, she affirmed to uncle Harper, only worked if 'you hit the fancy of a few' who then kept others from forgetting the newcomer; otherwise, once the first flush of almost indiscriminate infatuation had faded, the English had few qualms about dropping new acquaintances – unless there was some special reason not to do so. And, in the sisters' case, that special reason was the Duke of Wellington. In Bess's experience, when the English 'once take you to their Friendship, there is no end to their *dévouement*', and also, in the case of their devoted friend the Duke, to their influence.[1]

The Duke of Wellington held an extraordinary position in France for a British soldier. Officially his title was Commander-in-Chief, Army of Occupation, with over 150,000 British and allied men under his command, and he also bore the title of duke in four countries and Prince of Waterloo in the Netherlands. Unofficially he was a powerful ruler, rather like an Allies Regent, and was consulted by ruling sovereigns, government ministers, diplomats and the military. In Paris he attended the Allied ambassadors' bi-weekly conference to supervise French internal affairs, and also acted as counsellor to the French royal family and government. It was hardly surprising that Mary Berry detected a note of regality about him, he talked 'quite as treating *de Couronne à Couronne*'.

Nor did he confine himself to words. Lady Malmesbury, wife of a former British Ambassador to France, was shocked to find Wellington acted in public as if he *was* a sovereign. Although access to the Porte de Sèvres was forbidden to all but the King after dark, the Duke insisted upon it. She put it down to the Irish blood – 'never was such a *childish* shew of power – The

Potatoes are *smothering* the Laurels very fast' as 'these Wellesleys cannot bear being at too great a height'.[2]

The conqueror of Napoleon had certainly been elevated to the height of a saviour of the peoples of Europe, and he bore the singular role remarkably well. But there was a great deal that the sisters had yet to learn about him. His indiscreet enjoyment of female company in 1815, for instance, had amplified the talk of gossipmongers and those with a political axe to grind. Harriet Arbuthnot wrote in her journal that 'The adoration of the ladies for the Duke was given the name *"la nouvelle religion"*'. When he was asked years later if it was true that he had received all that female adulation in Paris, he replied, 'Oh yes! Plenty of that! Plenty of that!'

His public favourites included a platonic friend, the lovely Lady Shelley, and a mistress, the admired Italian diva, Giuseppina Grassini, which upset his duchess, who was very short-sighted but not enough to miss seeing his attentions to Grassini. Some of the high-born English ladies could be as familiar in matters of love as the Duke: '*horrid Charlotte Greville*', condemned Charles Percy from Paris in 1815, 'makes the most filthy & *disgusterous* love to the Duke of Wellington, sitting on his knee, patting his head & *wrinkling* her face into lascivious smiles.'[3]

None of these women threatened his reputation in the wider world; the same could not be said of his relationship with twenty-two-year-old Lady Frances Wedderburn-Webster. She was described by Byron's friend Scrope Davies as 'that beauty over whom the eye glides with giddy delight'. The *St James's Chronicle* claimed that 'a distinguished commander has surrendered himself captive to the beautiful wife of a military officer of high rank' and, over successive weeks, continued to drip speculation until the Wedderburn-Websters brought a joint action for libel against the paper on 16 February 1816. Wellington was usually indifferent to what was said of him ('Publish and be Damned' he supposedly later told the courtesan Harriette Wilson) but Lady Frances was a relation and heavily pregnant. When he read the libellous article, he had reacted angrily: 'That's too bad – the writer's a walking lie – never saw her alone in my life – this must be checked.'

It was checked – the court found for the Wedderburn-Websters, awarding them damages of £2,000. It also checked the Duke who, described in court as 'looked up to by Christendom as the titular saint of the world', became if not more saintly then more circumspect. When an emotional missile like Lady Caroline Lamb launched herself at him he deflected the attack into friendship and a campaign to reconcile her with her husband William Lamb. 'Nothing is more *agissant* but Caroline William in a purple riding habit, tormenting everybody but I am convinced ready primed for an attack upon the Duke of Wellington', Lady Granville wrote of her cousin in Paris in

1815. 'Poor William Lamb hides in one small room while she assembles lovers and tradespeople in another.' By 1817 Harriet Granville noted of Caroline and the Duke: 'I see she amuses him to the greatest degree, especially *her accidents*, which is the charitable term he gives all her sorties.'

By 1817, he was also more adept in handling people. British and French factions fought over policy, and his admirers, Lady Shelley, Lady Charlotte Greville, Lady Jersey, Mrs Arbuthnot, and his nieces, Lady Fitzroy Somerset, Lady Burghersh, Lady Worcester, fought over his company. 'You are all Syrens!' he had written to Harriet Arbuthnot from Cheltenham in July 1816. '& want to keep me from where I ought to be' as they vied to have him as their guest of honour. These women, with whom the Duke formed his closest friendships, were distinguished by their beauty and rank. It was among this circle of light-hearted rivalries revolving around the Duke and the British Embassy that Marianne, Bess and Louisa found themselves in Restoration Paris in the New Year of 1817.[4]

They lodged with Robert at the Hôtel de Bourbon in the rue de la Paix where many English visitors chose to stay. The hotel was situated in the *quartier* adjoining the Tuileries, the royal palace of the restored King Louis XVIII. It was close to the rue des Champs Élysées, where the Duke had his residence at the Hôtel de la Reynière, a handsome mansion with large gardens. 'What a fine spectacle!' exclaimed Lady Shelley of the view from these gardens, with 'the Dome of the Invalides rising above the trees, under whose shade are pitched countless canvas tents, gleaming through the blue smoke of their camp fire'. Paris was still the garrison city it had been in 1815 when the glimmer of English campfires and the music of Scottish airs recalled to Walter Scott, as he walked back from the Duke's to the Hôtel de Bourbon, that 'an English drum had not been heard in the capital of France since 1436 when the troops of Henry VI were expelled from Paris'.[5]

Shortly after their arrival in Paris, the sisters went to the Tuileries to be presented to the King, and in an adjoining suite to the Duchesse d'Angoulême, the only daughter of Louis XVI and Marie Antoinette, then, in different suites, to her husband the Duc, to Monsieur (the King's brother), and finally to the Duc and Duchesse de Berry. The following night they went without Marianne to the Duchesse d'Escars, who received for the widowed king as wife of his chamberlain, at the Tuileries. Her apartments were perched up so high that guests arrived breathless after climbing a staircase of 140 steps, potentially dangerous for Marianne. They entered a long gallery which opened into a suite of little low apartments 'most beautifully hung, some with tent drapery', and the rooms 'swarmed with old nobility with historic names, stars, red ribbons and silver bells at their button-holes; ladies in little white satin hats and *toques*, with a profusion of ostrich or, still better, *marabout* powder-puff feathers'.[6]

In place of the soft background chamber music heard at an English court came the continual tinkle of bells. These tiny silver bells were worn by the old nobility, the émigrés who had returned to France and were mostly entitled to wear the Croix St Louis. Many decorations had been destroyed or sold during the days of revolution and terror and, as they could not immediately bear the expense of replacements, a bell costing only about half a franc was worn to denote the missing croix.

The peal of other bells, church bells, was also to be heard throughout Paris. The sisters delighted in the public observance of their religion. Their letters home are full of the music and processions. They also visited the hospitals and convent schools run by the Sisters of Charity, the Soeurs de St Vincent de St Paul and other orders, some of whom had sent nuns to Baltimore. Paris thronged with returned émigrés. Many had passed their years of exile in America so that in the salons, at the Tuileries, at the balls and the theatre the sisters met people who had come with introductions to their grandfather, others they had seen in Maryland and Philadelphia, and some who knew of their family only by repute. Thus, the French did not regard American women as a race of strange, even savage, beings as Britons often did. The sisters had arrived in France already acquainted with or carrying introductions to a wide circle of French people ranging across the political spectrum from the *royalistes ultras* on the right, the constitutionalists in the centre, to whom belonged the Comte de Menon, still in love with Bess and eager to escort them around Paris, and the Independents on the left, including liberals and *Bonapartists*, such as Lafayette.

Audiences signalled their partisanship at public entertainments. When the sisters went to the Théâtre français to see Madame Mars in *Tartuffe*, to the Comédie française to see the great Talma and to the opera and the ballet, the performances were often delayed when the audience repeatedly sang 'Vive Henri Quatre' as an expression of loyalty to the Bourbons. By 1817, the *royalistes* were also more aggressive and 'Vive Henri Quatre' became a taunt to a suspected Bonapartist. Allegiance was also conveyed through the language of flowers. The sisters had to be careful when shopping for *à la mode* headdress ornaments. At the Tuileries the *ancien nobilité* looked askance at violets, the favourite flower of Napoleon.

Shopping was a necessary occupation in Paris, everything was so '*comparatively* cheap', except, Louisa told aunt Harper, for fine Cambric and India muslins which were easily bought in London and were only to be had in Paris at an enormous price; a muslin gown cost 10 shillings in London but 40 shillings in Paris in 1817. Silk, though, was a better buy in Paris either by the metre or made up by a dressmaker into gowns. It was such a bargain that the sisters had a couple of gowns made up for their ladies' maids to wear on English country visits when, Louisa had observed, a lady's maid was just as well dressed as her mistress and was expected to pin herself 'up neatly & look smart'.

The place above all others 'delightful' for shops was the Palais Royal at the other end of the Champs Élysées from the Tuileries. A walk through the arcades and a browse in the myriad shops full of jewels, silks and lace was 'most amusing' according to Louisa. Bess bought a silk cashmere shawl there and left it with Alexander Baring's sister Mrs Labouchère to be washed by a specially recommended *blanchisseuse*.[7]

If, by day, the Palais Royal could boast the finest shops in Paris, by night its boasts were of an altogether different order. It was, said Betsy Fremantle, 'the scene of everything most depraved in Paris'. The elegant shops were transformed into houses of gaming and prostitution. The most notorious gambling house was the Salon des Étrangers, from whose dangerous double doors no one emerged unscathed. Lord Thanet lost his great fortune of £50,000 a year: he threw away £120,000 [£7 million] in a single night but could only exclaim with the recklessness induced by the Salon, 'Well, I consider myself fortunate in not having lost twice that sum!' Men from the Allied armies and foreign visitors were also directed to the Palais Royal by guidebooks, such as *The Englishman's Mentor*, which described the *cabinets noirs* where there were scenes 'such as no Englishman can conceive . . . of frightful and unimaginable sensuality'.[8]

There were so many English in Paris that the talk that January was, as in London society, of money and marriages. 'Parkins Rancliffe's sister is going to be married to a Frenchman, a young Choiseul', Colonel Felton Hervey, military secretary to Wellington, wrote from Paris. 'I envy a Frenchman her £80,000 [£4.7 million].' The Parisian winter air seemed to make young officers attached to Wellington's army of occupation think of marriage. They, in turn, acted as a magnet drawing mothers with marriage-able daughters to Paris. How could the Duchess of Richmond with at least four unmarried daughters, or Lady Conyngham with two, resist an invita-tion to stay at the Duke's country headquarters at Cambrai, and then to join him in Paris to attend the balls given before and after Lent?

The Duke liked the young and enjoyed being involved in their lives; they blurted out confidences, liked to be active as he did, and delighted in his company. He entered particularly into the flirtations and teasings of his staff and the children of his close friends. 'You never told me you had bewitched my Secretary [Felton Hervey]!' the Duke teased Lady Georgiana (Georgy) Lennox at the time of the sisters' arrival in Paris. 'He is going about very poorly!' The Duke took a fatherly interest in his young staff, worked them hard and watched them play hard, enjoying the stories of their scrapes and infatuations. When asked whether he would ever be able to settle down after a military life, he answered, 'Oh! yes I shall, but I must

always have my house full. For sixteen years I have always been at the head
of our army, and', looking at his ADCs as he spoke, 'I must have these gay
fellows round me.' He liked to see them dancing, saying to Lady Shelley,
'How would society get on without all my boys?'[9]

Society in Paris would not have been nearly so enjoyable for Bess and
Louisa without his boys. The flurry of balls given almost every night added
to the heady atmosphere of carnival. 'The French dance as if they feared
they might not live to begin again after Lent', commented Mrs Spencer-
Stanhope. Everyone danced during carnival: at the *bals public* open to anyone
who paid a nominal sum; at the cabarets or *guingettes* outside Paris where
the poor could escape the tax on wine; and at the private houses of the
beau monde.[10]

The Duke gave 'a most brilliant ball', as he himself described it, on 27
January at the Hôtel de la Reynière where the French and British *ton*
mingled and danced until five in the morning. Louisa danced all night,
Bess proudly told their mother, and was thought 'very well' and 'very pretty'.
As the Duke always permitted his Cambrai staff to attend, about 300 Guards
officers in dress uniform twirled and whirled the young ladies around the
ballroom. The most fashionable dances were the waltz, polka, mazurka and
polonaise and the officers passed a certain amount of time practising their
dance routines. 'Today I practised the *Mazurka* in this room and *fancied* I
succeeded', wrote Lord Charles Fitzroy from Cambrai before one of the
Duke's costume balls. [11]

'This is a dancing generation', Marianne Spencer-Stanhope decided. 'I
think people's wits live in their heels' such was the devotion shown to
dancing and the reluctance to stop at five or six o'clock in the morning.
As one ball succeeded another, Louisa danced divinely and sparkled in
society, her vivacity and seductive charm proving extremely effective. The
Duke noticed that more of her partners were becoming 'poorly' and were
seen to be composing poems the next day. It was fashionable in that romantic
era for young beaux to be seen to be pining and assuming attitudes of love.
Charles Percy described how a mutual friend had returned from Paris in
love with one of the Stapleton girls '& when anybody is attending to him,
sighs & looks forlorn; not so, when unobserved!' The Duke was delighted
by Louisa's conquests, and did not mind being surrounded by sighing *soupi-
rants* as long as they obeyed his commands. He was most amused to discover
that one of his 'boys', his secretary Felton Hervey, had transferred his attentions to Louisa with surprising swiftness.[12]

When, in February, Wellington went to the château at Mont St Martin,
some fifteen miles outside the garrison town of Cambrai, the Caton party
accompanied him. The dullness of Cambrai after the gaieties of Paris
was felt by all the headquarters staff, who bemoaned the lack of public

entertainments. Private entertainments were another matter. The merriment of château life had become a by-word amongst Wellington's guests, who enjoyed his prodigious hospitality for months at a time. As if to compensate for the loss of external society, everyone set to work to provide amusements: there were no end of theatricals, concerts and dances; there were pranks and high jinks to appeal to the schoolboy and girl lurking in even the most august general and dowager duchess; and there were uproarious hunts and rides when, like children at a funfair, officers and young ladies ran screaming through the long passages of the château.

The Duke, as always, took the lead, saying of giving one lady 'a ride in the coach': 'I was the coachman and her fright was capital.' Riding the coach consisted of harnessed gentlemen dragging ladies on rugs through the corridors as fast as possible. On another occasion described by the Duke, there was an unusual twist to the hilarity: 'they hunted Lord Conyngham through all the corridors even that in the roof. At night we had an improvement on the coach. Two Goats were brought in and harnessed.'[13]

After the exertions of the château, the sisters and Robert accompanied the Duke on one of his routine visits to Brussels. Bess could think only of their proximity to the field of Waterloo, which she longed to visit. Such was his attachment to the sisters that Wellington overcame his reluctance to revisit the scene of his last battle. He had not been there since that June day of victory two years before but, uniquely, he bowed to their entreaties and escorted them. The road from Brussels approaching Waterloo passed through a fine wood but on each side mounds of earth still covered dead horses. In the village they visited the Duke's old headquarters and saw the door upon which the Prince of Orange had been carried off the battlefield.

At the farm of Hougoumont the marks of battle remained as clear as when Georgiana Capel saw them in the autumn of 1815; the walls perforated by balls and blackened by fire, 'one end a mass of black and smoke, broken rafters, dust, cinders, old bones, bricks, shattered windows' and many other sights evinced 'the horrid scenes which this once peaceful farm had witnessed'. The scene the sisters and the Duke witnessed in 1817 was as horrid for other reasons. It resembled a macabre fair with treasure seekers still scrabbling in the fields for souvenirs of buttons and bullets, and stallholders selling badges and bits of torn uniform and caps. The party saw the high garden wall through which the Guards fired upon the French, the house in whose defence so many guardsmen were slaughtered, the orchard where the Grenadiers fought and the garden containing a guardsman's grave. At La Belle Alliance, where the Duke met Blücher after the battle, stallholders were selling more trinkets and ragged pieces of 'uniform'.

On their return to Brussels they dined with the Duke. Marianne noticed that during the whole evening he scarcely uttered a word and 'by his deep-drawn sighs' showed how sad were the memories evoked. She afterwards confessed that, much as she had desired to visit such a famous place with him, she would never have proposed it if she had realised 'the mental anguish' it would cause him.[14]

Chastened by the experience, the sisters drove to Cambrai and left for Paris the next day. Their latest plans were to return to London in March, make their way to Liverpool and meet some of their Caton relations before sailing to America around 1 May. Word had already reached Paris, however, of their visit to Waterloo and was taken by gossips as more evidence of the Duke's 'unnatural' interest in the lovely Mrs Patterson. In Paris as in London, everyone treated Marianne as a reigning beauty, remarking especially upon the way the Duke was so 'lover-like' in his attendance. As the sisters prepared to leave Paris, the Duke wrote on 6 March to his niece Priscilla Burghersh, 'I shall be very sorry to lose the poor Americans!' He was not to lose them as soon as he thought – even as he wrote, their plans suddenly changed.[15]

Louisa in Love

Louisa had been in soaring spirits during the whole of their stay in France. She was swept off her feet by the glamorous aura of danger and the superb regimental dress uniform of the officers who danced with her all night; except that, unlike a Lydia Bennet, she knew the difference between a respectably rich aristocrat and a dashing penniless Wickham. Louisa, aged twenty-three, had already given one of the Comte de Menon's friends, an impecunious French nobleman, his *congé*. Then she received another proposal. This time there was no thought of any *congé*: Louisa was in love and she immediately accepted Felton Hervey.

Her delight enthused everyone else. 'Louisa believes there never was such a marriage before!' Bess exclaimed. Louisa had scarcely enough hours in the day to receive the congratulations from everyone in Paris, let alone to write about it. It was left to Bess to tell the family and their friends at home; and to Marianne and Robert to unravel their travelling arrangements. It was also from Robert, in the absence of any other male member of the family, that Felton Hervey had to ask formal permission for Louisa's hand and to open the marriage settlement negotiations.[1]

Louisa and Felton had known each other for only seven weeks but, as his stepfather explained, she and her sisters 'were so entirely in the Society of the Duke of Wellington in Paris' they saw Felton almost daily there, allowing Louisa a greater opportunity to become acquainted with him than was then customary. Felton had remained in Paris during her visit to Cambrai and Brussels and he proposed almost immediately upon her return. It is not surprising that Louisa was unable to resist his swift courtship; he was a presentable, intelligent, eligible man with much besides to recommend him. Aged thirty-four, Felton Hervey was spare, tall and long-limbed, with pleasant features and fair wavy hair. His father Felton Lionel Hervey, a grandson of the first Marquis of Bristol, had committed suicide when Felton was three years old. His mother Selina Elwill, an only child and heiress, was left pregnant, with four children under five. She had, however, the support of numerous Bathurst relations, in particular her uncle General Peter Bathurst of Clarendon Park in Wiltshire, who provided handsomely for her and her children in his will in 1801.

At the age of nineteen Felton inherited the Lainston estate a few miles west of Winchester in Hampshire, and other property in the old county of Southampton on condition he assumed the name of Bathurst; so he became Felton Bathurst Hervey while his next brother became Frederick Hervey Bathurst when he inherited the Clarendon Park estate. Felton also stood to inherit settled property on his mother's death: land in Wiltshire and £3,000 Bank stock and a house in Grosvenor Street from his Bathurst grandmother's will; large estates in Devonshire and Somersetshire and a smaller estate at Englefield Green, and £5,000 Bank stock from his Elwill grandfather. On coming of age he had, as the eldest son, already inherited an estate in Warwickshire and other property and bank stock. As Louisa later told Emily, she had entertained no thought of being married when she had first come to Paris but 'I certainly have married *admirably*', she concluded.[2]

She was also marrying a brave and distinguished soldier with excellent career prospects as one of Wellington's trusted coterie. Felton was born and bred to command, which he always did in the nicest possible way. The Duke called him 'the so amiable Colonel'. He had left Eton in 1800 aged eighteen and was 'extremely happy' to be given a commission as a cornet in the 3rd Dragoon Guards by the Prince of Wales; a mark of the especial favour in which the Herveys stood with the royal family, as the regiment was the Prince's own. In 1803, however, Felton transferred and purchased a troop (a captaincy) in the 14th Light Dragoons, was gazetted major in 1806 and in November 1808 embarked for the Iberian Peninsula.

The following year Wellington decided to take Oporto in Portugal, which was occupied by Marshal Soult and 11,800 French troops. The Douro River lay between them but all the bridges had been destroyed. On 12 May 1809 in a daring, victorious battle Felton, as his mother wrote, 'lost his right arm in a glorious way in leading his squadron after crossing the Douro against the French'. It was not until 2 June that she received a letter from him, 'the first he wrote with his left arm saying he was going on well'.

He sufficiently mastered the skill of being one-armed to be able to rejoin the regiment in October. The following year he became lieutenant-colonel, and was again injured in May 1811. 'That unfortunate fellow Hervey', Admiral Berkeley informed Lord Buckingham from Lisbon, 'has again been wounded in the leg, and I fear severely.' Such were Felton's powers of recovery that, on 25 October, his stepfather was writing, 'Felton Hervey has again distinguished himself greatly. He made several charges' and his bravery was 'the theme of the whole army'. He commanded the 14th through the roll-call of decisive battles in the Peninsular War, and then as they fought their way over the Pyrenees into France and up to Toulouse. After the defeat of Napoleon in 1814, Felton was promoted a colonel in the army. When the 14th were sent to fight in America, however, he did not accompany them.[3]

Instead he joined Wellington's staff and was at his side at Waterloo. As he related to Louisa and her family, at around half past seven on that summer's evening of battle, Wellington sighted the Prussians and Hervey called to nearby troops: 'The day is our own! The Prussians have arrived!' Wellington then rode off on his horse Copenhagen, exhorting each regiment to charge the French. It was to be the final decisive advance. As he drove Copenhagen over the flattened cornfields, soaked in blood and strewn with the dead, horses and men, Hervey was alongside him and urged him to go to a safer position, saying, 'We are getting into enclosed ground, and your life is too valuable to be thrown away.' 'Never mind,' answered the Duke, 'let them fire away. The battle's won; my life is of no consequence now.' About an hour later, in the dusk, they reached La Belle Alliance where Wellington and Blücher rode forward to greet one another in victory.

Thereafter, the Duke kept Hervey close to him, appointed him an ADC after Waterloo, recommended him as an extra ADC to the Prince Regent, and chose him to become Military and Private Secretary during the Occupation. Hervey possessed an equable temperament and a courteous manner, both of which remained unruffled by either the demands of battle or the Duke's odd explosions of temper. His administrative talents, firm and conciliatory in communications with others, and his complete discretion served Wellington well. The Duke was extremely attached to him and reposed entire confidence in him.[4]

This was the man whom Louisa loved and wished to marry without delay. It was customary to complete all marriage settlement negotiations and to sign the deeds before the marriage but, given that the mails could take up to ten weeks to reach Maryland, this did not suit Louisa at all. Nor did it suit Robert Patterson, who had no wish to remain indefinitely abroad. Etiquette demanded, however, that Louisa could not remain or travel in Europe without the chaperonage of Robert and Marianne.

Louisa managed to arrange matters, thanks to the Duke. Indeed, he and the Duchess treated her as a daughter and her wedding as in their charge. The Duke was delighted that Hervey, his young whipper-snapper, as he sometimes called him, was marrying her and wrote to Mrs Fremantle to advocate the match; he also took responsibility for its occurring before the settlements were completed. The wedding, he decided, was to be at Apsley House, which he had just purchased from his eldest brother Lord Wellesley, and the Duchess would present Louisa as a new bride at the May Drawing Room.[5]

Under his auspices, the marriage arrangements were *en train*. 'I propose to go over for the Regent's Birthday & Col Hervey's Marriage which will have surprised you not a little', he told Georgy Lennox on 8 March. 'I like the Lady very much indeed.' The Lady was bustling about among dressmakers, milliners, shoe-makers and more, having fittings for her wedding gown, buying the finest lace and trying to have everything ready within a fortnight. Leaving Hervey and the Duke to follow in April, she started out with Marianne, Bess and Patterson from Paris on 22 March and arrived four days later at Thomas's Hotel in Berkeley Square. News of the match was warmly received by Mrs Wellesley-Pole who immediately undertook to give a dinner and a party on the eve of the wedding. The Duke gave Mary Bagot the news on 9 April, writing that he had passed a good deal of his idle time that winter with the sisters: 'I never saw any people that I liked better, and I have regretted their departure much.'6

Their grandfather was with their parents at Brooklandwood when Bess's letter of 5 March arrived. Its news gave them conflicting sensations of pleasure and pain, he explained to her, 'of pleasure from Louisa having attracted and attached to her a man so universally esteemed & beloved as Col. Hervey; of *pain* from the apprehension that I shall never see her again'. Although Felton promised in his letter to them to bring Louisa to see them when the Occupation would be ended, Carroll of Carrollton knew that military men were not masters of their own time and that many incidents could arise to defeat Hervey's benevolent intentions. Mary Carroll Caton's longing to be with her beloved daughter and meet her new son-in-law was equally mixed with feelings of joy at Louisa's happiness.7

Congratulations from Felton's mother Selina and stepfather William Fremantle and the rest of his family were not less effusive, they were just not forthcoming. Mrs Fremantle noted tersely, 'heard of Felton's intended marriage' and then, 'rec'd letters from Felton & ye Duke of Wellington' and 'Mrs Patterson & c arrived in England'. Marianne had written a courteous letter to her, as had Louisa, but the first dialogue of any kind between them occurred on the Wednesday evening after their arrival in London when the Duchess of Wellington and Mrs Wellesley-Pole presented them to the Fremantles at Almack's. The support of the wider Wellington circle conveyed a clear message to the Fremantles, one it would be difficult for them to ignore without harming Felton's position, their own connections with the Wellesleys, and one of their sources of patronage. Louisa thus emerged in a strengthened position from this first encounter with her future in-laws.

Conformance to social forms undoubtedly eased the situation. Marianne and the Duchess of Wellington left cards the next day at Selina Fremantle's house in Great Stanhope Street and she, in turn, left her cards upon them; Marianne, Louisa and the Duchess called upon Mrs Fremantle the following day. On 29 March Louisa was bidden to dine with the Fremantles. The ordeal was intensified for her by the absence not only of Felton but also of her uninvited sisters; the evening ended pleasantly, though, hearing *Don Giovanni* at the Opera. It was much less of a trial the following evening to return with her sisters, Robert and the Duchess of Wellington.

The proprieties were thereby sufficiently maintained to satisfy everyone that the Fremantles welcomed Louisa as a daughter-in-law. In private, however, the Fremantles were aghast. 'You will have heard of Felton's marriage,' Fremantle wrote to his brother, 'it is not a match we like but hope it will turn out well, she is very pretty.' To them it was a *mésalliance*. In the first place, the idea of marrying an American was regarded as extraordinary by rich landed families who deemed rank and position as important as fortune. An American republican family possessed no rank and therefore held no position in society other than by its money. The concept of 'dollar princesses' would not become popular with the British aristocracy until the last quarter of the nineteenth century when agricultural depression and plummeting rent rolls led many British aristocrats to marry American heiresses as a means of preserving their encumbered estates and expensive tastes. In 1817, however, Mrs Fremantle was faced with a marriage between her heir and an American heiress arranged solely to satisfy their affections; their marriage was entirely a love match.[8]

The Fremantles' misgivings about an American in the family were by no means unusual. Augustus Foster's half-sister Mrs George Lamb (known as 'Caro George') had promoted a match between him and Annabella Milbanke (who eventually married Byron) because she felt 'a great horror at the possibility of an American Mrs Foster' becoming an intimate of their circle. Anne Bingham Baring was treated with disdain for being an American and not even invited to the wedding breakfast when her son married the daughter of the Earl of Sandwich.[9]

Their feelings about Louisa were coloured by the British belief that Americans were 'not safe in Society' or were all 'Yankees', signifying an ill-bred, vulgar person. Thus when Fremantle described Louisa as Felton's 'Yankee' wife, and spoke of the 'Yankee' marriage, he was conveying an unflattering opinion. They were also upset about Louisa's religion. Catholic emancipation had yet to be achieved in Britain, unlike in America, and if the children were brought up in that proscribed religion they would clearly be disadvantaged. Fremantle's patron was the Marquess of Buckingham, whose wife, the Marchioness, had converted to Catholicism in 1772, and their daughter Lady Mary Grenville was received into the Church of Rome in 1809. Lady Buckingham's religion had created difficulties for both her family and the Whig Party. Buckingham loved his wife but he tried to forbid her religion and, as his sister Lady Carysfort observed, her Catholicism

Apsley House, London, where Louisa was married in 1817. The Duke gave her away and he and the Duchess remained very fond of her.

was a situation 'over which my dear Brother always tried to throw a veil'. Reports of a papist chapel at Stowe, the Buckingham seat, and that the whole family was closet Papists were used as ammunition by political opponents of the powerful Grenville interest. William Fremantle had risen on the Grenville largesse to lucrative political preferment and, when Louisa first met him in March 1817, he represented Buckingham. Louisa's Catholicism was therefore a considerable problem. It was fortunate, however, that Fremantle generally deferred to his wife in matters concerning her children and Felton was her favourite son. Fremantle therefore surmised that she 'of course don't like the match much, but will be perfectly reconciled to it, if Felton secures his happiness'.[10]

Felton, however, was still in Paris so that it was left to Louisa to try to reconcile her future mother-in-law to the match. But on 1 April, two days after Louisa dined at Great Stanhope Street, Mrs Fremantle removed to her country house, Castle Hill at Englefield Green in Surrey. It was not until 12 April that she returned to Town, 'very ill'. Her unnamed illness was serious enough to prevent her from joining the company when, after Felton's arrival in London on the night of 20 April, a party including Louisa, her sisters, the Wellingtons, Lord and Lady Verulam and John Fremantle dined at her house on 21 April.[11]

Louisa and Felton were twice married on 24 April 1817. Shortly after two o'clock in the afternoon Felton and the Duke collected Louisa, Bess

and the Pattersons from Thomas's Hotel in Berkeley Square and drove not
to the Spanish Chapel at the Spanish Embassy as planned but to the Bavarian
Chapel in Warwick Street. The priest at the Spanish Chapel had refused
to marry them without their oath that any daughters of the marriage would
be brought up as Catholics. The Bavarian priest was not so scrupulous –
according to the American Minister, 'his indulgence was propitiated by a
hint that it would be politic not to indispose the Duke of Wellington
against the Catholics'.

Louisa, now Mrs Hervey, and Felton dined in a family party at the
Fremantles', with Dr Goodall, retired Provost of Eton, who was to marry
them in an Anglican ceremony later that evening. Meanwhile her sisters
dined in a family party at the Wellesley-Poles. The other guests had been
invited by the Duke to attend the second ceremony at Apsley House at
nine o'clock but the specified time was not allowed to interrupt the family
dinners; punctuality was never a quality thought worth cultivating by the
ton in Regency England.

John Quincy Adams was infuriated by the disregard of time in Britain.
He had learnt to arrive uncharacteristically late for an American, yet still
found only empty rooms to greet him. Louisa's wedding was no exception
and kept to English rather than punctual American time, Adams noted in
his diary. The Adamses still arrived too early. It was not until nearly eleven
o'clock that the guests managed to assemble in the salon at Apsley House,
and shortly afterwards Louisa entered the room on the arm of the Duke,
who was giving her away. She wore a simple white Parisian gown lightly
trimmed with exquisite Mechlin lace, gold slippers on her feet and, eschewing
her love of jewels, confined herself to a headdress of pearls, which on her
dark hair appeared luminous in the candlelight of the chandeliers and
candelabras.

After the Anglican service, Louisa distributed her favours, roses of silver
ribbon, to all the company which included many Caton friends such as
Thomas Coke and his daughter Elizabeth Coke, the Mansfields and the
Wellesley-Poles; and the Hervey family, Lord Liverpool, the Prime Minister,
and Lord and Lady Bathurst, as well as the Duke's whipper-snappers. Louisa
and Felton then set off for his mother's house at Englefield Green where,
as was customary, they would remain quietly for at least ten days. Neither
of their mothers, usual visitors on such occasions, was able to call upon
them; one far away in Maryland 'dreaming' of the emotional occasion, and
the other not well enough to attend the ceremonies or enjoy a drive to her
country house to see the newly weds.[12]

Marianne and Bess returned to Savile Row where other guests joined
the party. John Sneyd reported to Charles Bagot, 'I was at Mrs Pole's the
night of the Murrica wedding, and saw all the Yankeys, except the Doodle

THE
FEMALE COMBATANTS

I'll force you to Obedience
You Rebellious Slut

Liberty Liberty for ever Mother
while I exist

FOR OBEDIENCE

FOR LIBERTY

OR WHO SHALL
Publish'd According to Act Jan.y 26·1776. Price 6.d

The Female Combatants, an anonymous cartoon of 1776, depicting a fashionable Britannia fighting a native American. Britons still denigrated Americans as savages when the Caton sisters arrived in London forty years later.

Charles Carroll of Carrollton by Sir Joshua Reynolds c.1763. Charley was painted in London while he was reluctantly studying law at the Middle Temple.

Mary 'Molly' Carroll by Charles Willson Peale, 1771. The sisters' grandmother is shown holding one of the books ordered from London for her own Lady's Library.

The Resignation of General Washington's Commission by John Trumbull.
Washington voluntarily tenders his resignation as Commander-in-Chief to the Continental
Congress at the State House, Annapolis, on 23 Dec. 1783. Behind him stands Carroll of
Carrollton, President of the Senate, with his hand on the chair. Mary and Kitty Carroll
are on his left while Martha Washington and the ladies watch from the gallery.

Henry Darnall III by Justus Englehardt Kuhn c.1710,
with a black boy standing behind. The sisters' grandfather followed Darnall and Carroll family tradition,
presenting each of them with their own body slave.

The fiery rebellion in Saint-Domingue
when thousands of slaves took a terrible
vengeance on their owners, many of whom
escaped to Baltimore. Eighteenth-century
engraving of the French School.

Elizabeth Caton, a painting
by Thomas Philipps, undated.
Bess, her eyes 'so kind and smiling',
wears a luxuriant, fashionable turban.

The Star Chamber at Carlton House.
When Bess arrived for her first ball here,
she felt at a loss amidst the grandeur, the
only time she was overawed in England.

Coke of Holkham in his country clothes
by Thomas Gainsborough.

Arthur, Duke of Wellington
by Sir Thomas Lawrence.
The Duke fell in love with
Marianne and had this portrait
painted for her in 1817.

Colonel Sir Felton Bathurst Hervey
by Thomas Heaphy, undated.
Felton, dashing in his glamorous
regimental uniform, swept Louisa
off her feet in Paris.

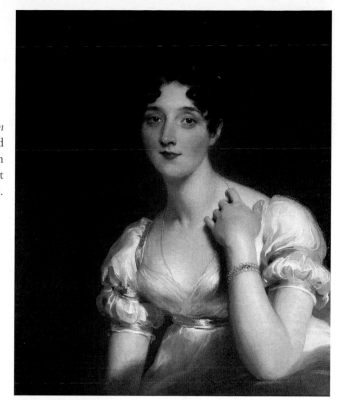

Marianne Patterson by Sir Thomas Lawrence, painted for the Duke, who kept it with him in France and then hung it in his study at Stratfield Saye.

Louisa Caton, a painting attributed to Sir Thomas Lawrence or his studio. She probably sat for it before her marriage in April 1817.

The Tea Party by Henry Sargent. A scene familiar to the sisters from the parties at their uncle Carroll's Homewood House.

A Society Ball, engraving by Charles Etienne Pierre Motte, 1819. Louisa liked nothing better than dancing till five in the morning at fashionable balls in London and Paris.

Emily, now a matronly thirty-seven, admitted to her sisters, 'I'm afraid when you all see my picture, I shall have altered so much, that you will not know me.'

The Muses of Painting, Poetry and Music by William E. West, 1825. Louisa holds a palette and brush, Bess a quill and Marianne strums a guitar in this composition painted in West's studio in Paris.

Marianne's second husband
Richard Marquess Wellesley,
Wellington's eldest brother.
Wellesley presented this portrait
by Sir Thomas Lawrence
to Queen Victoria.

Charles Carroll of Carrollton by Thomas Sully.
The sisters' beloved Grandpapa was
over ninety when he was painted for
Marianne and Richard Wellesley.

[Felton] who was just married.' He went on to ridicule Robert Patterson who apparently 'showed no better than as a lump of cobbler's wax'; Lady Charlotte Williams Wynn divulged that the Hervey marriage had 'richly supplied the town with small talk'. Louisa was said to have left the Bavarian Chapel on the Duke's, rather than Felton's, arm and insisted upon going to see the Waterloo Panorama 'in the hour of interval between the two ceremonies'. Felton was said to think her an 'unsophisticated Being'; and at Apsley House, not being a Protestant, she supposedly, 'burst out into loud laughter, & then began tittering the whole time' – whether to the exclusion of the groom saying 'with this ring I thee wed' and any other words of the marriage service was not related. 'In short,' Lady Charlotte concluded, 'the stories are endless & hold out no encouragement to the Election of unsophisticated Beings for Wives.'[13]

18

Marianne and the Duke

In England, the 'ridiculous falsehoods' circulated about the Hervey marriage and the Duke's prominent role in the sisters' lives reinforced the interest in his relationship with Marianne. When Charles Percy, junketting incessantly in London, met the sisters again after their arrival in Town from France they told him that nothing ever equalled the Duke's kindness to them in Paris: indeed, Percy observed to Ralph Sneyd, 'a pair of brilliant yet melting black eyes have been a very efficacious support to Mrs P[atterson] everywhere'. Those unable to judge the effect of her lovely eyes for themselves, such was the crush around her at Almack's, could console themselves by wandering into Lawrence's studio on Bond Street where they could gaze instead at her portrait, a work in progress.[1]

The Duke had commissioned Lawrence to paint two portraits in oil that spring, one of Marianne for him and one of himself as a present for Marianne. Lawrence had already produced several portraits of the Duke, including a splendid equestrian one the previous year. It was common practice to have engravings made of existing portraits to give to family and friends, as Wellington would do of his sombre portrait by George Hayter commissioned as a gift for a godson. For Marianne, no engraving would suffice. The large flattering portrait he gave her has become one of the most reproduced in the vast Wellington iconography. He is seen standing with folded arms, as he fixes the viewer with the assured level gaze of a commander, a man at the height of military fame wearing the field marshal's uniform of red coat and gold braid, the blue Garter sash and the orders of the Golden Fleece and the Grand Cross of the Bath. Marianne's picture is slightly smaller. Her lovely oval face bears an expression of sympathetic interest and the merest suggestion of a smile. She is shown seated, wearing a simple gown of white muslin with golden sash and ribbons, and is raising her left arm as if to hold the long delicate chain of tiny seed pearls and diamonds falling around her long neck.

No evidence survives to show what Robert thought about the portraits and Marianne's being so much with the Duke. She was in Bond Street for the sittings throughout April and the Duke sat for his portrait after his arrival in London on 21 April when they no doubt passed time together at the studio. On 9 May the Duke made a note of his initial payment to Lawrence. 'For my Picture for Mrs Patterson £78-15 [£4,600]' and 'Mrs P's for me £52-10'. He travelled to Brussels with the newly wed Herveys on 10 May and they all returned to London on 15 June for the opening of the Waterloo Bridge, various balls and Louisa's presentation as a married woman by the Duchess at the Drawing Room. On 4 July the Duke recorded: 'Paid £158-7 [£9,300] for the second half of my Picture for Mrs Patterson and of her Picture for me and the Frames'. The Duke took Marianne's portrait to France when he returned there in July and the French artist Marie-Victoire Jaquetot would paint a minature of Marianne from it for Bess in 1818. When the Duke returned to England after the Occupation ended, he always kept Marianne's picture hanging in his study at Stratfield Saye. Marianne, in turn, always kept his picture with her. The two paintings were reunited only upon her death when she bequeathed his portrait to his eldest son, the second duke, whom she had known from boyhood. In the present day, the portraits are again separated: the Duke's hangs at Apsley House and Marianne's at Stratfield Saye.[2]

The existence of these portraits at Lawrence's studio did little to divert the public from further speculation. Before the sisters had left France, the Duke had been concerned enough about the gossip flowing across the Channel to write to his niece Lady Burghersh, 'You must *for my sake* protect them against their host of enemies when they will go to England.' Anti-American prejudice and social envy were a combination powerful enough to provoke even the well-disposed. Lord Glenbervie, who met them with the Duke at the Wellesley-Poles in May, was more charitable than many when he recorded that 'the scandalous have been busy in imputing more than flirtation to him with Mrs Paterson' as the Duke's reputation resulted in his attentions to Marianne being taken 'as proof of an absolute intrigue' with her. Yet Glenbervie's description of Bess and Robert was hardly good-natured. Bess was 'very transatlantic indeed' [*not* meant as a compliment] while 'her brother' Robert 'still beyond her in that national characteristic, and also more of a clown and a lout than the most remote village or farmhouse in this country could supply'.

Whether in Brussels, Paris or further afield, everyone assumed Marianne and the Duke were enjoying a delicious, scandalous love affair. In Brussels, where Mrs Calvert attended a rout at the Duke of Richmond's on 24 May, she saw Louisa with the Duke and Felton and thought her 'a genteel looking young woman. It is the fashion to make a fuss about her because the Duke of Wellington is in love with Mrs Patterson.' It was from America and from Americans abroad, however, that the gossip was most damaging and the reports of it caused Marianne great distress.[3]

The chief culprit was Betsy, who hated Bess and apparently had previously abused her 'in the blackest and most infamous manner' at a public dinner in New York. Other members of the Patterson circle warned her against denigrating Bess in Europe. 'I hope you will not recommence hostilities with the belle – She certainly never can be considered a rival of yours', advised Edward Patterson, and Eliza Godefroy told her 'you cannot but injure yourself' in showing 'your unmerited dislike'. The Catons were at a loss to understand Betsy's motive for damaging Bess's reputation. Mary Carroll Caton, however, cautioned an indignant Bess to say nothing in the interests of Marianne's relations with the prickly Patterson family and her friendship with Betsy.

While Betsy was being fêted in Paris, she remained in contact with Marianne but once the sisters were in London, and everyone, even her brother Edward, was telling her about their amazing reception and the Duke's love for Marianne, her dormant jealousy and dislike were revived. Anxieties about money, the lack of a husband of rank and her own powerlessness to change the conditions of her life were, no doubt, compelling factors. Her envy of those more fortunate but, in her opinion, less worthy than herself, was vindictive. As someone said of her, 'She charms by her eyes and slays with her tongue'. Now, the chief recipient of her deadly remarks was no longer Bess but Marianne.[4]

The sisters' reception in Paris and their kindness to her did nothing to lessen her 'immoderate hatred'. She poured invective about Marianne into the ears of her friends, writing to Lady Morgan, the novelist, about Marianne: 'You would be surprised, if you knew how great a fool she is, at the power she exercises over the Duke.' Betsy next threw in the fib that Marianne 'had, however, no success in France, where not speaking the language of the country was a considerable advantage to her, since it prevented her nonsense from being heard'. Then, she instructed Sydney Morgan: 'Do not tell what I have written to you of this affair, since I should pass for malicious and unfriendly towards my compatriot and relation.'

Lady Morgan was only too happy to contribute her own views about the Mighty Bey and his Sultana, as she called the Duke and Marianne. Writing on 26 May 1817 from Dublin, she could not forebear to comment to Betsy:

> all you tell me of the *reigning Sultana* of *Mighty Bey* is *precisely* what I expected to hear – *vanity & folly* could not fail to *dove-tail* well, with *ostentation* & *ignorance* – he is a sad Let-out but of *such stuff* are *Hero's* made – *en attendant* what says the Husband! The whole is a monstrous *Esclandre* – for the English papers hear every time the *Missi* drops the handkerchieff – & *kiss & tell* is no longer a scandal in either parties.

The 'kiss & tell' referred to a wild accusation Betsy had made that Marianne wrote all the paragraphs appearing in the press and 'might revenge herself by saying some spiteful things of me through that channel'. In his memoirs, Lord William Lennox defends the Duke against the hostile gossip of these two 'fair adventuresses'. When the Duke, 'who did not particularly admire either of them', paid attention to Marianne, 'straightaway Madame Patterson-Bonaparte and Lady Morgan did their best to ridicule the sensible Duke and the favoured lady'.[5]

Marianne was understandably distressed. She knew that the ensuing accounts would upset her family. In response to a letter from uncle Harper about the gossip circulating in Maryland, Marianne revealed that she was under no illusions about her position in the public eye. She had to act with a degree of care and prudence, she wrote to him on 26 August 1817, 'knowing as a stranger more was required of me, and particularly as my own countrymen, and women, were disposed to be much provoked *at their merits* being overlooked, and *mine more than* appreciated; I have frequently sacrificed both pleasure and vanity (in not doing what every body else did) to prudence'.

She believed the gossip resulted from 'the inconceivable degree of envy and malice' the Duke's attentions excited, as 'all the fine ladies are ravenous for the least civility and outrageous against those who receive it'. In contrast, the attentions she had received from the Prince Regent were less dangerous because they produced less envy; though she observed that not having as much refinement and respect for women as the Duke, the Prince Regent required to be kept much more in order (clearly, not safe in carriages). Seeking to allay family concerns about her close friendship with the Duke, Marianne assured uncle Harper that 'The Duke has a most sincere regard for us all and is quite a Father to Louisa. I have felt all you say; and attentions from him must be attributed to an improper motive *most unjustly.*'

Although Marianne then claimed that the Duke 'never had any particular admiration for me; at least he never thought of me but with the same respect' as her uncle did, this was not an opinion with which either the Duke or his friends could honestly concur. Neither Marianne nor the Duke left behind their long intimate correspondence; bundles of empty envelopes and references to letters received and sent are all that testify to its existence, with the exception of several private letters which provide a glimpse of their feelings. It is not a fabrication to claim that the Duke was, indeed, madly in love with Marianne and that, while observing the proprieties, she was becoming attached to him.[6]

They were both married but, whereas Marianne was patient and gentle with her 'boorish' husband according to Lady Holland, Wellington was impatient and uncivil to his foolish wife according to Mrs Arbuthnot. Arthur Wellington was unhappily married and, in general, lived apart from his duchess. As penniless Captain Arthur Wesley (the family name reverted to Wellesley in 1797), he had proposed to Catherine Pakenham, the pretty and popular daughter of Lord Longford, and been rejected by her family;

as General Sir Arthur Wellesley, he had returned to marry Lady Catherine (Kitty) Pakenham unseen for twelve years. When he did see her in the Dublin church, he could only whisper in shock to his brother Gerald Wellesley: 'She has grown ugly, by Jove!' Maria Edgeworth, a friend of Kitty Pakenham's, was in raptures over the romance of such a marriage but most people who heard the tale thought Wellington a fool, as he later admitted he had been. 'Would you have believed that anybody could have been such a *d—d fool?*' he exclaimed to Mrs Arbuthnot in 1822. 'I was not in the least in love with her. I married her because they asked me to do it & I did not know myself.' He soon knew it was a mistake, that she could not support him in society and provide the companionship for which he yearned; as he confessed, 'at his home he had no creature to speak to, that discussing political or important subjects with the Duchess was like talking *Hebrew* to her'.[7]

The Duke yearned for a true consort, someone like Marianne who was everything his duchess was not: beautiful, well educated and well dressed, informed about current topics, possessed of charm and humour, an experienced hostess who moved effortlessly in society. It is no wonder that when he came to know Marianne, he loved her passionately.

They were unable to pass much time together after he returned from France with Louisa and Felton for the opening of Waterloo Bridge on 18 June. Fremantle was not pleased that the Duke's presence in London until the end of the month entailed the presence of Felton and Louisa at Great Stanhope Street. 'This makes a terrible worry & bustle *chez nous*, & rather annoys me & puts me out of my way, however it will not last long', he decided. 'I can't say I like my *belle fille mais c'est entre nous*,' he admitted to his brother Admiral Fremantle. Having recovered, Selina Fremantle was now able to become better acquainted with Louisa during their ten-day stay in London. On 25 June Louisa and Felton drove off for Englefield Green and then to Cheltenham where they remained until 16 July.[8]

The Duke was then engaged in the nation's purchase of a country estate for him. Lord Rivers had offered to sell Stratfield Saye House in Hampshire and Benjamin Wyatt, the Duke's architect, believed the estate 'capable of being made a princely place'. The house, nevertheless, remained largely untouched, the Duchess moving into a small bedroom and sitting room in the north-east corner of the top floor while the Duke took the south-west corner of the ground floor. By the middle of July, however, he was back in Paris but not before having set *en train* a baronetcy for Felton and a settlement for Louisa.

'Finding that your mother & sister were desirous that you should be made a Baronet, to which you have a Claim from your Grandfather,' the Duke explained to Felton on 5 July, 'I took the opportunity of mentioning the subject to Lord Liverpool.' Although Felton was 'not sufficiently anxious about it' to proceed if it caused difficulties, Liverpool was 'very happy' to give him one. After Louisa heard from the Duke that, in the event of another war, Felton would be awarded 'something higher', she confessed she wished Felton 'very much to leave the army, for he says if he should be so unfortunate as to lose his other arm – he should beg someone to shoot him'. The Duke would not hear of Felton's leaving the army, promising him even higher command in the event of another war, as was then expected.

The Duke suggested that the baronetcy afforded an ideal opportunity to finalise the settlements. Louisa knew very well that her father had not the £14,000 [£819,000] to settle on her. She had arranged to use a share of her Carrollton Manor estate which, with her existing annuity of £800 [£40,000], would bring £2,200 [£129,000] a year to the marriage, aside from other investments. Although not a princely sum, it would keep a moderate gentleman's establishment with carriage, liveries and servants in London. When Felton's income and capital were taken into account, though, it would do very well and allow Louisa to maintain a financial independence.

She became anxious only when difficulties arose between Felton's trustees and her grandfather over her jointure. A deed upon Carrollton would allow her to settle her share upon her children, whereupon Hervey 'could, and would settle upon me 3,000 Pounds [£175,000] a year in case I survived him'. Without such provision, in the event of Felton's death she was told she could be left destitute. 'It would really break my heart to see all the fortune, and all the beautiful diamonds, go to the nephew [if she had no children], while I was left starving.' The Duke stepped in. 'I believe you & I are pretty nearly of the same opinion upon this subject', he wrote to Felton. 'A Man cannot allow his wife to starve if any accident should happen to him, even though his friends should not be as liberal, and have as much confidence in him as he deserves.' Felton asked his mother to join him in providing for Louisa, which in due course she did.[9]

In all these arrangements Louisa looked to the Duke for advice as much as Felton did. And the Duke was delighted to oblige them. They now both belonged to his 'family' and he enjoyed their companionship and newly wed happiness. The nature of his affection for Louisa is clear from his letters. He addressed the daughters of his family and closest friends by their Christian names, and he did the same with Louisa. In spite of his busy life, full of reviews and official business, he took endless trouble over her small commissions; acting as courier for a pair of shoes or ascertaining that her new comb was ready. He gave her presents, Francisco Goya's portrait of him (now in the National Gallery) and a valuable gold medal he received for the battle

Marianne, a miniature enamelled by
Victoire Jaquotot, 1818. The Duke always
kept a miniature of her with him.

Arthur Duke of Wellington by Francisco
Goya c.1808–14. The Duke gave this
portrait as a present to Louisa.

of Vittoria which, she gleefully reported, he ought not to have done. 'My
Sisters say he spoils me, indeed if I was his own Child he could not appear
more fond of me', she told uncle Harper. When Mary Bagot confided in the
Duke that she and Bagot wished to leave America so bored and homesick
were they, he advised against it and joked: 'Besides how can you complain
when you have such elegant amusements as a *barbecue*?' He had read her
account of attending a barbecue to Louisa, who was much entertained by it.
'But,' he told Mary Bagot, Louisa 'swears she was never present at such an

amusement, but she knows what apple toddy is, and whiskey sling and a shote [a little pig]. She is very entertaining and we all like her excessively.'¹⁰

He left England in July with a heavy heart. He knew that Louisa was joining him in France but that it was unlikely he would ever see Marianne again. He had given Felton permission to stay behind with Louisa until the Pattersons and Bess left for Liverpool in early September. After taking the waters at Cheltenham, the Herveys joined the Patterson party at Holkham on 28 July. 'I am full of hope that Bess will marry either the uncle or nephew, any thing to keep her here', Louisa joked to uncle Harper in August. Coke, in fact, was trying to promote a match between Bess and his nephew and heir, young William Coke of Derbyshire, and thereby delay the departure of the Pattersons. On 12 August, Louisa and Felton left to join the Duke in France. 'You know by this time Mr P's determination to remain the Winter at Holkham where he is most happy,' Marianne explained in a letter home on 26 August, 'and indeed Mr Coke will not mention the subject or hear of our returning this Winter – In order to make it too late to think of it this Autumn he has proposed a tour of the Highlands to shoot Grouse, and we set off in the morning, and shall be a very pleasant party.' Although Louisa reported that 'every one will have it that Bess is certainly to marry Mr Coke', the match suited neither party and came to naught.¹¹

Marianne and Bess were dejected during the remainder of their stay in England. On their return to Holkham, they were plunged into the gloom of mourning. Princess Charlotte was delivered of a stillborn son on 5 November and died early the following morning. The *Observer* reported, on 9 November, 'numbers of females have been troubled with hysterics and other fits' since her death. Every woman about to undergo childbirth, always a life-threatening business, now felt the hand of fate hovering. Soon afterwards, Lady Albemarle was taken ill, miscarried and died seventeen hours later at Holkham. 'This is a most melancholy day in this Country, poor Princess Charlotte is tonight consigned to her tomb with all the state and pomp of Royalty', wrote Marianne on 19 November. 'Today is also the one on which poor Ly Albemarle was seen for the last time by her disconsolate husband, and the coffin closed for ever. You may well imagine the deepest gloom pervades every thing, and every body in this spacious Mansion.'¹²

When Louisa became unwell in Paris, Hervey insisted upon bringing her back in December to London where the sisters were reunited. Mary Carroll Caton suspected Louisa was in the family way 'by her husband's wishing her to be stationary, & in a former letter, she speaks of having given up hunting', a sacrifice Louisa would only make if pregnant. Her 'delicate health' reinforced the family's wish for Bess to remain with her when the Pattersons returned to America; it would be comforting to have a member of her own family with her in childbirth. Bess, though, wanted to go home.

Throughout that autumn and winter Bess's travel and marital plans fluctuated. 'B. Caton will find all her Beaux married upon her return', declared Ann Spear, as she announced the recent marriages of four of them. The only one that mattered was John Howard and he was still waiting for her return. Now, however, Bess had an English beau. In the course of their lengthy Holkham visit Squire Coke, who had first lost his heart to Marianne, found himself becoming increasingly attached to Bess, who was taken by his attentions. Her sisters and, indeed, Robert, thought she would become the next chatelaine of Holkham. She had once declared that nothing would induce her to forsake her parents and friends in Maryland – but that was said before Louisa's marriage and before she had become so well acquainted with Thomas Coke. Louisa told aunt Harper that Coke's daughters, especially Lady Anson, were never kind to her sister 'because they were afraid of her' becoming their stepmother. It is not clear exactly when Coke proposed, probably some-time in December or January. Bess, plunged into emotional turmoil, pleaded for time to consider. Should she stay with Louisa or go home, should she marry Coke or not?

Eventually, Louisa's illness in London (she had probably miscarried) decided Bess to stay with her for a year. She knew it would be impossible to go home if she married Coke, whose life was rooted in Holkham. And she did not know if she loved him enough to sacrifice returning to Maryland and John Howard. And so, Louisa reported to their mother, Bess rejected Mr Coke. On 4 February 1818, after a sad leave-taking from Marianne, Bess crossed to Calais with Louisa and Felton. Once in Paris, where they joined the Duke, Bess intimated she was not so sure about her decision after all.[13]

The Duke had only been able to see Marianne briefly after Christmas but he remained in regular correspondence with her throughout these months. Marianne's health now deteriorated, probably reflecting her emotional state. She might never see her sisters and the Duke again. On 6 February she left for Cheltenham on Dr Scott's insistence. 'I have been enjoying the society of Mrs Patterson', Charles Percy told Ralph Sneyd. 'I regret to say how very unwell she looks', but Percy would not be seeing her again as she was leaving England for America at the beginning of April. Bess had assured uncle Harper the previous year that Marianne's 'head & heart [are] both safe – notwithstanding the attention she excites'. But were they still? The same was not admitted by those who knew the Duke. Lady William Russell, whose husband was on the headquarters staff at Cambrai, regularly saw the Duke and the Herveys. She reported that the Duke looked 'horribly ill, *si dice* that it is not the present *combinazione* but love; that he declares he never knew the meaning of the word until he saw Mrs Paterson, & her departure for America *déchire son tendre coeur* in a terrible manner. He really looks mighty sick.'[14]

Emily's Return

While her sisters were in Europe, Emily had been trying to settle into married life in Montreal. Newly married Louisa would never have recognised herself as 'unsophisticated' but Emily aged twenty-one increasingly felt she was. Her first experience of the long Montreal winter had done little to reconcile her to living there. As Adam Hodgson wrote of a visit in 1820, Montreal differed 'so widely from the airy, expanded cities of the United States, that an American feels as far from home, on his first arrival, in a Canadian city, as I did in the forests of the Mississippi'. Emily was more forthright, in the course of asking aunt Harper not to abuse Montreal too much for her sake, declaring 'entre nous it is a miserable place'.[1]

The short frozen days, the outlook from her windows on to a narrow dark street, more like an alley than a smart thoroughfare, with closed iron window-shutters, made her feel imprisoned in bleakness. Homesick and depressed, she had suffered a miscarriage in January 1817 and was 'a good deal indisposed'. All her mother could say in answer to an enquiry about her youngest daughter was that Emily was 'as happy as she can be, separated from us all, in the *coldest* climate you can conceive'.[2]

John's love and care of her made all the difference, bolstering her morale and keeping her from utter despair. As the weather became more moderate, bringing early signs of spring, she wrote to uncle Harper: 'eight hundred miles from home robs every object of its charms except my excellent husband who is devoted to me', and they were 'in all respects very happily married'. Mac 'is everything I could desire' she affirmed; Montreal and her way of life left everything to be desired. While he was with her she quite forgot this and her aching homesickness but John could not always be with her and more often than not was absent. 'As soon as he leaves me, for the counting house,' she confessed, 'I think of nothing else.'[3]

This, of course, was not quite true for she thought a good deal of moving to New York, indeed, pinned all her hopes upon that eventuality. During their courtship, John had mentioned that they might not have to live permanently in Canada as he might be needed in New York. At the time it had not seemed so important, may even have been a lover's sop to soften the pain of leaving home, but now it meant everything. So much so that she started to read the New York newspapers regularly and even broached the subject at a family dinner with William McGillivray, long since released without charge from a Montreal prison after Selkirk's attack on Fort William and arrest of the NWC partners were declared unlawful. To her delight, it transpired that the company was indeed considering such an option. Owing to the disruption caused by the fur wars, it made sense to spread their operation outside Canada and re-establish an agency in New York. John, an experienced partner with an American wife, was the obvious candidate to establish and direct the new agency.

Buoyed up by the realisation that her exile from America was finite, Emily set about trying to relieve her boredom. She was used to being kept busy at home but Montreal offered ladies no scope for participation in any form of public life. She was a practical person, though, and she decided she would educate herself. Unlike her sisters, Emily had managed to slide out of learning at an earlier age than, she now realised, was desirable. John had also, as she put it, 'observed a deficiency' and suggested various classical works for her to read. As she explained to her family, 'you know I never did like to go out' and, with less inclination than ever for society, she discovered the world of books. 'I read history three hours every day and am trying to teach myself French besides the time I devote to music and I flatter myself when you see me you will think my mind greatly improved', she informed uncle Harper. By May 1817 she was writing home that 'reading has become a favourite occupation'.

Then, one morning, she read in the New York paper that Congress was debating a bill to prevent any subject of Great Britain residing in the USA from trading with the Indians. Astor, bent upon keeping Canadians out of the American fur trade, was, apparently, the driving force behind a bill being put before the House. Emily was upset. This would prevent their living in New York, as John was a British subject. 'I have cried my eyes out since dinner,' she told uncle Harper, 'the folks are very kind to me here but it is so far from home, that I confess the idea of residing here for ever is very unpleasant.' Although John assured her he would move to Maryland if she wanted, she knew that he could not afford to give up his partnership. 'Judge then what I must feel to have all my hopes blasted by a law.'

She begged her uncle to use his influence to prevent the bill being passed. Harper might have been in a stronger position to help if he had not resigned as senator for Maryland in order to contest the 1816 election as the vice-presidential candidate on the unsuccessful Federalist ticket. 'I wish you were in the Senate,' she wrote, 'at all events use your influence my uncle for you know how much I love my home.' Harper was able to reassure her that

the bill before Congress was separate from the Astor issue. John also
confirmed that the Navigation Act had nothing to do with the NWC. 'You
know I am very awkward on this subject', she wrote, excusing herself by
saying she had no one to apply to 'for Mac always answers me by telling
me I know nothing of business'. The episode was not one calculated to
increase her self-confidence, at a time when she was trying to broaden her
mind. As it transpired her concern about American trade laws, however
muddled, would be justified.⁴

More imminent, though, was the terrifying prospect of McTavish
departing for Fort William, to deal with the aftermath of Lord Selkirk's
illegal occupation. 'I have some hope that Mac will not be sent', she wrote
home. 'I cannot bear the idea of his going amongst savages, and to contend
with an outlaw that will go all lengths.' Selkirk was at the Red River Colony,
striding out on the prairies among his people 'like a kilted messiah' while
the NWC, supported by the government, had issued murder charges against
him. 'The Selkirk party look very downcast here, Lady Selkirk quite ill',
Emily informed uncle Harper on 22 May 1817. 'I would pity her from my
soul if she had not acted with such a want of delicacy.' Lady Selkirk was
trying to lobby people who might be chosen as jurists in her husband's
forthcoming trial. 'Only think of a Lady of her Rank . . . drinking tea with
the grocer's family', Emily exclaimed in a letter home, and 'she in her turn
condescending to tell them the most ridiculous falsehoods which these
ignorant people religiously believe'.⁵

By July Emily knew she was pregnant again and, determined to do everything to keep the baby, she arranged with Mac to go home in September.
This change in her life compensated for the end of her hopes about New
York. 'I am afraid that is now out of the question; and I am trying to resign
myself to the work of Providence', she had written wistfully to her eighty-
year-old grandfather. She was thrilled at the thought of seeing him again.

> Oh my dear Grandpapa how often how fervently do I pray for you, you
> have all your life been such a kind tender parent to me, my happiest
> years have been spent under your roof. When I think of them I almost
> regret I ever left you dear Grandpapa but heaven has blest me with such
> a kind tender Husband I should be ungrateful if I was not happy.

She was happier still when she was once more in Maryland. 'Emily is now
with us, as good humoured amiable and cheerful as ever, altered in nothing
but her shape', wrote uncle Harper on 14 November. The whole family was
excited at the prospect of the birth of her child; it would be Carroll of
Carrollton's first great-grandchild and Mary Carroll Caton's first long-desired
grandchild, which, Marianne said, meant it would have a good chance of
being spoilt, given the way their mother doted upon the young Harpers.

Just before Marianne and Robert left England they received letters from home with the news that Emily had given birth to a son on 18 January 1818. And, Emily affirmed, it was impossible that he should be named anything other than Charles Carroll McTavish, in honour of their beloved grandfather. As Emily was due back in Montreal at the beginning of June, her grandfather declined paying visits elsewhere saying, 'I wish to be as much as possible with Mrs McTavish while she remains in Maryland. I may never see her again when she leaves it.' Emily's Canadian sojourn had convinced her that she could never live happily there. Anywhere outside America was a foreign country, she was now satisfied, it was best never to know. Of the sisters, Emily was the one whose life would remain firmly rooted at home in Maryland.[6]

20

Unfulfilled Hopes

In Maryland Marianne was reunited with her family: her grandfather aged eighty; her father busy with a new mining venture; her mother delighting in a first grandson. Emily was still on an extended visit from Montreal, and her uncle Carroll was enjoying a period of stable health. Absent from the circle were John McTavish, who was visiting relations in Scotland before attending to NWC business in London; her aunt Carroll, still living in Philadelphia; and her uncle and aunt Harper. She was 'surprised and *gratified*' to find the Harpers had just gone to Europe, after young Mary's sad death in Poitiers, but she considered it the best means of diverting their minds and restoring aunt Harper's health, 'after such a soul harrowing event'.[1]

Marianne's year abroad had turned into two years so that she had a great deal of news to exchange. The era of 'good feeling' pervading the country when she left, reflecting a greater political harmony and financial optimism, had continued after President Monroe's inauguration in 1817. Her mother and Emily were full of the Monroes' stately and far more formal style of entertaining. Marianne, however, hoped to be quiet again after being the cynosure of all in London and Paris. Her mother thought her 'very thin & languid' though in better health and Robert 'much improved' in manners and conversation from his European tour. Marianne's reunion with Robert's family was, however, anything but tranquil. 'I fear great vexations are preparing for her from the Patterson family', Bess wrote about her sister's return home.

It was customary to welcome back family members on their arrival but William Patterson did not do so. 'Wd you believe,' asked Mary Carroll Caton on 16 August, 'that old Mr P. is quite cold to Robert, & to M[arianne] totally neglectful. She has seen him but for a few minutes since her return.' And when he did call upon her, his manner was icy, and did not thaw with the summer heat. The reason lay in Betsy's scandalous tales about Marianne and her admirers. When taxed by Robert about Betsy's stories, his father retorted that in Europe 'people did not pay such attentions without a motive', and Betsy was only repeating what was generally believed everywhere.[2]

It did not help Marianne that James Creighton, her cousin William Woodville's partner based in Liverpool, was upset at Louisa's refusal to give him an introduction to Wellington and was also fuelling Betsy's stories. As Mary Carroll Caton explained to Harper,

> 'Louisa has *repeatedly* requested us not to give letters to her, situated as she *is* at present. She cannot introduce any one to the Duke of W, his time is so much occupied, & he has necessarily so many people to receive, that she *knows* it is disagreeable to him – & as he is so kind, she does not like to encroach upon his goodness – therefore she means only to introduce to him, her own connections.'

And Creighton was no relation.

He took his revenge by telling Robert that Louisa 'had called him *brute* & c' in her letters; she had certainly chafed against Robert's diktats about their travelling plans but not to that extent, her mother said. Creighton also announced that Robert 'knew nothing that was *going on*' with the Duke and Marianne whereas he knew all about it. Her mother easily dismissed Creighton: 'I fear he has a low mind', she warned her sister, '& is very mischievous & vindictive withal, I *very* much suspect that he has *written* & said many things which he ought not.'

The Pattersons, though, took his words as confirmation of Betsy's remarks about Marianne's improper behaviour with the Duke, and continued to cold-shoulder her. Robert was so incensed that he refused to speak to Betsy and, as Mary Carroll Caton reported, '*all* this has soured Robert exceedingly'. Marianne was hurt, and distressed that her reputation was being torn to pieces. Furthermore, far from being able to sink back into anonymity, she had become a symbol of social success. She was inundated with calls and requests for introductions after girls plagued their parents to send them to Europe where they, too, could dazzle all the grand people who loved American women.[3]

She caught cold and developed a fever due, she said, to bathing at the Manor without wearing an oilskin cap, and the time it took to dry her long thick hair in the sun. She was under a great deal of emotional strain, though, and her asthma returned more severely than ever. She had to leave the Manor in early July to seek a respite at the Glades in the cooler Alleghenies. They were not cool enough, and after two weeks of violent attacks, Robert and her father decided to move her to higher mountains. It was a long jolting journey when they were frequently obliged to stop for several days as she wanted the strength to go on. Eventually, they reached the cold mountain air of Bedford Springs in Pennsylvania. Asthma continued to torment her every night so that, without sleep by day or night, she grew still weaker. 'How can she bear such continuous suffering?' Bess wailed from France. 'It makes me very unhappy.'[4]

After two months, their grandfather could report that Marianne was beginning to respond to the waters and cool air. By October, she was able to add a postscript in weak handwriting to a letter to uncle Harper and confirm she was much better. 'I hope it is so, but I fear that she deludes Herself, or what is more probable that she wishes to spare us pain as much as she can', Harper replied to her father. 'What a pity so charming a woman, so good and amiable in every respect, should be so afflicted. Give our tenderest love to her.' Everywhere they travelled abroad they found Marianne was remembered; everywhere they heard her praises.

The Duke added his own paean. He wrote long journal letters to her, conveyed – as were those from her sisters – in the diplomatic bag to Charles Bagot. The Duke also kept Marianne abreast of British current affairs by sending out the latest newspapers as well as books, such as the last work of Mme de Staël, which Carroll of Carrollton eagerly started reading. Marianne had brought home with her a small golden spaniel given to her by the Duke. 'Honey' became her constant companion. And, on her return from Bedford Springs in late October, the young Harper children were in and out of her bedchamber where little Bob Harper hugged 'sweet Honey' and romped with her on the sofa. They were soon joined by Emily and little Carroll: 'they have afforded me great happiness and amusement, as I am unable to leave the House, and frequently my room. I do not know what I should have done without her – She has a lovely Baby and [he] is as strong and intelligent as a child of a year old', the doting aunt wrote from Annapolis on 22 December 1818 to the Harpers.[5]

Letters, such as this one, were written with little thought of literary style, often in great haste to catch the ship, and as if carrying on a conversation. Their mother would write to them when they were abroad, 'I have taken up my pen to have a little chat', and then cram in every snippet of family and local news, using up every inch of space. They were all nevertheless constrained from writing freely about confidences and love affairs by the fear their letters could fall into the wrong hands. Thus the all-important subject of Thomas Coke's courtship with Bess was left if not in epistolary limbo, then in opaque sketchiness. 'Impress upon Lady Bessy – the more I hear upon that subject the more necessary I am sure it becomes for some friend to open her eyes – for I should not like to write upon the subject for fear of accidents', her frustrated mother begged Kitty Harper shortly after Marianne had returned home with the latest news, by then already two months old. Bess, though, did not even mention Coke in her letters.[6]

During her first summer with the Herveys at Cambrai, Bess began to regret her decision not to marry Coke. Louisa described her as 'out of spirits' to which their mother remonstrated, 'What a simpleton! I now more than ever regret her *conduct*, as it would have been the means of restoring Marianne,' – for, if Bess had married Coke, then Robert 'would have staid a year or two longer in England'. Coke, however, thinking perhaps that Bess preferred his nephew after all, had turned again to a match between them. The nephew, to please an uncle from whom he had considerable expectations, wrote to Bess. 'I do not like to write of C – implore B [Bess] not to *suffer* herself to *be a second* time *grilled* – which I have no doubt the *person* will *try* to do by following her – he has *not* & never had *serious* intentions & if he had he is unworthy of her', was her mother's opinion of William Coke. And Bess, if she still thought of either Coke, thought not of William but only of the eminently worthy Thomas Coke and of the attractions of English life.[7]

'Is not England nearest to paradise than any thing in this world?' she declared to her aunt Harper, now in England. 'I love the [English] more than ever since I have contrasted them with their Gallic neighbours. There is a moral justness among them unknown in France', Bess decided. She had found the French to be often 'excellent family people & truly kind hearted but a high spirited disinterested public character, is a thing they cannot understand or admire'. Louisa thought there was no country and climate as healthy as England where the people looked so neat and clean compared to France. Bess also admired the English character above all other and Holkham had given her a taste for, and an insight into, the best of life on an English country estate. Yet if she was to lead that style of life by marrying into it, she had not taken the opportunity provided by Thomas Coke. It transpired, though, that it was not Coke's Holkham that she was contemplating but Cholmondeley's Houghton.

'I can not help telling you a foolish thought that has come into my head & which never can be realised unless we make Grand Papa twenty years younger', she confided to her aunt. 'When you go to Mr Coke's you must go & see Houghton, a magnificent seat', not because she would like to marry Lord Cholmondeley, who was already in possession of a wife, but because she wanted to live there with her grandfather. Dream it might be, but Lord Cholmondeley talked of selling Houghton, which yielded £7,000 a year and could be bought for the sale price of the Carrollton estate. Her grandfather could keep all his funds in America for security at 6 or 7 per cent, 'that is if he is worth a million sterling as I have often heard'. And, there would be more room at Houghton for all of them to live with him as he liked them to do, while the climate would suit him better as he disliked the heat. 'I can not get it out of my head – we could have our townhouses & spend all the autumn & winter with him', she continued; it would be perfect also for Marianne's health and for the Herveys in London. 'What a goose, uncle Harper would think me – yet there is nothing but the ocean to prevent it,' – and the matter not only of her grandfather's advanced age but of her uncle Carroll and his family.[8]

She had already released John Howard Jr. from their understanding, given their enforced separation; she was now vacillating over Thomas Coke. Her grandfather advised her, 'whatever may be your decision my dearest Bessy, God grant it may eventuate in your lasting happiness, & that your choice may be directed as much by reflection & prudence as by love – let not a romantic fancy influence too much this most important crisis of your life.' On this occasion, though, Bess could not concur. Romantic love was paramount and she could never marry without it.[9]

The arrival of the Harpers at Cambrai had brought a longed-for link with home, as well as London news. Louisa insisted to them that 'Nothing can exceed the dullness of Cambray'. Provincial garrison life was beginning to pall even for her: 'I am quite tired of *army concerns*', she now dismissively said. She nonetheless entered with accustomed gusto into Felton's concerns, making plans to attend military reviews, to go to Paris and to entertain the Harpers. She and Bess still had to endure the condescension of visitors, attracted to Cambrai by the Duke's presence, and to ignore the anti-American comments and jealousy of the Duke's attentions to 'the Americans'.

Thomas Creevey, the diarist and former MP, was convinced that the sisters had no right to the Duke's friendship as *parvenues* Americans. He was walking with the Duke when their conversation was interrupted by Louisa and Bess 'coming up to the Duke with a Yankee general in their hands – a relation of theirs, just arrived from America – General Harper, whom they presented to the Duke'. Creevey crossly sniffed:

> It is not amiss to see these sisters, Mrs Harvey and Miss Cator [sic], not content with passing themselves off for tip-top Yankees, but playing much greater people than Lady C Greville and Lady F Cole – to *me* too, who remember their grandfather, old Cator [sic], a captain of an Indiaman in Liverpool; their father an adventurer to America, and know their two aunts now at Liverpool – Mrs Woodville and another, who move in about the *third-rate* society of that town.

General Harper might be 'a man of sound learning and polished style', classical scholar and legal expert, who advised his students to temper Blackstone with Spenser's *Faerie Queene*, but he was an American. Dining at Sir George Murray's one night, Creevey sat next to Harper 'who quite came up to my notion of a regular Yankee. I touched him upon the late seizure of the Floridas by the United States, but he was as plausible, cunning and jesuitical as the very devil.'¹⁰

Marianne, all too aware of the slights meted out to Americans abroad, was highly gratified to learn of the Duke's kindness to the Harpers whom he entertained at Cambrai and Paris and provided with introductions. The icy weather kept nearly everyone indoors in Annapolis during Christmas week so that letters were a welcome diversion; both the Duke's, written on 10 October, and Bess's, undated, brought accounts of the recent European congress at Aix-la-Chapelle. Expectations were high that it would replicate the famous Vienna 'dancing Congress' of 1814–15 and Louisa and Bess hoped to be allowed to accompany Felton there. Harper surmised that 'knowing the D of Wellington's wish to gratify them, they will not be disappointed'. In the event, Castlereagh and Wellington represented Britain and included in the Duke's suite were the Herveys, Bess and the Harpers. The Tsar, the Emperor of Austria and the King of Prussia along with suites of lesser royalties, the *grandes dames* of European society, endless diplomats, courtiers, financiers, and those with designs upon the rich and powerful also swept into Aix. There was ample scope for dalliance – Countess Lieven began a passionate affair with Metternich, for diversion – Lady Castlereagh and Countess Nesselrode threw lavish balls, and for leisure – Lawrence painted full-length portraits of the Tsar and the Emperor for the Prince Regent.

Bess wrote home that she and Louisa had been presented to 'the illustrious Tsar Alexander and many of the great statesmen of Europe' and had met up with Benjamin Ogle Tayloe, a Maryland friend who, as secretary of the Legation, accompanied the American Minister, Richard Rush. On 15 November the Allies signed a declaration that included the evacuation of foreign troops from France by the end of the month. At the ball given by the allied sovereigns on the last night, young Tayloe was gratified to see that 'amid the extraordinary constellation of European beauty there assembled' were his 'beautiful countrywomen' Bess and Louisa who 'attracted universal admiration and received marked attention from the Emperor Alexander'. From such dizzy social heights, the return to humdrum Cambrai was made bearable by the knowledge they would shortly be departing for England.¹¹

The end of the Occupation of France saw the Herveys and Bess return with the Duke to London on 20 December. They spent Christmas and New Year at Englefield Green with the Fremantles with whom Louisa now felt more comfortable; largely, she said, because 'Hervey's family seem to be quite reconciled to their *Yankee* relation'. Louisa, as a married woman, would also be able to relieve her mother-in-law from chaperoning Felton's younger sister Eliza Hervey. On 9 January 1819 the sisters joined Felton in Town to settle taking a small house in Piccadilly for 20 guineas [£1,300] a week, a price which shocked Louisa: 'there never was any thing so enormous – I shall get out of it as quick as possible', she exclaimed.

She was in excellent spirits and enjoying her new position. Felton's baronetcy had been granted at the beginning of December so that she had become Lady Hervey, 'to her very great satisfaction' her uncle Harper noted. She took greater satisfaction, however, in Felton's promotion. 'I cannot resist writing once more to tell you that the Duke of Wellington has made Felton his Secretary with 1000 Pounds [£62,500] a year,' she announced jubilantly to aunt Harper on 20 January, 'and I believe he will also be entitled to a house adjoining the Ordnance office – this is not quite arranged but it will be in a few days.' The duke, who liked to be kept busy, had accepted the post of Master-General of the Ordnance with a seat in Lord Liverpool's Cabinet. Although the Duke was careful to stress that he remained a servant of the country rather than any political party, it was inevitable that he was understood to support the Tory government's policies.

Where the Duke went Felton loyally followed, advising and assisting the new Master-General in both military and civilian matters. There were two branches in the British army: the cavalry and infantry under the Commander-in-Chief, the Duke of York, at the Horse Guards; and the Ordnance Corps of artillery and engineers under the Master-General, the Duke of Wellington, who also controlled the civilian Ordnance Department. Felton managed confidential correspondence, patronage requests and acted as the Duke's emissary. Wellington's extraordinary position at the centre of British and European public life gave Colonel Sir Felton Hervey a role of power and influence.[12]

Louisa, accordingly, was accepted as a woman with an assured place in British society and access to power and patronage. At the beginning of 1819, she was immersed in decorating their new London house in Pall Mall. Bess could only call this protracted exercise 'the agony of furnishing' as they drove about London from morning till night hunting for requisites. Louisa rushed off on expeditions to Moor field to find servants and bedding; they drove to Marylebone to look at a round table for the drawing room but Louisa judged it far too expensive at eighty guineas [£5,250]. 'We have spent hours at auctions to buy cheap things which we found afterwards were dearer than in the shops', lamented Bess. Bustle and chivvy as Louisa might, the house was still 'in confusion' at the beginning of May. Bess described it to her aunt:

> We have just got into the lower part of the Ordnance house – the drawing rooms require alteration & painting – it's small but exceedingly

comfortable, the bedrooms particularly small – Louisa's is very good because there are large doors that throw two little rooms into one – mine is large enough for one person, a dressing room for Hervey & a very little bath fill up the sleeping floor

but it would be another two months before the decorators completed painting and papering and everything was to Louisa's satisfaction.[13]

Felton's family came to dine on 3 June before they all went on to Lady Stafford's assembly. Later that week the Wellingtons, the Wellesley-Poles, Lord Westmorland and the Fitzroy Somersets dined before attending Almack's. Louisa and Bess were still treated as Mrs Wellesley-Pole's honorary daughters and thought the world of her: 'really a kind-hearted person, added to all her attractions of manner'.

Louisa's friendship with Emily Somerset, who used to like her particularly, had not remained so close. They had been good friends in Paris where Lord Fitzroy Somerset was Secretary at the British Embassy, Louisa thought her 'very pretty' and him 'amiable and delightful'. He and Hervey were old friends; they were both members of the Duke's 'family', had fought in the Peninsular War and at Waterloo, and each had also lost an arm in his service. The Duke, to please Emily Somerset, had arranged a place for Somerset at the Ordnance. While Somerset did not mind that Felton held the senior position and would be the first to be promoted, Emily disliked being in a junior position vis-à-vis Louisa and was annoyed by Louisa's friendship with the Duke. Louisa confided to aunt Harper that Lady Fitzroy had become '*ill natured and envious*' and 'since the Duke is more attentive to me than to her, I am not in her good graces'.

The other friend with whom Louisa had to be a little careful was the Duchess of Wellington. On 17 June the Prince Regent held the first Drawing Room of the Season at which Louisa, as the wife of a new member of the peerage, had to be again presented. The Duchess, kind and protective as ever, was more than happy to present Louisa. Yet for all her goodness, the Duchess could be 'tart and quick to take offence' with those she liked, especially when they received more attention from her husband than she ever did. Louisa realised that the Duke's neglect lay at the heart of her behaviour: 'The Duchess of W is excessively envious of me – because the Duke is kind to me – but poor *little Soul* I don't wonder at it – She is very good and I like her very much.'

As she settled into her new home with her devoted husband and sister, Louisa felt she had nothing to wish for but the society of her own family, 'a loss that nothing can compensate me for', and a baby. Since her probable miscarriage in 1817 she had not become pregnant. 'Lou is well but not as she wishes to be', was how Bess put it. Their mother, in writing

Catherine (Kitty) Duchess of Wellington, the kind and long-suffering friend of all three Caton sisters.

of her grandson Carroll McTavish, who *'grows* a fine fellow & does every thing *but* speak', added: 'I wish my dear Louisa had just such another.' Louisa, too, wished for it, and more and more as the months passed without any further signs; she had 'no hopes' which made her 'absolutely unhappy'.[14]

'Plunged in Sorrow'

Louisa and Bess were made unhappy by the news from America of Marianne's deteriorating health and Robert's disinclination to bring her back to Europe at a time of economic uncertainty. Marianne had written that 'Things in Balt are in a dull way, the Bank stock speculators are terribly alarmed, and everything seems to partake of their distress'. Even their grandfather was '*really* so pushed for *Cash* (for it is a general distress) that he says he can give his children *only* 8000£ [£500,000] a year', their mother had informed the Harpers. The speculative fever, financed by eruptions of dubious paper money that had fuelled the boom, had run its course and by 1819 the country faced economic paralysis. Prices collapsed, commerce dwindled, counterfeit bills circulated and depression engulfed Americans.

Baltimore suffered greatly after a congressional committee investigating the Bank of the United States unearthed evidence concerning the Baltimore branch, which was directed by Messrs Buchanan, McCullough and Williams. 'But the worst of it is', Mary Carroll Caton wrote, 'that they have by their *dishonesty* defrauded the US Bank of a million and a half of dollars certain!!!' – and maybe '3 *millions* & that the Bank will not make a dividend for two years', which would lessen her family's income from its large holding of bank stock.

Mary was in the centre of Baltimore a few days later when news emerged of the failure of the City Bank, where the cashier and some directors had also helped themselves to funds. 'You can have no idea of the confusion & distress,' she told her sister on 3 May 1819, 'they wanted to excite a mob – placards were stuck up at the Market House inviting the *people* to *hang* the President & directors before their own Banks, whenever they refused to pay *specie*, & to help themselves!' Emily was the only one of the family to lose money from the City failure: 'Poor Emily had six hundred dollars of stock of which she will certainly lose two – perhaps the whole.' Then a 'dreadful run was made upon the Mechanics Bank, & all the others'. Law-abiding citizens were in despair: 'what with the privateering, the slave trade – piracy – and the *dishonesty* of the leading and principal men of the Town, poor Balt^e is *degraded* to the lowest ebb', she declared. The crash lowered the return on investments so that Carroll of Carrollton 'must *reduce* & will *reduce* us – Heaven knows what we shall do,' she wailed, 'Papa is confounded by the *magnitude* of these *crimes* & is very uneasy'.[1]

All too soon, as John Quincy Adams noted in his diary, 'The House of Smith and Buchanan, which has been these thirty years one of the greatest commercial establishments in the United States broke last week with a crash which staggered the whole city of Baltimore and will extend no one knows how far.' As a senior politician, General Samuel Smith had long since left the operation of the firm to his partner Buchanan, who had speculated in the firm's name but ring-fenced his own assets; not so Robert's uncle, the innocent Smith, who lost everything. 'I never saw anyone so broken down in my life', his daughter-in-law wrote. 'The dread of disgrace, the stings of ingratitude, the loss of fortune altogether is too much for his sensibility and pride.' For many years he could not even travel to England to see his daughter Mary Mansfield in case one of his creditors might have him arrested upon the expectation that John Mansfield would pay the debt.

The shock of his uncle's reversal did little to encourage Robert to undertake extra expense. He had said that he would take Marianne to Florence but only if her father paid him £3,000–£4,000 [£187,000–£250,000] a year to do so. Caton, of course, had no such sum to hand: 'you know the utter *impossibility* of giving that sum without leaving ourselves greatly embarrassed', Mary Carroll Caton admitted and she knew that Marianne did not want to leave America, '& nothing but dire necessity will compel her'.[2]

By the spring of 1819, however, Marianne felt so ill that she would agree to anything to find relief. 'I suppose you know the plan Mr Patterson has fallen upon to get into possession of the property which my Grandfather has given her a deed for,' Louisa wrote in May to uncle Harper, 'he promises to come to Europe for 18 months provided she gives it up in fee simple to him.' Marianne could not sign over more of her Carrollton estate without her sisters' consent and agreement to relinquish all claims to it. Louisa had no objection to Marianne raising money on the security of the land. She did have objections though, and strong ones, to Robert's proposed ownership. If he owned the land he could sell it or give it to one of his brothers, for instance, and Marianne would be powerless to do anything about it. Louisa thought her 'very wrong to put herself so completely in the power of Mr Patterson'. She also objected to Robert's gaining control when she was prevented from using her own share of the estate as she wished.

The Baltimore crash put paid to these plans,. Her mother continued to hope that 'dear Angelic' Marianne's terms about Carrollton were 'so *advantageous* that Mr P may raise money by the spring to take her abroad'. Mr P, however, complained that even so, he could not afford it owing to his bank losses. Louisa's tart response was that he could come very easily if he really wished it as 'he has lost *nothing*, and the only difference the bank makes to him is to diminish his dividends for July – the 3 pr cents'. She would not sign anything for him until she heard from Marianne.

Her eldest sister, ill and in pain, was not able to write anything for some months. She was moved to Bedford Springs but her condition did not noticeably improve. The family was becoming resigned to the inevitable, drastic conclusion, first voiced by her grandfather in mid-July.

> I fear if the air of the mountains & Bedford waters do not strengthen her constitution she must live in Europe. I have no expectation that a residence of 18 months or 2 years in Europe will so improve her health as to enable her to live in this country with any comfort to herself and family: nothing can be more painful than to see a person so dear to us all, sinking gradually under a most distressing disease.[3]

To her concerns about Marianne, Louisa added solicitude about Hervey's health. 'We have been out no where since you left Town,' she told aunt Harper, 'I do not like to leave Hervey alone, he continues to be at times very unwell.' Several severe attacks of gout had left him 'pulled down' after a busy six months at the Ordnance. The prorogation of Parliament on 17 July allowed them to go to Hampshire where Louisa felt certain that the beauty and tranquillity of Lainston and a few months of country pursuits would restore him. After the busyness of moving into the Pall Mall house and a London season she looked forward to settling into their country house, taking long rides around the estate, paying visits in the neighbourhood and becoming acquainted with the tenant and estate families.

Lainston House, which exists today as a fifty-five-room country-house hotel, was in Louisa's time considered a fine rose-brick manor house set in parkland, its terraces falling away to a circular pool at the head of a mile-long avenue of quadruple lime trees. In its twelfth-century church the secret wedding of Elizabeth Chudleigh and Augustus Hervey in 1744 had led to one of the most celebrated bigamy trials when Mrs Hervey also married the Duke of Kingston. After those months of unfamiliar notoriety ancient Lainston slid thankfully back into the slow regular rhythm of a pastoral existence, one sustained for centuries throughout the feudal villages of the south of England. Everywhere the sturdy trees and clear rivers, the woods and fertile fields added to the impression, as Irving wrote, of 'a calm and settled security' and 'an hereditary transmission of unchanging virtues and attachments'.[4]

The glorious appearance of the English countryside, so frequently remarked upon by Bess and fellow Americans, belied the extent to which it was also a troubled place. The country folk around them scrabbled to earn a livelihood at a time when the prosperity that British farmers enjoyed during the Napoleonic Wars had evaporated. Corn Laws passed to protect British farmers from the foreign importation of corn, had not ensured stable prices and markets. Whereas the government and landowners viewed them as a short-term duty, radicals saw them as a tax on the food of the poor and demanded reform. The 'bust-and-boom' years of 1816–18 had witnessed corn riots, collier strikes and protest marches accompanied by shouts of 'Bread, or Blood!'

Across the land in 1819, dozing after the harvest in the August sunshine, fell the shadows of further unrest as numerous field meetings urged reforms. On 16 August, around 80,000 men, women and children converged for a monster reform meeting on St Peter's Field, Manchester. They were *en fête* rather than *en révolution* but the chairman of the magistrates panicked and ordered: 'Disperse the meeting!' A bugle sounded the charge of the 15th Hussars into the crowd and 'Swords were up and swords were down', wrote an impartial eye-witness, as terrified people stampeded to escape, leaving eleven dead and nearly 500 wounded bodies at 'Peterloo'.

As public indignation mounted, the Duke set to work on plans to contain future confrontation. The government was convinced that the next monster meeting of the 'agitators', as the Duke called them, would result in revolt unless regulated by military force. Hervey hurriedly left Lainston on 20 August for Stratfield Saye where, a few days later, Louisa and Bess joined him. While this crisis did not convert the sisters to Tory policies, it did place them at the heart of British political life. Messengers came and went with correspondence between the Duke and senior cabinet ministers. And the sisters were able to participate in serious political conversations with the Duke and Hervey. It was the nearest they had come in Britain to the 'petticoat politicking' of women's lives in Washington City. In London, they had been barred from being able to hear the political debates as women had been banned from the House of Commons gallery since 1778. Bess had been maddened during the previous session by not being able to attend the debates on Catholic emancipation and even more so by the outcome: 'The Catholic question was lost last night. I feel in a great rage about it', she had fumed to aunt Harper on 4 May. She had not yet managed to find an acquiescent MP to smuggle her into the House – through passages and over the chapel roof into a tiny room containing the ventilator shaft through which she could peer and hear the Commons debate below.[5]

In early September further meetings held in London and the trials of arrested reform leaders added to public disquiet. At a time when he had a large amount of business to transact, Felton became unwell again. On 17 September city authorities 'with a vast display of civic pomp', according to Lord Buckingham, went in procession to Carlton House to present an address requesting an enquiry into the outrages to the Prince Regent and the government. Hervey could not be there. His mother, arriving that day at Stratfield Saye, found him 'very ill'.[6]

They took Felton back to Englefield Green. Dr Pope, the family doctor, applied leeches and diagnosed 'a violent inflammation on the Wind Pipe' which could only be 'subdued by great bleeding & blistering & lowering of the system'. So successful was the lowering that Felton grew weaker by the day. The family took specialist advice but none of the reports was cheering and Dr Pope remained in attendance, even sleeping in the house. Then, on 24 September, doctors 'Baillie came twice & Pope & Furnival were constantly here,' Felton's mother wrote, 'but at Eight o'Clock it pleased the almighty to release my Dearest son from his sufferings'. Felton died cradled in Louisa's arms.

At first she could not believe he was dead. She held him in her arms and 'she began to sing him to sleep, as she said, and sang three hours incessantly'. Bess told her sisters that Louisa was stopped only by strong opiates. The shock almost killed her; indeed, at times throughout the succeeding months, she wished it had. She was 'out of her senses', collapsing into paroxysms of grief, and such was the alarming state of her convulsions that she could only be subdued with large doses of laudanum. The effect was to keep her 'in a kind of Torpid state all day & night' but, as soon as the dose wore off, a distressed Selina Fremantle observed, Louisa suffered such an attack that Dr Pope and Dr Furnival saw her and sent for a priest. Louisa habitually entered into all her feelings with exuberance. The priest, who came on 26 September from Weybridge, was more successful in containing her excessive display of deeply felt grief, and in helping her to withstand the agony of her beloved husband's death.[7]

'I cannot describe to you the scene of distress & misery,' wrote Fremantle, 'his Wife who was very fond of him is distraut, and the blow to my wife I am afraid will never be recovered, he was her favourite son, and her whole mind & soul was wrapped up in him.' Two days after his death the coffin was closed and his mother went to Egham Church to give directions to prepare the Hervey family vault. The outer coffin was brought on 29 September and Louisa had Mass performed by the Eton priest then and on successive days. Saturday 2 October was, Selina Fremantle recorded, 'a dreadful day. my Beloved son was enterr'd in ye Vault at Egham at two o'clock The Duke of Wellington, Ld Fitzroy Somerset, Sir Andrew Barnard, Sir Colin Campbell &c attended as did the principal tradesmen of Egham all the shops there shut', as a mark of respect.

Louisa remained secluded for two months in her bedchamber at Englefield Green. She lived only with Bess and the rest of the Fremantle-Hervey family could almost have been absent from the house. At the beginning of December Bess wrote that 'Louisa was still plunged in sorrow and never left her room – not even to take a little exercise'. Bess believed that Felton's use of quack medicine to treat gout had caused his death; she grieved for the brother-in-law she had come to love. 'You will find him the best of men & husbands,' she had advised the Harpers before their first meeting in 1818, 'though he has not the softest manner, his disposition is as tender as a woman's.'[8]

The sisters were now marooned in a family without the usual deep-seated ties of affection and sympathy. 'Alas for Poor Hervey's death. How wretched a lot awaits the poor widow desolate & disliked by his family', their friend Charles Percy had commiserated. It was a situation made more wretched by the lack of letters from home. Bess learnt that her letter breaking the news of Felton's death had reached America before 8 November. 'I think they would have written immediately if everybody was well', especially as she knew how shocked they would be. Comforting letters from home had, unfortunately, miscarried; the sisters were desolate.

While Louisa could turn to her religious faith and memories of Felton and their married life, she could not turn to their children for consolation. Her childlessness became more poignant in widowhood. William Fremantle, though, thought 'it is fortunate there were no Children' so that Felton's next brother inherited his estate and title. Louisa had lost a great deal: Felton, and any hope of having his children; Lainston; the Pall Mall house; her life and social position in London; and her place in the unofficial sphere of patronage and influence. She was left with only broken hopes and memories of a short era of happiness. Felton's prestigious office was filled by Lord Fitzroy Somerset and Emily Somerset now held all the advantages and hopes of Louisa's former position. It is no wonder that she told Bess that she thought her life had completely disintegrated and that she was 'dead to the world'.[9]

Into this abyss of grief rode the Duke. He told them the Duchess expected them at Stratfield Saye where they should proceed immediately to live for as long as it suited them. 'The duke is as kind to me as possible', Bess wrote from Stratfield Saye on 8 January 1820. She was relieved that Louisa's spirits were a little improved but, apart from going to church, her sister still refused to leave her room. Bess tried in vain to persuade her to see friends but Louisa seemed to think it an agony to suppose that she could ever receive them again. The Duke was an exception; she saw him as her link with Felton and all that their life together had been.

She discussed her affairs and the settlement of Felton's estate with him, though on bad days she asked Bess to deputise for her. The Duke was concerned about the fall in her income and prospects. None of the arrangements for a settlement upon her had been completed when Felton died; a state of affairs that left Louisa dependent upon the goodwill of Selina Fremantle. As one legal adviser explained, her annual income 'was not sufficient to maintain her according to her station in life as the Widow of the said Sir Felton Elwill Bathurst Hervey'. She could not inherit most of his property, which had provided the majority of his income, because it was entailed and automatically passed to the new baronet Sir Frederick Hervey Bathurst.

As a result, Fremantle explained, 'Felton was enabled to leave her very little, all he had to leave she possesses'. This amounted to an estate at Kingsbury in Warwickshire which he left in trust to provide her with an income of £400 [£25,000] a year and bank stock, shares and cash at Hoare's Bank. The contents of their London house, so recently furnished by Louisa, had to be sold and the proceeds returned to his estate. This exercise was overseen by Fremantle and, although Louisa could buy back items she wanted, her spirits were so low that she took no interest in it.

The Duke was determined to protect the interests of The Widow, as he now called Louisa. He asked Mrs Fremantle to Stratfield Saye on 3 February 1820 and she then agreed to provide a further sum of £400 a year so as to take Louisa's income up to £1,000 [£67,000] a year without including her American income. This would enable Louisa to take a house and live comfortably, if quietly, in town. Louisa, however, could not bear the idea of London without Felton so Bess arranged with the Duke to take Park Corner House, the dower house on the Stratfield Saye estate, until Felton's estate had been settled and they were ready to return to Maryland.[10]

The winter of 1820 was full of incident. Lord Holland gave his son a summary, writing in February: 'A King's death, a Queen's character, a French Prince's murder, and an assassination plot to sweep away a whole Cabinet at once, seem such grand subjects, that it appears preposterous to say one has nothing to write about.' The Duke had a good deal to say and to do about the Prince Regent who, on the death of his father, had become

King George IV in January. He celebrated his accession by the removal of his detested wife's name from the liturgy and by divorcing her. 'You'll see that we have had a good deal of trouble with our Master about his wife', Wellington wrote to Marianne, assuring her that they had 'settled the point in a very satisfactory manner'. Events would prove otherwise; the future of Queen Caroline absorbed government time and public interest throughout that year. The assassination in Paris of the Duc de Berri, ultimate heir to the French throne, was quickly overtaken by a similar event much nearer home.

Of this incident, 'the most desperate & bloody that ever yet entered the Minds of Men', the Duke wrote at great length to Marianne on 27 February. As the ministers met at Lord Harrowby's house in Grosvenor Square for a Cabinet dinner on 23 February, Arthur Thistlewood, a known Radical, planned to gain access under pretext of delivering a despatch box and to let his band of twenty-five revolutionaries into the house whereupon they would rush into the dining room and slaughter every member of the Cabinet. 'We were saved certainly by Divine Providence' when an informant stopped Harrowby in the Park to alert him. As an arrest based upon the testimony of informants would not stand up in court, the Cabinet had to pretend nothing was amiss.

The Duke and Castlereagh came up with a plot of their own: each minister should arrive armed with a brace of pistols inside his despatch box. When the assassins entered, the ministers would hold them up in the hall until the military arrested them. 'My colleagues, however, were of a different opinion', was how the Duke put it, rather regretfully, some years later; 'and perhaps they were right' for, as he told Marianne at the time, it was 'really quite shocking to read the reports of the Miscreants. They talk of Murder & Blood as they would of their common occupations; & two of them actually prepared Sacks to carry off our Heads after we should be murdered.' On the day itself, carriages were ordered for the ministers, in case they were being watched, while nine radicals were captured in their hide-out in Cato Street; five ringleaders were hanged on May Day and others transported to Botany Bay.[11]

By then Marianne and Robert had been deputed to go and bring her sisters home. When they landed in England at the beginning of June, Queen Caroline had just returned from exile. She entered London to a tumultuous welcome from the British public led by one of her supporters, the radical Alderman Wood. What would Liverpool and the King do? As the Queen stood firm against the government's offer of £50,000 [£3.4 million] to return to exile and not be crowned, mobs hurled stones at ministerial carriages and houses. Marianne and Robert were staying in Louisa's house in South Audley Street, though she could not be persuaded to live there, and

Alderman Wood was a neighbour. The queen's followers massed outside his house by day to cheer her and by night to break the windows of any residents who refused to 'light up' and illuminate their houses as a symbol of support.

Bess had earlier accompanied the Duchess of Wellington to Apsley House, leaving Louisa with Eliza Hervey, and she thought the Duchess nervy and 'very anxious for the Duke's safety'. Many others, not least the government itself, were frightened by the escalation of violence; a radical meeting at the King's Mews required a reading of the Riot Act and a charge of the Life Guards to disperse the crowd. Many of London's society leaders left for the country.

Robert Patterson likewise decided to leave London for Stratfield Saye. He was not in the best of spirits, having endured an uncomfortable passage from America despite the services of the Harpers' major-domo, Auguste, who was to escort young Harper and Carroll home from school in Paris. Auguste complained to the boys that on the voyage 'Mr Patterson was never contented and had always something to be offended at'. He had no intention of lingering in England.[12]

His mood was not improved by Louisa's refusal to leave Stratfield Saye and accompany them to Cheltenham where they proposed to take a secluded house. Although she had been warned about Louisa's mental state, Marianne was alarmed to find her so dejected and uninterested in life – except on one subject: she was adamant that she would never return to America, that she could not possibly leave Felton. She could visit him at Egham Church, and keep his memory alive by being near the places and people they had known together, but in America she would be cut off from everything associated with him. She was also a co-executor of Felton's will and there remained his estate to settle and her own business affairs. Bess had to agree there was 'no prospect of their being soon wound up'.

Louisa was condemning herself to a life of exile. She was also condemning one of her sisters to the same fate. The obvious candidate to stay with her was Marianne. Yet Robert would never allow it, however unfair to Bess, who had been abroad for four years. It was possible, Marianne mused, that their mother, who longed to visit Europe, would agree to come over and by then Louisa might have become reconciled to returning home. These were questions that could not be resolved without protracted family discussion.[13]

In the meantime, Robert was impatient to leave for Cheltenham with or without Louisa. Mindful of the gossip that attended Marianne whenever she and the Duke were together, Robert was uneasy at Stratfield Saye. Countess Lieven noticed the Duke's delight over Marianne's return. When he wrote about it, 'his letter radiates happiness'. She knew Marianne only by sight, she told Prince Metternich, 'and certainly that is the best way to know her; she is superb'. She then asserted: 'Wellington does not bother himself much about the rest.' Brought up in Russia, she found the English people particularly frank about their own affairs. When the Duke took her into his study, she was amazed to see the two portraits of Marianne and Lady Charlotte Greville: 'How can one have two passions at the same time, and how can one bear to parade them before the world at large?'

The Duke was outmanoeuvred, though, over accompanying Marianne to Cheltenham. Robert announced a sudden change of plan. They must go to Brussels and then take the waters at Spa, which the Duke was not free to do. Bess went with the Pattersons, leaving Louisa in the care of the Duchess and Eliza Hervey. They returned at the end of September to find Louisa still opposed to going home. Marianne wanted to remain but Robert again refused to allow it. Bess therefore stayed in England when Marianne and Robert sailed for home at the beginning of November.[14]

Bess's positive attitude carried her through circumstances that might otherwise cause resentment. She alleviated the monotony of Louisa's mourning with her books and, as her letters home testify, an abiding interest in political and financial news. She started reading Ricardo's *Principles of Political Economy and Taxation* (1817), and endorsed his views about the restoration of a stable currency, influential in the reintroduction of sovereign coins, which had begun in February. She noted, though, that the over-sharp contraction of the note-issue (paper-money) had jabbed the country where it hurt, writing: 'There is great distress among the farmers – their rents are high & prices exceedingly reduced from the return to specie payments whilst the taxes and the poor are as burthensome as ever – a ministry of angels if they had not the power of working miracles would not relieve the country.'[15]

The country was also writhing under the indignity of royal scandal with the 'trial' of the Queen. When Liverpool, facing defeat, withdrew the doomed Bill of Pains and Penalties intended to deprive the Queen of her powers and privileges on the grounds of 'outrageous' adultery with her Italian major-domo, the furious king threatened to dismiss the government. But he did nothing – except interest himself in his new mistress Lady Conyngham, the 'Vice-Queen' as she was generally named, and his coronation for which Parliament had voted the enormous sum of £243,000 [£16.3 million]. Louisa took no part in the coronation but Bess was given a coveted voucher of attendance by the Duke, who was officiating as Lord High Constable of England.

At six o'clock on the fine, warm morning of 19 July 1821, in full dress and plumes, Bess left Apsley House with the Duchess for Westminster Hall where they took their seats in the Lord High Constable's box immediately above the royal family. It was a splendid scene, Bess reported home, with the ladies in feathers and diamonds and the gentlemen, in uniform, arrayed along the galleries of the hall. The peers arrived from the House of Lords and at ten o'clock the King entered and, after the presentation of the regalia to the officers of state, the huge procession slowly started for Westminster Abbey. The ladies were spared the hour's march in the hot sun and instead went by a narrow passage erected from the Lords' entrance to Poets' Corner, which gave them ample time to be seated before the procession arrived at the North Door.

Bess and the Duchess were so near the King that, Bess wrote, they could hear him whisper to his attendants. His conduct with Lady Conyngham inside the abbey – 'The eyes they made at each other, the reciprocal kissing of each other's rings, which everyone observed! and God alone knows what!!!' exclaimed the Duke – was as universally decried as the Queen's outside. When she was barred at three entrances, the crowd turned against her. Crying to the sentry at Westminster Hall: 'Let me pass; I am your queen' she had the doors slammed shut in her face by the pages. The uncrowned queen had no option but to retreat; her health and spirit worn down after the long fight for her rights, she became ill and died within a month.[16]

After George IV was crowned, the Tower guns were fired, the peers put on their coronets and the band and trumpets sounded 'God Save the King'. As the royal procession returned to Westminster Hall for the public banquet, Bess and the Duchess made their way to the Lord High Constable's apartment where a table for forty awaited them. In looking for it they were ushered by mistake into another apartment where the royal princesses and various royal relations were dining, all of whom insisted the Duchess and Bess join them, which they did, very glad of the dinner after a six-o'clock-in-the-morning start. They then returned to the Duke's box for the toasts when the peers drank to the King; he in return to the peers and the good people; whereupon the whole assembly again sang 'God Save the King'. People stood up in the galleries, waving their hats, fans and handkerchiefs, and shouted 'God Bless the King!' in a surge of loyalty disavowed by most of them six months before. 'The Spectacle', Bess wrote home, 'exceeded anything on this side of Eternity.'

London erupted with grand illuminations, fireworks, celebratory theatrical performances and a fair in Hyde Park. The coronation festivities continued with a Drawing Room on 26 July where everybody had to be freshly presented to the crowned king. Bess wore a French gown of pink tulle embroidered in pink with a train and a headdress of fifteen feathers and pearls but reported home that she had often dressed for a cotillion ball at dear little Annapolis with infinitely more goût. The women all wore slim-fitting gowns as, after his mother Queen Charlotte's death at the end of 1818, the King had abolished the traditional court dress of hoops.

The family had been inundated with enquiries about Bess's attendance at the coronation festivities after letters had been received in Maryland from the American Minister and Mrs Rush. At his audience to present his credentials in February 1818, Rush had been surprised when the Prince Regent had asked, not about the President, but if he knew the ladies from America who had made such favourable impressions, naming Mrs Patterson and the Miss Catons. 'You are very kind to mention Mr Rush's amiable letter respecting dearest Bess', Mary Carroll Caton answered Nancy Chase. She was quick to pass on how popular the Rush couple were, '& how deservedly so', as she knew Nancy Chase would circulate them. And, aware of the envy produced in America by her daughters' social success, she was sure Bess's presence at the coronation would excite a similar response. She therefore emphasised how Bess's letters, far from revelling in the social whirl, were filled 'with elevated & pious feelings – altho' she occasionally moves in the *great* World, she views all these *things*, as they *deserve*', in the grand scheme of God's will. This was for public consumption, to protect her daughter's reputation; in private, Mary Carroll Caton delighted in her social success. Emily once mischievously sent uncle Harper a vignette of the family at the Manor on a summer's afternoon: 'Grandpapa is at this moment playing chess with Mr Marechal, papa asleep with a book in his hand on the Sopha & Mama on her own bed dreaming of the great folks in London.'[17]

22

Afflicting Circumstances

Emily had some good news to share with her sisters in 1821. The McTavishes were now permanently settled in Baltimore. The continuation of the fur wars eventually led to pressure from the British government for a merger between the NWC and HBC to form a single trading company that would extend British influence across North America. With profits falling and the partners at odds, McGillivray had travelled to London for talks in 1820. The final deal, concluded on 26 March 1821, provided for the amalgamation of the companies' assets, and a joint board operating under the Hudson Bay Company name and charter.

That summer John travelled the familiar route from Lachine to Fort William for the annual meeting, one like no other he had ever attended; it was a wake for forty years of NWC history, a grim farewell to the McTavish legacy in Canada. As McGillivray parted from his old colleagues, he understood that something more valuable had been surrendered, that 'the Fur trade is forever lost to Canada!' The individuals who had come together as proprietors of Canada's first national enterprise had lost their independence to absentee London-based committee men serving only British imperialism. Late in July, the *voyageurs* took the remaining partners, including John, away by canoe across Lake Superior, for the last time. 'The feudal state of Fort William is at an end,' Washington Irving wrote, 'the lords of the lakes and the forests are all passed away.'

Emily shed no tears for the demise of the NWC and thus the necessity of living in Montreal. John retained strong links with the new HBC as he had a share of its profits and a shareholding in McTavish, McGillivray & Co, which became the HBC's Montreal agency. He remained a director of the Bank of Montreal, and retained investments and property there. None of these interests required his undivided attention so that he and Emily were able to commit themselves to living in Maryland. Ensconced with their baby son and her family in Baltimore, Emily's happiness would have been complete but for the ill-health of one sister and the unplanned absence of the other two.[1]

*

When cholera invaded Maryland during the fever season of 1822, Robert, who lived for his horses and dogs, was engrossed in a new horse at Tuscarora plantation. He had no sooner returned to Brooklandwood, where he heard of John Howard's death, than he was struck down with cholera. From the first his illness was severe and dangerous, though as a fit and healthy man, he was thought to have a better chance of recovery than most. Emily immediately took the precaution of sending four-year-old Carroll with his nurse to the Manor. Robert had been delirious for two days when Carroll of Carrollton gave Harper a bulletin on 22 October. 'Mr Patterson had a better night, slept some time, and during the latter part of it he was more composed than he has been for several nights past, the Doctors say the medicines have operated just as they wished.'

The doctors, however, had no effective medicine to prescribe for cholera, though they gave Robert Peruvian bark. Marianne and Emily nursed him constantly and thought he was pulling through when, on 25 October, he had no delirium, his fever appeared to abate and he enjoyed a good night. At eight o'clock the next morning, his condition deteriorated so quickly that he died within a few hours. The funeral and burial were held as soon as possible to prevent contagion, after which the entire family went to the Manor.

Marianne bore her grief with customary composure but was nevertheless in deep distress. Robert had long been more companion than lover; the interesting dandyish beau of their early marriage disappearing into the dull, impatient husband of most of their sixteen years together – Stratford Canning called him 'her ill-matched husband'. She endured her loss 'like a pious and resigned Christian', her uncle Harper wrote on 3 November, and 'with a dignity and good Grace becoming to her character'.[2]

She was to need all her good grace to contend with the Patterson family's opposition to the settlement of the will. Besides landholdings, Robert left a personal estate worth an inventory value of $103,352 [£1.84 million]. In his will he left Marianne all his personal effects; his stocks; the dividends for life in his large holding of US Bank stock; and the 600 acres of Carrollton Manor, which had originally belonged to her and which he had already contracted by deed to return to her on his death. He also gave his brother John Patterson some property and Georgia lands, the residue of all his estate and made him remainderman to his US Bank stock on Marianne's death. He appointed both of them co-executors of his will.

At first all was harmony. In the beginning, in early November, John Patterson wrote in the affectionate style of the brother-in-law he was and was willing to do all he could to process the will without delay. By mid-December, though, he was distinctly frosty: he was consulting lawyers, addressing her as 'my dear Madam' and signing off with 'I am with great respect.' What can have happened?[3]

Although Marianne had been content for him to settle the will, several contentious issues then emerged. The first concerned the right of dower, enshrined in Maryland law, giving her the right to claim a third of the value of all property. Uncle Harper advised her that she might be better off renouncing the will in order to claim dower right in the whole estate.

Her grandfather, however, provided an equally strong argument against renouncing the will. It would involve legal expense, acrimony and delay. He could recall the well-known Maryland case in which the Ringgold family was embroiled in an acrimonious legal dispute that not only lasted for years but also absorbed much of the wealth of the estate. Marianne took her grandfather's advice and did not renounce the will. But she did take her uncle's advice to claim dower in the landed property that Robert had left to John Patterson.

On 21 November, uncle Harper urged her to join in the administration of the estate. Robert had wished her to do so and she should attend to her own affairs, and make herself thoroughly acquainted with them, as she had been brought up to do. 'I have no idea, that a woman in your situation fulfils her duty, by moping or crying in her room', he continued. 'She has active duties to perform; which she ought to attend to, without bustle or affectation indeed, but with care and diligence.' Harper was confident that Marianne could manage Robert's affairs as successfully as she did her own. Marianne took his 'little lecture' in good heart and assumed the co-executorship as any 'man of business' would do. It was fortunate that she did so.

She learnt that there was a problem with the US Bank stock. Robert's holding was valued at $52,500 but it transpired that he had pledged $33,000 of it to the bank as security for two loans. And one of them was for John Patterson, taken out only shortly before and not accounted for in the will. These were debts on the estate that had to be repaid. Marianne wanted to sell all the US Bank stock but John Patterson wanted to sell the personal estate and use the dividends of the stock to mop up any deficit. If they sold the personal estate, it would absorb everything that Robert had willed to her, including shares and property held in her own name. If they sold the stock then John Patterson would not inherit any capital after Marianne died.[4]

Patterson was furious that she would not submit to his wishes. He demanded the keys and papers of Tuscarora, which together with the whole estate had been ring-fenced as 'her own absolute property' by a deed of 8 February 1821. He then disputed her ownership of Tuscarora, alleging the claims of creditors came before her interests so that everything at her house in Baltimore and at Brooklandwood, apart from her clothes and shoes, must also be inventoried.

She remained calm against this barrage. To his insinuations that as a
woman she could know little of Robert's business affairs, she replied that
she was well acquainted with his concerns and books. 'In the settlement
of the Estate I only wish to have what he gives me and the Laws confirm
– I therefore must ascertain what are my rights, and having done so I will
maintain them' were her ringing words. It was, however, a wearying business as John Patterson was determined to obtain as much as he could of
his dead brother's estate through the courts. Roger Taney, her lawyer and
a future Chief Justice of the Supreme Court, writing to her on 1 March
1823, was sorry to hear that she was 'still harassed by the unpleasant controversy about the estate'.[5]

It was the Patterson family, rather than the estate, which brought her
the most grief. She had lost Robert, was already estranged from Betsy and
John, and was now to be in bad odour with her father-in-law. On 4 March
William Patterson wrote her a formal but huffy letter. He had received her
packet of legal deeds to be forwarded on to John Patterson and took
exception to her request for a receipt.

Marianne was taken aback. If she had been sending deeds to her grandfather she would have asked him for confirmation of their arrival, and she
told William Patterson 'you are too much a Man of the World to take offence
at what is always done'. It was simply good business practice. Whereas she had
believed him to be her friend, she could not say the same for the rest of the
family: 'It has been my misfortune to have no friends in my husband's family,
and by any act of my life to give them dissatisfaction.'

Betsy, needless to say, concurred with this opinion. She had been living
since 1819 in Geneva so as to afford to educate her son to his rank and
had recently sent him back to America to attend Harvard. She was in Paris,
however, in 1823 when she learned that a small portion of Marianne's land
was to be divided among Robert's heirs. 'No feelings of romance or false
delicacy shall prevent my taking what the law allows me, and I only regret
it is not more', declared Betsy. 'I consider the will, which left her mistress
to dispose after her death of the whole as highly unjust.' John Patterson's
erratic behaviour over negotiations with Marianne apparently stemmed
from drink; when William Patterson left him some brandy, Betsy commented:
'a Joke with which to amuse the Public because John was a Drunkard &
known to be such'. Mary Carroll Caton reported indignantly that he was
now taking the case to the Orphans Court 'merely to gain time & harass
– you would shudder if you *knew* the whole of his *conduct*! but the judges
decide I believe upon the intentions of the Testator'.[6]

Unfortunately the judges would not decide anything for some years to
come. The family urged Marianne to live in England but she insisted she
could not leave Maryland until her affairs were satisfactorily arranged;

she also admitted to her mother and Emily that she would rather have feeble health with them at home than good health abroad. Her grandfather, though, believed that another winter of ill-health combined with a desire to relieve Bess would persuade her otherwise.

By the following spring, as he had guessed, the strain of fragile health and dealing with the Patterson family had taken its toll. After leaving her affairs in the hands of uncle Harper and John McTavish, Marianne informed her father-in-law that her physicians advised her to leave America for two years. Mr and Mrs Alexander Brown, of the banking family, had offered her their protection on the journey and so, on 22 April 1824, she sailed on the *Alexander* for Liverpool.[7]

PART III
Anglo-American Wives 1824–34

*One must cross that vast Atlantic Ocean to know how to value –
Country – Home – & friends.*
                              Sallie Coles Stevenson, 28 April 1837

23

Marianne's Return

'We have received no tidings of the *Alexander* since the Pilot took leave of her beyond the Capes of Delaware', John McTavish informed his friend George Jackson on 17 May 1824, but Mrs Caton 'has been pleased and displeased about fifty times a day both with wind and weather for the last three weeks.' She was especially fidgety because Marianne's spirits had been uncharacteristically dejected before she sailed. The voyage did little to raise them. 'I cannot describe the feeling of forlornness & desolation which came over my heart when you left me,' she confided to her mother. At the age of thirty-five, widowed, ill, and reluctantly leaving home, she was also, for the first time in her life, unaccompanied by a member of her family.

She was not alone, though, for she was travelling with friends and servants, including Henny, her trusted personal servant. Henny was probably a Doughoregan Manor slave, brought up in her own slave family like Marianne's body maid Anny (whose fate is unrecorded), and given to Marianne by her grandfather; a number of slaves called Henny are listed in the family inventories – Henny Sidman, for example, who belonged to Emily. Yet Marianne's Henny, whose full name was Henrietta Johnstone, does not appear in them. If Henny was a freed slave then, at some stage, Marianne had freed her by an act of manumission; in the same way as, after Robert's death, she freed his valet. If Henny had not been freed before she left America, once she landed on English soil, where the slave trade had been abolished, she legally became a free woman.

Henny was tall, slim and strong and supported Marianne through the long nights of asthmatic attacks. She remained a constant companion and Marianne cherished her. On the voyage, they shared a cabin and when the ship encountered a storm off the Irish coast that seemed like a hurricane and lasted three days, the two women clung together, shouting fervent prayers as the waves lashed the berths. Marianne put her trust in God, 'who orders *all* for the best', and the *Alexander* captain, 'an excellent one who never left the deck for a moment'. He steered them safely into the harbour of Liverpool at the end of May. Exhausted by seasickness, the extreme cold of the cabins and a want of food, she disembarked.[1]

Her reunion with her sisters in London on 6 June brought great happiness. Although Louisa had recovered her spirits and come out again into
the world, Marianne's health precluded going into society before they took
the waters at Cheltenham. She could receive visits from old friends, who
'were all glad to see her among them again'; especially her sisters' circle of
American friends, glad of a fresh link with home.

They were eager to learn more about Lafayette's tour in America with
Fanny Wright. After visiting the country in 1818 this volatile and flamboyant Scotswoman had published *Views of Society and Manners in America*
(1821) in which she enthused about the great republic, claiming 'the liberties of mankind are entrusted to their guardianship'. In Paris, she attracted
the attention of another champion of America, Lafayette, and moved with
her sister Camilla to live with him and his family at La Grange, where she
began to write his life but, after she asked him to adopt her, his family,
distrusting her influence, tried to separate them.

The means seemed to be at hand when Lafayette was invited to the
United States in June 1824 as 'Guest of the Nation'. Marianne left America
in a fever of Lafayette worship and preparations. Uncle Harper was immersed
in arrangements for the military reviews and receptions to be held in
Maryland. Ann Royall, the Maryland author, recalled that long before the
illustrious guest arrived 'we had the Lafayette ribbons, Lafayette waistcoats,
Lafayette feathers, hats, caps &c. – everything was honored by his image
and subscription – even the ginger cakes were impressed with his name,
and nothing was heard either in the streets or in the houses but Lafayette!
Lafayette!' Even so, he would be pilloried if two young single women accompanied him. The land of liberty was remarkably restrictive where matters
of convention were concerned. The Wrights, therefore, sailed on a different
ship, travelling in the wake of his progress through the country. They had
not yet arrived in Baltimore when Emily accompanied her grandfather and
mother to the festivities held for Lafayette.[2]

Offended by continued fierce English criticism, like the famous onslaught
on American culture and slavery from Sydney Smith in the *Edinburgh
Review*, American counter-attacks came not just in periodicals – the *Port
Folio*, for instance, calling Great Britain 'a jealous and cruel step-mother'
– but also from Congress itself. In a Fourth of July address the Secretary of
State John Quincy Adams denounced the 'unrelenting war of slander and
invective, waged by almost all the literature of Great Britain against the
good name of this country'. Only one criticism drew no American response:
slavery.

Yet, notwithstanding appearances, political relations between the two
countries had undergone a change since Marianne's previous visit. While
American politicians remained suspicious of British leaders and the British

questioned American motives, both now regretted the undermining 'warfare of the mind' that nagged at peace. It was in Britain's interest to sustain a rapprochement with America; first, to continue to benefit from her trade, which provided Britain's largest overseas market, and second, to safeguard her Canadian colony. Castlereagh's policy of conciliation was followed by his successor George Canning. Yet continued American distrust underlay President Monroe's isolationist message in 1823 which stated that, while the USA would not intervene in the affairs of the European powers, they must recognise that the US sphere of influence now encompassed the whole American hemisphere.

By 1824, Anglo-American relations could be said to have stabilised, if not improved. The sheen of political respect and friendly relations covering a mutual antipathy spilled over into private lives which, with faster, more frequent transatlantic travel, brought more Americans to England. Rich American women, though hardly numerous, were less of a novelty than Marianne, Bess and Louisa had been on their arrival in 1816.[3]

They continued to enjoy the affection and protection of the Wellingtons, although without Felton they naturally saw a little less of the Duke. Marianne also found the Duke more circumspect than in 1820, though she kept her place in his heart and he called every day to see her at South Audley Street. She was free to marry again but he was not. He had fallen passionately in love with Marianne but no evidence survives about the exact nature of their love affair. There is evidence, though, of his earlier sexual affair with Lady Charlotte Greville, mother of the diarist Charles Greville. She is the dark-haired beauty whose portrait hung alongside Marianne's in the Duke's study. Discovery by her husband brought an end to the liaison, though not the friendship. Her son, however, retained a grudge against Wellington. In his published diaries Greville dedicates a long passage to the Duke's love affairs featuring the usual suspects, Harriet Arbuthnot, Lady Jersey, Lady Shelley and Lady Georgiana Fane, but not either of the serious candidates: his mother and Marianne.

Although Marianne and the Duke were deeply attached and she enjoyed what Lady Charlotte Greville called 'a thousand acts of kindness, friendship, & attention with professions of regard & affection for me and all belonging to me', Marianne found in 1824 that another woman was determined to keep the Duke away from her. Harriet Arbuthnot was devastated by Lord Castlereagh's suicide in 1822, which left her without access to high-ranking political power. She swiftly transferred her considerable energies to the Duke of Wellington. 'He has promised to fill the place of the friend I have lost', she wrote in her journal that year.

The Duke enabled her to feel close again to power and patronage and her husband Charles Arbuthnot, a junior minister, close to cabinet decision-making, and the Arbuthnots provided the Duke with a safe, supportive place to talk freely about his concerns. Their friendship gave rise to gossip that she and the Duke were lovers, but Harriet, a conventional, prudish woman, was a devoted wife. It is clear from their correspondence that the Arbuthnots and the Duke were a trio of friends, not a *ménage à trois*. She, nevertheless, wanted the importance of the Duke at *her* side, away from all his other close female friends and, especially, his American ones. She tried to influence the Duke against Marianne, telling him she was 'insignificant', nothing but 'the widow of an American shopkeeper'. On surer ground, she disliked Marianne for her politics. Mrs Arbuthnot was an ultra-Tory: she did not want the Duke being influenced by Marianne's intelligent and informed Whiggery.[4]

Marianne and Louisa differed from these women, and, indeed, most Englishwomen in high society, in their reluctance to use their influence with the Duke to further, or ruin, other people's interests: as Marianne once declared: 'I for one have promised him never to ask for anything.' The Duke, needless to say, instructed them in the arts of British patronage, Louisa over time proving an adept pupil. Her first quest was to increase her army pension. The Duke helped her to compose a formal address to the Duke of York, Commander-in-Chief, arguing that Felton's illustrious military career entitled her, 'an unprotected stranger', to a larger sum than the 'very inadequate' pension of £80 [£5,800] a year ordinarily allowed. The petition was to be submitted to the King but first it would be a courtesy to send it to Lord Liverpool, who was interested in his wife's family, the Herveys. Louisa certainly had powerful friends. His Majesty was indeed pleased on Liverpool's advice to bestow a pension of £368 [£27,000].[5]

In addition to seeing her old friends, Marianne had a new one to make: Thomas Coke's young wife Lady Anne Coke. Marianne had been concerned about Bess's reaction. Did she have regrets? Was it to be the end of their friendship with the Cokes? Not at all, Bess reassured her sister. She wished 'dear dear Mr Coke all the happiness in the world' and in the first autumn of his marriage paid a long visit with Louisa at Holkham. It was not quite as light-hearted as former visits, at least judging from Eliza Coke's description. 'Such a dreadful *glum* dinner today; my father having caught cold, Lady Anne with a bad headache and nearly as white as powder, Tip [Viscount Titchfield] cross, William [Coke] having shot ill, Lady Smith *précieuse*, Miss Caton chilly, Sir James Smith [president of the Linnaean Society] eating himself sick with a *load* of preserved pine-apple.' She was disconsolate, Eliza Coke told her fiancé John Spencer-Stanhope, until Louisa's 'utter folly' nearly choked her with laughter.

Louisa had re-entered the world determined to have fun; she set about enlivening the company by practising her somewhat rusty southern-belle coquetry upon some of the male guests. 'I wish you had heard Captain Spencer last night,' Eliza Coke continued, 'declaring that Lady Hervey made her *first* attack on Fidèle Jack [Lord Althorp, an old hunting friend of Felton's], who was so terrified that he had serious thoughts of leaving the house, shooting and all. She is too great a goose!' It was the captain's turn the next night. The other guests laughed at the delight of Althorp and the discomfiture of his brother Captain Robert Spencer and, as Louisa intended, the rest of the visit was much more amiable.[6]

By the time Marianne met her in 1824, Lady Anne had borne Coke a son and heir. Seeing the contented Coke ménage might have caused Bess a pang of regret. In replying to Marianne's account of the Cokes, her grand-father wrote of Bess: 'she had it in her power to make happy the man of the greatest merit in England: what errors do we commit when we suffer *passion* to get the better of our judgment! errors generally irretrievable & frequently lamented.' Several family letters contain tantalising hints about the existence of a mysterious suitor, one Lord G or Lord C (the handwriting is illegible), to whom Bess was attracted. Whether he proposed or not, or was ineligible, remain unknowable.

Her extended residence abroad concerned the family. Louisa now had less need of Bess's attention, her grandfather pointed out to Marianne, having become closer to all the Hervey family, who were 'friendly & very attentive to her', and the Wellingtons also looked after her. Bess, now aged thirty-three, impressed her grandfather as being more indecisive than ever. There had been plenty of offers and opportunities to marry if she had been so inclined, he reasoned, but now she must come home with Marianne.[7]

He was eighty-eight and he missed his granddaughters more as the years went by and longed for them to come home. The American doctors' verdict that Marianne had to live abroad to stay alive had, however, been confirmed by the Duke's physician, Doctor Hume. After a long dose of Cheltenham waters, the sisters had decamped to France on 21 August 1824. Marianne received an epistolary rap on the knuckles from her grandfather when he saw that her next letter was not dated from the South of France. She felt better, however, and they were being painted by the American artist William West, whom they had met through another recent arrival, Washington Irving. West's studio in Paris became a gathering place for Americans. The sisters whiled away their sittings by chatting to other friends and visitors and, as Irving recalled, the talk was all of art and poetry. Byron's death earlier that year lent West's recollections poignancy and his Byron portrait, the last from life, fame. It would appear, from a later remark of Bess's, that the sisters commissioned separate likenesses from West for their grandfather.[8]

Writing to Emily and McTavish from Paris on 1 December, Bess passed on the latest English news: Canning had recalled Sir Charles Stuart, the Ambassador in Paris, who had been 'very angry' at being given only a fortnight's notice to make way for Canning's old friend Lord Granville. Bess had met the Granvilles at her friend Betty de Rothschild's latest party where Harriet Granville received her in the most gracious manner and spoke of Marianne as 'the most perfect being, so amiable &c.'. This was gratifying but surprising, because hitherto Lady Granville had made 'a point of always behaving towards them all with a very great distance, not to say rudeness' in the *de haut en bas* manner that some aristocratic ladies still extended to Americans.

The reason for the volte-face emerged the following week when Harriet Granville called upon Marianne 'in obedience to the Duke of Wellington's entreaties', of which the sisters had been quite unaware. 'She seems a very charming person, very handsome with *l'air noble* and not a shade of her mother-country', Harriet Granville reported to her sister Lady Morpeth on 13 December. 'She shook all over when I went into the room, but if for grief at the loss of Mr Paterson, sentiment at the recollection of the Duke, or the coldness of the room, I do not presume to judge.' Marianne's trembling was the sign of an imminent relapse. She was able to sit for West on 22 December but an evening at the opera with Maria Bingham Baring provoked a severe asthma attack.[9]

When Irving called at West's studio on 17 January 1825 he found only Louisa and Bess there. By the spring, however, all three sisters were at the studio. West was working on an allegorical triple portrait, *The Muses of Painting, Poetry and Music*, using Louisa and Bess who, as the Muses of Painting and Poetry look to Marianne, the Muse of Music. Irving remembered those days fondly. 'How are the dear Patterson and Catons? God bless them', he told West. 'I . . . would give all the money in my pocket to have your painting room and all its frequenters back again.'[10]

In the event, their gaieties were quickly curtailed. 'We have been plunged into the deepest distress', McTavish wrote. Their beloved uncle Harper had been standing reading the newspaper after breakfast when he was felled to the ground by a heart attack and died instantly. It was impossible to grasp as the previous day 'he spoke in Court for several hours', McTavish explained. 'At night he attended the dancing assembly, and was in excellent spirits.' Her grandfather wrote on 25 January to Marianne: 'on this subject it is painful for me to dwell, my forebodings of the future events in this family bereft of its head fill me with distressing anxieties.' They had all relied upon Robert Harper's wise counsel and affectionate interest and his death removed a pillar of support from the family so that when troubles came, its unity crumbled. At Carroll House the family enveloped Kitty Harper and her three surviving children. Marianne, Bess and Louisa longed to be at home with them.

When her grandfather wrote to Bess on 27 April he made no mention of the second death in the family: their unfortunate uncle Carroll Jr had died three weeks earlier, attended only by Emily and McTavish. By the time they heard, the sisters were in London. Marianne felt so much better that she decided to sail early for home with Bess in October 1826. Their grandfather was overjoyed: 'I already anticipate the delight yours & her company & conversation will afford me', he owned to Bess. He also made his views known: 'I depend on your coming with her; if you should not, I shall be grievously disappointed & displeased.' Bess understood that she was on no account to remain abroad any longer.[11]

Someone else who thought they should return home, despite her own hatred of the place, was Betsy Bonaparte. Irritated beyond measure by the accounts of their still having Wellington's protection and living in style while she had to economise, she ranted to her father, first, that 'the Duke is said to be tired of the Catons; but tired or not, they pursue him, live on his estate, and until he gets them husbands he will never be rid of them'; then, that they were considered '*mere* adventurers and swindlers', asserting 'E— and L— both made their way to Europe by impudence; two more ignorant, unprincipled asses never left their own country'. Her parting shot was to accuse them of ruining the reputation of Americans abroad by 'the fraud they practise to get husbands, in affirming they have forty thousand pounds fortune, besides great expectations from grandpapa'.

William Patterson must have remonstrated with her. In Betsy's next letter from Geneva on 11 December she accepted that 'abusing the C—s can do me no good, and have resolved not to speak of them again . . . At all events I leave them to their fate, here & hereafter.' But she could not resist scratching away at them with her pointed nib for years to come. As late as 1867, she called them 'the most pernicious foes of my life' and scribbled on an old letter: 'The Catons, of whom Mme Godefroy speaks were, out of my own family, the greatest Enemies I ever had, & like my father and his sons omitted nothing to injure me.'[12]

24

His Delinquency

While Louisa was occupied with the Hervey family, Marianne and Bess decided to visit Ireland before the three of them went to Italy for the winter. Marianne had promised her grandfather that, should she ever have the opportunity, she would endeavour to discover more about some of the Gaelic names dotted about the Carroll genealogies kept in the family's 'little Irish Manuscript Book'. She and Bess hoped to catch echoes of their Irish fore-bears, echoes that resounded in Maryland through land connected by name with an Irish past. Doughoregen Manor, for instance, took its name from Déuiche Uéi Riagé ain, a valley nestling at the foot of the Slieve Bloom Mountains.[1]

If the sisters held any fanciful notions about their heritage, they were swiftly disabused when they landed in July 1825 at Kingstown Dun Laoghaire and drove into Dublin. What could Marianne and Bess first say of Ireland but that they rejoiced every hour that their ancestors had emigrated to the happy land of America when they saw 'the misery, poverty & filth around them'. Nothing, neither the English poor nor the Continental peasantry, could have prepared them, they said, for the wretched sight and smell of the Irish people. Elsewhere the penurious were penned together in slum areas but in Dublin they were everywhere, 'lying half naked and apparently half dead from cold and hunger on the parapets and steps of the houses of the well-to-do'. Prosperous Dubliners merely stepped over the bundles on their doorsteps as if over a puddle, or sent their servants to clear the way as if stamping down some undergrowth.

Dublin was a city of 'lamentable contrasts', as Lady Gower pointed out, 'its public buildings beautiful, its quays putting one in mind of Paris'. A capital city 'splendid beyond my expectations' affirmed Sir Walter Scott that very month, with its broad paved streets and Georgian squares. The fine Georgian mansions of the nobility were proud sentinels of an Anglo-Irish heritage, monuments to the Protestant power of the Ascendancy that dominated Ireland and ignored the penalised and larger Catholic population.

Looming over the city was the castle, the seat of the Lord Lieutenant of Ireland and his large staff who governed the Irish on behalf of the British Crown. This office was held by the Duke's eldest brother Richard, Marquess Wellesley who also had a country house about three miles away, the Viceregal Lodge in the Phoenix Park. Arás an Uachtárain, today the residence of the President of Ireland, is a graceful long white Palladian mansion set in ninety acres of parkland.[2]

Marianne and Bess dined at Viceregal Lodge in the second week of August. Lord Wellesley had already invited them to drive out with him and to an evening party, which Marianne had to forgo for fear of catching cold in the changeable weather. Lady Osborne told her cousin in July, 'we have fires constantly and are very glad to eat strawberries and cream by a blazing hearth'. The sisters wanted to meet Sir Walter Scott, who was being lionised in Ireland, and they were entirely satisfied: 'his stories and his kindness were exemplary', Bess reported home. In mid-August, the sisters left Dublin to stay at Mount Shannon with their friend Julia Burrell, who had recently married Lord Clare.[3]

On their return in September the Lord Lieutenant became so taken with them that they found that nearly every day some excursion or amusement drew them together. 'The charms of his conversation, drawn as it was from a boundless store of political and literary knowledge, and pointed by his long and varied acquaintance with the world' proved as attractive to them as to Lord Cloncurry. There can have been few Foreign Secretaries of that era who would have merited the Persian envoy's description of Lord Wellesley in 1809 as 'well versed in the literature of Hind, Rum and Farang' and 'fluent in the idioms of Arabic, Turkish and Persian'. He mesmerised the sisters with tales of India, where he had been Governor-General, and of men such as Pitt to whom he had been devoted.[4]

As the castle and the lodge were being refurbished, Colonel Talbot, an Irish landowner, had offered Wellesley the use of Malahide Castle, his mansion outside Dublin. Lord Wellesley invited Marianne and Bess to join him and his secretary Colonel Shawe there for walks and drives in the sea air. 'I have too agreeable a recollection of a visit to Malahide not to have great pleasure in the thought of seeing the Lord Lieutenant again', Marianne replied to Colonel Shawe in response to yet another invitation. In the face of what was becoming a barrage of Lord Wellesley's notes, invitations and marked attentions, Marianne's ability to date her letters deserted her. She was flustered by his Lordship's ardent pursuit.[5]

There were further drives and walks and dinners at Malahide in the course of which Lord Wellesley proposed. Marianne, agonised, asked for time to reflect. Lord Wellesley, remarkable for his mastery of poetic language, composed a love letter that overpowered her. She capitulated. 'I believe I am as frank, as unaffected', she wrote:

'A Couple Strolling', as Lord Wellesley and Marianne did on their 'delightful walks' in the sea air at Malahide Castle, Dublin. Anonymous watercolour 1825.

I was fully convinced of the feelings of my own heart, and the conflict of giving you up, or of leaving my own family for ever, who are inexpressibly dear to me, was too much for my health. You have triumphed, and I confess all that you wish. Let me entreat you to keep this a profound secret, as my situation is one of peculiar delicacy – I am convinced there cannot be a more feeling and honorable heart than yours, and in making you the guardian of my happiness I feel that I have secured it.

Wellesley, elated, told her that they must immediately request the King's consent. Marianne agreed. 'I venture to hope he will not condemn your choice, and shall be proud and happy to be considered among the number of his subjects.' There were to be compensations for such drastic action: 'I will drive to Malahide tomorrow to pass an hour with you, and will dine with you the next day.'

There were also tears of painful regret when letters arrived from home, written in ignorance of these Irish developments. 'Mama says she shall be miserable until she hears I have left Ireland, she dreads every thing in that unhappy Country, and my venerable Grandfather writes that he cannot bear me to remain longer from home. What can I say to them for leaving them?' she cried to him. Yet the tie of her family was not strong enough to pull her away from the magnet of Lord Wellesley's love. 'I hope you have not got your cold today. And that you did not forget your Cloak again.' She was already becoming a wife.

By the fourth note she was also entirely his. 'My dearest Lord you make me love you every day more and more, as your noble, and amiable character, is *disclosed* to my view – My family indeed will be proud, and happy to confide me to you and glory in their alliance to a person so distinguished in every respect. I shall not marry a stranger, for you are just as well known in America, as in Europe, and India.' She had sent him a draft of her letter to the King: 'I am glad you like my note to the King, though you could have expressed my sentiments for me much better than I can myself', and she referred to a comment about her in the press:

> I will obey you dearest and never look at a scandalous News Paper, and if possible never be annoyed at their attacks – but it is easier for one like you, of unquestionable superiority to despise them, than for me a woman and a stranger. I look forward with *childish* impatience to our next meeting. When shall it be? But above *all* do not delay writing to the King.'[6]

Already the threads of flattery, dependence, self-effacement and procrastination, which would be woven into the fabric of their marriage, are apparent. How easy would it be for Marianne to throw off her American independence and exchange it for British subjugation? How easy to replace the Duke in her heart! And already their marriage was no longer a matter of private delight but in the public domain.

Their announcement of this unexpected marriage drew forth some equally unexpected responses. Her family was overjoyed at her happiness and flattered by the marquess's attentions. Bess's opinion carried weight, as she at least had met the bridegroom and she was thrilled both by Marianne's delight and Wellesley's romantic behaviour. 'I confidently anticipate a great deal of happiness for her', she assured William West. 'She will be one of the loveliest Vice-Queens the Irish ever had, and I have no doubt will be extremely popular.' Bess enjoyed sparring with Wellesley and once again having proximity to political events. Marianne light-heartedly told Wellesley that Bess sent her love and 'says she wishes she was going to be married *to you herself*. I am very glad *she is not.*' Bess also told Emily and McTavish that it was clear Lord Wellesley 'was very deeply in love for a man of 62' (he was sixty-six) because he had declared that if the government objected to his alliance he would instantly renounce the vice-royalty; that the prospect of Marianne's fortune could not be entirely discounted in his unselfish offer was not apparent to Bess.[7]

Louisa, caught unawares, was nonetheless delighted. She would waste no time in crossing the Irish Sea, after her round of country visits. As her mother repeated to Nancy Chase, 'this Marriage is so important to her – it secures at least the residence of one of her sisters in England – she adds she always felt assured there was a brilliant fate in reserve for her beloved Maryanne – she was so much admired'. Marianne's return home, so keenly anticipated by her grandfather, was now abandoned and he voiced his profound regrets that he would never see her again much as he rejoiced in her felicity. It was especially reassuring for the family to feel that such a match would have the Duke of Wellington's entire approval and support. But, did it?[8]

Marianne wrote at the earliest opportunity to tell him she was going to marry his eldest brother and to ask him to act as her trustee. The Duke was devastated. Nothing had prepared him for such an event, she was *his love*. He reacted like a rejected lover. At Stratfield Saye Mrs Arbuthnot listened aghast while he revealed his true feelings for Marianne, railing against such a preposterous match with his estranged brother. Wellesley, he said, was 'a man totally ruined; when he quitted Ireland, which he must soon do, he wd not have a house to take her to or money to keep a carriage; he had not a shilling in the world &, moreover, he was of a most jealous disposition, a violent temper & had entirely worn out his constitution' by his profligate habits.[9]

The Duke's views were quite at odds with everything Marianne knew of Lord Wellesley. Could they be true? 'The truth is, he is a great *compound*', Liverpool once wrote of Wellesley:

> and if one is to have the use of him it must be by making as little as possible of some of his absurdities. We have known him for thirty years. The acquaintance of Peel and Goulburn has been but recent and they therefore cannot see as well as us, that a man may be wise in some things and most foolish in others.

It was more difficult for a younger brother to show the same under-standing towards a brother whom he had once revered. The Duke had seen Wellesley injure a brilliant political career by his private habits, of which even Lady Liverpool could write that Wellesley 'is going on sadly with his *Ladies*, quarrelling with his wife & Lavishing thousands on his mistress – pity pity!' His estranged first wife had known all about these women, who included the celebrated Regency courtesan Harriette Wilson. The only record of Wellesley ever following in Wellington's footsteps was to Harriette's door, as she relates in her notorious memoirs: 'His Lordship appeared the very essence of everything most *recherché* in superfine elegance. He was in fact all essence!'

Wellington, a more regular visitor, was concerned less with his brother's 'essence' and more with his reputation, ranting to their brother William:

> I wish that Wellesley was *castrated*; or that he would like other people attend to his business & perform too. It is lamentable to see Talents & character & advantages such as he possesses thrown away upon Whoring. Then the ruin to his Private Fortune which at his time of life is dereliction of his advantages; & the Injury which the Publick & his Party must suffer from this folly.

In their early careers Wellesley was the leader and statesman of the family. There had always been a strong bond between the brothers, indeed they worked so well as a team in public life in India and the Peninsular campaign that Cobbett decried their powerful influence as 'the arrogance of that damned infernal family'. That Wellington was not exaggerating is clear from other accounts. Lord Galloway, writing about Cabinet appointments, thought:

> Wellesley would do famously but he is *lost* by women. *Debt* and its disgrace approaches him fast, and *flogging*, I fear, will be necessary to him as a Minister, as they say it is to him *as a man*. He shewed us a very *brilliant specimen* of what he by *nature* was in the House of Lords upon the Spanish question, but like a meteor after a blaze disappeared.[10]

The knowledge of Wellesley's undisciplined character coupled with his own abiding love for Marianne stoked the Duke's distress. Mrs Arbuthnot tried to downplay this, writing that Marianne 'was some years ago supposed to be the Duke's mistress & with whom he was certainly very much in love. I have never seen the Duke more annoyed. His love for her has long been at an end, but he had a great interest for her.' But his lovelorn outpourings could not be stemmed. He was sure his brother, from feelings of jealousy, would never allow Marianne to associate with him. He believed that he had now lost her for ever. In his reply to Marianne's letter, he told her that 'a wise man would hold his tongue' rather than point out the fatal consequences of such a marriage but that he felt he must do so; he was hoping to prevent it and thereby save her from a fate far worse than widowhood.[11]

His warning came too late. Marianne could not believe that marriage would keep her away from him and, confused and dismayed by his response, had to dissemble to Wellesley about the letter, saying: '[T]hrough life he will always feel the greatest interest in your happiness and mine – did I not tell you he loved you?' The Duke managed to congratulate his brother on 13 October in a letter that revealed his deep love for Marianne:

I have long known Mrs Patterson intimately, and have felt the greatest regard and affection for her; but I don't think that I have been blinded by my partiality for her when I state that in disposition temper sense acquirements and manners she is equal if not superior to any Woman of any country with whom I have ever been in Society.

The proposal could have been coming from him; sadly for both of them it was never possible. 'The Duke's letter is most gratifying to me,' she told Wellesley, 'and I am the more pleased with it, as I am confident he thinks what he says, and that no one can have a better opinion of one another, or feel a more sincere friendship than he does for me.'[12]

Marianne knew very little about Wellesley's past or his finances, except what he imparted which, because she trusted the Duke and the Maryboroughs, she believed. There were many who could enlighten her. Lord Clare called the viceroy 'His Delinquency' and wrote of the marriage: 'Seriously she is an excellent well behaved woman & in my opinion very attractive but how she can bring herself to marry an old ruined battered rake is to me incomprehensible.' Eliza Godefroy described Wellesley as 'a libertine of shattered fortunes'. And Betsy, who heard from Lady Morgan that he was 'so much in debt that the plate on his table was hired; had his carriage once seized in the streets of Dublin', thought that, even 'with all these drawbacks to perfect happiness', the match gave the sisters 'a rank in Europe; and with Mr Carroll's money to keep it up, they may be considered the most fortunate in the United States of America'. None of them spoke out to her.[13]

Marianne was now unable to disentangle herself from such a charming rake. And, when he chose to be, there was no one as charismatic as Richard Wellesley. A slender man of distinguished looks with pure white hair and thick black eyebrows defining compelling blue eyes, he was highly intelligent, highly strung and highly sexed. He possessed 'a natural flair for leadership, great gifts and bounding ambition', and was liberal, courageous and far-seeing – he was an early advocate of both the Peninsular campaign, as a means of defeating Napoleon, and Catholic emancipation. Yet he was also vain, arbitrary, self-absorbed and arrogant.

Born in 1760, Richard was the eldest son of Garret Wesley, first Earl of Mornington, whose family had long been settled in Ireland, where they held estates in the counties of Meath and Kildare. His mother, from whom he and some of his six siblings inherited strength of will and violent temper, was Anne Hill Trevor, daughter of the first Viscount Dungannon, so that Wellesley was born into the Protestant Ascendancy. He was an outstanding classicist at Eton where his closest companion there and at Oxford was William Grenville (later Prime Minister). When Lord Mornington died in

1781, Wellesley, then aged twenty-one, assumed his father's large debts as well as his title and, as head of the family, responsibility for his brothers and sisters. He had to leave Oxford, sell Mornington House in Dublin and liquidate other Irish interests. He took his seat in the Irish House of Commons and was then elected to the English one in 1784 as member for Bere Alston in Devonshire, a borough so rotten that he was not required to attend the election. In 1786 he was appointed a junior Lord of the Treasury.

While travelling with Grenville on the Continent that year he fell passionately in love with Hyacinthe Roland, a beautiful French actress who bore him five children, Richard (1787), Anne (1788), Hyacinthe (1789), Gerald (1790) and Henry (1794), before they married in 1794. It was not a match that found favour with his family; Richard was their star, their fount of patronage who had already settled his brothers Arthur and Henry, and who was supposed to marry a rich aristocratic woman, not a mistress who could never be received in society. Then, at the age of thirty-seven, he was appointed Governor-General of India and, leaving Hyacinthe and children behind (at her choice), served there from 1798 until 1805, returning to England with an Irish marquessate, which he denounced as the 'gilt potato'.

His ego wounded, he clashed with Hyacinthe. Service as Special Ambassador to Spain in 1809–10 only prolonged their marital agony. On his return home he signed a deed of separation from her: 'Continue to live with vile and depraved characters who by flattering your extravagant vanity dominate you, dishonour you and ruin you' were some of her words when she left Apsley House that February. Wellesley became Foreign Secretary in 1810 and reached the peak of his political career when the Regent asked him to form a government in 1812 but he was not successful in uniting the different political factions and Liverpool came to power.

From then until 1821 Wellesley was out of office, deeply offended with Liverpool for refusing to serve under him. They were unfulfilled and embarrassed years. With creditors at the gates, a large part of his estates, some 13,000 acres, had to be sold at auction to meet his debts and he still owed £183,000. He sold Apsley House to his brother the Duke for £42,000 in 1817, the year after Hyacinthe Wellesley died. In 1821, having become reconciled to Liverpool, he was appointed Lord Lieutenant of Ireland; it was a last chance.[14]

Marianne's family, however, was fed another version, probably by Bess. As Mary Carroll Caton related:

He is sixty four in May – in excellent health & in the habit of taking powerful exercise & hunting &c – not looking more than forty-five –

very fair – soft blue eyes – intelligent – eloquent – gentle – the best bred
man in Europe! – the most amiable temper – & a feeling heart . . . a
blended likeness of Lady Bagot & the Duke of W. He has *never* been
divorced or separated from his Wife who was taken from the Opera when
very young to be his *Mistress*. She bore him three children (*all* now
married into high life and affluence), after she had ceased to have children her conduct had been so *exemplary* from the time she *lived* with
him, that his mother & his family persuaded him to marry her – he
never gambled & his difficulties have arisen from a magnificent, & liberal
temper fostered by living in situations that imperiously called for splendor
– & a long residence in the oriental state, which he was obliged to
support in India – he in fact was plundered by his servants.

The Carroll Catons did not understand how relatively poor Wellesley was.
They believed that their precious Marianne was making a grand match
with the Duke's brother. Her mother wryly wrote: 'I suppose now that
Marianne will not *want* her income, John Patterson will come to some
arrangement, such is the world.'[15]

Impulsive as her nuptial plans were, Marianne was, nonetheless, well
prepared when it came to protecting her financial interests. She had placed
her fortune and property in a trust before she left Maryland, appointing
McTavish and Roswell Colt, the Carroll broker and financial adviser, as
trustees, and giving them a power of attorney. Safeguarding her estate was
easier in widowhood because she was in law a *feme sole*. By marrying
Wellesley, however, Marianne would revert to being a *feme coverte* whereby
all her property would automatically pass into his ownership.

Colt, fortuitously, was in Liverpool and she asked him to travel over to
advise her in October, telling Wellesley: 'I hope you will talk over the
subject with him, & have it finished at once, that nothing may defer our
union.' The final settlement was all that she wished. It invested her property in her trustees to ensure she received all the income from it for her
sole use and benefit freed from the debts and engagements of Lord Wellesley.
It also gave her the power of disposal and of appointment of her heirs and
it ensured that she retained the same powers over any 'after-acquired property' inherited. She brought a portion, or capital sum, of £40,000 [£2.7
million] to the marriage and Lord Wellesley also undertook to provide
£40,000; thus from a total marriage settlement of £80,000, half would be
settled in trust for her and invested at 4½ per cent interest in the government funds to yield an income of £1,800 [£125,000] a year, which she could
choose to receive either as an annuity or as a pension on his death, and
half would be invested to provide portions for any children of the marriage.
She would not be dependent upon her husband and had no need to be

concerned with his arrangements; nor for his part would he have welcomed it. With the settlements satisfactorily negotiated, the business aspect of their marriage was completed.[16]

There was, though, a serious political dimension. Lord Wellesley had notified the Prime Minister and the King on 9 October of his intention to marry 'a person, in every respect worthy of my heart & hand & possessed of every excellent & amiable quality'. Marianne had already told Wellesley that: 'The only person I have really felt any anxiety about has been Lord Liverpool's opinion, as he might raise some objection to the King.' He had, indeed, immediately sent a copy of Wellesley's letter to the King and, writing on 11 October to his Home Secretary Robert Peel, he described the marriage of his Lord Lieutenant as a 'very strange and awkward event'. Marianne's political antennae were to prove just as sensitive as the Prime Minister's, and with reason.

The talk of the castle and Dublin society that autumn had one refrain and one only: 'the Lord Lieutenant, they say, is going to be married . . . the Lady is Mrs Patterson who is visiting here . . .' and then, the four-word *coup de grâce*: 'she is *a Catholic*'. The most controversial domestic political issue, the one that posed the greatest threat to the stability of government throughout Liverpool's long premiership, was the question of Catholic emancipation. This was why Liverpool could only write at first of Marianne's marriage: 'The most awkward circumstance in this connection is, that the lady is a Roman Catholic, and I need not add, that under the circumstances in which he [Lord Wellesley] is placed at present, this may add to all the other embarrassments connected with the Catholic question.'[17]

After the Act of Union between Britain and Ireland in 1801, Pitt's proposal to grant Catholics equal political rights – a Catholic had no right to sit in Parliament or to hold any official office, for instance – had foundered upon the rocks of royal and Protestant opposition. George III was persuaded it would breach his coronation oath to uphold the rights and privileges of the Church of England, and staunch Protestant MPs believed that it would divide the Anglican Church from the state. Thereafter, the Catholic question had remained a running sore. Religious exclusion polluted every aspect of ordinary Irish life with a great miasma of suspicion and fear 'mixed up with everything we eat or drink or say or think' as a correspondent of Peel's wrote.

While opponents of emancipation thought the suffering of the Irish should first be alleviated by improved living conditions, Irish Catholics felt that the oppression and injustice of their unequal treatment should first be removed. When Wellesley became Lord Lieutenant in 1822, Catholics were still excluded from the political process and from professional advancement, from being buried by their own priests in cemeteries and from being able to maintain their own clergy (ministering to six million Catholics), and being forced to pay tithes to a Protestant clergy (ministering to 800,000 Protestants) when the poorest of them could not pay their rents and faced eviction and starvation. Creevey discovered that the Catholic priest in a large Kilkenny parish received £70 a year whereas the Protestant parson received £500 a year for ministering to two Ascendancy families, the only Protestants in the parish.[18]

Despite numerous parliamentary committees and bills, the conditions of the Irish Catholics remained unchanged. Desperate with frustration and poverty, they resorted to forming secret societies and to violence. Dublin Castle correspondence books are full of reports from local magistrates about disorder and unrest in the countryside. It is no wonder that, as accounts reached America through the priesthood grapevine, Mary Carroll Caton wanted her daughters to leave such 'a dangerous country' where discrimination and retaliation formed part of daily existence, and people took the law into their own hands.

Daniel O'Connell, a skilled barrister precluded from sitting on the bench and holding senior legal office by his religion, found the legal loopholes by which to challenge minority Protestant rule. In 1823 O'Connell and Richard Lalor Shiel, a barrister and dramatist, founded the Catholic Association, and O'Connell thereafter dominated the movement for Irish Catholic rights, his oratory and passion capturing the hearts and minds of the Irish priesthood and peasantry. Caroline Fox, Lord Holland's sister, told the story of a group of travellers passing a large stone post belonging to the post office and inscribed GPO. To an enquiry about its meaning, an Irishman immediately answered: 'God Preserve O'Connell.'[19]

Political agitation had escalated in 1825 after Parliament banned the Catholic Association, and the Catholic Relief Bill wound its way through Parliament but was thrown out by the Lords. 'We must begin again', said Daniel O'Connell. By the time Marianne and Bess arrived in Ireland that July, he had found a fresh loophole and formed the New Catholic Association. The news of Marianne's marriage heartened Catholics in Ireland. A Catholic at the Irish court of King George, as consort of the Lord Lieutenant, was an extraordinary prospect; the expectations of a downtrodden race were suddenly vested in the ethereal figure of an American woman.

'The only thing talked of is the marriage of Lord Wellesley with Mrs Patterson who is the widow of the brother of the lady who married Jerome Bonaparte', Daniel O'Connell reported to his wife that October. 'She is a Catholic and a strict one.' He told her that Marianne had dined with the former Attorney-General for Ireland, the Protestant champion William Saurin, who had been removed from office by

Wellesley. According to O'Connell, someone at the dinner mentioned Catholic politics whereupon Saurin 'at once damned the Pope and Popery to the lowest pit of Hell'. Marianne 'said nothing at the time, but before dinner was quite over she took occasion to mention her being a Catholic just as a matter of course. You may judge of Saurin's confusion.' The next day, however, Saurin sent her a long apology, which O'Connell was sure she disregarded but which it is far more likely she politely acknowledged.[20]

The Irish government at Dublin Castle operated what Lady Gregory called a sandwich system of government whereby if the Lord Lieutenant was a 'Catholic', i.e. pro-Catholic emancipation, as Lord Wellesley had always been, then the Chief Secretary must be a 'Protestant' i.e. anti-Catholic emancipation, as Henry Goulburn was. 'What can exceed the ridicule of this systematically coupling together a friend and an enemy to toleration,' asked Lord Grenville, 'but certainly never before introduced into politics as fixed and fundamental systems for the conduct of the most difficult and dangerous crisis of a country.' It was, however, one of the many balancing acts of Liverpool's long years of government.

Goulburn found the Lord Lieutenant tiresome enough at the best of times but Wellesley acting 'like a true lover' and neglecting ordinary business to plan a wedding was a development only sent to try him further. 'The thing is absurd enough in itself – Her being Roman Catholic & a bigotted one will prove a serious inconvenience here', he told Peel, also a 'Protestant'; they feared the Lord Lieutenant would come under papist petticoat influence. 'If Mrs P shall connect herself with R.C. Politics she will do infinite mischief', contended Peel. To the staunch Protestant castle officials, the advent of a Catholic Lady Lieutenant brought the spectre of sedition into the heart of government. They could only view Marianne, whatever her personal qualities, with deepest suspicion.[21]

The King, however, could only view her with delight. He was quick to remind Lord Maryborough that it had been at Savile Row that he had first met Marianne and 'he had been then struck with her appearance, and manner, which he thought particularly distinguished'. The King waxed lyrical about her to everyone, telling Joseph Jekyll that she was 'one of the most sensible and highly bred women he ever conversed with'. Such praises did not necessarily signify his sanction of the marriage for he was infuriatingly capricious, as Wellesley knew. Without regal sanction they could not marry; with it they were better equipped to overcome objections. Liverpool's opposition was purely on a political level; on a personal one he, too, thought Marianne would be good for Wellesley, not only would she 'draw him forth from those secluded habits which are wholly incompatible with his public character, and are in many ways discreditable to him' but 'she will govern him better than he will govern himself'. The King, amused by this extraordinary romance, disregarded his ministers and gave Wellesley his approval. The couple made plans to marry before the end of the month.[22]

25

The Lady Lieutenant

'I learn that His Excellency is desperately in love and regularly writes three times a day to his inamorata', Goulburn reported to Peel on 16 October 1825. Much of the smooth running of Irish affairs would depend, they decided, upon Marianne's behaviour. 'She is clever & well informed, a little too much so as to be agreeable', but would, nonetheless, Goulburn reasoned, make a tolerable Lady Lieutenant.[1]

Dining in Norfolk at three o'clock on Saturday 29 October, Thomas Coke proposed a toast to Marianne. He wept, Louisa reported, and said there was not a man on earth deserving *such a treasure*. In Ireland, Marianne and Bess, escorted by Colonel Shawe and Edward Johnston drove to Viceregal Lodge in Phoenix Park. After they dined with Lord Wellesley and the household and officers of state, the marriage ceremony was performed at eight o'clock by the Lord Primate Beresford, Archbishop of Armagh. Marianne wore a fine India muslin and white satin dress, elegantly worked in gros cotton and lace and made in Paris, and a splendid point lace veil given to her by her mother. Roswell Colt, the only outsider present, wrote to the Catons that Marianne 'never looked more beautiful'. After the ceremony the new Lady Wellesley withdrew with her lord, favours were distributed and the company dispersed.[2]

As the guests were passing out of the Park they met one of His Excellency's private carriages driving the Most Rev. Dr Murray, the Catholic Archbishop of Dublin, to the second ceremony. He married Marianne and Wellesley according to the rites of the Catholic Church in the presence of Bess, the Blakes, Dr Hunter and Colonel Shawe. It was a very short and simple service after which the small wedding party dined and the bridal couple retired. Almost immediately 'Protestant' Mrs Arbuthnot was writing: 'Lord Wellesley is married; he had a most extraordinary set of low people present at the ceremony, which does not look as if his lady had cured him of his love of inferiors. He had the *Catholic Archbishop of Dublin* to perform the ceremony, which I think a scandal as his assuming that title is contrary to law.' The Duke even asked Peel: 'Is not the appearance of the Roman Catholic archbishop *in pontificalibus*

contrary to law? It is at all events very improper, considering what the
King determined on that subject.' ³

Marianne had barely been married a week before she had to tiptoe
around her religion. It became all the more constraining after an outburst
from the King. He had heard that there had been a celebration of *Mass*
at Viceregal Lodge on the Sunday following the wedding. 'That house is
as much my palace as the one in which I am,' he fumed from Windsor,
'and in my Palace, Mass shall not be said; Upon this I positively insist.'
He also objected to Lady Wellesley's donation to a Roman Catholic chapel
after her marriage.

Goulburn was instructed to investigate. He reported back to Peel that
the donation was a fabrication. In the case of the Mass, he had ascertained
that Lady Wellesley had debated whether she should attend Mass publicly
in Dublin. There was a precedent as Lady Buckingham had worshipped at
the Liffey Street Chapel, her carriage waiting for her at the door. The political climate had since deteriorated and, Goulburn stressed, if Lady Wellesley
attended a regular chapel it would give rise to worse than scandal; it might
precipitate rebellion.

Marianne, as it happened, always travelled with a box containing a
crucifix and missal. She had already suggested that she could celebrate Mass
in her private rooms, Henny would arrange the crucifix and, rather than
use an Irishman, she would have her own American priest. He had therefore come on that Sunday in a hackney cab to the lodge to celebrate Mass
in her room, which only she, Bess and Henny attended. Goulburn could
thus assure Peel that, from what he could judge, Lady Wellesley would will-
ingly adopt any course to avoid controversy and her tactful compromise
was by far the best solution.⁴

As she settled into her new roles of wife and Her Excellency, she told
her mother that she prayed and read for guidance more than she had ever
done before; her elevated status would not make her less of a Christian but
would enlarge her sphere of usefulness as she hoped to alleviate some of
the poverty and misery in Dublin. She soon won over the castle old guard;
William Plunket, the Attorney-General, told Canning she possessed 'a
considerable sheen of prudence & good sense'; Colonel Merrick Shawe
became a firm friend, describing her as an 'admirable Vice-Queen – and,
what is still better, a Most Excellent woman'. Best of all was her effect
upon the spirits of His Excellency. In the first month of marriage the
Wellesleys were 'very happy', Marianne owning that 'Ld Wellesley was
certainly the *most agreeable* man in the world – all acknowledge his talents
& *perfect politeness*'.

There was a busy programme of formal entertainments with dinners
of twenty to thirty people every night at the Lodge. George Montgomery

gave his cousin an account of one. Arriving at seven o'clock, they were ushered by sundry ADCs into the drawing room, where after waiting at least half an hour 'the Royal approach was announced when in walked His Excellency in ribbons, stars, Diamonds and a *good deal of Bronze* leading in the Mss who I think very handsome, plainly dressed, and therefore a great contrast to my lord. They were *very gracious* spoke to every body and at dinner sat next to each other.' Montgomery was struck by Marianne's profound curtsy to His Excellency, which the ladies copied, in preference to the usual perfunctory bob; at about eleven o'clock 'the 2 Royalties said kind things to all, and left us to our fate, and our Carriages'.[5]

In early January 1826 Marianne held her first Drawing Room at the Castle when society had the opportunity of judging the new Lady Lieutenant. One of the first with praise was Lady Morgan, who had never before been able to attend a castle event, previously open only to Protestants. She wrote how a Catholic by law had been prohibited from crossing the castle yard and 'until Ld Wellesley's time the Castle parties only admitted the orange party – many of those worthies would not meet me – & for O'Connell they would have deemed the roof not safe that afforded him a friend'. So it was with exultation that she enthused to Betsy on 13 January 1826: 'I was *there* last Monday. It was the *first presentation* to the new *Vice Reine*. The impression was highly favourable – wonderful considering that she stood in a circle of *orange protestants*.' Marianne was 'easy, graceful & just enough of *dignity* for the station, with no smiling familiarities as I called or rather *reconciled* Mrs P with Lady W'.

Marianne wore a gown of white satin with a tulle overdress richly worked in gold, with a long train of scarlet Irish tabinet also richly worked in a deep border of gold embroidered in shamrocks of green, purple and gold. She had ensured that her clothes were of Irish cloth and made in Ireland, a policy that gave work locally and also brought in orders from those who admired her gowns. It was a small but significant start to her career as Lady Lieutenant. Lord Wellesley was 'enchanted by the manner in which she acquitted herself – & so were all the guests', Bess reported. 'Marianne looks as humble & placid in her new state as when plain Mrs P. She *understands* that a great part of the adulation she receives is to her *station*.' Lady Morgan was struck by the contrasting symbolism of Marianne's new position. At the St Patrick's Day ball at the castle, for instance, 'when the vice-regal procession marched up the great Hall amidst hundreds of full dressed *royal loyal* Protestant-ascendancy orangemen & women, & when at the end of a string of pages, aid-decamps [sic], battleaxes &c &c, the representative of Majesty led up a papist – american – *Republican* . . . we are now all toleration and conciliation – & *botheration*' – for this, after all, was Ireland; it also proved to be a prescient description of the state of Marianne's marriage.[6]

On Goulburn's return from England in early January he had found, he wrote to Peel, that 'all the rumours which had prevailed as to domestic differences in the Lord Lieutenant's family were not by any means exaggerated'. In public Marianne played the part of Lady Lieutenant to perfection. In private she was being bullied and made wretched; she did not think she could bear to remain in Ireland with Wellesley. In distress, she sent a *cri de coeur* to the Duke, divulging that 'all the evils he had predicted had come upon her even to a greater degree than he expected'. She was miserable, 'very unhappy and only anxious to *die*'.

The chief source of Marianne's botheration was the cuckoo in her marital nest, one Edward Johnston. She had received 'a repetition of insults' from him, he had obstructed her wishes and abused her over trifles ever since her marriage; in short he had treated her in a manner no gentleman would condone: yet her own husband appeared oblivious. Her problem was made more intractable by Johnston's position: he was not only Wellesley's private secretary but also claimed to be his son.[7]

Johnston's origins are dimmed by the shadow of illegitimacy. There is some connection with Devonshire, where his mother lived and which Wellesley represented, and with Sir William Knighton, who began as a Plymouth *accoucheur* and, through Wellesley, became the Prince Regent's physician, Keeper of the Privy Purse and was a conduit to the royal ear. Johnston first appears as 'le J' whom Hyacinthe Wellesley dismissed as part of the 'seraglio' kept by Wellesley. After her death, a furious Lord Wellesley broke off communications with their children because they would not hand over to him the legacies she had carefully left to them. Young Richard wrote to Gerald out in India that their father had 'taken a young man to live with him as his Secretary, whom he takes pains to declare his natural son'. Relations were not improved when the Duke held a family dinner to reconcile Wellesley with his children and the uninvited Johnston appeared, to the Duke's evident annoyance. Johnston, seeing an opportunity for advancement, had no doubt plagued Wellesley to take him. The Duke had even cautioned Wellesley *not* to take Johnston to Ireland – advice unheeded.[8]

This was the young man who was making Marianne's married life unbearable. He had been in England when Wellesley was wooing her and had returned just before her marriage. Determined not to forfeit his financial lifeline and suspicious of the new marchioness in case she weakened his influence, the egregious Johnston sought any occasion both to ridicule her and to manipulate Wellesley so as to drive a wedge between them. On one occasion, she told the Duke, Johnston manufactured a quarrel about her retiring ill to bed 'without *wishing him goodnight!*' properly.

Others at the castle could not abide Johnston's 'presumption and want of judgment'; nor could they fathom his hold over Wellesley in place of 'a beautiful refined wife' with a sweet disposition. 'The torment that this fellow is to me is not to be described', Goulburn moaned to Peel. Johnston was at the head of a small group of amusing but disreputable young spongers – the 'Parasites' or the 'Banditti' as the Duke called them – surrounding Wellesley. Johnston's unorthodox meddling caused Peel to deplore 'such a worthless coxcomb as Mr Johnston exercising an influence over Irish affairs'.[9]

Johnston's malevolent interference took on a greater significance when, in the tense political situation, it could be the means of destabilising the authority of the Crown. Marianne now found that her marital problems were being discussed at the highest levels of British government after Goulburn asked for adjudication at ministerial level and gave Peel a 'terrible account of the feuds in Lord Wellesley's family'. As Peel told his wife, on 6 January, 'a separation was very nearly taking place between Lord and Lady W. on account of Johnston; that Johnston after a very severe struggle has been quite triumphant; that Lady W. is very much to be pitied, and everything is in sad confusion, their family affairs being the exclusive topic of conversation in Dublin.'

One way to avert the scandal suggested to the Prime Minister by Peel and the Duke would be to keep Johnston in London at his sinecure post at the Board of Stamps. Liverpool, as placatory as ever, hesitated from raising the issue directly with Wellesley 'out of delicacy'. The outcome of these initial high-level consultations was that Johnston, who could have been as easily dislodged from the castle as a limpet from a rock, remained clinging onto Their Excellencies' household.[10]

It took Louisa to make sense of this extraordinary situation and help Marianne. Unlike the three Cabinet ministers, Louisa felt no circumspection about interceding in the Wellesley household. Bess, busy trying to comfort their eldest sister, was still vacillating over the best course to take. Irresolution had never been one of Louisa's characteristics; she had no compunction about tackling anyone who threatened Marianne's happiness for, as she would tell Lord Liverpool that summer, 'though she is my Sister, I must gratify my heart by saying never were more purity, integrity, piety, gentleness and kindness united in woman'.

Although Louisa had yet to meet her new brother-in-law, she knew far more about the Wellesley family than her sisters; partly as a result of the Wellingtons and partly because she could be privy to gossip withheld from unmarried Bess. When it came to love, sex and money, the Regency was an age of profligate scandal; elopements, adulteries, debts, 'crim cons' and divorces provided amusement for spectators and often misery for participants. And no family conformed to the mores of the age more strictly than the Wellesleys. Louisa knew what had happened to Lady Charlotte Wellesley, wife of Henry Wellesley, the youngest brother, when she eloped with Lord Paget (later Marquess of Anglesey), the distinguished cavalry officer. Wellesley and Lady Paget divorced their spouses and Lady Paget married the Duke of Argyll. 'What a complication of infamy & vice!' the Duchess of Wellington exclaimed, as Lady Charlotte the new Lady Paget was ruined and forced to live a secluded life. Another Wellesley wife, Lady Emily, had married the fourth brother, the Revd Doctor Gerald Wellesley, and then, betrayed by Lord Anglesey, left him for a little-known short dalliance. Thereafter, as an estranged wife, she was consigned to an existence in the shadows while her husband was denied a vacant bishopric on moral grounds.

Louisa had also learned that, contrary to what her family in America had been told, Lord Wellesley *had been separated* from his first wife and had treated her and their children badly. She had met their elder daughter Anne who possessed 'a flirtatious nature and a French gaiety' as well as her father's violent temper but had been saddled with Sir William Abdy, a rich, dull husband. One day she decided to change her life and, using her dog as the pretext, she stepped out of her town house, tripped along Hill Street to the corner at Park Lane, climbed into a smart gig and eloped with its occupant Lord Charles Cavendish Bentinck. After being divorced Anne returned from France to marry him on 23 July 1816, when she produced 'the *damning* evidence of Sir William's impotence, she was within 3 weeks of her confinement', her brother wrote. She was never again received in society but she would become the great-grandmother of the late Queen Elizabeth the Queen Mother.[11]

Primed about the irreparable damage to a woman's virtuous reputation if she left her husband, Louisa was clear about the options available to Marianne; options, which the Duke affirmed, were severely limited. 'Dearest Louisa', he wrote on 1 January 1826 admitting that he felt the greatest difficulty over what to do about Marianne for, much as he would always help and protect her, there was only one course open to her as a virtuous wife. While he feared that she would not be able to endure her humiliating position for more than another year, he urged that she do so for 'the first of all worldly Duties for a Wife and her connections is to endeavour to raise her husband and at all events not to lower him in the eyes of the World'. He was quite certain 'there is no husband in existence who would resent a forgetfulness or omission of this duty so much as that husband under discussion'. Marianne must stay in Ireland and try to save her marriage. He entreated Louisa, indeed all the sisters, 'neither to write nor speak of what you see and hear in Ireland. You will only make bad insupportable.'

His advice about Johnston was even more pessimistic:

I certainly hoped for the sake of your sister but more for that of Lord W that she would have been able to banish from His Presence for ever all the Parasites. I know how uncomfortable her life must be, that which is to her a want is good company. I don't mean that of Dandies, but that of clever, sensible men. No man of sense will nor can go to a house in possession of such a Banditti as that which surrounds Lord W.

If Marianne had known about them, she could have made their removal a condition of marriage but an attempt now 'would fix their Empire over him and destroy her'. To retain her respectability and not injure her husband, she 'must make up her Mind to do the best she can' with all their support.[12]

When Louisa crossed the Irish Sea she knew that to antagonise Wellesley and the Parasites would hinder her own ability to improve the situation. However forewarned she was about 'his weaknesses', as she called them to Lord Liverpool, she was entirely unprepared for the onrush of Wellesley's boyish charm with which he proceeded to disarm her. Wellesley, the eternal brilliant adolescent who could infuriate with foolishness one moment and nurse with tenderness the next, was immensely lovable: 'the very *sort* of man, that a woman could adore' Bess had written to their mother. She also told her that 'Louisa was *charmed* by the respect & kind attention paid her by her new Brother – & that they were all as happy as possible'.

The three sisters had decided to say nothing for the moment about Marianne's problems in their letters home. Bess wrote instead of the formality and grandeur of castle life. When relating this, their mother wrote *private* on her letter 'as you know how things get *distorted*'. In the American Republic where 'exterior conduct mirrored inner virtue', such regal trappings and etiquette would be perceived as corrupting influences on her virtuous republican daughters.

When her grandfather wrote to Marianne: 'The homage & deference paid to rank, not founded on the merits & esteem of the person to whom it is paid, and all the frippery & parade of high life never did or ever will reach & satisfy the heart', he was reminding her of the obligations of a good republican wife. And in their hearts the sisters remained true to the ideals of the American Republic, Marianne speaking 'of her pride in being an American'. Their mother heard that Marianne was 'a *great favourite* in Dublin' though 'people are surprised that a woman not born in your station can acquit herself so admirably'.[13]

She told Marianne in March of reports reaching them that 'Lady Hervey is very much admired *and* thought extremely beautiful', adding: 'But why does not the lazy Lady Hervey write herself and tell me the thousand and one tales that we should be too happy to hear.' Louisa, however, felt they would be anything but happy to hear of the strain Marianne lived under and of her deteriorating health. It was all the more puzzling because Wellesley's love for Marianne was undoubted. He wrote love poems to her and respected her opinion as he talked through his political problems. Alone with her and her sisters, he was quite the tender lover, writing of her looking 'more wondrous than ever, and is adored, impossible to describe how much'.[14]

In spite of her growing affection for Wellesley with whom, she told Lord Liverpool, 'it is impossible to live without loving him', it did not take Louisa long to have the measure of the Johnston problem. She decided to act contrary to the Duke's advice and appeal to Liverpool, though she knew better than to request Johnston's removal; it would only make Wellesley suspicious and obdurate. She wrote to Lord Liverpool as the senior member of her married family, who would oblige her with an interest and who would like to hear about castle affairs as they affected her and her sisters' comfort.

Thus, in voicing her concern about Marianne's poor health, she mentioned Johnston's contributory role and spoke of her plan to remove Marianne from Ireland during at least part of the time that Johnston was there. Marianne could return with her to England to take the waters, her health providing acceptable grounds for her absence. Louisa undertook to speak to Wellesley. Her sisters could return to Dublin shortly before Johnston had to leave for duty in London so that, she reasoned, further rows would be avoided.

She also discussed Johnston's unfathomable hold over Wellesley.

When he [Johnston] fears he has gone too far, he becomes all penitence and grief, and if that does not do, *falls ill* that the fear of losing him may revive Lord W's affection – he is always alluding to the misfortune of his birth, and represents himself to Lord W *as one* who lives upon his favour, and who *must sink* the moment he abandons him. It is by these acts, and by unblushing falsehood, that he extricates himself from all the scrapes he gets into and holds Lord W in bondage.[15]

Liverpool's response was all that Louisa could desire. He was not just generous in his sympathy for Marianne but he removed Johnston from the

Board of Stamps and placed him in another office that demanded more regular hours. Johnston's 'scrapes' had come to concern the Prime Minister. Johnston might have persuaded Wellesley that '*his extortions* are only the extravagance natural to youth' but others were more specific: he was accused of accepting bribes to procure office and honours. Frederick Lamb warned the Duke to be 'upon his guard about Johnson, there being no doubt that He took large sums of money in Ireland for his influence, and that he must be kept away from Ld W'. He also took large sums from Wellesley who could ill-afford to lose them.

Even worse, Liverpool was being urged by other ministers to recall Wellesley owing to Johnston's behaviour. Liverpool therefore intimated to Louisa that Wellesley might have to move to another post. Replying from Stratfield Saye on 10 August 1826, she was quick to emphasise the necessity of Wellesley retaining his Lord-Lieutenancy for financial reasons. She pointed out that Marianne took nothing from him financially and even put part of her own money to defray a Lady Lieutenant's expenses which, she owned, were considerable.[16]

Part of Johnston's hostility towards Marianne might have stemmed from pique at being unable to tap into her fortune; most nineteenth-century Englishmen would agree that it should belong to her husband (and thus be available to Johnston). Young William Wellesley-Pole, next Lord Maryborough, provided a notorious case of male plunder. His wife, Catherine Tylney-Long, 'the richest female commoner in England', had possessed estates worth £30,000 a year and £200,000 [£10 million] in the (Government stock) funds on their marriage. It took 'Wicked William' a mere ten years to necessitate a sudden removal to France to escape creditors and, after her death in September 1825, he tried to gain his children and their inheritance by threatening to murder their guardian the Duke 'as a notorious adulterer: everyone knew of his intrigues with his sister-in-law Lady Wellesley'.[17]

As Marianne faced up to the consequences of her impulsive marriage she realised now that she could never leave her husband without causing disgrace. Besides, he was often the most attentive companion and lover. 'Be assured my beloved Life that you are ever in my heart & soul & mind', reads one of his notes; at his worst he expected her to bend to his will and she could never rely upon him for anything. Louisa convinced her that eventually she would dislodge the Banditti. In the meantime she embarked upon the first of the short separations from him, so vital to her health and to the continuation of what was a semi-detached, mostly unhappy marriage.[18]

When she left Dublin with Bess in April 1827 to stay with the Duke at Apsley House, her stepson Gerald Wellesley read it was 'owing to a misunderstanding between her & her husband in consequence of the intrusion of some one who, from the way it is mentioned, I suppose to be understood as Mr Johnston'. Joseph Jekyll also saw through Louisa's plan, telling his sister-in-law: 'Under the pretext of resorting for health to the waters of Leamington, the Lady-Lieutenant of Ireland is said to be separating herself from her Lord.'

Throughout these years of separation portraits formed an important link in the chain of familial affection, a means by which they could feel closer to each other. Marianne had commissioned portraits of herself and Wellesley from Lawrence with the idea of sending copies to her family. In London she sat for her portrait, which was never finished, while Wellesley's was never started. Lawrence had painted him before, in 1811 and 1812–13, the diarist Farington recording how: 'Lawrence has noticed when His Lordship sat to him for His Portrait, that his *Lips* were painted.' Marianne knew one of these portraits for it hung at Dublin Castle, though it no longer belonged to Wellesley; he had long since acquiesced to Johnston's pleas and given it to him. She would be thwarted twice in her desire to buy it back. Johnston refused her offers though she feared he 'would no doubt sell it the first time he wanted money'. Johnston, according to Edward Littleton, later did exactly that, 'having through abuse of Lord W's attachment and confidence pillaged him of all he could obtain from him, at length quarrelled with him about money matters' and sold it. On learning it was in a dealer's shop, the Wellesleys decided to offer £200 for it, only to learn it had already been bought; Marianne's equanimity was ruffled for, typically, 'Wellesley was so pleased at M[ontgomery]'s conduct in giving his last shilling to obtain the picture that he would not take it from him'. Littleton said, 'I would myself have given 500 guineas for it.' Marianne consoled herself by having a copy done for her grandfather.[19]

At the same time, Carroll of Carrollton commissioned a portrait of himself from Sully for her and Wellesley. Thomas Sully, an Englishman but brought up in South Carolina, dominated the field of American portraiture and had already produced a superb portrait of Marianne's aunt Carroll. It was not until January 1828 that Sully sent the 'Wellesley' portrait to be varnished in Lawrence's studio where Marianne was still intermittently sitting for her second portrait.

The 'Wellesley' portrait with its preliminary work, sketches and studies would provide the basis of the famous portrait commissioned in 1834 by the State of Maryland. This still hangs in the State House in Annapolis and is considered by curator Ann Townsend to be 'one of the most magnificent state portraits in American art – moving and eloquently expressive of the understated elegance which Carroll himself would have approved'. Marianne, however, was looking for a true likeness of the grandfather she might never again hug. He reminded her of his advanced age: 'You write

Sully's portrait fails in expression of my countenance, which, you fancy, spoke the idea of the mind before words gave it utterance; that look which partial friends thought intelligent and expressive, has lost whatever lustre it once might have had.'[20]

At nearly ninety, though healthy and sprightly, he was feeling aged. Three years had elapsed since he had last embraced Marianne, and eleven for Bess and Louisa. 'I never cross, my dear Mary[e] your portrait by Sir Thomas Lawrence, without thinking it represents one I shall never see again,' he lamented. Their mother, though, lived in hope of being reunited with them. Her friends declared her life was now 'one of *imagination*, that I live in expectation from Packet to Packet' and, she admitted, 'it is very true my heart is *too* much absorbed by you my children, & I am in a constant state of anxious solicitude', now heightened by reports in the press of a Wellesley separation.

While her grandfather assured Marianne on 15 May 1827 that 'the ridiculous paragraphs, perhaps malicious, give us not a moment's uneasiness – we know you too well & the character of the Marquis', her mother had already discerned something was amiss. Constrained by the post, she tried to comfort her beloved Marianne and, ardently as she wished to take her daughter 'to shelter in the fond bosom of your devoted Mother', she could not leave her elderly father who, at the very mention of her undertaking the transatlantic journey, paled and became unduly agitated at the thought of being without her for at least a year, during which time he might die.[21]

Uncertain Futures

Emily was now gradually growing into Marianne's role of plantation mistress and hostess for their aged grandfather. When her cousin young Charles Carroll married Mary Digges Lee in October 1825 Emily oversaw the week-long nuptial festivities at the Manor. Although young Charles 'the Heir Apparent' (as Mac called him) was ready to take over the management of the Carroll estates, his grandfather retained control with the help of a bevy of agents, overseers, legal and financial advisers, and relied upon the services of Caton and McTavish to conduct daily business. Nor did the newly married couple assume any responsibilities for the running of his houses; he looked instead to Mary Carroll Caton and Emily for his domestic happiness.

Emily was kept even busier the following autumn of 1826 when Mac severely sprained his arm in a riding accident and needed her help with everything. She organised a large house party on 12 September for her grandfather's 89th birthday. Two days later Mary Lee Carroll gave birth to a baby girl there, while a week later the little girl of Emily's cousin Elizabeth Carroll Tucker fell ill and died the following morning. As Mac recorded, 'what with children coming into the world and children going out of it, bilious fevers, dinners & visitors, poor Mrs Mac in her capacity of Lady of the House was fagged to death'.

This was hardly surprising for Emily was herself due to be confined in early November. In the eight years since their son Carroll's birth, she had endured several miscarriages and become 'delicate'. Her excellent health throughout this pregnancy delighted the family and Lord Wellesley wrote that he would be happy to stand sponsor. They left the Manor for Baltimore earlier than usual that year and, on the afternoon of 21 November, Mac could proudly announce 'little *Mary Wellesley* popped into this breathing world about two Hours since. Both mother and daughter are doing well.'[1]

Mary (she would soon be called May within the family) was a thriving and endearing baby. 'Dear little Mary Wellesley is growing daily more engaging', her great-grandfather acknowledged to her aunt Marianne almost a year later. 'I leave her mother and grandmother to describe her little winning tricks; they can do it better than I can.' Carroll, aged nine, was long since a schoolboy; his great-grandfather thought him 'strong & active, indeed he is a fine boy, and dear to us all'. Their absent aunts, hungry for every morsel of intelligence, urged Emily to send likenesses of them in the diplomatic bag and she obliged them with some drawings.

Emily also commissioned a portrait of Mac from the American artist Charles Bird King, who had already painted her grandfather. King also copied one of the replicas of Lawrence's portrait of Wellesley, sent in the diplomatic bag from London to Washington City. Both portraits were delivered to the McTavish town house in South Street, Baltimore but whereas Wellesley's was judged excellent, Mac's was not and Emily 'took it into her head to be terribly out of humour' with his picture, which she had hoped would raise his spirits.[2]

McTavish was undergoing a trying time. The family firm McGillivrays was causing concern. In 1825, Simon McGillivray had arrived in Montreal to find it in fiscal chaos and the resident partner Thain in a state of mental collapse. Declaring that no one else could understand the books, Thain locked the door of his office, took the key and sailed for Britain where he was confined in a Scottish asylum for the insane. Such unusual corporate behaviour was more than offset by the McGillivrays' ample resources, so that McTavish and Carroll of Carrollton happily increased their shareholding in the firm in early December.

Then came a letter from London written in October by 'Bear' Ellice, English politician and NWC partner, announcing not only the sudden death of William McGillivray but also the dire state of the markets: London was gearing itself for the December 1825 financial crash, of which Wellington later recalled, 'had it not been for most extraordinary exertions – above all on the part of old Rothschild – the Bank [of England] must have stopped payment'. Many banks and trading firms in England and America failed and, in a system of unlimited liability, investors were plunged from riches to penury overnight. 'I have had no spirits to write', McTavish confessed to George Jackson on 12 January 1826. He had learned of McGillivrays' bankruptcy. His cousin Simon concluded that, with the plunging value of his £100,000 [£7.2 million] personal fortune and his £100,000 HBC stock pledged to pay the firm's debts, 'it was useless to put off the evil day'. By the summer they knew the worst: McTavish had sustained severe losses and his fortune was ruined, though he retained HBC stock and land in Montreal. His cousin was left penniless. A settlement with creditors for 10 shillings in the pound was only made possible by a contribution from 'Bear' Ellice. Thus rose and fell in two generations the magnificent McTavish fur venture.[3]

It was now all the more important for Emily that Mac had paid occupation in Maryland. His quarterly salary of £877–7s–7d [£63,500] 'came most opportunely' that February from the British Foreign Office. McTavish's salaried appointment as an Arbitrator had arisen through the good offices of 'Bear' Ellice who, without office, held a remarkable sway over transatlantic affairs. Emily Eden never could see why: '"The Bear says the country does not like it"; "the Bear thinks Lord Grey a fool" &c &c.' And the Bear had determined that Mac should belong to the Joint Anglo-American Commission appointed in 1821 to settle all Anglo-American claims relating to property, including slaves, damaged in the 1812 War. He worked with his old friend George Jackson, the British Commissioner, and two American colleagues.[4]

Emily asked her sisters about finding another Foreign Office post in America; McTavish was a British citizen, as by marriage was Emily. Marianne, who now understood the patronage system, hoped to obtain one through Wellesley, reassuring Emily in August 1826 that no one else's demands would be allowed 'to clash with Mac's Interests' and that he 'could rest quite secure on that point'. Access to patronage was never secure, though, and soon Wellesley's future was as uncertain as McTavish's. Marianne's letter of 12 May 1827 received in Baltimore on 5 July reflected this, being 'of rather a sombre tone'.[5]

Uncertainty, about their future and their marriage, was not the only dispiriting aspect of Marianne's life in Ireland. Her grandfather had sent an extract about her from a sketch of his life written by John Latrobe, which stated:

> it is a singular circumstance that one hundred and forty years after the first emigration of her ancestor to America, this Lady should become a Vice-Queen of the country from which he fled, at the Summit of a system which a more immediate Ancestor had risqued every thing to destroy; or in the energetic and partial language of Bishop England 'that in the land from which the father's father fled, his daughter's daughter now reigns as Queen'.[6]

Marianne had never felt less queen-like. At the time of her marriage she had cherished hopes that she could fulfil her grandfather's wish: 'May God who has elevated you to so high a station make you his instrument for restoring good will, the spirit of conciliation between parties, and the suppression of discord, the bane of poor & oppressed Ireland!' In her role of wife and lady hostess, she had hoped to emulate Dolley Madison's entertainments, to hold parties where political and religious enemies could meet socially. Her grandfather believed she was peculiarly well-placed to make a difference; a belief, he wrote, 'founded not merely on personal charms but on the sweetness of your temper, excellent understanding, discretion and discernment which eminently mark your character, qualities at all times and in all situations essential to gain & retain the esteem & confidence of those with whom we associate, and particularly so in the one you now occupy'.[7]

Yet all their aspirations for her vocation of public service foundered on the 'botheration' of religious bigotry and adverse publicity. There could be no open house at the castle, as there was at the President's House, and, although the Wellesleys welcomed Catholics at castle functions, entertainments were politically resonant. Moreover, the press in Ireland was highly partisan and in the pay either of the castle or of the Catholic opposition. As a Catholic and Lady Lieutenant, Marianne attracted the invective of both sides. The Orange newspapers regularly issued snide invitations on her behalf: 'There will be a Rosary at the Lodge on the Evening of Monday the 20th inst. The Ladies and Gentlemen who attend are requested to bring their own beads' ran one of the milder announcements in the *Dublin Evening Mail*. The attacks in the Protestant press became so insulting that the only way to avoid provoking prejudice was to confine herself to official duties and make any charitable donations anonymously.[8]

In the event, her time in Ireland was short. In 1827 Liverpool suffered a severe stroke and his resignation removed a long-standing placatory influence from the government; he never recovered and would die the following year. When Canning succeeded him, the 'pro-Protestant' Tory wing, the Duke, Peel and Goulburn, resigned from the largely 'pro-Catholic' government. The appointment of William Lamb, a 'pro-Catholic', to succeed Goulburn in Ireland led the King to insist upon a new 'Protestant' Lord Lieutenant. Thus, although Wellesley and Canning were old political friends, protégés of Pitt and supporters of Catholic emancipation, Canning could not keep Wellesley in Ireland.

Marianne was still in England and wanted to see Canning about the Johnston problem and a post for McTavish; now it became more important to discuss her husband's future. Wellesley had been offered the important Vienna Embassy but doubted he could afford the higher expense involved. When Marianne undertook to provide funds, Wellesley asked her to clarify with Canning the terms of the post. Canning, however, would not see her. On 27 June, he told Wellesley the reason: 'It is because, without doing any good, our interview would only place us both in an embarrassing situation.' What he then went on to say showed a want of confidence in Marianne's discretion and did not improve Wellesley's humour.

Lady Wellesley sees the Duke of Wellington (as it is natural that she should do) almost daily. If we (Lady Wellesley and I) meet, am I to stipulate that what passes between us is *not* to go to the Duke! – or am I to discuss matters with Lady Wellesley at the risk of their being communicated to the Duke in his present temper of bitter political hostility?

Without any helpful input from Marianne, who had left for Dublin, Wellesley refused Vienna. Negotiations were still pending when Canning suddenly died on 8 August 1827. Although Wellesley liked to think that he would now be offered the highest office, the King's command to form a government went to Lord Goderich.[9]

Marianne wrote to her stepson Richard about their intended departure. 'We are to remain here until December and Lord Anglesea is to succeed your father as Ld Lt.' Now that she was to leave official life she allowed herself a private comment on the immoderate political situation. 'I think the Catholics are very ungrateful to Ld. Wellesley', though it was 'quite impossible for an impartial, and upright man to please the violent, and factious of either party'.

Before she left unhappy Ireland she also paid a public visit to a Catholic church; she was prepared to attract the derogatory comments of the Orange faction so as to please herself and her family, for once. Her grandfather's delighted reaction made it all the more worthwhile: 'Bessy's letter gave the account of your attendance at the Oratorio in the R. C. church; you made an effort, great indeed in your situation, to honor your religion, in doing so, as in all you do, you acted with propriety, guided by the dictates of good sense & rectitude.' She would need to draw on these qualities in the year ahead. She and Wellesley were returning to London to begin a life together without a large staff to do their bidding; and without a landed estate upon which to retire. They had no position and faced an uncertain future.[10]

27

Perplexing Positions: Marianne

When Marianne returned to London just before Christmas 1827 she moved with Wellesley into one of the new stucco houses built by Nash at the Regent's Park, having turned down a larger house nearby as 'out of the question, for those who have no money', such as her 'dearest Lord'. They took it in Wellesley's name though Marianne paid for it as he had lost his £30,000 [£2.3 million] a year salary on leaving Ireland; the income from his remaining estates and a small pension were easily swallowed up by charges, such as his mother's jointure. Marianne also took the precaution of asking her American trustees to sell 203 shares of US Bank stock and transfer the £5,000 [£380,000] proceeds to her English trustee, the Duke. Wellesley was thereby settled in London but, she worried, 'not *placed*'. He was, 'you may well suppose, a little fidgetty', she told Richard Wellesley. It was impossible to rely upon any promises of public office while Britain was in the throes of the political crisis caused by Canning's death.[1]

A Prime Minister as 'vacillating and weak' as Lord Goderich, was unable to impose his authority upon a coalition government. The Ultra-Tories [Ultras] were angered by Wellington's reinstatement as Commander-in-Chief, thereby bolstering a Canningite government they opposed; to which the Duke retorted that he 'was *no politician* but a soldier'. The government was in a sorry state, 'quite at *sixes & sevens*, some for peace, some for war [over Greece], and all despised and derided by everybody', noted one Tory MP. News of the battle of Navarino – the English naval routing of Turkey, an ally, in the Greek war of independence – and of dissension between Cabinet factions heightened the sense of a continual political crisis. On 11 December Goderich tearfully told the King of his wish to appoint Lords Wellesley and Holland to the Cabinet. Later that day he wrote tendering his resignation unless the King accepted the Duke or Lord Hill at the Ordnance and Wellesley as Lord President of the Council. The king, busy redecorating Windsor Castle, could think 'of nothing but his upholstery & his buildings' and was irritated beyond measure by all these ministerial issues.[2]

When the Duke arrived in London on 15 December, he found the Cabinet leaking like a sieve and London flooded with stories about these appointments. Michael Prendergast MP had it that Wellesley was hovering on the threshold of Downing Street only to be swatted away by a more influential colleague: 'Mr Huskisson is and has been for several days the sole cause of your Excellency's not having been summoned by the King.' Huskisson declared he would resign if Wellesley came in and his support, as leader of a large group of Canningites, was essential for any future administration to survive.[3]

The king, having been advised that the only way to keep out the Ultras was to reinstate Goderich, did so on 20 December. Whether the two Wellesley brothers were also to come in remained unclear – as did the government's future. 'I understand that the Government is tottering to its foundations', the Duke informed Peel. 'They are all going for some reason or other. Huskisson will not stay if Herries does. Lord Goderich will go if anyone resigns.' Fresh rumours circulated that the King wanted both Wellesleys in the Cabinet. The Duke, fed false stories by Mrs Arbuthnot about Wellesley's low opinion of him, retorted: 'You know that I have always suspected this scheme of bringing Lord W & me together . . .' He meant politically, not personally, for he was a 'Protestant' Tory whereas Wellesley was a 'Catholic' Canningite; yet hearsay concerning their political views was often interpreted as defining their private relations.[4]

Marianne acted as a conduit between them as she still loved the Duke, as he did her. This is clear from Canning's correspondence and the few surviving notes the Duke was sending her. His letters begin 'My dearest Lady Wellesley', notable in itself as it was most unusual for him to write to a married woman in this way; his other close sister-in-law was 'My dear Mrs Pole', and a good friend was 'My dear Mrs Arbuthnot'. He was able to give Marianne the latest political news when he called on 2 January as he came straight from attending a Cabinet meeting. She must have spoken to him on other subjects too because two days later, after receiving another note from her, he assured her that he would call upon her husband that afternoon. He felt 'for what has passed as much as Lord Wellesley does' and 'I sincerely lament the lasting state of things', but 'I hope I shall not have occasion to say anything upon that subject. If it should be necessary I must speak out.' He never clarified on paper what 'that subject' was.

Over the next few days it became clear that the government must fall. At his audience with the King on 8 January 1828 Goderich resigned again, shedding such copious tears that His Majesty had to lend him a handkerchief. Whom would the King now send for to become Prime Minister? 'We have not the slightest hint from any quarter', Marianne admitted as they, like other aspirant families, waited in suspense.[5]

The king kept none of them waiting much longer. On the following morning, Lord Chancellor Lyndhurst returned to Windsor with the next Prime Minister. 'Arthur,' said the King, sitting up in bed resplendent in an elaborate turban nightcap, 'the Cabinet is defunct!' and he invited his 'dear Friend' Wellington to form a government. The only conditions were that Catholic emancipation must not be made a Cabinet issue, there must be a 'Protestant' Lord Chancellor and Lord Lieutenant in Ireland and no office given to the Whig leader Lord Grey.

The Duke sent for the one man whose leadership in the Commons would be crucial to the success of the new government: Robert Peel, who reluctantly agreed to become Home Secretary. Peel had to insist upon the inclusion of Canningites with speaking talent to strengthen his control over a difficult Commons. Wellington's was thus to be a coalition government, with all the attendant disunity and manoeuvring of its predecessor.

Wellington, used to the inflexible hierarchy of military command rather than the malleable cabal of political negotiation, found the business of Cabinet-making uncomfortable. On the one hand he had the King, who cared for nothing but keeping the Duke of Devonshire as Lord Chamberlain; on the other, he had Lord Bathurst, who cared for nothing except bringing back his old colleagues; and finally he had all the Tory grandees, who cared for nothing except their rightful places in his government. One did not, he had to remind the latter, form a ministry as one did a dinner or house party. That was the easy part. The exigencies of coalition government meant that he had to refuse or give junior office to the Ultras – men such as Charles Arbuthnot who had followed him out of office over Canning and now expected to follow him back in.[6]

In the wintry landscape of the Regent's Park, Marianne was confined to her room with asthma and worrying about her husband. 'I am very anxious to hear how the Ministry will be settled,' she confessed to her stepson Richard, 'as yet I know nothing more than we read in the Papers. Whether Ld Wellesley is to form part of the New Govt is *really without affectation* more than I can tell you.'

Wellesley, an experienced candidate, awaited his call. He had signalled his wish for office, stating he would not object to serve under anyone approved by the King. It was now expected that the Duke would retain him; they were 'on good terms, and, prior to the break up [of the Ministry] had seen much of each other', as Marianne affirmed. Richard Wellesley, giving her the latest reports from the younger backbenchers, assured her: 'There is a very general wish that my father should be in the Ministry, and the Duke must be aware of this fact.' His father's ambitions were bolstered by Peel's stated intention 'to promote the reunion of the old party' of Liverpool's Cabinet, and the warm assurances of mutual regard in their recent correspondence.[7]

On 21 January the Duke settled his Cabinet and Marianne wrote to her stepson: 'From the list in the *Courier*, Ld Wellesley is *not* I perceive to form a part of the New Cabinet.' She pinned her remaining hopes on the frayed thread of Ireland: 'As he is still Ld Lieut of Ireland perhaps they wait until he is free to accept office.' He was already free, for 'Protestant' Lord Anglesey's Irish appointment was confirmed that very day. Marianne's reaction to the Duke's behaviour was one of utter shock: 'I cannot think The Duke would be so unkind', especially in a coalition government, to overlook Wellesley's claims. And this was at the heart of it: the Duke had chosen to cast aside the natural claims to preferment, throwing off the mantle of obligation, kinship and alliance, customary in Georgian England. 'I know nothing,' Marianne admitted to her stepson, 'but I will not believe he can forget Ld Wellesley's merits & services.' Not to notice one brother was extraordinary but not to notice two was unnatural; the Duke had also forgotten his elder brother William Lord Maryborough, also once a member of Liverpool's government.[8]

Lord Wellesley was astounded. It had never occurred to him that he would be left without even the merest crumb of preferment, by a younger brother so much in his familial debt: the considerable financial support, military commissions and preferment in Ireland, India and the Peninsula, had all flowed to Arthur through Richard's patronage. It was inconceivable that the Duke should reciprocate in this extraordinary manner. Such public humiliation was unbearable, as was the absence of any communication. Writing on 26 January to announce the death of Lady Caroline Lamb, he admitted to Marianne: 'I am worn down with visitors to day – No news – Every matter respecting me of the most gloomy aspect.' He was dejected and wounded.

It was not until 3 February that the Duke got in touch. He would have been so glad to ask assistance 'and to have been the means of giving the King and his Councils, the benefit of your powerful services and able advice'. But he could not and he spared him the reasons, if any, in his letter. Wellesley was furious: he was being overlooked and that was all Wellington could say. This reaction was by no means unusual for someone of Lord Wellesley's station with a chain of other people dependent upon him for preferment. 'What a strange family they are!' Marianne sighed. 'God made men, women & Wellesleys.'[9]

Although there was much to recommend Lord Wellesley as a statesman, there was also much to veto. He was a pro-Catholic Canningite and Goulburn, the new Tory Chancellor of the Exchequer, voiced doubts, coloured by the Johnston business, about Wellesley's efficiency and commitment to playing an active parliamentary role. More damaging still was Huskisson's continued determination to keep him out; although known to be an arch-intriguer – the Duke said 'he was a good bridge for rats to run over' – Huskisson's word still carried weight in the Cabinet. Unaware of this, Wellesley blamed first the King, who appeared to expect his appointment but did not insist upon it, and then Wellington.

Public reports of an estrangement between the Wellesley brothers were widely believed. The family looked to Lord Wellesley as an authority, with that respect accorded by British families to primogeniture; he had provided financial support, negotiated their marriages and been an important political figure for patronage. Although Wellington had overtaken him in fame and riches, Richard was the politician in the family, not Arthur. It was a difficult adjustment for all the brothers to make but the Duke's decision not to notice them in public life made it much harder. As the channels of communication between them closed, frozen with resentment and misunderstanding, some of the family looked to Marianne to reopen them whilst others felt that she had not sufficiently used her influence with the Duke. 'We shall, I assure you, feel the sincerest pain if my father is not placed in the Cabinet', wrote her stepson.[10]

Over the ensuing months, Wellesley himself began to feel that there was some tenuous connection between his ill-treatment and Marianne: that she was somehow implicated in his political exile. Dejected and without occupation, Wellesley became suspicious and angry with her. She could no longer easily see the Duke every day in such circumstances. He was her oldest, most constant friend in England and she felt lonely without his company. Her customary discretion slipped during a tête-à-tête with her younger stepdaughter, Marianne telling her that Wellesley was very much out of spirits; 'she says it is a wretched life she leads & that as Mrs Patterson she was much better off, & had more friends than now', Hyacinthe Littleton reported to her brother. Hyacinthe wished their father 'would rally a little bit' for Marianne's sake.[11]

He rallied as soon as he had something to do. The repeal of the Test and Corporation Acts encouraged supporters of Catholic emancipation. 'I hope the yielding this, what used to be called *Bulwark* of the Church, is only the prelude to the great question of Catholic liberty being carried', wrote Lady Holland on 17 April 1828. Marianne was relieved to find Wellesley rallying support for the great cause and Bess was hopeful of victory at last. Four days later, voting on the motion for Catholic emancipation the pro-Catholics obtained a majority of six, the first time in the life of the 1826 Parliament there had been a Commons majority in favour of Catholic liberties.

When Wellesley rose to speak in the debate on 10 June he had no inside information about what the Duke was minded to do but their views were long-standing and well known. The Duke was on record as opposing and

Wellesley as supporting Roman Catholic claims. Marianne also supported them but she continued to admire the Duke, telling her grandfather that the Duke was doing everything wise and good for his country. 'I beg to differ with you; I cannot believe him to act wisely, who acts unjustly; to keep a large portion of the empire in a state of distrust and degradation is a most singular aberration of mind in a man, who is not a religious bigot', he replied from America where, he thanked God, Catholics had long been emancipated.

Lord Wellesley spoke in a 'clear and forcible manner' for several hours. As he sat down, the Duke immediately rose to oppose. Commentators, then and afterwards, have made much of this occasion as evidence of the brothers' dislike, if not hatred, of one another. The press might delight that the Duke differed from his noble relation but the words he chose contained a message of strong affection, an uncommon component of his parliamentary speechifying. It was most unusual for Wellington to say 'I feel particular concern' at having to 'differ in opinion from him whom I so dearly love, and for whose opinions I entertain so much respect and deference'. The Wellesley family understood them to come not from a prime minister but from a younger brother to the head of the family; the Duke was publicly signalling familial atonement.

He led the 'Protestants' in flinging out the motion by forty-four votes and dashed Catholic hopes again. The New Catholic Association then persuaded Daniel O'Connell to stand in a by-election in County Clare. When he was elected by a large majority, the spectre of an Irish Washington embarking upon a War of Independence suddenly haunted the British political mind. The Duke began secretly to move towards Catholic emancipation so as to put down 'the rebellion that seems hanging over our heads' and preserve the Union.[12]

After the exertions of this extraordinary session, the Wellesleys retired to Brighton. Marianne's stepson Richard enjoyed composing Greek and Latin verse with his father but noticed that 'poor Lady W. seems quite grateful for *anything* that inspires him with better humour & better spirits'. Wellesley owned to being deeply mortified by his reception in England after his Lord Lieutenancy – by which he meant the lack of notice by the King. There had been no ribbon or medal of honour, no sinecure or pension; none of the gifts the sovereign was usually minded to bestow upon a successful returning pro-consul or statesman. Wellesley smarted from neglect and wounded pride.

Edward Littleton heard that the Wellesleys were 'in a sad state of pecuniary distress and of course both unhappy'. Marianne's money, nonetheless, allowed Wellesley to take a 'villa' in Twickenham, the palladian Marble Hill built for the Countess of Suffolk, for his own separate use, owing, he declared, to the dampness of the Regent's Park and his need for retirement. A trickle of conjecture once again began to spot the pages of diaries, letters and newspapers. Joseph Jekyll wrote of 'That little spendthrift Wellesley [who] has not £4000 per annum' keeping two establishments. 'There is no regular separation' but they live apart.[13]

The trickle gradually reached America where, for once, it was not Marianne's health but her situation that worried her mother, who noticed that the London society pages never seemed to mention Wellesley, even in accounts of family events. 'I almost put out my Eyes to see yr name or Ld W & to *see* them *together* as others are in the newspapers.' When Marianne mentioned attending a Wellesley family wedding, her mother scanned the London papers for details. 'I see the Duke of W gave away the Bride – was Lord W invited – he seems to shut himself, or is shut *out*, by all his family', she observed. 'Lord W's interests must be nothing, he never appears.' Why did he not ever accompany his wife? She was filled with dismay as the latest accounts regaled gossip about the Wellesleys' marriage and his removal to Twickenham: 'the distress, various reports in general circulation here, have given – & if Ld W has a spark of feeling, he will not hesitate a moment to write to me – to relieve my intense anxiety – & to *refute* the *lies* that are in every person's mouth!!' She was almost beside herself when a Mrs Skinner, newly arrived from London, confirmed that Marianne was 'delicate & out of spirits'. 'Oh!' Mary Carroll Caton moaned, 'it is so strange that we do not know that which concerns you *so intimately* & all the country are talking about it!!' She was convinced that her eldest daughter would soon be deserted by an errant husband.

They were already bewildered by the political news of Wellesley. 'The Duke's conduct to his brother astonishes me; that brother he once esteemed & loved; how has he ceased to be deserving of that esteem & love? does he disapprove of his administration in Ireland – that administration has been publicly praised by his successor', her grandfather asked Marianne. She could give him no straightforward answer. In the late 1820s, she was more in need of her family and the Duke than she had ever been, saddled with supporting an unemployed prima donna of a husband, a man described in Croker's inimitable phrase as 'a brilliant incapacity'.[14]

The Duke was now able to help her and bring peace to her unhappy marriage. Notwithstanding her mother's anxious question 'have you, my beloved one, a *friend* or even an intimate acquaintance &c, I fear not', Marianne did have the Duke as a confidante and 'that amiable, excellent' Colonel Shawe as a friend and trusted go-between. Merrick Shawe was devoted to Marianne and his pivotal, if unobtrusive, role in the

Wellesley family enabled him to act as her chevalier without arousing suspicion. He was born into the Anglo-Irish Ascendancy and, after the Mysore War, he was appointed ADC in 1799 to Wellesley in India, became his Military Secretary in 1801 and then Private Secretary from 1803. He had remained with Wellesley ever since, a discreet and popular member of his staff.

Merrick Shawe is known as the original Major Pendennis, in Thackeray's semi-autobiographical novel *Pendennis*, the retired Regency gentleman with a position in the London world – one who 'lived in such good company that he might be excused for feeling like an earl'. Shawe was Thackeray's uncle by marriage and obtained a post for Thackeray as a book reviewer for *The Times*, providing franks for Thackeray's letters through Wellesley. Moreover, the stories he supplied Thackeray of the fashionable Regency world featured people Marianne and her sisters knew well.

Shawe could tell them about Wellesley's unpopularity with the East India Company civil servants, who complained because he would not don a congee cap, smoke a hookay and hobnob with them at Government House. Wellesley preferred to converse with maharajahs about Indian literature and his collection of botanical drawings, to create beautiful gardens at Barrackpore and to build a Government House at Calcutta – places where in 'magnificent solitude' he could 'stalk about like a Royal Tiger' preparing for the next India campaign. And Shawe also spoke about how Canning had told Wellesley 'he had walked into the House the greatest man in England, and had walked out the least' in 1812 after he failed to explain his resignation from the Cabinet to an expectant House. Wellesley never felt he needed to account to anyone; used from an early age to taking responsibility for others, he essentially walked alone. What Marianne had to accustom him to do was to walk with her in uxorious companionship without the Johnston brothers.[15]

During the first eight months of the Duke's premiership Johnston continued to pester Wellesley about a post. Wellesley asked Shawe to see the Duke about it on 9 August. While the Duke had no desire to serve Johnston, he agreed to give him employment; partly because Wellesley had asked for it and, he told Shawe, at present he had no other means of obliging him. Much more importantly, though, he did it to help Marianne. For here at last, he and Shawe agreed, was the opportunity to send Johnston as far away from her as possible. Wellesley was, indeed, pleased by his brother's kindness. Yet the Duke's response placed Marianne in a predicament. Wellesley now believed that the Duke was not ill-disposed towards Johnston. This, in turn, made him suspect that everything he had been told about the unfavourable opinions held by the King, Liverpool and Canning was a malicious intrigue. He now suspected Marianne of inventing everything.

Convinced she was behind his disfavour at Windsor, he subjected her to 'ungovernable bursts of temper'.

In despair she turned to Shawe and the Duke. She was so miserable and ill with asthma her doctor Sir Richard Hunter believed she might never recover. The Duke was distressed to hear of this sorry episode. He knew that, without the Johnstons, Wellesley would be much nicer to Marianne. Shawe confirmed this: 'He likes her society and seems to place great confidence in her, except when these suspicions, which are confined to this sole topic, are infused into his mind.' The Duke responded with alacrity. To clear Marianne, he sent Shawe a letter which could be shown to Wellesley. In it, the Duke made clear that the adverse view 'generally entertained' about Johnston had existed before Marianne's marriage, had been held by himself, Liverpool and Canning, and that no one should be misled by his help 'to suppose that he had altered his opinion regarding Mr Johnston'.[16]

This did the trick. Wellesley asked Shawe to remove the banditti: the game was up. Shawe told Johnston 'his conduct . . . had done great mischief – he had better therefore be quiet – Be satisfied with whatever may be done for him.' Johnston, in disgrace, must live quietly elsewhere and 'wait respectfully for whatever notice may be taken of him'. But he did not go without some struggle, despite Shawe's impression of a docile penitent.

The thorn in Marianne's marriage had been removed at last and the quality of her life improved immeasurably. She told Shawe that Wellesley was 'very much relieved and at ease'. By the end of October Hunter gave a more favourable account of her, which Shawe passed on to the Duke: 'Lady Wellesley is said to be quite recovered, a sure indication of the removal of the uneasiness which affected her health.'[17]

Perplexing Positions: Louisa

Marianne had been without the regular company of her sisters throughout much of her first six months back in England. Bess had joined Louisa at South Audley Street from where they embarked upon the social whirl of the Season. While political upheaval over Catholic agitation also kept Bess engrossed, its prominence in English public life proved unexpectedly harmful to Louisa's prospects. Bustling about on visits, riding to hounds and indulging in society again, Louisa had largely emerged from that deadening fog of bereavement. And now, suddenly, she became caught up in another man's existence.

Sometime during the previous year, a young Guards officer appeared quite captivated by her. Louisa, who at thirty-three retained her vivacity and seductive charm, was diverted by his attentions but not enough to pander to them. In July, while she was staying with the Fremantles, he followed to renew his suit. A certain amount of secrecy, for reasons unspec-ified, surrounded their growing friendship. Louisa continued her life as usual, dividing her time between Town and Stratfield Saye. There are hints in letters of one proposal, and she may have refused him more than once. Then, at the beginning of April 1828, he proposed again and this time she accepted him.[1]

Up to this moment only two people were caught in the gentle ebb and flow of this courtship: Louisa and her beau, Lord Carmarthen. From then on, however, his family, conscious of rank, religion and fortune, directed the strong current of disapproval to try to pull them apart. Louisa still confided in the Duke but, on this occasion, she did not ask him to inter-vene; partly because he had no close connection to Carmarthen's family, and partly because he was the Prime Minister and she did not wish to place him in an awkward position. And awkward it would be. When Carmarthen did what every dutiful son should do and sought his father's consent to marry, he was refused.

Francis Godolphin D'Arcy Osborne was twenty-eight, a captain in the 2nd Life Guards and MP for Helston in Cornwall. As a 'Protestant' Tory he had supported Liverpool and now supported the Duke. Lord Carmarthen,

or 'Car' as Louisa always called him, was a handsome, fair-haired, tall man
with an engaging manner, likeable and straightforward – some said too
much so, for he lacked any great ambition and intellect. Kind and depend-
able, he was happiest leading the active life of a country gentleman on his
estates, ferreting and shooting out on the Yorkshire moors and stalking and
fishing in Scotland. Horses were also a great pleasure and he lived for
hunting, racing and the turf. He had received the education of a nobleman's
son at Christ Church, Oxford, and was given a cornetcy in the 10th Prince
of Wales's own Royal Regiment of Hussars, the exclusive regiment in which
Felton had started his military career. He liked good pictures, fine wines
and visits to Paris. Foreign travel he otherwise considered overrated, much
preferring his own country.[2]

Carmarthen might be considered an ordinary specimen of lordling but
the world judged him to be far from commonplace; indeed, he was the *beau
ideal* if not of every Regency ingénue then of every Regency mother. By
marrying him Louisa was making a splendid match, a match such as no
American woman had ever made before. She was marrying the heir to a
dukedom and a duke, as all the world knew, was an exalted being, above
the law and beyond arrest, above every other non-royal person in the land.

> Flattered, adulated, deferred to, with incomes enormously increased by
> the Industrial Revolution, and as yet untaxed, all-powerful over a tenantry
> as yet unenfranchised, subject to no ordinary laws, holding the govern-
> ment of the country firmly in their hands and wielding through their
> closely-knit connections an unchallengeable social power, the milords
> of England were the astonishment and admiration of Europe

was how Cecil Woodham-Smith described dukes of the nineteenth century.
This would be Lord Carmarthen's inheritance as the eldest son and heir of
the sixth Duke of Leeds.

Louisa, a foreigner, would be a duchess, the world exclaimed in admiration, conjuring up visions of that desirable ducal coronet adorned with
strawberry leaves that would crown her dark curls. The lady grandees, who
better understood the mores of ducal society, knew more than to applaud.
It was a 'very bad match' the Duke of Portland's daughter agreed. Lord
Carmarthen had so far forgotten his duty as to think of marrying an older
childless American widow without suitable rank and religion, and with
little fortune by ducal standards. With one voice society concurred: 'it was
a *mésalliance*'.[3]

Their Graces the Duke and Duchess of Leeds were horrified by their
son's choice and set out to prevent the marriage. The Duchess of Leeds
refused to receive Louisa or to meet her. The Duke of Leeds threatened
Carmarthen with a barrage of financial penalties: disinheritance, severance

of patronage and blocking whatever income possible from the Leeds estates. Chamberlains, advisers, trustees and lawyers were dispatched to dissuade Lord Carmarthen. Would he waver? Were the consequences of such a straightforward act too great for an heir to such splendour to bear? Lord Carmarthen stood resolute. He again wrote to ask for his father's permission to marry.

Louisa had only to hear about Carmarthen's sister to realise that there would be no quick resolution to the affair. 'How does dear pretty pretty Lady C Osborne? is she recovered, is all that sad story about Mr Capel true?' asked the Marchioness of Bute after the Duke of Leeds had sent the Earl of Essex's heir packing. Two years later, after Lady Charlotte Osborne announced her marriage to the relatively impecunious third son of a county neighbour, plain Mr Lane Fox, the Duke of Leeds was incensed. 'Do you know anything of dear little Lady Charlotte Osborne – I am so sorry to hear she and her family are divided and no longer friends', Lady Bute observed to Ralph Sneyd. It was not until the following year that Sneyd could announce a reconciliation shortly before the arrival of a first grand-child.[4]

The Duke of Leeds was sensitive about family marriages. He had been only nine when his mother died but he knew of the notoriety she had brought upon the family. Amelia, Baroness Conyers, most delectable of heiresses, only child of Robert D'Arcy, Earl of Holdernesse, beloved at court through her mother's close friendship with Queen Charlotte, and wife of the fifth Duke of Leeds, had wilfully thrown away her reputation when she conceived a grand passion for 'Mad Jack' Byron, father of the poet. They flung their liaison with astounding recklessness in the face of the world. Divorce was inevitable as was the publication of all the details. Ostracised after their marriage they went to live in Paris where Byron spent his way through her remaining fortune. She returned to Holdernesse House in 1783 for the birth of her third and only surviving child by him, a daughter Augusta Mary Byron, known later by her married name as Augusta Leigh, Lord Byron's half-sister.

The fifth duke had behaved impeccably over the divorce: helping to arrange it, allowing Lady Amelia to keep her carriage and favourite horses and footmen, refusing to claim damages awarded to him for injury and even paying for the confinement of her first child by 'Mad Jack'. He did, it was true, retain control of her Holdernesse fortune from which he allowed her £1,500 a year, when other cuckolded husbands were by no means as generous. Most important of all, he allowed her to see their Osborne children. After she died of consumption and unhappiness in 1784, having already separated from the feckless Jack Byron, her children George (the future sixth Duke of Leeds), together with his brother

Lord Francis, sister Lady Mary and half-sister Augusta remained with their grandmother Lady Holdernesse and the kind, affectionate fifth duke. But where his father had been sympathetic and forgiving, the sixth duke was tyrannical and steadfastly unforgiving to his own son.[5]

The sixth duke was also 'great at his liquor' which made him unpredictable. 'Does the Duke enjoy Champagne as much as ever' Lady Bute had asked, whereas Lady Granville put it stronger. 'Ascot was a beautiful sight on the Cup Day', she wrote to the Duke of Devonshire of the June 1829 meeting. 'The dinners not very long or hot, though Leeds sat on one side of me, drunk as a fish, quite incoherent. "I don't know if you will quite take my meaning, see my view, but it has always struck me that scarlet strawberries in private conversation are very agreeable to meet with occasionally."' Although Leeds's meaning and his opinions varied with the level of alcohol in his blood, he was always entirely coherent about opposing his heir's marriage.[6]

As Louisa and Carmarthen waited for his answer, Marianne prevailed upon Wellesley as head of their family to write in support of Louisa. 'I hope his answer to Ld C may be favourable, otherwise the situation will be awkward', Wellesley remarked to Marianne. A few days' later Carmarthen was summoned to the family's London house in St James's Square where he found his father somewhat less angry after receiving Wellesley's letter but now using the duchess's feelings as the reason for his opposition. She would never agree to the match and Carmarthen would ruin her health and happiness if he went ahead with such a marriage. The duchess, so 'good and kind' to Lady Bute, was feeling anything but good and kind towards papist Louisa, Lady Hervey.

The Leeds family held estates in Cornwall and in Yorkshire, the chief seat being at Hornby Castle in the North Riding. Among their county neighbours were some of the Catholic aristocracy and gentry, towards whom the duchess had never previously displayed anti-Catholic prejudice. Yet the idea of having a Catholic daughter-in-law was now made profoundly disturbing to her by the prominence accorded to Catholic agitation in public life. Protestant suspicions of Catholics, as people who would always obey the Pope first and subvert the Crown and the established religion of England, were being roused by the current debates, while lurking underneath lay the more intangible emotional and cultural superstitions.

Women like the Duchess of Leeds could not bear the thought of their grandchildren being subjected to an alien 'foreign' religion, one based upon confession in which, they believed, priests could ask questions of a most 'improper and revolting nature'. Anti-Catholicism was built into British national culture. Protestant schoolboys stuck pins through the eyes of Queen Mary Tudor in their history picture books. During a journey, the architect

Pugin once crossed himself while engrossed in private prayer – to the horror of a lady seated opposite who cried out: 'You are a Catholic, Sir; – Guard, Guard, let me out.' The inability of the British to relinquish these beliefs astounded Carroll of Carrollton. 'What! does the stale bugbear of the Devil, Pope & Pretender still haunt the minds of Englishmen?' he asked Marianne.

The Duchess of Leeds did not wish to be parted from her son and alienated from her future grandchildren. If Carmarthen insisted upon marrying Louisa then the only solution was for her to renounce her religion. It was now Louisa's turn to be horrified. She wrote indignantly to the Wellesleys that the Duchess 'still insists on my becoming a Protestant or urges *me* to back off the marriage "out of delicacy for the feelings of the Parents" which would insure me their good opinion and friendship – this proposition I think nearly as absurd, as that of changing my religion'.[7]

Gaining no success from this ploy, the Duke of Leeds's next move was to secure the King's disapproval and prevent the marriage. The Duke of Leeds, a Master of the Horse, would have been surprised by the royal reaction. The king already knew of the match and the Leedses' opposition from the Fremantles, who had been informed by Louisa on 10 April. Lord Conyngham told Fremantle about Leeds's letter and reported, 'The King has not ceased laughing' – the Carmarthen marriage had the seal of royal approval. Louisa announced to the Wellesleys: 'we have not the least intention of breaking off the marriage, but mean to have it conducted as soon as circumstances will permit.'[8]

On 24 April she called upon Wellesley, while he was still in bed, to announce that it was her wedding day. He immediately scribbled a pencilled note to Marianne to tell her that Louisa's marriage would take place that evening and she had asked him to give her away. Louisa and Carmarthen were married at St Luke's Church in Chelsea by Gerald Wellesley in the presence of her two sisters, Lord Wellesley, and her trustee Major-General Sir Colin Campbell – without any single family member or connection of the bridegroom.[9]

Quiet as the wedding was, reports caused a discordant spate of comment in England and America. Marianne and Wellesley had dined at Holland House on the eve of the wedding but, as Lady Holland did not know Louisa, Marianne had not said anything about the Leeds family. Lady Holland, in announcing the marriage to her son, wrote that the Duke of Leeds was 'deeply mortified; & his friends have no consolation to offer but the improbability of her having any children'; she caustically added, 'They say Lady Hervey wanted six qualifications, youth, beauty, character, fortune, birth, sense. She is nine years older than Ld C., & has only assurance for sense.' A lady's age was never published and often even close relations were uncertain. Henry Addington had Carmarthen losing three years and Louisa

Louisa painted by Ann Mee shortly
after her second marriage. Engraved
by Thomson c. 1828.

'Car', Francis D'Arcy Godolphin
Osborne, Marquess of Carmarthen,
shown in his Militia uniform.

gaining two in his account to Vaughan in Washington City. 'How Mother
Caton will chuckle at a ducal coronet sitting on the brows of her fiddle
faddle daughter, who however with all her mawkish affectation, can see
into a millstone in the true Yankee fashion.'[10]

Mother Caton was, indeed, delighted with the prospect of Louisa's match,
announced by Marianne on 8 April. Neither she nor Louisa's grandfather
could consider the event as viable, though, without the consent of the
groom's parents. They feared that she might be jilted, for 'should his passion
cool (in the love of young persons there is always passion) may he not
repent an alliance without the approbation of his parents?' asked her grandfather. Marianne's description of Carmarthen as most amiable, honourable
and devoted to Louisa somewhat allayed their fears.

Once letters reached them of the marriage having taken place, however,
her mother could announce it. She was reassured to learn that 'Louisa's
marriage bids fair to be as happy in domestic life, as it is brilliant & distinguished'. Louisa, she told a Carroll cousin, had suffered too severely from
Felton's early death to be led away by 'the allurements of Rank and station'.
They were sanguine that Louisa's 'amiable qualities' would overcome the
prejudice and opposition of Carmarthen's parents.[11]

While Louisa and Carmarthen remained estranged from his family they
might also face financial ruin. Louisa was receiving letters of congratula-
tion about her splendid marriage bestowing exalted rank and fortune at a

time when, in reality, she possessed less, not more, worldly goods. As was customary, the income she received as a widow from Felton's family stopped when she remarried and, as Carmarthen's income had not increased, they had to consider their position. Carmarthen would normally have obtained a substantial settlement and a suitable house from the Leeds estates upon marriage but, until he and his father were reunited, neither would be forth-coming, nor could any provision be made for Louisa. In the meantime, though ducal families might sniff at her 'meagre' fortune, she provided the marital houses by keeping on her town house and Park Corner House, and drew upon her funds to support the marriage by directing Hoare's Bank to sell some of her shares.

Lord Carmarthen had been a rich bachelor and he could raise large sums against his inheritance and reversions on the Leeds estates. He was also a man of probity – 'the inspiration of stolidity' as Addington described him – possessing sound financial habits to match Louisa's, ensuring bills were promptly paid and estates maintained. His rectitude about money matters, not typical of the Regency, boded well for the future of the Leeds estates and pleased Louisa, herself so correct about finances. He did not therefore welcome using her funds and houses and being unable to provide properly for her, when his father had an annual rent roll of £37,000 [£2.7 million] as well as a large personal wealth and additional income from the unen-tailed estates.

From the first days of their marriage Carmarthen consulted Louisa as an equal partner and came to rely upon her acumen. Indeed, many of the most important letters and memoranda written under his name, about the contested resettlement of the Leeds estates, were drafted by her and are equal to documents prepared by professional lawyers and advisers. In the early summer of 1828, as an interim measure, Carmarthen instructed his man of business William Stephens to arrange a loan for £2,000 a year from one of his bankers against the security of two new life insurance policies for £10,000 and £20,000 taken out to protect Louisa.[12]

The newly weds then embarked upon a leisurely continental tour that kept them abroad for nearly eighteen months. Marianne and Bess met up with them on several occasions and they were together in Paris the following March just after Peel had introduced the government's Catholic Relief Bill in the Commons. The sisters were thus absent during the exciting debates about emancipation and Bess had to glean as much news as she could from the British Embassy and the French Rothschilds. Bess and Marianne arranged to join the Carmarthens again during May at Spa where Louisa, desperate about not yet having conceived, was taking the water cure. She had always assumed Felton's ill-health had prevented further 'hopes', telling a friend

Harriet Chew Carroll,
painted by Robert Field
in 1800, the year of her marriage.

The sisters' uncle
Charles Carroll of Homewood
by Robert Field, 1800.

Robert Goodloe Harper, by Charles Bird King. The sisters' uncle Harper, a prominent lawyer, was a US Senator and unsuccessful Federalist candidate for Vice-President in the 1816 election.

Betsy Patterson Bonaparte by Jean-Baptiste-Jacques Augustin, 1808. When asked to dress more decently, Betsy nonchalantly draped a gauzy scarf around her shoulder.

Jerome Bonaparte, by Jean-Baptiste-Jacques Augustin, 1808. Jerome incurred his elder brother Napoleon's wrath by marrying Betsy in Baltimore in 1803.

Dolley Payne Madison, who took the sisters and their female friends to hear debates in the Capitol and put a stylish stamp on public life in Washington City.

John McTavish
by William J. Hubbard, 1829–32, shown as a country gentleman.

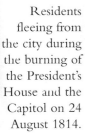

Residents fleeing from the city during the burning of the President's House and the Capitol on 24 August 1814.

The Company attending a Drawing Room at old Buckingham Palace during George IV's Reign. Lithograph published by G. Humphrey in 1822.

La manie de la Danse. The sisters danced the night away in Paris during Carnival 1817. Engraving by Philibert Louis Debucourt.

Marianne and
Lord Wellesley at
Dublin Castle, 1826.
This was Marianne's
first official Drawing
Room as the
Lady Lieutenant.

President Jackson's Inaugural Levée or All Creation going to the White House.
Caricature by Robert Cruikshank, 1829, depicting people storming the President's House to
get at the refreshments and see the new President, who was nearly crushed in the melée.

Queen Adelaide by Sir Martin Archer Shee, 1831.

King William IV, in his coronation robes, painted by Sir Martin Archer Shee.

Marianne in her coronation robes with Carroll McTavish, one of the pages holding her train. The unfinished painting is attributed to Sir Thomas Lawrence.

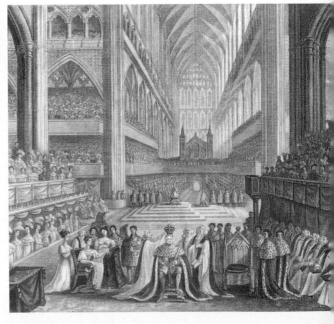

The coronation of William IV, 8 September 1831.

Bess painted in the 1830s
when she was busy as a
Lady Speculator.

The sisters' astute friend Hannah
de Rothschild at her writing desk.

Joshua Bates, the Barings' partner
who looked after the sisters'
investment portfolio.

Hornby Castle as Louisa would first have seen it in 1828.
Anonymous watercolour.

Marianne watched with the Wellesley family from Apsley House as the Duke of Wellington's funeral procession passed on its way to St Paul's. Lithograph after Louis Haghe, 1853.

that 'the want of children arose from no defect of hers'. She was now being proved wrong and Emily's announcement of her imminent third confinement, with wishes that dear Lou would also have 'a sweet infant' on the way, deepened her torment.[13]

By the time they returned home the excitement caused by the achievement of Catholic emancipation had largely abated. Wellington's government survived and he emerged with enhanced prestige. 'He is the only Man living who could have carried the measure', Sir Colin Campbell wrote to his duchess, '& he has saved his Country from a Civil War by his firmness & manliness.' The Duke, now looking upon Ireland with fonder eyes, opened negotiations to buy the last of the family estates that Wellesley, pressed by creditors, was trying to sell.[14]

The political rehabilitation of Catholics brought no change in the Duke and duchess of Leeds' attitude to their daughter-in-law. Eventually, Lord Wharncliffe, a trustee and Yorkshire neighbour, learnt of the Duchess's desire for a rapprochement with her son and volunteered to broker an agreement. He arranged for the three of them to meet in London and Carmarthen was reunited with his mother. Nine months later, Wharncliffe sent out an agreement based upon Carmarthen's terms of receiving an additional income of £10,000 [£700,000] a year secured on the Dukedom and a jointure for Louisa, and upon the Duke's terms of retaining the power to raise £120,000 on the estates resettled on his son. Carmarthen was so anxious for a full reconciliation that, on 24 July 1830, without consulting Louisa, who was away, or his legal advisers, he consented to the terms. This, it transpired, was a mistake.

Louisa examined the supporting accounts and discovered a large discrepancy in the figures. She calculated that the agreement would not provide Carmarthen with at least £10,000 a year but only at best £3,000 and at worst about £700 a year; that no consideration had been made for rents falling and, should they do so even slightly, 'the whole income of the Estates would not be sufficient to pay the charges upon them'. Moreover, she asserted in her memorandum, Carmarthen had not been given the power to sell an acre of land so that he could 'be left *literally* without the means of existence, a situation to which no one could expect him to reduce himself'. Louisa's memo was found to be correct by Carmarthen's legal advisers. He therefore withdrew his consent on the basis that the agreed terms had not been met.

Wharncliffe was far from happy: 'I will not disguise from you that the contents of your letter gave me great pain', he replied on 2 October and, refusing to accept the sums were inaccurate, insisted that Carmarthen 'was by every feeling that actuates men of honour and gentlemen in their dealings with each other pledged to do what may be necessary to carry into effect the terms'. Carmarthen, rueing that he had taken the figures to be

correct, was 'very indignant' at reading 'expressions offensive' to his feelings. He now saw no alternative but to inform his father that he had been
deceived about the terms of agreement and could no longer consider himself
bound by them. In order to bring to an end their differences, he told his
father, he was happy to present corrected figures to effect more equitable
terms for a settlement. It was 'of no *Use*', responded the angry duke, 'to
make any Comment, & the more so as I beg to be understood as fully coin-
ciding in every Word Lord Wharncliffe's Answers convey'd to you. There
is therefore an End of the Matter.' And there the matter would have ended
but for a tragic accident.[15]

It was said that the sixth duke had never looked favourably upon his heir
and that all his hopes were vested in his younger son Lord Conyers Osborne,
'a very fine young man', Lady Holland affirmed. Lord Conyers, fourteen
years' younger than Carmarthen, was accidentally killed in February 1831
while wrestling at Christ Church, Oxford. The Duchess of Leeds could not
endure the additional sorrow of a breach with her only surviving son. The
Duke of Leeds made no objection to their conciliation though he became,
if anything, more hostile to Carmarthen for having outlived Lord Conyers.
'I hope the Duke will come round by degrees', wished Lady Bedingfeld,
advising Marianne that 'Grief softens some people, but those who have no
resignation generally become more hard – they are *angry* and *impatient* under
the Tryal'.[16]

That summer the Carmarthens were taking Huntly Lodge in the
Highlands for the fishing and stalking. Louisa decided first, to take the
waters at Harrogate at a time when the Duchess of Leeds was known to be
in the neighbourhood. What could be more coincidental than that they
should meet; an event that would please Car and satisfy her. She described
her first impressions of Harrogate to her sisters: the weather in July was
predictably cold and rainy and 'the place frightful and desolate looking'.
As for the Granby Hotel, it was 'not what *I call comfortable* – no Carpets
– no *window Curtains* but beds – small rooms, low ceilings – doors not shut-
ting – very inn kind'. The next day she drove to High Harrogate which
was not so pretty but cooler, 'however in this *detestable* climate there is no
danger of our being too hot'. The water 'exceeds in *nastiness* any thing you
can imagine – imagine a combination of Gunpowder-Sulphur-Salt and rotton
Eggs – I really fear [Marianne] will never get it down – or keep it down'.
The only good point about Harrogate was that the Duchess had taken a
house there. 'Car has just gone to see his mother & know whether she
returns to Hornby tomorrow', Louisa wrote excitedly to her sisters, '& if
she means to see me.' After three years of marriage was she at last to meet
her mother-in-law?

'Car has just come in – says the Duchess has asked me there to Luncheon

– & is coming here to see me – Adieu dearest Sisters', she scribbled in haste. Her state of distraction was not to be imagined; her face was too flushed and her maid could not find the right white crêpe sleeves . . . At last, the waiting was over: 'Well, she has been to see me and we went back in the Carriage with her to Dinner – She was very kind & told Car she liked his dear Wife.' Louisa thought her mother-in-law 'a very sweet creature – so very like Car – the same eyes & fine head & skin – & the most beautiful teeth'. It was a relief to know her at last, she told her sisters, and to see 'precious Car smiling in delight at us both'. The duchess insisted that they leave the Granby and take the house next to hers and so they passed the whole week in her society, greedily making up for the years of estrangement.[17]

The Duke of Leeds was not a party to this happy reunion. He was not to be so easily won over and Louisa had to resign herself to a continued exile from Hornby Castle. In the course of their pleasant drives the two women agreed that 'nobody thought of Lord Carmarthen' and that he was not noticed. The Duke of Leeds certainly showed no inclination to do so by offering his heir any of the county positions in his patronage, such as command of the Militia or a Deputy Lord Lieutenantcy, roles Car would have been expected to fill almost by right. Louisa was able to assure her mother-in-law that she had every hope of furthering Car's career. In spite of his father's damaging disregard she would use her influence to obtain a position for Car through her own dearest connection, her sister Marianne.

Petticoat Politics

In the early 1830s Marianne and Emily found themselves in unexpected circumstances. They had not seen each other for six years and their lives now ran along very different lines. In Washington City, the society that the sisters had enjoyed changed so radically during the late 1820s and early 1830s that Emily, who would normally have attended entertainments in the capital, stayed away. 'Our society is in a sad state', Margaret Bayard Smith, a resident, affirmed; the local gentry and established families did not mix in political circles. They left social events to the 'democracy' and refused 'to mingle with the very lowest of the people'.

The catalyst for this change was General Andrew Jackson, the hero of the battle of New Orleans, 'man of the people' and leader of a new movement called the Democrats, *'emphatically the cause of the people'*. The rising middle and labouring classes in both the USA and Britain were demanding greater participation in their electoral systems. Although in both countries the term 'democracy' had long signified violent 'rule by mob' – Carroll of Carrollton told Alexis de Tocqueville, 'a mere Democracy is but a mob' – at the 1828 American presidential election it came to denote 'a sacred political goal'. This election was notable for being the first instance of universal white male suffrage in every state (except South Carolina) and, when Jackson defeated President John Quincy Adams, it seemed to inaugurate a new era, the Age of Democracy.[1]

During the debates about democracy and suffrage, age-old anxieties about 'petticoat politics' and female sexuality emerged in both countries, with the perceived influence of a woman at the centre of power: in republican America a barmaid. The effect of Jacksonian democracy in Washington City was, according to one historian, 'the breakdown of the republican aristocracy in which the women of Washington had flourished'. On Inaugural Day, 4 March 1829, a rabble stormed the President's House, 'the people forcing their way into the saloons' and breaking china and glass in the struggle to reach the refreshments. The mob swelled to over 2,000, all eager to see the new President, who was nearly pressed to death against a wall.

'Ladies fainted, men were seen with bloody noses, and such a scene of confusion took place as it is impossible to describe', recorded Margaret B. Smith. 'Ladies and gentlemen only had been expected, and not the people *en masse*. But it was the People's day and the People's president and the People would rule.'[2]

The Ladies, however, not the People, ruled the social world so necessary to the smooth running of the machinery of politics. When John H. Eaton, senator of Tennessee and good friend of the President, chose to marry Margaret 'Peggy' O'Neale Timberlake, a local tavern-keeper's widowed daughter with a reputation, he thereby removed himself from polite society. 'Eaton has just married his mistress, and the mistress of eleven doz. others!' declared Senator Louis McLane. When Eaton was appointed to the Cabinet as Secretary of War, however, since Jackson and his Secretary of State Martin Van Buren were both widowers, Peggy Eaton could become the leading lady of society. The ladies of Washington were aghast.

At the grand Inaugural Ball, which McTavish and the Catons attended, 'the other ladies of the official family tried not to notice' as Peggy Eaton swept into the ballroom; Floride Calhoun, wife of the vice-president, cut her dead and no woman spoke to her. Thereafter, with Jackson insisting upon her virtue and the ladies upon her vice, the scandal escalated into a social boycott, known as the 'Petticoat War'. The irritated President even discussed the issue at a Cabinet meeting and tried to force her society upon his colleagues. He forgot that invitations were the business of the ladies and, as Adams noted on 6 February 1830, Cabinet families gave large dinner parties 'to which Mrs Eaton is not invited. On the other hand, the president makes her doubly conspicuous by an over-display of notice.'[3]

This culminated in a large party which Charles Vaughan, the British Minister, was asked to give for the Eatons by Van Buren. 'Fifty guests, one hundred candles, lamps, silver plate of every description and for a queen, Peggy O'Neale, led in by Mr Vaughan', one eye-witness recorded, 'and sitting between him and the president.' The few ladies present nevertheless snubbed her. Vaughan was a good friend of McTavish, who was also there, although Emily stayed at home. Her attitude was shared by the ladies during Jackson's early presidency, which was a period of great social upheaval throughout the country – the levelling of the ranks, in de Tocqueville's phrase. Whereas family and breeding had previously been the determinants of social position, in a more democratic and mobile society wealth was becoming the sole arbiter of status. Even using this new criterion, Emily through her grandfather had no difficulty in retaining social distinction in a country becoming richer and more capitalist.[4]

The McTavishes were also growing wealthier. On the death of his consumptive cousin Simon McTavish in 1828, John inherited the entailed McTavish estate, which included the Dunardary estate in Argyllshire, the McTavish mansion in Montreal (between the present-day McTavish and Peel Streets) and British and Canadian family trusts. The bequest was timely as the McTavish nursery was expanding. 'I have begun a long letter to you my darling but must postpone finishing it, as I feel too nervous to write', a heavily pregnant Emily confided to Marianne on 18 March. 'Mama says it is keeping Lent but I don't subscribe to that opinion.' Her second son, Alexander, appeared later that month.[5]

In 1830 McTavish decreed that his elder son Carroll, now twelve, was old enough to be sent to school in England. Whatever misgivings Emily might have, she kept them to herself. She and John had long agreed that their children would be brought up in her faith and that their sons' education would be his decision. Carroll once appealed to her about military school, only to be told, 'Your father will act as his judgment dictates – he has left me in charge of Mary's [May's] education but I never give an opinion respecting that of my boys.' She had sent three-year-old May the previous year to the Infant School in Baltimore 'to keep her out of mischief', she said, though she did concede, 'I could not give her the attention she required.' While Emily's time was taken up with helping her nonagenarian grandfather and nursing baby Alex through bouts of fever, McTavish took Carroll to be educated at Stonyhurst College, a Jesuit boarding school in Lancashire. [6]

However painful for them to part with Carroll, a lovable, personable boy, it was necessary 'to make a *good* and well Educated Man' of him, and reinforce his Britishness (he was, after all, only a quarter American). His progress and well-being thereafter pervade family letters. His father encouraged his 'dearest Boy' to ride like a gentleman. 'I hear you were fined half a Crown at the Riding School in London for falling off your Horse. Sitting (or rather Sticking) on a Horse is one thing – but riding well and gracefully is quite another affair; and one which is entirely neglected in this Country.' His aunts were overjoyed to have him in their care during the holidays, though Emily was sure they would spoil him as much as his grandmother had done, sighing 'there is no one like an anxious Mother, who is clear sighted to every defect'. She missed her 'darling boy' dreadfully and prayed to bring him to her arms once more.

His grandmother Caton meanwhile urged: 'Hold up your head my beloved Boy – it gives a gentleman like air & will expand yr chest & be the best safe guard against consumption, that fatal malady in your family.' She sent him chatty letters full of family news. His 'Grandpapa' Carroll's failing eyesight prevented him from reading anything – she and Emily now read to him alternately every day and Emily dealt with his letters – though he remained otherwise in excellent health. Alex and May, however, were thriving. 'Your dear little Brother is a fine boy & I love him the better for being so much like you, he crawls about the floor', Mary Carroll Caton informed Carroll on 23 April, while dear little May was 'so very engaging & often makes a speech to your Portrait!' It was also a blessing to know that Carroll had his aunts to protect him 'in a foreign Country'; he was always to remember, she told him, that 'aunt Wellesley & Bessy love you very much'. His presence in England provided a new interest for Marianne who cared for him as for a son, fussing over his health and letters, arranging dentist appointments and travels in the school holidays and, as Emily had surmised, spoiling him just a little.[7]

On midsummer's day that year, Marianne, comfortably settled with Bess in the bower of the Regent's Park, read her husband's latest note from Marble Hill. After hearing a bad account from Windsor of George IV's relapse, he had driven over to nearby Bushy Park to call on the King's brother the Duke of Clarence and his wife Princess Adelaide of Saxe-Meiningen. He found the Duke of Clarence 'very much affected' by the King's illness', he repeatedly shed tears in describing it', and the Duchess 'a very agreeable woman, & told me some very amusing stories' as they promenaded round a garden full of flowers, noble oaks and chestnut trees. The road to Bushy was, he learned, unusually busy. Many an aristocrat had been unaccountably struck by the need to savour the unfamiliar delights of Bushy Park and seek out the Clarences.[8]

George IV died early on the morning of 26 June 1830. The Duke of Clarence was asleep in bed when, at 6 a.m., Sir Henry Halford arrived to announce his accession. He received the news that he had become King William IV and decided to return to bed, purportedly saying that 'he wished particularly to do so, having never yet been in bed with a Queen!' Within a few hours, though, he was driving to Windsor, bearing 'a bit of crape on a white hat, grinning and nodding to everybody as he whirled along'. He could not hide his happiness and, compared to 'the last unforgiving animal', Emily Eden wrote, 'This man at least *wishes* to make everybody happy', including his Prime Minister.[9]

The new king assured Wellington that he desired his government to continue as before. On 3 July, however, the Lord Chamberlain resigned and the King proposed his friend Lord Wellesley. The Duke demurred. Wellesley had 'uniformly & bitterly opposed the present administration', except over Catholic emancipation, so that the Duke 'could not conscientiously recommend him to make such a choice'. The inexperienced king immediately agreed. It is no wonder the Duke said he could do more business in ten minutes with the new king than in ten days with the old one; wily George IV had informed his ministers only after he had made the appointments.

This was the second occasion that the Duke had thwarted his eldest brother's ambitions for office but there was, this time, political justification for his actions. In the long course of Wellesley's public career, as political alliances had regrouped, he moved from being an ardent Pittite to a moderate Whig. As he made clear to Marianne: 'I have felt it to be my public duty to oppose the present Administration, & that accordingly I have voted against them in Parliament, & that I am determined to oppose them in the next Parliament.'[10]

Yet, where it would have been impossible for him to accept office under the present Tory government, it would be entirely feasible for Marianne to do so. Early in July the King's brother the Duke of Sussex wrote at the behest of the Queen to offer her the appointment of Lady of the Bedchamber, usually referred to as Lady-in-Waiting, with a salary of £500 [£38,000] a year. She would be asked to attend the Queen at court twice a year, usually for a month or two at a time but sometimes for longer at her Majesty's pleasure. Marianne, honoured by the Queen's notice and pleased to have the occupation, wrote to announce it to her husband. Wellesley, somewhat startled, replied that he would have to explain to Lord Grey that it would not change his Whig allegiance. Marianne knew that she did not owe her appointment to political consideration, 'it was the Queen's own kindness that prompted her to confer such a flattering mark of favor on me.' She had come to know her through Charlotte, Lady Bedingfeld, also at court and a fellow 'Cat' (Catholic). Marianne was determined to accept the appointment. 'I see no reason why I should not take a situation so agreeable to me', she reasoned to her husband.[11]

The style of the new court was in marked contrast with the previous one. The bonhomie of the sixty-five-year-old William IV endeared him to the public as much as it ruffled office-holders. 'He behaved with great inde-cency', pronounced Greville after George IV's funeral, where the 'Sailor King' unregally darted around shaking hands with people and could be heard calling out, 'Generals, generals, keep step, keep step! Admirals, keep step!' At St James's Palace, the presentations of new brides 'were conducted in a very *unceremonious* manner, as you may imagine with our *citizen King*', Lady Elizabeth Fielding recounted. 'The King forgot to kiss my sister Louisa, and shook hands with her instead. Some he kissed on both cheeks, some not at all, just as the fancy took him!'[12]

He entertained a large company on a scale which alarmed his Treasurer, Sir William Fremantle. There have seldom been less than forty at dinner, Fremantle groaned, 'I am in dread at the expense.' But the King had no intention of emulating George IV, he was temperate and kept in check by the Queen's practical qualities. Harriet Granville returned from an audience declaring she was 'quite enchanted with her' and thought her 'the merriest, most natural, most sensible person she ever met with'. Others were disenchanted with her commonplace majesty; 'a little insignificant person as ever I saw', claimed one lady spectator at an inspection of the Tower. 'She was dressed "exceedingly plain" in bombazine, with a little shabby muslin collar, dyed Leghorn hat and leather shoes.'

Fremantle explained to the Duke of Buckingham that she 'does not want to be a Queen'. But a queen she had to be and the cultural flourishes and showmanship of George IV's entertainments were smothered by the homeliness of sitting around her mahogany needlework table while the King snoozed. The Queen, however, was trying to instil some respectability into the British Court and, as Mary Frampton expressed it, to draw 'some degree of line as to character in those she invites' and receives.[13]

Yet Queen Adelaide's course was strewn with the debris of Regency mores. She was herself living with the illegitimate FitzClarences, born of the King's long liaison with the famous actress Mrs Jordan. While the daughters married and settled down in the nobility, the sons had an unhappy time shackled to the court but deprived of royal status and tormented by innuendo. 'Can anything be more indecent than the entry of a Sovereign into his capital, with one bastard riding before him, and another by his carriage?' ran one press attack by the *Morning Post*. Their aunt by marriage, the Duchess of Kent, did not wish her daughter and their cousin Princess Victoria to be contaminated by their company – which made for strained gatherings at court.

Marianne also shared the problem of a husband's irregular family, which both women managed with perfect charity and tact. They also shared the misery of being left childless. The Queen became extremely fond of Marianne and her 'kind feeling Heart'. Marianne was devoted to her and had a copy of Audubon's book *Birds of America* specially bound to present to her. Wellesley, a keen ornithologist, thought it magnificent. 'I fear the Binding (which is the grandest I ever saw) will be very expensive to you; I hope Grandpapa is to pay.' He teased her about the illustration for the Penanted Grouse, shown with a pair of extra wings to its head, 'it appears to me to be a *Yankee* Fib'.[14]

The new reign opened with a succession of entertainments. 'I hope you are sufficiently gorged with reviews, balls, dinners & breakfasts', wrote Wellesley to Marianne and Bess. It had been many years since the British public had enjoyed the presence of a queen consort. When Wellesley arranged to send Queen Adelaide a posy of violets from the garden he had to ask his American wife: 'Not having written to a *Queen* since Queen Charlotte's time I forget the Address; do you begin Madam? or how?'

He had warned Marianne that she would find being a lady-in-waiting 'troublesome enough, although honourable'. Not just from the 'waiting' duties of attendance on the Queen when she would have to sit or stand for hours. But, Wellesley also knew, from an impetuous or careless remark that could give offence for, as Lady Louisa Stuart would write in 1835, 'if once a prejudice gets into a Royal head, it can never be got out again to the end of time'. Marianne, nevertheless, enjoyed the court where her discretion and tact were held in high esteem and her skills of diplomacy were such as to make an American of a son of George III. King William, who had visited America as a sailor, would astonish guests in 1833, when he declared that 'it was always a matter of serious regret to him that he had not been born a free, independent American, so much he respected that nation, and considered Washington the greatest man that ever lived'.[15]

Marianne had been the first American marchioness and she was now the first daughter of the American Republic to become a courtier. Her fellow courtiers and their visitors could not quite believe that she was, indeed, a Yankee at the court of King William and, as such, she naturally invited condescension. Lady Wharncliffe, wife of the Leeds estates' trustee, saw her in waiting at the Royal Pavilion in Brighton and marvelled to her daughter: 'really it is quite remarkable to see the perfect *ease* & propriety of her manner in her *place*. It is as if she had been born at Court, & certainly never for a moment reminds one that she is a Yankee.'[16]

Marianne was at Windsor when the conversation turned to the best-selling book *The Domestic Manners of the Americans*, which Frances Trollope had written after being enticed to America by Fanny Wright, who had stayed on after Lafayette's triumphal tour, and founded a colony at Nashoba, Tennessee, to educate and emancipate slaves. Mrs Trollope, however, had disliked her stay, first at Nashoba, and then at Cincinnati. Both women failed in their American projects and returned home, Fanny Wright after taking her slaves to freedom in Haiti and Fanny Trollope after her business ventures folded.

Fanny Trollope inflicted further critical blows upon the battered body of the American Republic. 'Other nations have been called thin-skinned, but the citizens of the Union have no skins at all', she avowed. And they became apoplectic when they read her book. Americans, especially East Coast ones, were astounded by her prejudice. There was not a single fault found by her in western manners – the spitting, table manners, too free speech – that was not complained about by the higher class of American.

At Windsor her account of American speech excited most comment. Marianne was asked 'Do you come from that part of America where they "guess" and where they "calculate"?' – To which the King swiftly interjected, 'Lady Wellesley comes from where they *fascinate!*' This vignette would often be repeated, not least by Bess who delightedly related it to Creevey. He had long since revised his opinion of the Caton sisters as *parvenues* and was much taken with Marianne. 'I have been *so* lucky in picking up a playfellow in Lady Wellesley', he wrote after meeting her at Buxton Spa. 'I have walked for an hour with her daily, and in my life I never found a more agreeable companion.' Wellesley could not refrain from teasing her: 'You must be a well trained Courtier, to go to Court to hear your own Country ridiculed; I *guess* & *calculate* you *are progressing.*'[17]

Emily, too, was progressing. On a spring day in 1831 a stream of well-wishers descended upon the Caton town house in Baltimore. Emily had given birth to her fourth child, a third son, Richard Caton McTavish. Her father had managed to dash off a few lines with the news to catch the sailing of *The Robin* to Liverpool but her mother knew that only she could furnish her elder daughters with the satisfying details of the confinement. 'You will have heard my dear ones three ere you receive this letter of Emily's safety & well doing – & that the little boy is perfectly well – She is better than I have ever known her to be at this period – altho' she has suffered for a long time – most severely.' As Mary Carroll Caton sat at her writing table on 29 March, she wished Marianne and Louisa had 'just such a sweet infant'. She sent them 'an infinity of love' from Emily, who attributed her fecundity to drinking lots of water. 'I wish you would drink every morning before you breakfast a jug of alkaline water, you cannot tell it from soda water, it is made of potash – or soda – but stronger, I will get the proportions from Grouche', she urged Marianne. 'It has been of more use to me than any thing I ever tried – I particularly wish you would try it, it cannot injure you, I think Lou would find it strengthening.'[18]

One of Emily's well-wishers was their old friend Susan Decatur fresh from Washington City and full of accounts of 'the Eaton woman' whom the President 'continually and mistakenly champions'. Political life was at an impasse with Cabinet members refusing to meet Mrs Eaton and the President refusing to part with Mr Eaton. When over a hundred congressmen threatened to abandon Jackson if the Petticoat War continued, a political crisis was under way. 'You ask how are things in Washington,' a bemused Benjamin Crowninshield replied to a friend, 'perhaps the strangest in the world, because for the first time, I believe the destiny of the nation hangs on a *woman's* favor.'

Would Peggy Eaton destroy an administration? Not quite, just the resignation of the entire Cabinet in April. The scandal continued to cling to the President even after the Eatons retired to Tennessee in September.

Thereafter official entertainments became small, modest affairs compared to the balls and receptions given by Dolley Madison and Louisa Adams. The unofficial sphere, where society and politics met, shrank as social events in official government circles were determined by political rather than social needs. The ladies of Washington politicked no more and became just like elite women elsewhere in America.[19]

The Reform Bill

As Emily retreated into her home and private life, in less democratic England Marianne was advancing into a political storm. Although she had assured Wellesley that her royal appointment was non-political, she was being proved wrong. During the Reform Bill crisis of 1830–2, she was subjected to press invective in the wake of her royal mistress – symptomatic of the hostility directed towards the perceived power of women to influence politics.

The issue of parliamentary reform, to extend the right to vote and abolish rotten boroughs, while not new, moved to head the British political agenda in 1830. Cobbett attracted large audiences at meetings to promote the subject, and so did the political unions. The first, founded in Birmingham in 1829 by a group including a prominent banker Thomas Attwood, became 'the most powerful political force in the Midlands', attracting press coverage and stimulating interest in the question of Reform throughout the country. None of which helped the Wellington government; already unpopular, it lost further support in the general election required to be held within six months of the King's accession. The Duke blamed the July revolution in France, which had placed the Duc d'Orléans on the throne. The new French king was none other than Marianne's old émigré friend Louis-Philippe, who walked about the streets of Paris with a tricolour on his hat and shook hands with passing citizens. The events in France were swiftly followed by a revolution in Belgium to secure independence from Holland. All this raised fears of revolt spreading to England.[1]

While London did sport its own tricolour ribbons and cockades at the monster Radical meetings held that August, of far more effect was the outbreak of violence in the countryside during the Swing riots. Agricultural distress and the fear of new threshing machinery erupted in the burning of ricks and buildings and the smashing of machines across England, including on Wellington's estate. Through this mêlée stalked a legendary bogeyman who sent farmers threatening letters signed 'Captain Swing'. No one had ever seen him, though all alike lived in terror of him. The Swing riots lasted sixteen days and added to the general feeling that the government had lost control of events.[2]

In London, petitions and meetings began to menace the government. On 2 November, in the debate on the royal address to the new Parliament, Lord Grey spoke of the need for moderate reform whereupon Wellington completely misjudged the political climate and declared that he was not prepared to bring forward any reforms: 'as long as I hold any station in the government of the country, I shall always feel it my duty to resist such measures when proposed by others'. The blunder was clear even to his supporters. When asked about what the Duke had said, Aberdeen answered: 'He said that we were going out.'

To everyone's surprise they did. On 15 November the government was inadvertently defeated over the Civil List and, although this was not an issue of confidence, Wellington resigned. The King was sufficiently unsettled by the unrest in the country to feel, he told Peel, that concessions over Reform were essential. He sent for his next First Minister, Lord Grey, and after thirty-three years of unbroken Tory rule, the Whigs returned to power. Greville, in attendance as Clerk of the Council, described the changeover of government on 22 November 1830 when after the old ministers gave up their seals of office, they met the new ministers arriving to take up theirs. 'The effect was very droll' with all the Cabinet there including 'Lord Wellesley his little eyes twinkling with joy, and Brougham, in Chancellor's costume'. Wellesley's appointment as Lord Steward of the Household, though a minor office, returned him to public life and occupation, thereby helping Marianne.[3]

Such feeling had been aroused by the Duke's declaration against any reform that the Whigs assumed office on a wave of popularity – and of expectation that they would deliver it. Proposed measures included enfranchising the large industrial towns such as Manchester and abolishing the small or rotten boroughs. When Louisa married Carmarthen, he was a member of Parliament for the small borough of Helston, Cornwall where the Duke of Leeds's interest was paramount as a large Cornish landowner. At the election of 1830, however, his father vindictively gave the seat to someone else, so opposed did he remain to Car's marriage.[4]

The struggle for reform started on 1 March 1831 when Lord John Russell introduced the first Bill in the House of Commons. Many MPs realised they were listening to their own extinction. Russell sat down in 'a profound silence'. Initial stupefaction was swiftly followed by cheers from pro-reformers and angry incredulity from the Tories for whom this was not Reform but Revolution. Throughout the ensuing seven nights of debate, the excitement generated was universal; it was as if the whole nation had suddenly become politicised. People waited hours to catch the latest news from arriving express coaches and Scottish labourers clubbed together to afford the newspaper, two days' old but at half-price.

News was also eagerly awaited in Maryland. 'I wish I cou'd know, my precious Mary^e, that all was well on the other side of the Water', Mary Carroll Caton wrote anxiously from Baltimore on the day of the second reading of the Bill. 'We hear such frightful stories of the state of England – the horrid state of the times, & the impossibility of the Govt making these reforms, which the disaffected require, without destroying every thing – tho' I make great allowances for exaggeration.' There was no exaggeration, however, about the tense proceedings in the House on the night of 22 March. As Creevey wrote from Brooks's, 'Devilish near, was it not?' The second reading of the Reform Bill was carried by a single vote.[5]

Illuminations lit up the country in celebration although the Bill was likely to be defeated during the committee stage by the Tories. The government now faced either the dissolution of Parliament or resignation when the vote went against it in committee.

The history of the struggle over the Reform Bill has concentrated upon men's political power, wielded in the official space of monarchy, government, parliament and union. Yet there is another, camouflaged, story about women's political power. This one is caught in the murmur of asides and the snatches of conversation floating in the unofficial space of drawing rooms, dining rooms and ballrooms as it drifts through calls, visits and dinners. Once grasped, though, the filmy threads of women's influence weave through the diary entries and letters about the Reform crisis, especially the diaries of Charles Greville. As Clerk of the Privy Council under the Wellington and Grey ministries he retained access to both Tory and Whig sides throughout the socially divisive period of Reform. Greville discloses that political negotiations were frequently conducted through women intermediaries who commanded respect, such as Lady Cowper.[6]

Marianne, Bess and Louisa found it easy to mingle with friends on both sides of the Reform divide as they were looked upon as foreigners and thus politically neutral. At this juncture, however, Marianne found herself singled out for being what the Duke called 'a female politician' in her role as a courtier. It is not simple to disentangle the threads of her perceived influence. Marianne flitted in and out of court, hovering in attendance on Her Majesty and resting in near anonymity behind the throne. As the soul of discretion, what she did tell Bess, Louisa and Wellesley only occasionally emerges in surviving correspondence. Where she was unlike her fellow courtiers was in the way she straddled the Reform divide, keeping confidantes in opposing camps. She was accused of intriguing on behalf of the Tories; and yet was herself that most unusual of Reform courtiers: a Republican and a Whig.

Unlike any other British institution, the court had always offered aristocratic women access to power through the ear of kings and queens.

The early nineteenth century was still an age of palace politics in that the monarch had an important role in the making and unmaking of govern- ments and in shaping their policies. It mattered, therefore, that William IV and Adelaide's court was, almost to a person, resolutely Tory and resolutely anti-Reform; Herries confirmed that 'all the Royal Family, and the FitzClarences too, are against Reform'. The King, however, was determined to support his ministers. The queen, a decided Tory, was said never to speak in public of her political opinions. When pressed about this by Sir John Malcolm, Marianne tactfully answered that although the Queen influenced the King, she 'never shows that she has any power. Never speaks on poli- tics nor the King either in his private society.'[7]

Yet she knew that Their Majesties did discuss politics. That March, after she relayed the latest reports from home to them – that some of the southern states might secede from the Union over the renewal of the Tariff Act, which had long favoured the North – they talked about what policy England should adopt. The King thought the right one was alliance with the northern states and instructed his Ambassador Charles Vaughan to see Lord Palmerston, then Foreign Secretary. Vaughan's scepticism about Marianne's information deepened when the Foreign Office confirmed no such reports had arrived. By the autumn, however, secession and even war loomed; South Carolina nullified the tariff and readied for secession, Vice-President Calhoun resigned to support his state, and, declaring nullification tanta- mount to treason, the President dispatched a man of war and arms to Charleston to enforce the tariff. Clay only averted the danger of the disso- lution of the United States by securing the passage of a compromise Tariff Act.[8]

In England, when the fate of the government, the bill and the peace of the nation rested ultimately with the King, it was not surprising that minis- ters, and the press, feared that he would be swayed by his family and courtiers to decide against them. The *Morning Herald* threatened 'Woe betide the Queen' if she used her influence against the people's will. The Prime Minister at first disregarded the rumours, writing to Lady Grey on 7 April: 'I believe implicitly in what Taylor says, as to her not wishing to interfere, and that the King, if she were so inclined, would not let her.' As tension over the fate of the bill mounted, the pro-Reform press attacked the Queen's suspi- cious foreign influence – *The Times* remarking that 'a foreigner was no very competent judge of English liberties, and politics are not the proper field for female enterprize or exertion'; while the anti-Reform press attacked Marianne's influence, speaking darkly of Yankee chatter and 'a certain lady Republican plaguing the King about Reform'.[9]

As the reformers had feared, a spoiling motion was carried in the Commons and, to forestall one in the Lords, on 22 April, a reluctant King was persuaded by Grey to dissolve Parliament immediately. When the King arrived at the House of Lords he could have been forgiven for thinking he was too late to prevent a revolution. Inside the stately Lords' chamber, the Ultras were hurling abuse, Londonderry was brandishing a whip at the Duke of Richmond while five other peers clung to his coat-tails. 'What was all the hubbub?' the King asked his Lord Chancellor. 'If it please Your Majesty,' answered Brougham, 'it is the Lords debating.'[10]

The Wellesley family went into mourning two days later when the Duchess of Wellington died, after being seriously ill since January. The sisters had paid visits, sitting at her bedside throughout the spring. She had been such a kind friend to them from their earliest days in London and her suffering, perhaps from cancer, was sad to see. 'It is a relief from the state of torture from which she suffered', sighed Lord Wellesley on hearing the news from Marianne on 25 April. The Duke and his sons went down to Stratfield Saye, leaving her coffin at Apsley House until burial arrangements were finalised. The house left in darkness presented a perfect target when the Lord Mayor ordered pro-Reform illuminations on 27 April and the mob smashed its windows and pulled up the railings. 'The people are gone Mad', the Duke shouted in indignation.[11]

The reformers' message 'The Bill, the whole Bill, and nothing but the Bill' captured the mood of the country. The election result was a landslide victory for the Whigs and Radicals. The King opened Parliament on 23 June, an occasion when the House of Lords was so full of ladies that the peers could not find places. The government introduced the second Reform Bill on 24 June, it passed the Commons by 136 votes on 7 July and was in committee until September.

As Steward of the Household, Wellesley was required to direct arrangements for the forthcoming coronation. Unlike George IV's extravaganza, this king's was to be a modest occasion. 'We have been doing everything to save expense at the Coronation & shall succeed', Wellesley pronounced on 16 July. Carroll was jubilant at the prospect of attending as Marianne's page; 'your Grandmother is very anxious that you should write her a full account', prodded his father. On 8 September the people of London so successfully pushed disorder and distress into the background for the coronation that a foreigner arriving that day would have thought all the reports about Reform disturbances were scaremongering. London was *en fête*.

It was 'a magnificent spectacle', wrote Marianne. 'The King looked well and happy. The dear Queen did her part to perfection; with Piety, dignity and grace.' The peeresses were admired for their beauty and elegant robes. Marianne's grandfather had thoughtfully sent her a present of $5,000 to help cover the expenses of her coronation robes. Lady Dover thought the grouping about the Queen beautiful; the maids of honour in white satin

trains with white wreaths in their hair and those who held the train were
also in white but with plumes and diamonds. Mary Carroll Caton needed
to make no allowance for exaggeration about her daughter's glowing description of the ceremony and the scene in the abbey when the Queen was
crowned and the peeresses in one orchestrated movement placed their coronets upon their heads.[12]

The coronation was but an interlude between acts in the Reform drama
being played out in Parliament. After an unprecedented struggle the
second bill passed the Commons by a resounding majority of 109. 'Now
that the Bill approaches the House of Lords, all its former interest revives',
Lady Wharncliffe's son remarked to her on 18 September, '& the crisis
must be to them most momentous & perplexing.' The Lords were likely
to inflict defeat as all the Tories were united at last against the bill. Where
a peer's inclinations were uncertain even the Duke relied upon the negotiating skills of the ladies to deliver the vote. 'What do you say to Lord
Gage?' he asked Frances Shelley on 24 September. 'Could you insinuate
to him to come up and vote against the Bill, or to give his proxy against
it?' The Duke knew she was 'a *sensible* woman' who would discreetly
manage the affair. 'You are delightful', he exclaimed after she obtained
Gage's promise.

The Whigs believed they were doing their best to preserve the social
order by passing the bill rather than having a more extreme measure forced
upon them later by a more Radical government. The intransigence of both
sides meant that confrontation was inevitable. 'The struggle will be violent
with the old Rogues', as Wellesley described the Tory peers to Marianne,
'but the Country is unanimous in favour of the present Ministers, who are
in very good spirits.'[13]

The ladies from both sides of the Reform question flocked into Town
for the 'intensely interesting' event. Their presence in large numbers was
an exceptional feature of the five nights of Reform debate, as before, only
a few ladies at a time had been allowed to attend the Lords' debates, bundled
behind a red curtain below the bar of the Upper House to hear but not see
the speakers. The insistence of the peeresses, determined not to miss a word
of the Reform debates, had persuaded the Upper House to admit many
more. A crowd of ladies thus piled into the enlarged space, where even
chairs had been provided and the curtain drawn back, to hear the debates.
They signalled their verdict on the speakers by either standing to listen,
raptly, or by sitting down, bored. 'Falmouth began, & spoke most funere-
ally – Rosebery followed, & was pompously dull. The ladies all sat down
till both these men sat down', noted Lord Ellenborough on 6 October. Some
of the women quite forgot themselves in their partisan excitement. 'There
are many anecdotes that would make you laugh, some disgusting of their

violence', reported Caroline Fox. 'One, during Lord Grey's beautiful & touching reply, was furious, using most opprobrious epithets, *Scoundrel, Villain,* & some too strong for utterance for female lips. Lady Mansfield was the offender.'[14]

Bess, the only sister to attend the Lords' debates, also heard Lord Grey. She managed to squeeze in with Marianne's sister-in-law Lady Cowley on two of the nights. 'It was wonderful to hear Lord Grey's moving words,' she enthused to Louisa, but Lord Londonderry shouted 'and was ridiculous'. She and her friends thrived on the late nights and the drama. 'I never felt so eager', admitted Georgiana Dover. 'Do you know the feeling of excitement which makes one feel as if everything depended on one's own individual existence.'

Emotions were so charged that Lord Chancellor Brougham sustained an eloquent defence of the bill for over three hours with the help of two bottles of port negus, but his effort was in vain. On 8 October the bill was defeated by a majority of forty-one, including twenty-one bishops. As the general public woke up to the result, grief and anger filled the hearts of reformers. *The Morning Chronicle* and other prints brought out mourning editions edged in black; shops remained closed; Consols fell nearly a point, there was a run for gold on the Bank of England and serious rioting. Bishops attracted widespread vituperation, and, in November, bonfires boasted a mitred figure.[15]

Into this fervid atmosphere the dismissal of Lord Howe, the Queen's Lord Chamberlain, at the request of the government, exploded with the force of a cannon ball, damaging relations between monarch and ministers, and being interpreted as proof of Tory plots at court to defeat Reform. Marianne was with the Queen at Windsor when Grey arrived on 10 October to see the King about a third bill. Grey asked for the removal of Lord Howe, a vocal anti-reformer who had just voted against the second bill, offering to explain to the Queen the effect that opposition from people in her Household to the King's ministers must produce. According to Grey, the King agreed and undertook to break the news to the Queen, who 'did not understand this country and who might take fire if a change in her family was notified by a Minister'.[16]

Unfortunately, Howe told her first. 'I would not believe it,' she wrote in her diary, 'for I had trusted in, and built firmly on the King's love to me.' She realised the strain the King was under over Reform 'but unfortunately he has not been able to resist the representations of his Ministers, and yielded, and I fear it will be the beginning of much evil. May God support us and protect and shield this country and save the King from ruin.' She knew that the King had previously differentiated between *his* Household, whose members had to support the government of the day or resign, and *her* Household, whose members' political preferences played no part in their appointments. The King shared her fondness for Howe and had said that Howe had the right to vote as he pleased.

She therefore blamed Grey. Just as he saw Tory courtiers in every closet whispering anti-Reform propaganda into royal ears, the Queen saw Whig politicians plotting to dismiss all her Household and isolate her from the King and their loyal subjects. She foresaw that, as the Radicals gained the upper hand with the Whigs, the monarchy would be overthrown.[17]

Reports of Howe's dismissal spread rapidly through the castle. The queen's ladies received them with disbelief, Marianne wrote to Louisa. What could possibly be achieved by depriving the court of Lord Howe, and 'if there was now some thing political about *his* appointment, might not all *ours* be considered so as well?' The Queen had kept to her rooms since seeing Lord Howe. That evening, five minutes before the dinner hour of seven o'clock, Marianne went with her friend Lady Westmeath to the Queen's private drawing room. There they waited with the other ladies and Howe. Her Majesty kept them waiting a long time and the reason was clear as soon as she entered: her pale face and red eyes revealing her distress. 'I had a hard struggle before I appeared at table, after this blow, which I felt deeply as an insult, which filled me with indignation. I felt myself deeply wounded both as wife and queen. I cannot conquer the feeling', she confided to her diary.

Even the King's usual geniality could not divert the company as they watched the Queen, and Howe, red-faced with suppressed indignation. He was being made a scapegoat for the defeat of Grey's bill. The King's reprimand to Howe had been leaked to *The Times*. A mortified Howe wrote angrily to the Duke that 'my Lord Brougham may yet find me a thorn in his side'.[18]

It was far more likely, though, that Brougham, a skilful political operator, would be a thorn in his or the Queen's side. In the months leading up to the Lords' October vote, he had been busy feeding the press with snippets of gossip to discredit Queen Adelaide and weaken her anti-Reformist 'Petticoat Ascendancy'. Brougham was not popular with the ladies. 'Dirty, cynical and coarse' the Duchess of Dino called him and Marianne was wary of his biting tongue. Wellesley, however, enjoyed his company and intellect. Once Marianne realised that he was regularly talking to Brougham in the Lords, she used this conduit to counter some of the wild stories spread by the Whigs about the Queen's politics, telling Wellesley that Reform was never discussed. She had been with the King and Queen hourly while the Reform Bill was debated in the Lords but that 'not a word was ever uttered on the subject at Court'.

Wellesley remained unconvinced. He believed the Queen, like all the other Germanic royalties he had known, was an ill-educated reactionary. She had, he told Edward Littleton, 'continually thwarted the King'. This of course was the Whig line but, Whig that she was, Marianne continued to take the Queen's part and believed and told her sisters that it was Lord Grey and the ministers who had ill-treated the poor Queen.'[19]

Three days later the Queen dined at the French ambassador's where the Whigs were out in force. Marianne, in attendance, gently voiced surprise that the Queen's personal appointments had been made political, and told Lady Grey of 'the Household's sadness over Lord Howe's removal' – sentiments she intended Lady Grey to convey to the Prime Minister. Lady Grey also appears to have conveyed them to Lord Holland whose diary entry for 14 October scornfully records: 'The Queen scarcely spoke to Lord Grey at dinner, and Her Ladies affect sorrow, indignation and surprise at the dismissal of Lord Howe.' Marianne wished only to protect the Queen. 'She is calumniated in all the papers and made ill with worry on behalf of the King', Marianne commented.[20]

On 20 October the Queen gave a formal party after the prorogation of Parliament. The immense drawing room at St James's Palace groaned as ministers, diplomats and their ladies stood for hours waiting for the Queen, attended by Marianne and Lady Albemarle, to complete walking round the circle. Suddenly the room bristled to attention as Queen Adelaide smartly passed by Lord Grey. 'I watched the Queen going round the circle, and as far as I could judge she appeared to *cut* Lord Grey', Georgiana Dover gasped to her sister. Others present confirmed that the Queen absolutely cut the Prime Minister and barely acknowledged the Lord Chancellor. Some ladies were convinced the influence behind the Queen's behaviour was of Yankee provenance. The Queen's 'mind has been poisoned by the bad entourage, who are doing their utmost to convince her the removal of Ld Howe is a *personal insult*', Lady Holland wrote the following day. 'All her ladies to a *man* are furious, & encourage her perverseness. The worst of them is Lady Wellesley, the Republican!'[21]

'A foreigner' remained a ready weapon of disparagement and, at this time of national crisis, it was inevitable that the two prominent foreigners at court, one 'a nasty German frow' and the other 'a silly petulant Yankee' according to the Morning Chronicle, were singled out for denunciation. Queen Adelaide clung to Marianne and confided in her. At the end of her period of waiting, she pressed her to stay. Although Marianne largely lived apart from Wellesley, it did not always suit him to have her at court. Before she left Windsor, the Queen kissed her and taking a long gold chain from around her neck gave it to her as a mark of her affection.

Henry Brougham, the Lord Chancellor, trying to persuade a sleepy William IV to create peers during the Reform Bill crisis. In the background, courtiers watch for the King's reaction.

On 3 January 1832 Grey went down to see the King at Brighton and proposed that additional peers be created to force the bill through the Lords. Marianne and Bess were staying at the Pavilion and so saw Grey. Marianne remained a Whig standard-bearer at the Tory court. 'Fortunately all the Court were not of the same side, so that Lord Grey was put on his guard', Le Marchant acknowledged. Louisa was in hopes that if any peers were to be made, and it was known that eldest sons would be the most acceptable candidates to the King, Marianne would speak to Lord Grey about Carmarthen.[22]

The question of peer-making remained tantalisingly unresolved throughout the spring as the bill ground its way through the committee stage in the Commons, where it was carried on 23 March, and at last, reached the Lords. The excitement was so intense that ladies set off at eleven in the morning to obtain a seat for the evening's debate. Their numbers had to be restricted again so crammed were MPs, as Littleton recorded on 10 April: '[I]ntense interest. Stanley, Graham lying on the floor at the end of the House of Lords opposite the throne, all night.'

The King was so nervous about the fate of the bill that he arrived in London two days' early. Grey was equally tense, writing: 'The rejection of this bill on the second reading would be to me such ruin as never fell upon a public man.' With the help of Tory 'waverers' and the odd bishop, the government carried the second reading by 9 votes on 13–14 April. It was an immense relief for the King, who admitted he never slept a wink till he learnt the result, and for Grey, who had succeeded without creating peers. Yet the Whig triumph was to be short-lived; in committee, the government was defeated on 7 May.[23]

Peers or No Peers was once again the question as the Cabinet agreed it was a resignation issue. Marianne relayed the news to Louisa at Huntley Lodge. 'Car writes in answer to you. It may be shown to Lord Grey. I do hope he will be made a peer', Louisa scrawled back. It was one thing for Car to apply for a peerage so as to be independent of his father and quite another to disown the political allegiance of his family. 'Pray do not let it get about what I am trying for, or that I am thinking of supporting Lord Grey', he entreated Marianne. '*Above all* I do not wish *my family* to know *any thing* about it, so pray endeavour to have it kept a secret.'

As it happened, all the eldest sons of the Dukes of Leeds, bar one, had been called up to the Lords but Carmarthen knew that his father would do nothing to help him. As it also happened, he admired Lord Grey and wanted to support his government. Unfortunately, Carmarthen was not alone. Grey later told Creevey that the applications made to him for peerages had been over 300 and for baronetages 'absolutely endless'. The King, however, refused to create the requisite number of additional peers to secure the bill. The government duly resigned and Wellesley went out of office. A month of near anarchy, the famous Days of May, followed. Alarming reports poured in from the country. Le Marchant heard that 'people were tired of signing petitions and addresses – they wished to fight it out at once, and the sooner the better' and 'a manufacturer offered to supply the Birmingham Union with 10,000 muskets at 15s a piece'.[24]

The King knew the necessity of passing a Reform measure. On 12 May he asked Wellington to form a government to pass the Reform Bill. Peel refused to support a measure he had just opposed and, without him, Wellington could not succeed. In any case the country would not let him. A meeting held at the radical Francis Place's house decided that towns were to be barricaded and placards printed 'To stop the Duke, go for Gold' to cause a run on the banks.

'The whole country is in a state little short of insurrection', recorded Littleton on 14 May as the funds fell and the barricades went up. The Duke did the sensible thing and relinquished forming a government. The King sent for Grey, who insisted upon the creation of peers as a condition of resuming office. The King tearfully agreed. As Tory peers 'skulked in clubs and country houses', the bill finally passed in the Lords on 4 June: 'this event which I have long wished to see, will be very pleasing to *some folks*', Wellesley scribbled to Marianne.[25]

That day Their Majesties attended a military review in Hyde Park to mingled hisses and cheers; by the evening they were being cheered enthusiastically as they arrived at Apsley House where the blinds of sheet iron screening the broken windows had been thrown open to allow a blaze of light to stream out upon the arriving uniformed and bejewelled guests, including Marianne and Bess. Using the family code to indicate that they were safe after all the disturbances, Bess wrote at the top of her June letter: 'All's well'.[26]

The Last Signer

In Maryland, Emily and the family were looking forward to a no less momentous celebration of their own. Grandpapa Carroll's ninety-fifth birthday in September would be a national occasion. The previous year, Emily had arranged a large party attended by the great of Washington City. Carroll of Carrollton had dined with forty guests and the family, 'amongst others the good old President, who stayed a day or 2 with us, we had 3 Cabinet Ministers also & a very large party of Gentlemen', Emily had told Carroll.

She was now a matron of about thirty-seven years and had relinquished any claim to elegance or beauty. Her lack of interest in fashion was something of a sisterly joke, as she intimated to Louisa: 'I wish you could have seen Mary's delight at receiving her aunt's beautiful present – the Child is very fond of dress, you will say she did not acquire that from me.' After sitting for her only surviving portrait, she admitted to her sisters, 'I am afraid when you all see my picture, I shall have altered so much, that you will not know me – but the heart is still the same, and clings to the dear sisters of early youth, who shared my joys and sorrows, and now my ardent prayers for an eternal union!'[1]

It was fifteen years since she had seen Louisa and Bess but, despite their long separation, their sisterhood remained close, flourishing on shared confidences, memories and long letters. Emily tied her sisters to their homeland and American identity. Americans assumed her sisters led more glamorous, exciting public lives, all three beautiful women moving in the highest circles, at ease in society, at court and mingling with famous people – such must be the happiness of heiresses. And, equally, they assumed that Emily, the stay-at-home sister, led a dull, secluded existence, devoid of diversion and out of society, such as would bore her sisters to death – as it did Betsy Bonaparte.

Yet Emily was contented. She was happy in her marriage, her family and her home life. None of her sisters could say the same; the misery of not yet having a baby still gnawed at Louisa who otherwise was very happy with Car. To McTavish's suggestions that they return to his native Scotland or visit her sisters in London, Emily always demurred. Although she longed to see them, in truth, she could not bear the thought of leaving home. Domesticity and caring for others fulfilled her. McTavish called her the Lady of the House, and so she continued to be, in her own house in Second Street, Baltimore, at the Manor and helping her mother at the Caton town house. Capable, serene and without any other ambition, Emily enjoyed looking after them all.

She might have appeared to live out of society in comparison with her sisters but the American world still came, in increasing numbers as the years passed, on pilgrimage to Caton House and to the Manor to pay their respects to her grandfather. In this way Emily saw more of the important people in American public life and more European visitors than most American married women outside Washington City ever could. Six years before, in 1826, the year in which Americans had celebrated the fiftieth anniversary of the signing of the Declaration of Independence, only three Signers survived of the original fifty-six. On that Fourth of July, John Adams had died at his farm at Quincy. His last words were 'Thomas Jefferson survives', not knowing that Jefferson had died earlier that same day at Monticello.*

As the last of that immortal band of patriots, the long-admired Carroll of Carrollton became a national treasure. 'That bright constellation the light of which has shone upon the world for fifty years, is now reduced to a single star, whose beams feebly twinkle on the horizon and soon will be seen no more', was the Revd Philip Courtland Hay's description. At the grand age of eighty-nine Carroll appeared anything but feeble to the streams of visitors and delegations calling on him. He retained 'all the vivacity and grace of youth', according to Macready the actor, and insisted upon accompanying departing visitors downstairs, telling Macready in the liveliest manner, 'Oh I shall never see you again, and so I will see the last of you.' He continued to plunge into his cold bath and ride every day at the Manor, telling Robert Gilmor that his horse knew the distance so well from habit that, without guiding him, he always turned at the fifth milestone.[2]

When he appeared in public people gathered to gaze at him and those with introductions brought their children to see him so that they could say they had spoken to the last surviving Signer. Captain Basil Hall, grandson of Lord Selkirk, and his wife Margaret Hall, were prepared to find the Signer by no means extraordinary. She had to admit she was quite wrong. 'He met us with as light and active a step as the youngest person in the room, and I cannot say that I discovered one single mark of old age either in his manner, appearance, or faculties.'

* This is Susan Boylston Adams Clark's account, 9 July 1826, cited by David McCullough. Another version is 'Thomas Jefferson still lives'.

She described how 'everything was in grand style and well arranged'. The Catons 'have a delightful house and a very handsome establishment, no less than three servants in livery, which I dare say you will laugh at to hear me mention as a thing worthy of remark, but except at Mr Harrison's and Mr Lenox's at Philadelphia, I have not seen a servant in livery in the country, and you cannot think how *grand* it appears to me'. Her only complaint was that Emily could not converse properly in Spanish or French with a Spanish guest. Her grandfather, however, remained fluent in the language and was delighted to hear that Carroll McTavish was applying himself at Stonyhurst to French and, most importantly, Latin.[3]

Wellesley assured Carroll McTavish that:

> Your scheme of making money by teaching Latin to Bessy is an extremely wise project; & I think you have managed very cunningly in fining her a penny for every mistake. You will make much more by this contrivance, than by the price you have put upon each lesson: Before she has mastered '*Propria quo Marisbus*' I have no doubt you will have made a fortune; which I hope you will lay out in the Baltimore Rail Way.

If he did he would be adding to the major Carroll investment in this new feat of engineering, the Baltimore and Ohio Railroad. For once the whole family was as convinced as Caton that it would make money. Carroll of Carrollton had laid the foundation stone in 1828 and he sat on the Board of Directors. The family, therefore, took a great interest in the development of this local railroad. 'You will be glad to hear that the Rail Road is now completed as far as Ellicotts Mills, a distance of 11 miles, & the journey is usually performed in one hour', McTavish informed his eldest son. 'The Cars contain about 30 passengers each, and are drawn by one horse, – a fresh one being put in half way. The price for a Drive to the Mills and back is 75/100 or ¾ 1/2d sterling – 12 Carriages starting every day.'[4]

Although Carroll of Carrollton continued to take an interest in these improvements, it was noticeable that, as the world was speeding up, he was slowing down. He was entirely dependent upon Mary Carroll Caton, aged fifty-two, and Emily. His eyesight had failed, she warned her sisters, 'he can walk, but cannot read or write, except sign his name – I read to him all day, and write all his letters for him'. This was not, however, apparent to the outside world, which continued to marvel at the longevity and good health of the Signer.

Friends and acquaintances also marvelled at the affectionate regard within the Carroll family, which struck Henry Addington at the Manor in 1826 and later in Dublin where he saw Marianne and Bess. 'I never met with people more devoted to each other than the whole of the Carroll folks,' he observed to Charles Vaughan, 'and believe it arises from their grand bond of Union, old Carroll himself, to whom they all look up as to a directing Planet.'⁵

By the summer of 1832, when Bess was writing 'All's well', it was evident at the Manor that the Planet was losing direction. Except for her time in Canada, Emily had lived with him her entire life. She looked upon the Manor as her real home, where she and her children were at their happiest. 'I long to breathe the fresh air of heaven in the Country', she would say about being there. 'We leave this dear and venerable Mansion in a week,' she wrote, 'it is always with great regret that I turn my back upon the old Manor, and with a feeling of apprehension, as if I never should return to it.'

Her apprehension deepened as her grandfather's health steadily declined. He was too frail to celebrate his ninety-fifth birthday, though he continued indomitably cheerful, propped up in an armchair at Caton House, making little jokes with the family physician and comforting Emily and her mother when they could no longer wipe away tears without his seeing them. When Reverend John Chanche came to administer the Sacrament, he greeted him by saying: 'Emily sent you to me. She takes care of both my body and soul.' Indeed, she had even convinced him in 1830 to provide Manor land and funds to build a large seminary, St Charles College.⁶

On 14 November Emily sent for Reverend Chanche for the last time. As she held Charles Carroll of Carrollton in her arms, he died in his sleep at four o'clock that morning, peacefully leaving his two daughters Mary and Kitty kneeling in prayer at his bedside. The rest of the family was summoned while all the servants gathered in the hall. Caton immediately wrote to Marianne. Grieved not to have been with her beloved grandpapa, she took comfort in the last preserved lock of his hair and the last letter he wrote himself to her; the shaky handwriting wandering across the page to end with the words 'God bless you my dear Maryᵉ and give you health: though so far and so long separated from you & your sisters you are always in my thoughts.'⁷

The news of his death caused regret throughout the United States. President Jackson declared official mourning, an honour only accorded to one other Revolutionary hero, George Washington. City newspapers appeared bordered in black and arrangements were made for a lying-in-state, a public funeral at the cathedral in Baltimore and a procession to accompany the funeral cortège to the Manor, where the last Signer would be buried in the family vault.

The family moved to the Manor, leaving a skeleton staff at Caton House. Charles Arfwedson, a Swede newly arrived in Baltimore, found that two black crepe-covered stakes at the entrance to the house gave the only sign of mourning at the lying-in-state. The room containing the bier had been stripped of all movable furniture except for four burning tapers around a bed covered with a white sheet. At the head of the bed was placed a crucifix and on the bed lay Carroll of Carrollton's body wrapped in a blue morning gown.

'Who could stand in the presence of the venerable patriot and not catch the influence of the holy flame which filled, illuminated and inspired him in 1776?' *Niles' Weekly Register* had asked. The jostling spectators crammed into the large room showed that they certainly could. They pushed and shoved, laughed and swore and shouted and 'even went so far as to examine the morning-gown, to touch the lifeless body, and to place their hands on the forehead'. Arfwedson shuddered at such impropriety. He was no better pleased on 17 November by the funeral ceremony: the 'grand' procession was without order or dignity in the pouring rain, with scarcely a black mourning garment to be seen. Was this the spirit of democracy at work; the democratic society which the Signer had helped to create but had also deprecated? By his standards it was a mob that surged noisily through Caton House to gaze upon him for the last time.[8]

Driving rain having cut short the procession, carriages collected the clergy and mourning party near the cathedral at 12.30 p.m. for the journey to the Manor. On arrival there at 4.30 p.m., Carroll of Carrollton was buried in the family chapel where, Reverend Deluol noted, the Carroll burial vault was under the spot where he had always prayed, on the gospel side near the altar. Refreshments were offered to the large party and it soon became clear that proprieties were not to be better observed at the Manor. Mr Hammond, a neighbour, became exceedingly drunk and when others failed to restrain him, George Howard, the Governor of Maryland, grabbed hold of the inebriated man, 'dragged him to the porch in the hall, shoved him to the ground, and fell on him with a crash'. As Hammond was carted off, Howard returned to the dining room, saying: 'I settled him.'

Although the McTavishes were at the Manor, Emily was not there to see this contretemps. Her horror of drunkenness remained potent. Writing to Carroll in May she had urged him after his education was finished 'to get into business of some kind, for laziness is the Mother of vice' and, she continued:

in this Country, where every one is of some profession, an idle man has no companion, but the vicious and those are drunkards – you know my beloved boy how much we have suffered from that vice, uncle Carroll died in the prime of life from the effects of it – I trust God in his mercy will spare me that affliction in any of my Children, it would certainly kill me.[9]

The torrential rain that poured over Maryland meant that after the funeral the family remained at the Manor and did not return to Baltimore until 19 November. At noon the next day a large group of family members and their advisers gathered in the drawing room of Caton House to see the will opened and read by the Carroll agent George Neilson. The thirty-five pages took so long to read that when McTavish and John White of the Bank of the United States went to deposit them at the court they discovered the Registrar had left for dinner.

Carroll of Carrollton had left a landed estate worth some $1.6 million [£22 m.]. In the will, as expected, he bequeathed the Doughoregan Manor estate, and much else, to his grandson young Charles Carroll, and a third of Carrollton Manor to his Carroll grandchildren. Catonsville, Brooklandwood, Carroll House, 15,897 acres in Pennsylvania, and a third of Carrollton Manor estate went to Mary Carroll Caton and her daughters. Gay Street and 5,897 acres in Pennsylvania went to Kitty Harper and, at her request, Oakland to Charles Harper and a third of Carrollton Manor estate directly to her three surviving children along with land in New York State. Carroll of Carrollton's personal property was nearly all bequeathed in line with the landed properties. His moneyed estate was divided equally between the three branches of the family, taking into account the annuities totalling $1.1 million [£15.4 million] they had already received.[10]

The surprising aspects were the three recently drawn-up codicils. They benefited one person only: Emily. The family immediately began to quarrel bitterly. In deep mourning, expecting to live in seclusion for the foreseeable future, Emily was vilified as a greedy, unscrupulous woman who had obtained property and large sums of money by undue influence over her grandfather when he was blind and with enfeebled understanding.

The row and ensuing legal battle centred upon Folly Farm, part of the Manor estate, formerly farmed by her uncle Carroll and now by her cousin young Charles Carroll. Harriet Carroll's marriage settlement had been secured on Folly Farm until 1830, when her son had reluctantly acceded to his grandfather's request for a deed of release – to build a house there for Emily. The Carroll branch was astounded by the codicils: the first bequeathed half of the personal property at Folly Farm (Folly Quarter) to Emily, together with *half* of the tobacco, corn, wheat, plate and furniture at the Manor; the second of 1830 left Emily 200 shares of US bank stock as an outright gift and one third of the slaves at the Manor; the third, dated 1831, confirmed payments of $6,000, $4,253 and $10,000 to her as well as the outright gift of all Folly Farm with further funds to complete the large plantation house her grandfather was providing for her. This was an enormous bequest. His long-stated purpose had been to divide his personal and moneyed estate equally between the three branches of the family. Yet Emily would benefit at the expense of all of them but especially the Carroll branch, now forfeiting Manor land and possessions amassed over generations.[11]

As details of the will reached Marianne and her sisters, Wellesley hoped that she was not likely to suffer, for 'anything is preferable to a Law Suit', but it was far too late to prevent expensive litigation. The first legal moves were made on 21 November and on 4 December aunt Carroll's lawyers entered a protest against the 1831 codicil. She felt she had been dispossessed and her children disadvantaged by Emily and her family, who had lived for free at the Manor for years. Young Charles Carroll joined her in seeking to show that his grandfather was unduly influenced to add the last two codicils.

The Signer, however, was said to have observed that 'it was strange that if he could give twelve thousand acres to his grandson from pride, he could not give one thousand acres to his granddaughter from affection'. If that had been all, it would have been quite acceptable. He had always been scrupulously even-handed with his generosity but in the last months of his life he had suddenly given Emily much more than any other grandchild. He had bequeathed his extensive library to his McTavish great-grandson but nothing to his Carroll ones, who would now live at the Manor without any library.[12]

It was, McTavish said, 'a most perplexing as well as a most provoking business', leading to a schism in the affectionate union of the Carroll family as the angry Harpers supported the Carroll branch against the Catons. Emily had told the Harpers that a power of attorney prevented their grandfather from paying for their education when, it now transpired, he had been paying large sums to her. 'Pray for your dear Mother, I have a great deal to vex me in the settlement of this Estate & require the assistance of Heaven to direct me', Emily begged her son. It would take over seven years, though, before the legal controversy surrounding Carroll of Carrollton's estate could be finally resolved.

After the death of Robert Oliver in 1834, she was appointed the sole executrix by the courts. McTavish had to become a US citizen on 26 February so that, as his wife, she could legally become an American (again) and execute an American will. She was largely ignorant of the duties involved and relied upon David Perine, her legal agent. 'Remember you are the staff of my support', she was still telling him in 1840, 'and if you protect me, the Heirs (from whom experience has proved that I need expect no indulgences) cannot molest me.' In the initial compromise settlement aunt Carroll did not succeed in overthrowing the third codicil by proving Carroll of Carrollton was of unsound mind; Mary Carroll Caton's share was increased by $100,000 [£1.8 m.] and the Carroll and Harper branches

Charles Carroll, the sisters' cousin
and heir to the Carroll estates, by
William E. West, 1825.

Charles Carroll Harper who
joined forces with young Carroll
to fight Emily over their grandfather's will in 1832. Painted by
Charles Bird King c.1830s.

received $120,000 each. And all the slaves and some property were returned
to cousin Charles Carroll.[13]

By this time Emily had a fine new country house. Set against wooded
hills with the Patuxent River flowing under the new arched bridge and
past the lawn terraces, it was built in a neo-classical design with Doric
porticoes of six pillars on the carriage and lawn fronts. Grandpapa Carroll
had spared no expense in the materials for the twenty-feet arched hall,
library and the spacious gallery. The three-acre garden spreading out from
the lawn terraces contained shrubberies, flower knots, greenhouses, fruit

gardens and an ice house. He had also built Emily two warm, plunging baths each with a dressing room, two dairies and her own small chapel. She now also owned all the stables and slave and farm buildings that stood on the Folly Quarter land given to her from the Manor estate. In keeping with 'the luxury, comfort and splendour of the house', described locally as 'a regal mansion', Emily renamed it Carrollton Hall. It was, she wrote, 'a very handsome establishment. I hope our Carroll will be a clever fellow and deserve to inherit it – it has cost his mother many agonies – for there is nothing so terrible to encounter as the *envy* of those you love.'[14]

The Harpers could not swallow her self-righteousness. Her cousin Charles Harper believed that 'in private life she has some good qualities being of an obliging friendly disposition in ordinary cases, with amiable manners & kind in her attendance upon members of her family who may be sick: but put *money* in view, there does not exist a more unfeeling & remorseless shark'.

Who is to say whether the fear of moving out of the Manor pushed her to take what she could from her grandfather? It is highly unlikely that if he had died earlier he would have given her so much money when he was previously fastidious in charging the sums advanced to the three branches of the family against their fortunes. In the usual way, gifts to Emily would have been charged to her mother's account. Nor was the timing of them helpful to Emily's reputation. Her grandfather was feeble, blind according to Emily, and witnesses testified to his loss of memory and inability to grasp everything; signing the Folly deed, his characteristic flourishing signature 'Charles Carroll of Carrollton' had been reduced to a single shaky squiggle.[15]

A Longed-for Reunion

In August 1834, Marianne was staying with Bess at Harrogate when she received a cryptic note from Wellesley. He was in attendance on the King and believed that he might 'get an offer'. Lord Anglesey wished to resign from the Lord Lieutenancy and Grey proposed Wellesley 'on account of his experience & knowledge of Ireland'. Marianne could, in fact, take the credit for it as she had encouraged the King to suggest him to Grey in the first place. Wellesley went ahead to Ireland in September as Marianne was going with Bess to join the Carmarthens in Stonehaven, Aberdeenshire. She wrote from there to tell Queen Adelaide who replied on 11 September with '*heartfelt congratulations* on the fortunate turn of your fate'. She begged her to come into waiting again on her return and hoped that Marianne would always consider herself as belonging to her.[1]

Although Greville thought the appointment disastrous: 'Once very brilliant, probably never very efficient, he is worn out and effete. It is astonishing that they should send' a man quite unfit for government, Wellesley was full of confidence, writing to Marianne on 2 October, 'I find myself more equal than ever to all my duties, which I am discharging in a way to terrify all enemies & subordinates.' Meanwhile, Palmerston's secretary Sullivan hoped that Marianne 'will have the good taste not to go publicly to the catholic Chapel, as she did when she was in Dublin before'. Wellesley thought she would be amused to hear that 'your former Enemies The Dublin Orangerie drank your health with *ten times ten* on the 30th Sep.'.[2]

She arrived in Dublin with Bess on 26 October to find him positively rejuvenated by office. He was immersed in business and even Greville now revised his opinion, writing on 14 November that Wellesley 'has astonished everybody by his activity and assiduity in business. He appeared, before he went, in the last stage of decrepitude, and they had no idea the energy was in him; but they say he is quite a new man, and it is not merely a splash, but neat and *bona-fide* business that he does.'

Without the Parasites to torment her, Marianne was able to take up her own duties with composure. Wellesley's new private secretary, Alfred Montgomery, was not at all like Johnston, though rumoured to be another of Wellesley's bastards. A handsome, amiable young man with whom Bess liked to match wits, 'Ally' Montgomery liked and admired Marianne and helped her to keep Wellesley in good humour. This was by no means easy when faced with O'Connell and the perennial difficulty of maintaining order in Ireland. Political conditions were much as on her last visit with priests stirring up trouble and O'Connell to the fore, this time launching a campaign for the Repeal of the Union. With two Irish bills under way, Wellesley was sanguine about Ireland but Althorp believed 'It will turn us out', and, indeed, it did in July 1834. When O'Connell leaked a secret understanding over the Irish Coercion Bill, in which Wellesley was involved, Grey resigned. 'We are in a Mess here,' Lord Wharncliffe acknowledged, 'the Government is broken up.' The King then asked Lord Melbourne to reconstruct the Whig Ministry and Wellesley stayed put.[3]

Marianne and Bess had already left Dublin and for the most wonderful of reasons. They could scarcely believe it but they were going to see their mother. The death of their grandfather had released her self-imposed ban on travelling abroad. When she landed in Liverpool, at the beginning of July, to be greeted by Marianne and Bess, who rushed into her arms, they were all quite overcome, oh! the delight of being together again. Over a month, with tender fascination they embarked upon an excavation of their lives over the eighteen years of separation. Every possible detail was extracted from their mother: about Emily, her family, and everyone they knew at home; their mother in turn piecing together everything about Louisa, and Car and Wellesley. They made plans and also calls on Caton relations in the neighbourhood. There were some upsetting discoveries. It pained them to find that their mother was losing her eyesight and, after they installed themselves at the Clarendon Hotel in mid-July, arrangements were made for her to consult the best London oculists.

When it came to the latest news of their father, though, Marianne was ahead of her. She had been warned he faced calls on stock that he could not meet. Marianne quickly wrote:

> [D]earest Papa, I have heard with great pain, the state of your affairs, and as I think the sum of two thousand pounds will relieve you from those most pressing demands that have been produced from the unsettled State of Grand Papa's affairs, I entreat you as *you value my happiness*, and that of all your family, that you will accept it as a loan, without interest, until you can pay me with *perfect convenience*.

It was imperative that he paid all his debts as soon as possible and she begged him to live upon his income, 'whatever it may be – your time of life requires repose'.

Marianne did not want to spoil their time together by telling her mother about his latest financial disasters. 'All's well', she wrote to her father on 12 July. 'I am sure Mamma will do every thing she can to make you happy' on her return. It was such a turn-about for Emily to be the one writing: 'I hope Mamma will come back to us next spring – I really feel lost without her' and for her sisters to have their mother all to themselves after so many years apart.[4]

After Marianne returned to her vice-regal duties, crossing the Irish Sea on 20 August, Bess and their mother collected Carroll from Stonyhurst and set off to see Louisa at Mar Lodge near Braemar. It was worth every minute of the long uncomfortable journey for their mother to be reunited with Louisa on 26 August – 'I had great pleasure in finding my dear Lou so well & happy' – and then meeting Lord Carmarthen, about whom she had received conflicting reports. 'I like Carmarthen *very* much, his reception was everything I could desire, it shows how necessary it is to judge for one's self', she told Anne Woodville. They lived in very good style with an excellent French chef and, most unexpectedly to her, could even produce from Dunottar, another Carmarthen house about six miles away, fine grapes, peaches and melons. She found Louisa 'active & attentive & has tact in managing & arranging everything to the best advantage'. Coming from the heat of Maryland she was surprised to find the gardens full of a variety of beautiful flowers 'for it is *very cold*, even now I have on all my winter clothes'.

Her romantic susceptibilities were stirred by the 'extremely beautiful wild & picturesque views' and the Highland customs. 'I *must* tell you,' she enthused to a niece, 'how charmed I was with the Highland meeting, although it Poured torrents of rain almost the whole time. The young Laird & Chief of Invercuauld (Farquharson) & his pretty wife, met us at the ancient Castle of Braemar, he was dressed in his *Kilt*' and 'made me fancy I saw a second Lochinvar ready to bound off with his fair lady'.[5]

She left Louisa sooner than planned owing to the damaging effect upon her eyes of the smoking peat fires in her bedchamber. In October Bess took her to Ireland to meet the Wellesleys at Viceregal Lodge, where she was much more comfortable: 'the Park, grounds & house are all *delightful*', she enthused to Carroll, back at Stonyhurst. 'I have seen a beautiful review, fine martial music & we dine at home or abroad every day in company & go sometimes to the Theatre.' She had also finally met her other son-in-law, all of seventy-five and her elder by ten years. He was at his most charming: 'I have never seen a more distinguished man in mind, manner or appearance,' she gushed, and his 'reception of *me* has been in the kindest manner'. He also produced the appointment of McTavish as British consul at Baltimore, arranged through Palmerston. She had been anxious about

McTavish, he seemed to have no judgement in stocks and accounts, she once told Bess, though 'Emily, dear soul, thinks he cannot err'; still 'upon the whole he has many good qualities & is a kind husband & Parent'. Marianne was amused to hear her mother jumping to defend Wellesley from the barbs of O'Connell, 'Lord W's intellect is as powerful as ever & *brilliant* to a degree – & indefatiguably industrious.'[6]

Unfortunately such brilliance was not enough to keep him in office. In November Melbourne resigned and Peel was summoned to form a Conservative (Tory) ministry. The Wellesleys prepared to set off once more for unemployment. 'Lou says you are a Goose to act for every thing or every one, until you *secure* a home over yr head at least for yourself', their mother told Marianne. McTavish was touched to learn that, in the midst of her own uncertainty, she had thought to ascertain that his consularship had been confirmed before Palmerston left office. 'We are all very well but sad – as we go on Thursday and Ld & Ly W on Wednesday', Mary Carroll Caton informed her grandson on 28 November.[7]

While the sisters and their mother stayed at the Clarendon Hotel, Wellesley took a lease on Hurlingham Lodge at Fulham, described by Littleton as 'one of the most delightful villas I have ever entered on the banks of the Thames'. Wellesley immersed himself in what he described as 'my own thoughts, my books & the comforts of a Country life [which] afford me uninterrupted enjoyment'. They were to be interrupted only by visits to the Lords and not by the *fal lal* of Marianne and Bess, who now used the Clarendon as their London house.[8]

'I have been so anxious', their mother declared after hearing on 25 April 1834 of the fall of Peel's government, as 'the Whigs have returned & *not* sent Ld Wellesley to Ireland – he has been offered the place of [Lord] Chamberlain to his Majesty'. Wellesley was mortified at not being reappointed to Ireland and had 'a ROUW' with Melbourne, after which he resigned, withdrew his support from Melbourne's Ministry and thereafter remained on the back benches of the Lords. Marianne believed he had been unfairly treated, telling him, 'I have renounced *forever* all my Whiggery.' The next family surprise, as Marianne explained to Carroll, was that 'Mamma has gone through the operation for cataract, and is doing as well as possible. She kept it a profound secret from us all, and let no one in the House know it, but Mrs Chaplin [the housekeeper], until she was safe in Bed. Who would have imagined dear Mamma to have so much courage?' By 21 July her eye had improved sufficiently to allow them all to leave London to pass two months with the Carmarthens.[9]

The family party made their sad way to Liverpool in October. The thought that they might never again see their mother deepened their emotional farewells. 'I shall return *home* not the less contented', their mother revealed,

'from having had so much enjoyment' and so thankful 'for the happiness
& health of my beloved daughters'. She was at last happy about Bess. In
a letter to Nancy Chase, she had emphasised that 'Bessy is *not* engaged –
nor do I *think* she will ever marry'. Bess was now in her mid-forties and her
mother accepted that she had no *wish* to marry. Their reunion had also
clarified another cherished notion: that Bess would return home. Bess now
made the choice she had evaded all these years between America and
England, and between home and her two sisters: she decided to stay and
live with Marianne in England.[10]

PART IV
Heiresses 1834–74

Fortunes are as frequently dissipated by negligence and inattention to pecuniary concerns as by vice and extravagance.
Charles Carroll of Carrollton, 7 April 1808

33
Lady Speculators

Throughout the years that Bess had lived abroad she seemed to pass her time bobbing gently in the wake of her sisters, discussing politics and rejecting suitors attracted by what her grandfather described as 'your sweet and arch countenance, so expressive of sense and sentiment'. Yet Bess, more often than not, had been engrossed in the business of managing her fortune and making money with and for her sisters and their friends in the financial markets. As her grandfather recognised: 'The speculations of my dear Bess are more in stocks and mines than on marriage.'[1]

It was not surprising that she should be familiar with the culture of investment. Her grandfather substantially increased his inherited investments with bank stocks, utilities and US government securities that yielded interest as high as 10 per cent annually. He held shares in canal, turnpike and water companies as well as local banks from their inception, and was a founder director of the First Bank of the United States and its successor the Second Bank. In consequence, Bess and her sisters had grown up hearing about the family's moneyed estate and its investments and any political or economic events that might affect them.[2]

They also grew up in a country seized by land speculation. From Washington, who started a company to purchase lands in the West, and Franklin, who entered into an Illinois land speculation, to their own father and uncle, who bought over 60,000 acres in upstate New York, everyone tried to play the national game. It continued to grip Americans throughout the nineteenth century; in the 1830s a speculative mania developed over lots of land sold by the Illinois and Chicago Canal Company, with people seemingly 'devoured by a passion for money'. While Bess and her grandfather had no wish to speculate in land, their correspondence often refers to her latest foray as a speculator in other fields.[3]

Bess was, after all, that most unusual of creatures in the early nineteenth century, a lady speculator. Like any speculator in the financial markets, she tried to buy when the price was falling or low and sell when the price was rising or high, dipping in and out of the market to profit from changes in the price. Unlike longer-term investors, whose surplus capital flowed into the stock markets to finance government debt, foreign loans, the building of canals, turnpikes, railways and mines, and joint-stock companies throughout the world in return for income, speculators' funds flowed in – and then strategically out again for short-term capital gain. Speculations were termed 'specs' by Bess and her friends, one of them asking, 'What do you say to a little Spec in Northern shares. They have had a great fall and if there is any hope they now must be worth buying. Would it be too speculative to buy a hundred.'[4]

The sisters and their friends disprove the contention that women possessed neither the knowledge and inclination nor the surplus capital to be active managers of their wealth and indulge in financial speculation in the early nineteenth century. They were by no means alone The financial revolution of the 1690s had introduced a number of innovations: the establishment of the Bank of England to finance the national debt, and the emergence of the London Stock Exchange to trade regularly in government securities issued by the bank and in shares of chartered companies, the East India, Hudson's Bay and the Royal African. Women invested in these companies and they are estimated to have provided between 20 and 35 per cent of the investing community in 1707–9. It was not long, however, before the female speculator first made herself known in the early eighteenth century.

Behind the bubbles and crashes, the booms and busts of the eighteenth and early nineteenth centuries lurked speculators of both sexes. And though money was made in a bubble, more often than not the bubble burst too soon for many, leaving behind heavy losses. During the notorious South Sea Company bubble of the eighteenth century, journalists attacked women speculators as prime examples of the stock market fever devouring the populace; there were, for instance, thirty-five ladies out of eighty-eight names on Lord Sunderland's list for the second subscription. Active female speculators ran from Lady Mary Wortley Montagu who bought stock in 1720 hoping to pay off a blackmailer, to Billingsgate Market women, who were said to turn 'to a merry Way of buying and selling South Sea over a refreshing cup of Gin'. While Lady Mary failed to sell out at the top of the market and pay off her blackmailer, Sarah, Duchess of Marlborough sold out in time to make a huge profit of nearly £100,000 [£14.5 m.]

The widespread depiction of women South Sea speculators as irresponsible victims driven to desperation by their losses served to heighten moral anxieties about women's role in investment and speculation, which continued well into the nineteenth century. Stock-trading was characterised in 1761 by Thomas Mortimer as 'an activity suitable for patriotic and prudent gentlemen, but ill-advised and dangerous for women' whose 'ignorance, joined to a propensity for gaming' made them fit to invest only through the medium of male relatives. By 1824 the Annual Register was emphasising the prominent role of females participating in the speculative mania: 'all the gambling propensities of human nature were brought into action', it began, with men from princes to poets 'intermingled with women of all ranks and degrees, spinsters, wives and widows, to venture some portion of their property in schemes of which scarcely anything was known except the name'.[6]

All of this fed into the nineteenth-century attempt to draw some moral distinction between gambling and investment and speculation. While invest-ment was seen as a legitimate means of holding capital and property for income, gambling was increasingly thought of as an illegitimate risk. Speculation was not so easy to differentiate. Alexander Baring's view came to be widely accepted. While the 'evil' of speculation deserved to be checked 'though he hardly knew how' he said during the 1825 banking crisis, 'he should be sorry to see any person drawing a line, discriminating between fair enterprise and extravagant speculation'. Most people did not bother trying to differentiate, indeed women like Harriet Arbuthnot used the terms somewhat indiscriminately and never let the words dissuade from the actions, though others might take a higher moral line on specs. 'I am very fond of these speculations & should *gamble* greatly in them if I could,' she wrote, 'but Mr Arbuthnot does not like them & will not allow me to have any of the American ones as their value depends upon political events, & he thinks in his official situation it would be improper.'[7]

For those women who sought a more conventional mode of investment there was nothing like Consols, the government-funded debt of consoli-dated annuities which paid a fixed rate of between 3 and 5 per cent annual interest. Their appeal lay in the ease with which they could be purchased by a down payment and then instalments; be traded by selling them in fractions; produce regular income with six-month or quarterly dividends; and provide the security of government backing. It is not therefore surprising that the proportion of women investors in 'the funds' rose from 34.7 per cent in 1810 to 47.2 per cent by 1840.[8]

The largest and most popular of 'the funds' was the 3 per cent Consols. In *Endymion*, Disraeli's Lord Montford so 'admired the sweet simplicity of the three per Cents' that he left his wife half a million in Consols. They were used as a barometer of wealth to determine a lady's income; when Louisa announced the astonishing marriage of the Duke of Somerset to Miss Shaw Stewart with 'only a fortune of seven thousand pounds' in the 3 per cents, the sisters knew this meant a pittance of only £210 a year. Thackeray's heroine Becky Sharpe certainly understood that 'the great rich Miss Crawley with seventy five thousand pounds in the five per cents' had £3,750 a year giving 'a balance at her banker's which would have made her beloved anywhere'. The sisters, however, had little in Consols; Louisa had only 1,000 in the 5 per cent Navy stock, yielding £51, which she soon sold and Marianne at one time had 5,000 in the 3 per cents. They might have invested in them for fun or as a practice run, as the income received was derisory. When her husband of just five days had to attend to pressing banking business, Judith Montefiore decided to divert herself: 'Most probably I shall have a few trifling transactions in the funds merely to amuse, I commenced yesterday by purchasing Consols, by which I have gained a few pounds.' Whereas in 1800 relatively little was listed on the London Stock Exchange, by the 1830s there was a more competitive market with over 100 stocks listed. The sisters, like some of their rich friends, wanted higher yields and so entered the expanding markets as lady speculators. It was a vastly amusing diversion and, at times, a most profitable one.[9]

The social whirl gave Bess and her sisters wonderful opportunities to promote their financial interests. As they paid calls and visited; as they dined and attended routs; as they circulated in company and danced in ballrooms: behind their nodding heads and animated faces, gossiping chatter and decorative fans, ran the thread of a more purposeful conversation. Leading hostesses gathered Cabinet ministers, influential politicians, foreign ambassadors, royalties, financiers, landowners – and their ladies. And what was on offer, besides romantic possibilities and proposals, was access through important people to the latest political and financial news and information. It is no wonder that Lady Holland moaned on 4 March 1834, 'I have not been well enough to go even *once* to Psse Lieven's Wednesdays, Ly Grey's Thursdays, Dsse Dino's Fridays or Mrs Baring's Saturdays.'

The soirée and grand salon provided an opportunity to obtain important information quickly, whether the result of a battle or the market coup of a new foreign loan, whereas dinners provided opportunities for more detailed discussion. Bess, her sisters and their friends proved adept at mixing business with pleasure wherever they were. Whilst participating in the 'dizzying' social round, they sought out the great men, their wives and sisters, alert to the latest reports which could affect their market strategies. When Bess wanted advice about her Spanish stocks in 1833, Marianne was able to oblige after sitting next to 'kind-hearted' diplomat Sir Robert Taylor at a large dinner in honour of the Austrian Ambassador; Taylor's opinion that 'there will be no general war, but there may be a fight among the Spaniards', was passed on to Bess and by her to their bankers before deciding whether to hold or to sell.[10]

Few men realised what these ladies were up to, though the Rothschilds were an exception; they understood the importance of the social side of a woman's life for business. After Charlotte de Rothschild married her cousin Lionel de Rothschild in 1836 and came to live in London, her father wrote about her new responsibilities: 'Business or just busy – find out what is happening in London . . . go visiting.' And this is exactly what Bess and her fellow lady speculators would do the day after a social engagement so that they could pass on whatever news they had gleaned.[11]

Bess and her friends emerge from their letters as part of a network of lady speculators. They talked and wrote to each other about the state of the markets and political news; deliberated about prices of particular stocks and shares, extolling some, disapproving the performance of others; suggested ways of making money for each other, and shared information about loans and stocks – Bess, for instance, writing, 'I hope our present affairs are going smoothly – Spanish the paper says is likely to rise.' It was most convenient that she could read the COURT CIRCULAR in *The Times* and the *Morning Chronicle* to discover what all her friends were doing and who was with Marianne at court and then in the next column MONEY MARKET and CITY INTELLIGENCE to learn the latest prices and financial news. The first column told her that Marianne went to dine and sleep at Windsor with other guests including the Lievens, Lords Grey and Palmerston and the Duke of Devonshire on 2 April 1832; the second that Consols closed down at 82 while in the foreign stock market demand for Brazilian stock rose on the dividend being paid and was quoted at 57 to ½, though Cortes bonds were lower.[12]

Through reading the newspapers the sisters were able to keep informed in an era as yet without specialist financial journalism. Lists of prices and commodities intended for merchants had been published in London and Europe since the seventeenth century, *Castaing's Course of the Exchange*, for example, provided information on London stock prices twice weekly from 1698. These were joined in the eighteenth century by polemical penny sheets while essays about the new commercial economy appeared in the *Edinburgh Review* from 1802. It is likely that Bess saw some of these articles as the family read this periodical. That she kept abreast through what she read – and she could rely upon having more up-to-date price information after the invention of the electric telegraph in the 1830s – is evident from comments to one of her financial advisers. She wanted to buy 10,000 more Chilean bonds, due to an article in the *Standard* newspaper reporting that there would be an early and equitable settlement of the claims of bond-holders. 'Now it is *possible* that this may not be true, but the public will think so for a time, at least,' she reasoned, at any rate, 'I can only lose a few hundred & if it be true, I shall make many thousand & a short time will decide it.' On this occasion she was buying with another friend, something she often did for her sisters and any friends who were married and legally prevented from buying stock in their own names; 'when I say I, I mean me & my partner who thinks with me', she explained to her adviser.[13]

Writing to an American friend the day after her arrival in Paris in April 1830, Bess related how

> the house is full from morning to night with visitors . . . – we dined yesterday with Ld Cowley who took Mamma to the Opera . . . – Paris is full of Americans – Mrs W[elles]'s new baby is a *remarkably* fine one – fat & fair as a lilly – tell dear Mr Bates I hope he has kept my Buenos Ayres for I think they will go higher. I cannot make out what the deferred Spanish stock, which I bought is now by the French papers – ask him to write to me & tell me the news commercial & political – the Queen went off to Belgium this morning to see her daughter the Queen of the Belgians who is confined but I suppose she will return in time for us to be presented . . . tell me at once if you wish me to bring you anything.

Such an interposition of topics, whether personal and business or formal and informal, is a constant feature of all these women's correspondence, an epistolary juggling act in keeping with the way they managed their busy lives. Yet this style might also account for the lack of notice given to the role of lady speculators in the stock markets, the seeming frivolity and domestication of speculation hiding their financial acumen and the evidence of their informed decisions about specs and investments.[14]

When Bess was discussing investments with her grandfather in the 1820s, the rage was for exotic bonds and mines in South America, fuelled by Bolívar's fight for independence from Spain, the anticipated economic progress of the new republics, and their high-interest payments compared with Consols. Bess could not resist a Columbian gold mine where, the promoters alleged, 'lumps of pure gold, weighing from two to fifty pounds, were totally neglected' but which, once worked by an English mining company, would yield considerably more gold than all Europe required. The mining boom had started in 1824 and British goods flooded into South America. Harriet Martineau wrote 'that warming pans from Birmingham were among the articles exposed under the burning sun of that sky; and that skates from Sheffield were offered for sale to people who had never heard of ice'.

After Canning, then Foreign Secretary, called 'the New World into exis-tence to redress the balance of the Old' by officially recognising South American independence from Spain, the mining market skyrocketed. 'Nothing was ever like it before, not even the days of the South Sea scheme', Rush recorded. 'Shares in some of the companies have advanced to seven-teen hundred per cent within a few months, and are bought with avidity at this price.' Bess bought in this rising market and sold at a good profit in early 1825. It was well she did. As the Duke foresaw, 'the greatest national calamities will be the consequence of this speculating mania, that all the companies are bubbles invented for stockjobbing purposes & that there will be a general crash'. And so there was; mining shares, like everything else, plunged in the 1825–6 banking crisis.

Bess, however, then bought again at the bottom of the market in late 1826; even so, her grandfather did not consider it a good speculation. In a message sent via Marianne he wrote that while Bess 'has great hopes & expectations from her shares in the Columbian mines, I fear she will be disappointed; the mines may be fertile in minerals and may be prodigiously worked' but without the establishment of sound government 'the chance of shareholders receiving dividends is precarious'. As for Louisa's spec in Columbian scrip, he could only surmise gloomily, 'I fear it will turn out a bad speculation.'[15]

None of this prevented either of them speculating again, though at one point Bess received a smart rap on the knuckles from him: 'you wrote that you have made yr fortune by the Loan of £500', an advance on her allowance for which Browns charged him interest! He would not tolerate an indebted granddaughter following in her father's footsteps. 'I earnestly beg you to repay them that sum when able without loss.' Louisa, always careful to invest surplus funds, did make a small profit by selling when bonds rose to 36½ in 1827. Both sisters knew full well, as their friend Alexander Baring stated in 1828 at a Latin America bondholders' meeting, that their investments entailed a high risk of non-payment, reflected in the high interest rates and the discounts at which the bonds were sold.[16]

They learned from their grandfather to play the markets only with money they could afford to lose, though Bess's enthusiasm sometimes initially clouded her judgment. She was vastly amused by 'playing', as she called it, and then being busy about choosing the next spec. For such investors, 'the charm was in the excitement', as the writer Harriet Martineau admitted, herself the victim of her father's near ruin in the 1825–6 crash. Benjamin Disraeli, who lost money on his Mexican mining shares, captured the mood of those times in *Vivian Grey*. At a party of 'the celebrated loan-monger' Mr Premium, everyone 'looked full of some great plan; as if the fate of empires was on his very breath'.

If it proved too intoxicating at times, Bess could rely not only upon her more practical younger sister but also upon their financial advisers to keep her from what she liked to call 'folly'. All three sisters had investment accounts with the two premier houses in the City, Baring Brothers and N. M. Rothschild, keeping banking (current and saving) accounts at Hoares Bank (Louisa and Marianne) and Wright & Co (Bess), and for American transactions at William & James Brown & Co in Liverpool. All this in an era when most women did not even possess a bank account – wealthy women might keep one at a private 'Town' bank, such as Herries, Farquhar & Co, Coutts or Drummonds – and only a very few women were either so rich or well connected enough to use Barings and Rothschilds. 'Who holds the balance of the world?' Byron asked in *Don Juan* in 1818 and decided: 'Jew Rothschild and his fellow, Christian Baring.'[17]

While rich women in the Regency period are traditionally thought to have been content with a passive rentier role, that is, merely receiving dividends and rents from their trustees; with being given pin money by their husbands; and with having hidden debts paid off secretly by bankers such as Thomas Coutts: the Caton sisters possessed investment portfolios and were active and informed players in the domestic and foreign markets. They showed a startling familiarity with market terminology and psychology. 'It is possible the Portuguese sixes may be paid off or converted into fives – if peace continues the fives will rise above a hundred & one wd now get very nearly 5 & ½ pr Ct interest buying at 92', Bess advised a friend about buying £2,000 Portuguese bonds with Barings. These are words used by financial markets' professionals in the present century but hardly recognisable as those of early nineteenth-century gentlewomen.[18]

After Alexander Baring retired in 1830, the sisters' investments at Barings were looked after by Joshua Bates, one of the three managing partners. 'His tone was dry, his words few', was how the son of Thomas Ward, Barings' American agent, described him. At first glance this dour banker of serious mien, called 'illiterate and ignorant' by Benjamin Moran, a secretary of the American Legation, appeared not only an unlikely ally in the sisters' speculating sorties but also an uncongenial man to befriend. Yet there was much in their eyes to recommend him. Bates was a fellow American, born in Weymouth, Massachusetts (thus a true Yankee), his wife Lucretia was part of their American tea-table, and they could rely upon his business ability and knowledge of financial markets in America and Europe. All their important countrymen visiting London called upon him, he was highly regarded in America (despite Moran's jaundiced opinion), and he could keep them *au courant* with the latest American political news.[19]

Although they were small fry compared to most of Barings' accounts, the US government, for instance, the sisters were deemed worth cultivating as private clients who lent the house prestige. Their grandfather had opened an account in 1807, sending Barings £500 as 'merely an experiment with a view to learn the form and expence attending purchases of stock in London' and going on from there to larger transactions. The sisters thus had the Carroll name and known fortune behind them; they also possessed an extraordinary position for Americans in English society while being socially revered in American society. In 1831 their friend Louis McLane, the American Minister, advised his successor Martin Van Buren [future

President of the United States] to use Schultz as his tailor, Adams as hostler and 'Lady Wellesley and Miss Caton will instruct you in the mysteries of fashion' [meaning fashionable life] while Mr Bates 'your Banker – whom you will find the kindest man in the world, will instruct and aid you essentially in all matters of business and housekeeping'.[20]

The sisters had 'connections', something most bankers did not possess. Snobbery about any association with commerce, even banking, was still rife in England. In 1830 Alexander and Anne Bingham Baring had married their daughter to Lord Henry Thynne, future Marquess of Bath, paying £50,000 [£3.8 million] for the privilege against his £10,000 contribution to the settlements. 'As the Barings want connection and he wants money, it was a natural marriage for all the world to insist upon', observed Emily Eden. The Baring agent Thomas Ward believed that one of Bates's few weaknesses was undue deference to wealth and rank; he certainly had a soft spot for the sisters.[21]

Bess usually managed their speculations with him throughout the 1830s. Her approach would have been found distinctly novel at any counting house. 'I have an *inspiration* about Buenos Ayres bonds & must have some, even though I have to part with some of my Spanish', she wrote in 1832 about buying £10,000 Buenos Ayres 6 per cents. This might seem an odd spec since in 1828 the Argentine government had defaulted on its interest payments but she must have reasoned that, as Barings was behind the loan and she could buy at a discount, once dividends were resumed she would make money. Her inspiration soon wilted. 'If I can get out of the Buenos Ayres [bonds] *without loss* I should like to do it', she would remind Bates three years later as the chance of getting any money back receded. In the end, though, she was able to take advantage of a slight price rise on the news of a partial dividend being secured by Barings in 1843, which enabled her to scramble out of them quickly. Such were the ups and downs of a speculating lady.

On another occasion, she asked for a statement of account 'to see how I stand poor simpleton!' For the sale of some of her railroad shares, she needed him to organise a power of attorney, then required for the transfer of American securities: 'It is only in case they think fit to treat me like a child & prevent me using my own property – I certainly am old enough to be a fool if it is my humour.' She found it irksome that she had to go to this extra expense and trouble each time she wanted to turn over her portfolio in America. Still, she enjoyed teasing her 'dear' Mr Bates, telling him that what with the land her grandfather had left her by deed and her Baltimore lots, 'you see I have made it as clear as mud that I am the best creditor you have, though my name would not bring much in the stock exchange'.[22]

Although Barings were the sisters' bankers, none of them had ever found it necessary to visit the counting house, which was in the City of London. When they had business to transact they either saw Joshua Bates at his house, 90 Portland Place, or, more usually, he or one of his partners called upon them. It was no longer socially acceptable for wealthy banking families to live above 'the shop'; as David Morier Evans would confirm in his survey of the City published in 1845, 'a dwelling in the City is a thing not now considered desirable – all move either towards the west, or emigrate to the suburbs, – the one for fashion, the other for economy and fresh air'. The richest, the Alexander Baring and Nathan Rothschild families, had lived since the 1820s in magnificent town houses at 82 and 107 Piccadilly, respectively.

Nor was it customary for gentlewomen to venture into the City's labyrinthine crowded streets. Hastening 'as quickly as possible out of the dirty City, swarming like an ant-hill', Prince Pückler-Muskau found it then a 'tumultuous' place, 'where you may be lost like a flitting atom'. As did Charlotte and Anne Brontë when, on a Saturday over twenty years later, they set out from their inn near St Paul's Cathedral for their publishers in Cornhill: 'they became so dismayed by the crowded streets, and the impeded crossings, that they stood still repeatedly, in complete despair of making progress, and were nearly an hour in walking the half-mile they had to go.'

The carriages of the wealthy made little headway as they vied with every sort of vehicle from loaded coal waggons to swaying stage coaches forming two close lines in the middle of streets, 'like great tides, going reverse ways, and reaching farther than the eye can see', Richard Rush had exclaimed on his first exploration of the area back in 1817. Even ladies arriving by carriage could not expect to meet with the usual courtesies, especially by the imperious East India Company. When Maria Edgeworth arranged to see the Mint's new double printing press and then went to the India House museum in 1831, 'a superb mock majesty man in scarlet cloak and cocked hat bedizened with gold motioned our carriage away. "Coachman! drive on – no carriage can stand ever before the India-house."'[23]

There was no deference to fashionable ladies on dividend days either, when all shareholders, male and female, had to attend the Bank of England in person to collect their interest; not until 1870 were warrants trusted to the post. One visitor described the scene:

> At least fifty clerks are sitting in a circle in a high vaulted saloon, well-provided with a cupola and lanterns. They do nothing whatever but pay and weigh, and weigh and pay. On all sides, the rattling of gold, as they push it with little brass shovels across the tables. People elbowing and pushing in order to get a *locus standi* near the clerks; the doors are continually opening and shutting.

DIVIDEND DAY AT THE BANK,

Dividend Day at the Bank of England. Anonymous engraving.

As an account published in *All the Year Round* noted, 'a handsome carriage and pair might, on dividend days, be seen waiting in Gresham Street while its mistress, with the greatest precautions to avoid being seen, made her way to the Bank to draw a quarter's annuity'. Ladies of means usually preferred their advisers, authorised by letter of attorney, or their trustees, to arrange such matters for them, as in the sisters' case, when their dividends were collected either by their solicitor William Stephens or a clerk from Hoare's Bank, and credited to their respective accounts.[24]

Yet, on 8 November 1832, Bess sent a note to Bates. 'Will you be so good as to receive me and a lady who wishes you to make an investment for her at your Banking house tomorrow between the hours of two & three.' Her companion was 'the lady of whom I spoke to you last spring and you are to keep it a profound secret'. Her friend, the petite, dark-haired Marchioness of Westmeath, was the daughter of Lord Salisbury, a Wellesley cousin and often at court with Marianne. 'A lively pretty little vixen' was how Henry Fox described a younger, happier Lady Emily; even her parents admitted her unforgiving, sullen, obstinate nature was more apparent in the older embittered Lady Emily. The Westmeaths had married for love in 1812 but had long been a warring couple; they had been fighting over a judicial separation and the custody of their daughter in a *cause célèbre* since 1818. Bess and Marianne, moved by their friend's unhappy situation, tried to help where they could. As common law did not then differentiate between the property of a married or of a separated woman (which still belonged to the husband unless already held by the wife's trustees), Lady Emily did not want Lord Westmeath to know about her surplus funds. To avoid discovery, the two women decided to brave the City and go incognito to Barings. Bess then had to ask Bates: 'Please to tell me where you are to be found in the City.'[25]

The following afternoon, the veiled pair went by carriage into the City, crawling along Cornhill and valiantly negotiating the traffic to turn opposite India House into Bishopsgate-street within. They proceeded through an archway into the open courtyard of No. 8, a solid Georgian house with stables at the side and a garden at the rear. Inside, the hushed atmosphere of the banking room, dimly lit and with a single candlestick fixed to every desk, belied the 'very hard work' absorbing over thirty clerks hunched over ledgers and correspondence but then, 'unnecessary conversation in the Office, one with another' was decried, as were personal visitors. Bess, however, was a private client, introducing a new customer to Bates and the three of them got down to business in the more comfortable partners' room.[26]

That Lady Emily had any excess funds was surprising given that she had already spent £12,000 on litigation and once claimed she had only bread, cheese and barley water to live on; she was, however, not only a speculating lady but also a calculating one. She had augmented her £250-a-year salary as lady-in-waiting to Queen Adelaide, then Duchess of Clarence, by 'humiliatingly obsequious lobbying' of the 'Vice-Queen', Lady Conyngham, to obtain a grace-and-favour apartment at St James's Palace. Then, in 1829, she had put her mind to obtaining a pension through Wellington's influence. When she was granted an Irish life pension of £385 it caused a public outcry. This was political corruption: an abuse of the Civil List and, from the magnitude of the sum and her connections, smacked blatantly of being 'a job'. Once the uproar subsided, the Duke secretly pushed through a warrant under the royal sign manual.[27]

Three years later here were Bess and Mr Bates equally anxious to help her increase her fortune. Bess had already suggested she invest in the Baltimore & Ohio Railroad in which Barings was also interested. 'The railroad is making more than five per cent on the money expended, after paying all expenses, though the steam is yet only used for passengers', she explained; besides which, she told Bates: 'It is at a great discount 28 or 30, for 50 paid', so now was a good time to buy. Lady Emily arranged to invest £1,000 in the railway, which would be kept in Bess's name. (Over a decade later, a divorcing Fanny Kemble would invest £3,000 in bonds kept in her friend Emily Fitzhugh's name.) Bess also fancied a Spanish spec, buying more £1,020 Spanish Cortes bonds at the bottom of the market. 'I shall clear at least a thousand pounds by my speculation,' she believed, for 'whatever party prevails in Spain the bonds will rise, & I cannot bear the thought of losing the opportunity.' She directed Bates to buy her ten bonds and ten for Lady Emily, who as a new client would provide collateral security of two Danish 3 per cents.[28]

Whenever they contemplated dabbling in Spanish bonds the sisters could take advice from another speculator, their friend Hannah de Rothschild. Spain, after all, was known in the banking world as a Rothschild preserve and her husband was that City phenomenon, Nathan Rothschild. His coups were legendary and his transactions in bills, bullion, government stock and foreign loans so profitable that by 1825 the capital of his house was £1.14 million – well ahead of Barings at nearly £0.5 million. Decisive, ambitious and impatient, he was 'the commanding general' among his four brothers, Carl writing: 'We owe everything, really everything to him.' Ever since Nathan Rothschild had been able to provide the gold to finance Wellington's Peninsular campaign, he had been entrusted by John Herries at the Treasury with all important government business. He had arranged subsidy payments to Britain's allies and with his brothers assembled £18 million required for the Allied military campaign that ended at Waterloo. And, like the Duke, Rothschild was involved in the sisters' errands. If Marianne needed to replenish her court headdress, Rothschild conveyed her request to Hannah in Paris. 'I will take care of Lady Wellesley's commissions, hoping her Feathers may come in time', she replied. Or if Marianne wanted a new lady's maid, Rothschild would tell Hannah or Betty de Rothschild to engage a suitable one in Paris.[29]

Louisa was not far behind her sister in placing orders for the latest Parisian couture and had confidence in Hannah de Rothschild's taste. The dresses reached Louisa via the Rothschild bank's white bag from Paris and were exactly what she wanted but other items failed to arrive. 'I will write to Hubault concerning the Hat and to the person who had the order for the Pelise [sic] and hope when they arrive you may have frequent opportunities of wearing them with much satisfaction', Hannah assured her. It is likely that, if they had not met earlier, the sisters came to know Hannah through her sister-in-law Betty de Rothschild in Paris during the winter of 1824–5. Louisa kept an account at the Paris bank which she could draw upon for her shopping bills, as is clear from a letter she wrote from Harrogate to ask her sisters to see if Charles Harper had 'paid that scoundrel of a frenchman, the bill for Carmarthen's waistcoats, and ask him to send back the bill with the *receipt*. There is money lodged with the house of Rothschild in Paris to pay that bill, & the one for my shoes.'[30]

Born in London of Dutch mercantile parentage, dark-haired Hannah de Rothschild was described by a granddaughter as 'striking in appearance, with very beautiful blue eyes, a fine brow, and a straight Grecian nose'. A poised, cultured woman she was not only intelligent and socially adept but she also played a significant role in helping Rothschild to build the London house into the most powerful of the five Rothschild banks. Her astuteness over Rothschild business and, indeed, her own speculations were recognised by him. Although women were excluded as partners from the family firm, as ordained by his father, in his final will Nathan Rothschild directed that she was 'to have a voice in all deliberations; moreover, it is my special wish, that my sons shall not engage in any transactions of moment, without having previously asked her maternal advice'.

This is understandable, for her letters to him are rich in strategic advice, opinions on political issues and news of the markets as well as wifely concern. 'I received your note as the Brazil stock fell upon a supposition of a new Loan and if that is not the case I dare say they will regain their price', goes one written in 1831. 'However, as Barbacena is Finance Minister I think it better to be prudent. A small purchase for money about 10,000 to gain your coffee might not be amiss. More I would not recommend. I will not detain your messenger longer than to say a little gruel would be good for you.'[31]

It was no easier to decide upon speculations closer to home and the sisters had more than enough reason to seek Hannah's advice: European countries were erupting with agitation and revolution in the early 1830s. Rothschilds sustained losses in the July revolution placing Louis-Philippe on the French throne in 1830 but, with the French 'political atmosphere brightening' as Hannah judged that August, 'I could not make up my mind to enter into any spec worth noticing after so material a rise, but I bought 3000 Ducats and 60,000 rentes. I must wait a little for the advantage but prospects are good.' As Louisa also increased her holding of *rentes* at this time, she might well have talked to Hannah about this spec as well as *haute couture*.[32]

Prospects might be good in France but later that month the discontented Belgians, stimulated by the July revolution, demanded their independence from the Kingdom of the Netherlands and were opposed by the Dutch who bombarded Antwerp in October. Despite several conferences of the powers it took an invasion by the French army the following August to force the Dutch army to retire. The havoc in the markets and sudden fluctuations in stocks, 'the Brokers come in every moment with different prices', Hannah explained from the Paris bank, made it difficult for anyone to make money;

especially after the Poles joined in with a rebellion against Russia in 1831. 'On account of the Polish defeat, last night and all today great agitation and alarm has existed which has had a bad effect upon the funds', Hannah alerted her husband from Paris that May. 'If there is any fall I would not sell but should the funds remain the same and you can sell French rentes *well* I think you would be doing right.'[33]

Even Hannah sometimes admitted: 'Politics are so puzzling that nothing can be done in the way of a spec', and nowhere was this more evident than in yet another European country in turmoil – Spain; and Bess and Lady Emily were speculating with its Cortes bonds. 'I have not yet heard if there is any political news to affect the funds today. We must expect little fluctuations during the contest between the different Spanish Grandees', Hannah advised. Bess and her friends held the bonds in a rising but volatile market, one only the brave entered in view of the deteriorating repressive regime in Spain. In June 1833, King Ferdinand VII assured the succession of his elder infant daughter Isabella by setting aside Salic law, thereby depriving the heir apparent, his brother Don Carlos, of the throne. On the King's death three months later, his queen Maria Cristina became regent for her daughter and, to obtain Liberal support, granted a constitution. Having followed these developments closely, Bess decided that this was the time to buy yet more Spanish, which she did. 'I have an inclination to fly at the Spanish threes', she wrote to Bates on 1 October 1833 just as she was getting into the carriage with her mother en route to join Marianne in Dublin, '& therefore if you wish sell my Peruvian, I should like you to invest them in Spanish shares which you must write to Paris for as they are not sold in the english [*sic*] market.'[34]

The bonds were, indeed, traded in Paris (to avoid British usury laws that limited interest charges to a maximum 5 per cent) where ladies became overwrought about the fall in Spanish the following year when Don Carlos refused to recognise Isabella and the Carlist war started. The Cortes bonds, which had risen from 14 to 36 in just six months, declined to 31 and the Spanish 5 per cents fell from above 80 to 28. 'The ruin on all hands among the speculators is enormous, and the papers show that many have balanced their accounts by suicide. The mania for gambling in the funds is vastly more extensive here than in London', observed Thomas Raikes that August 1834. 'The women are deeply engaged in it, and had established a parquet for themselves in one of the galleries at the Bourse from whence they were expelled by an order of the Minister of Commerce, but they still continue their *agiotage* to the same extent in the outer passages.' Raikes recalled that when a man was arrested on the Exchange for 'supposed communications with Don Carlos, and aiding his escape from England, which produced a panic among bondholders, these irritated viragoes would have torn him to pieces, if the arrival of the gendarmes had not saved him from their fury'.

In London, Bess and her fellow women speculators were more composed. After all, Britain and France had signed an alliance on 22 April 1834 with Isabella's government and diplomatically isolated the Carlists. The country needed to borrow more money, though, and returned to the market for three loans of 5 per cent active, deferred and passive bonds even though the interest on previous debt remained unpaid. 'I think you ever so right to have nothing to do with the loan. The price was much too high for the present state of Europe', Bess concurred with Bates. By the new year of 1835, however, prices in London of Cortes bonds had risen to 47 and were continuing to advance. 'I am glad to see that my Spanish Cortez [sic] bonds are rising', a pleased Lady Emily wrote to him on 18 February 1835. As Spanish, Portuguese and every other kind of foreign security became wildly popular, John Francis, a Bank of England official and City author, noted: 'All was excitement in the foreign market.'[35]

Early in May, Bess happily took a profit on some of her Spanish. It was well she did. At the end of the month Spanish stock plunged from 72 to 50. Rothschilds, the greatest holder, turned bear, and the Stock Exchange 'groaned beneath the burden' of desperate sellers; the 'Spanish panic' was under way. Many fell into difficulties and 'like card houses in a puff of wind brought down others'. Within a week 'the ruin was so comprehensive', recorded one of the principal jobbers in Spanish stock, that over half the members of the Stock Exchange had defaulted. Bates was being economical with the truth when he sniffed, 'My House has nothing to do with it – we have never touched Spanish or any of the speculative stocks, and never intend to do so.' Barings bank might not but Bates and some of its clients clearly did.

Rothschild was soon ready to re-enter the market at the lower prices. As Bess and her friends learned through Hannah, there was money to be made in Spain. Quicksilver or mercury was an essential element in the refining process of gold and silver and the best source was in Spain. The Rothschilds' eldest son Lionel was in Madrid successfully negotiating with the Spanish government for control of the industry at the Almadén quicksilver mines. This information convinced Bess that it was time to increase her holding of Spanish stock. Hannah de Rothschild advised her to buy and told her that the Almadén mines 'were very cheap at the price they had bought them . . . & that Spain had great resources if they were properly applied'.

Before proceeding with her purchase Bess, as usual, asked her sisters if they wished to join her spec; as married women, to preserve their legal ownership, they always put their speculations in Bess's name. Marianne 'does not like to sell the Spanish stock she has in my name as she feels confident it will rise', Bess had told Bates at the end of 1834. After Marianne agreed to come in with this latest spec, Bess sent Bates an order to buy 10,000 deferred stock. She gave her reasons, mentioning that 'Rothschild I am told has bought immensely' and that 'Mrs De Rothschild told me the longer I kept my Spanish stock, the better – she never speaks but when she is almost sure & quite serious'. Bess then added the caveat: 'Do not mention what Mrs De Rothschild told me for her husband might be angry – she did it out of kindness to me.' What Bates made of this early instance of female insider dealing is unrecorded.[36]

He did for once resist her entreaties about increasing her holding of Spanish. 'I cannot help making one more attempt to soften your flinty heart and get you to buy me ten thousand Spanish', went just one of her letters. It was fortunate he resisted for the deferred did not prosper. 'Alas! The Spanish!' became a refrain in all her letters of this period. 'Alas! the Spanish! My deferred stock has fallen 50 per cent from what it was when I bought', Bess wailed on 16 September 1835. After a small rise in prices, she was ready to cut her losses and go for something better. 'If I sell out my Spanish, I have some thought of buying myself into the Birmingham & London road, because there must be immense returns' – already she is being caught by a new area of speculation.

The City was in the throes of a railway boom. The first bout of speculative enthusiasm for railways had been ignited by the opening of the Stockton and Darlington Railway in 1825 but then swiftly extinguished by the financial crash at the end of the year. The second bout occurred alongside the euphoria for foreign bonds and joint-stock banks in 1835. 'I have done everything to stop the gambling in our shares not to the satisfaction of the Stock Exchange here or of the share brokers elsewhere', the bemused banker and railway director George Carr Glyn wrote in October of the London to Birmingham railway – for the line had yet to be built. The fever for railway shares was fanned by the success of the Liverpool and Manchester Railway Company [L&M].

The second L&M Railway Bill was introduced early in 1826, the first having been defeated. Although the chief danger remained in the Lords – 'What chance can we, a few Liverpool merchants, have against Lord Derby?' cried one of its chief supporters – Louisa did not wait for the result but (possibly through the Duke) bought ten shares for £3 each on 22 April, a month before the bill passed the Lords. Harriet Arbuthnot reported that shortly afterwards L&M shares rose to £58. Louisa would increase her holding tenfold in due course and was probably the first of the family to invest in railways.

It was not until the following February that a charter for the Baltimore

& Ohio Railroad Company was granted by the Maryland legislature, and in April Carroll of Carrollton was elected a stockholder director. Although the sisters secured 120 shares each and their grandfather 410 shares in the oversubscribed stock at par value of $100, Louisa's investment in the L&M Railway brought an earlier and more profitable return. The English railway opened in 1830, it recorded profits of £71,000 the following year and she was soon receiving a dividend of 10 per cent. Louisa often took a long-term investment view, unlike Bess who preferred the short-term approach.[37]

Some of the women they knew eschewed the stock market altogether when it came to managing their fortunes. Betsy Bonaparte, for instance, disparaged money-fixated Baltimore society, telling Lady Morgan: '[W]hat could I write about except the fluctuations and consequent prices of American Stocks.' Yet her cousin Ann Spear's letters show that Betsy was deeply engaged in the money-making business. This was especially true after the death of her father in July 1835. The ninth item in his long will read, 'The conduct of my daughter Betsy has through life been so disobedient that in no instant has she ever consulted my opinions or feelings; indeed she has caused me more pain and trouble than all my other children put together.' It would therefore be most inconsiderate of him to treat her equally with them; Betsy in consequence received only a house at South Street and four small properties, which she rented out. 'Do you know that having been cheated out of the fortune which I ought to have inherited from my late rich and unjust parent, I have only ten thousand dollars, or two thousand pounds English!!' she exclaimed in disgust. She was annoyed enough to have forgotten the $23,000 lent to Russell Colt at 5 per cent a year together with $17,000 rolled over for another year which Ann Spear confirmed in February 1827. Betsy, unlike Bess, was risk-averse and sought safety first. She made a great fortune from investing in property and lending money out on mortgage. 'Once I had everything but money,' she would sigh in old age, 'but now I have nothing but money.'[38]

Whatever their chosen investment vehicle, however, none of these women could be regarded as 'does in the city', vulnerable to predatory male brokers and fraudulent company promoters. Widowed Elizabeth Powel, aunt of Bess's beau, was just one Philadelphian woman who sold stock against male advice – and profited. Along with a common belief that widows and spinsters had no business speculating and were 'guilty victims', ran a deep vein of sympathy for the 'helpless' victims of fraud, male and female, in public prints. Bess and Marianne were certainly not 'does' although in the course of speculating they did once come unstuck with an investment in a company promotion for the Pneumatic Railroad invented by an American compatriot, Jacob Perkins, that turned into a Bubble of their own.[39]

William West, acting as his agent, approached the sisters but whereas

'A Doe in the City', a caricature in *Punch*, 1 November 1845.

Louisa refused, Marianne invested £200 to help a fellow American. 'No one will feel more proud that an American should have the glory of the invention', she assured him and agreed to obtain an Irish patent for the steam engine. Bess was immediately transported into speculative heaven. 'My imagination is haunted with Railroads and Patents', she revealed in October 1833. Letters flew from her pen as she succumbed to what Walter Bagehot identified as 'the mere love of activity' so fatal to speculators. 'I want to know what Mr Perkins has done with his glorious Railroad', she wrote from the Highlands. 'Pray ask Mr Perkins if his Road can go over the Alps', ran another undated note to West.

She wailed about being unable to put a large amount into the Pneumatic Railroad because litigation on her grandfather's estate had frozen her regular allowance and his bequests. 'I already have so many irons in the fire that I cannot venture more than two or three hundred pounds.' She could drum up potential investors from her richer friends and, in the spring of 1835, announced 'Mr de Rothschild the father and Mrs de Rothschild have promised me to go on Saturday to see the Rail Road', and that Hannah would get as many people to go as she could.

This was the high point of the Pneumatic Railroad venture. Reminding Marianne that autumn to send their bankers Wrights £250, Bess wrote: 'We are very low at Barings & owe a great deal. I think you can easily pay that out of the money Lou has repaid you', and then begged her: 'Do not do anything for Perkins scheme and West.' It fast became 'Alas! the Pneumatic Railroad!' Perkins absconded with company funds, and the project failed. Socially and financially embarrassed, West returned to America where, armed with letters from the sisters, he settled as an artist in Baltimore. No more was heard of the Pneumatic Railroad. For all her cries of financial woe, Bess's unsuccessful spec did not much matter. In May 1835, McTavish was able to send bills of exchange drawn on Browns for £2,066–5s–8d [£200,000], the equivalent of $10,000, which the court had ruled was due to each of them under the first division of their grandfather's personal estate. The balance would not be distributed until the end of 1835 when there would also be a further remittance due on account of the interest. Bess was looking forward to more fun as a lady speculator, when her prospects altered once again.[40]

34

Plantagenet

Just as her mother came to terms with Bess's unmarried state, Bess changed her mind and accepted a proposal of marriage. 'I have just had a very serious conversation with Bessy & she has promised me to accept Plantagenet immediately', that unlikely, and doubtless unaccustomed match-maker Lord Wellesley divulged to Marianne in the spring of 1836: 'She has enjoined secrecy (except to you).' Aware of Bess's propensity to be capricious in such matters, he advised Marianne to bring the matter to a close and to fix the day without delay. There was also a practical reason to move swiftly: 'Rely on it, it is most important to secure good settlements while it is in her power; God knows, what events might happen to frustrate the whole.'[1]

This time, though, Bess had no desire to delay the arrangements – and anyway Louisa would not let her. A more experienced match-maker than Lord Wellesley, she made certain that their legal man Stephens quickly prepared the necessary documents. She and Plantagenet – George William Stafford Jerningham – were well acquainted; when Sir Colin Campbell was posted abroad and resigned as a trustee of her own marriage settlement in 1834, she had asked Plantagenet to replace him. Her only concern over the marriage was his lack of fortune; she called his initial offer of jointure 'a pittance'.

Once this was increased to £800 [£63,000] a year – better, though not what Louisa thought sufficient – the final marriage settlement could be drawn up and then witnessed by the American Legation on 7 May 1836. It reflected Bess's wish to retain control over her own property, notwithstanding her coverture; her American property (including Carrollton Manor land, Baltimore land and rental properties, shares in railroads and future share of her mother's large estates) was conveyed to McTavish and her father in trust, and her British property similarly to Carmarthen and Bates. All remained for her sole and separate use and she retained the power and 'absolute authority' to do with it whatever she wished, as if she continued to be an unmarried woman.

She was not marrying into great wealth. 'You had better pack up and make the best of your way, as the Post Boys say, to France' where they could

Costessy Hall in Norfolk, always known as 'Cossey' in the Lord Stafford's family.

live more cheaply, Louisa advised. She had consulted her friend Lady James Hay who had a friend Lady Grannard living very handsomely in Paris in an apartment in the Faubourg Saint Germain for £2,000 a year. Louisa reasoned that her sister would not want many servants as the porter and his daughters could clean the place but a cook at £25 a year was essential, 'it is more wholesome & comfortable & cheaper' than to send for food. Louisa was already making a plan to help the newly weds by placing Plantagenet's mortgages in Scotland at 3½ per cent rather than his present 5 per cent.[2]

It might be thought that Bess was marrying a pauper. Society, however, would hardly have ascribed that description to Plantagenet, the seventh Baronet and eighth Baron Stafford of Costessey Hall, Norfolk, and in possession of other large estates in Staffordshire and Shropshire. Tall with a pleasant countenance, large hooded blue eyes and a straight nose framed by a full head of dark, greying hair, he was a widower of sixty-four with a large family and, as Bess told Wellesley, descended from the Plantagenets, hence the nickname.

Fluctuating fortunes under the Tudors and Stuarts had bedevilled Bess's illustrious new family down the ages, but the fluctuations in Plantagenet's own fortunes arose largely through heavily mortgaged estates, costly building and the barony. His first wife, Frances Sulyarde of Haughley Park in Suffolk, was a great heiress but she became dissatisfied with Cossey, as the family called it, and persuaded him to rebuild. The Tudor mansion and the neo-Gothic chapel were subsumed into an edifice of ornate chimneys and turrets above which rose a tower, its pinnacles soaring 130 feet, whilst below a new library and drawing room flanked by a 108-feet picture gallery spread almost to the River Tud's edge. It was, indeed, a *folie de grandeur*, the scale matched only by the ruinous cost. Plantagenet also had to bear the expensive restitution of the old Stafford barony, which was eventually allowed by the House of Lords in 1826. When Frances Stafford died unexpectedly in 1832, the family estates were saddled with heavy charges and Cossey left uncompleted. He no longer had the use of her fortune and his ten surviving younger children were due their share of her marriage settlement.[3]

It was to these circumstances that Mr Gordon, an acquaintance, had alluded when he said of Bess's marriage: 'I am sorry for it, – a large family & embarrassed means that nothing can compensate – She is too good & too clever to marry even a Lord to be pressed all the days of her life by so many masters & mistresses.' While Bess would no doubt have agreed with Eliza Godefroy's remark about happiness, 'I think *Independence one of its primary ingredients*', she was prepared to sacrifice it for Lord Stafford. He was, Marianne agreed, 'a most amiable and kind-hearted man', unselfish in his attentions to others with 'that plain unaffected goodness so peculiar to him' in his sister's opinion. Moreover, he shared Bess's political allegiance, supporting the Whig party and voting for Reform. As a country gentleman, he was characterised in Norfolk as 'an excellent landlord, and full of beneficence and charity to the poor and needy'; this is borne out by a list of the expenses of his establishment at Cossey Hall including nearly £200 a quarter for people sustained by his charity and over £60 a quarter to provide bread and faggots for the poor.

Bess was also marrying a Catholic and a devout one. The Jerninghams had been at the forefront of the wearying struggle for Catholic emancipation and had long been a leading family in the intermarried old English and European Catholic world. At a ball for about 500 people given by Lady Kenmare, 'half of them were in masks but as there were a very great assemblage of Cats that all knew one another intimately, it was really very pleasant', Stafford's mother Lady Jerningham decided. The Carrolls in Maryland helped émigrés from France just as Stafford's mother did at Cossey. Her generosity sometimes tried the family; when she sheltered all the Blue Nuns, forced to flee from their convent in Paris, she had to admit to her daughter, 'Your poor father has been a little impatient about them.' It was exactly the manner of benevolence Bess admired.[4]

She chose to have a French wedding and arrived with Marianne on 22 May in Paris where Lord Stafford met them. Their mother still could not quite believe that Bess would get married. In announcing the match, Mary Carroll Caton added the caveat: 'If Bessy did not change her mind.' Bess was married on 26 May at the Church of St Roche and afterwards at the British Embassy. 'Lord Stafford is a Man of such an Excellent character that I have the most entire reliance in confiding the happiness of this darling child to him', her mother informed Nancy Chase. On 1 June the married couple set off for Brussels where some of her new stepdaughters, Charlotte, wife of Thomas Fraser (created Baron Lovat in 1837 and twelfth Lord Lovat when the attainder was reversed) and Laura Petre, and several of her step-sons had gathered to welcome them. 'I have been very kindly received by all the family who are here & I have no doubt we shall get on very well together', she reassured Wellesley, who was agog to hear the details. The Staffords took a house with a pleasure garden at the back and the park in front, 'so that we are about as rural as you are at Hurlingham. I make my first appearance [as a married woman] in public tonight at the Palace. The Duchess of Gloucester is here & the King is doing all he can to make her visit agreeable.' Although enjoying her new life, she found it overwhelming to be without Marianne. 'I miss my beloved sister most dreadfully & cannot imagine how I am to get on without her', she confided. Marianne would be joining them after taking the waters at Vichy.[5]

Writing from Mar Lodge to Marianne on 28 July, Louisa hoped 'our dearest Bess is happy but I fear they are much distressed from "the ways and means"'. She and Carmarthen were trying to find a way of raising extra funds on Stafford's encumbered estates (£154,000 [12 million]) of mortgages and bonds in one schedule alone. It was some relief to learn from Bess that Stafford's income was not to be as reduced as they had feared; nevertheless, after a tour of Italy over the winter months, they planned to live economically in Paris for two years. [6]

Louisa was also busy getting to know Plantagenent's grown-up children so as to help Bess in her new role as a stepmother. 'She has three daughters to matromise now', her mother noted. Bess was not ideally suited for bringing out young ladies; her bonnet and pelisse were found to be torn minutes before her wedding but she had never noticed: 'it was so like her', her mother commented. What she and her sisters did notice was that some of her step-children looked coldly upon her. Henny Johnston remembered later that once, when they were talking, Bess asked her: 'Why do you think I married Lord Stafford?' – 'I don't know my lady but I suppose because you loved him.' – 'Well that was one reason,' she said, '& you know what a good saintly man he is.' There was, however, another reason: 'His children are not so kind to him as they ought to be so I pitied him & thought I would marry him & take care of him.' And, Henny affirmed, Bess and Stafford 'were very happy'.

That autumn Louisa invited two of his unmarried daughters to one of the large parties she and Carmarthen held throughout the autumn months at Mar Lodge. Barred from any of the Leedses' houses, they increasingly divided the year between Scotland and London. While Carmarthen was out all day shooting, fishing or stalking – and sometimes all three – Louisa rode and walked with the ladies. She was always urging her 'indolent' sisters to take more exercise, writing to them in September: 'I am certain that riding a Pony regularly every day, in the open air will be of infinite use. It shakes the Bowels, – & the Limbs – keeps them in a healthy state – I find by experience.'[7]

After bidding farewell to the Staffords in Brussels that autumn, Marianne returned to London. Queen Adelaide asked her to go into waiting and she afterwards visited Lord Wellesley at Hurlingham before installing herself at the Clarendon Hotel. There was an addition that year to their American circle: Sallie Coles Stevenson, who had called out 'Peace' to the Madisons' servants in 1815, and her husband Andrew Stevenson, the newly appointed American Minister. Marianne was happy to help her old friend through the transition from being a republican wife in America to a diplomatic one in England, which Sallie found 'a procession of social and regal magnificence "so splendid it dazzled one's eyes to look upon it"'. She thought Marianne 'an elegant creature' and appreciated her kindness.

When it came to Sallie's first Drawing Room in April 1837, she turned to Marianne for advice. Marianne supplied names of the best hairdresser, a mantua-maker who would also come to dress her on the day and the Frenchman who would supply the plume of feathers. Although confined to the hotel with a cold, Marianne then sent for the Frenchman to satisfy herself that the feathers were correctly set in a plume. When the great day arrived, Sallie Stevenson described in a letter home on 22 April 1837 how Mary Mansfield 'in her sober quiet way said "Your dress is perfect – it could not have been in better taste" – rouge and all'. Marianne insisted upon Sallie Stevenson wearing some. 'Lady Wellesley sent to Paris for a pot of the best. I was somewhat puzzled to know how to put it on, whether it was to be wet or dry or how? But they all said I managed it very well, only not enough so that I had to go back & re-touch. It is, they say, considered a part of Court dress as much as the train.'[8]

Despite appearances, all was not so well in the American community. At home, whether on land, urban lots, banks or cotton, in the inflationary 1830s: 'Everybody is speculating and everything has become an object of speculation . . . From Maine to the Red River, the whole country is an immense [stock market]. Thus far everybody has made money as is always the case when speculation is in the ascendant', wrote the French writer Michael Chevalier. By 1837 everybody was more likely to be losing money. During the preceding six months an economic storm fuelled by wild speculation and the reckless extension of credit had broken over the United

States and was moving rapidly across the Atlantic to batter the leading firms engaged in the American trade. In the ensuing financial crisis the sisters not only saw the value of their American investments collapse but also their regular remittances delayed or lost. Of their bankers, Rothschilds was seeking to steer a steady course without the brilliant hand of Nathan Rothschild at the helm. He died aged fifty-nine in July 1836 leaving his sons to carry on the London bank. In October, Hannah rightly judged affairs to be 'quite as precarious as they have been for some time', to the extent that the bank made a loss that year.

It was much worse for the Anglo-American houses. 'A very disastrous state of things is expected in New York & every one seems alarmed', noted Bates in mid-November. Unable to remit the large sums owing to their European creditors, American merchants started to fail and brought others down with them on both sides of the Atlantic. The sisters' accounts were all right at Barings, as Bates had seen the storm coming and battened down the hatches early on; Barings 'were never in danger' despite rumours circulating to the contrary. Others were not so lucky and, in early March 1837, the Bank of England had to agree to a rescue package for three over-extended houses, the 'three Ws', to avert a panic; Bates in all his sixteen years in London 'never knew such a state of things before'.[9]

It was no better in the United States where Baltimore, like everywhere else, was caught in the eye of the raging financial storm. Unregulated state banks had recklessly extended credit, lending against the inflated collateral of shares and bonds; reports from New York of the failure of about 350 mercantile firms, due to the sudden lack of credit, shook Baltimore. There was a run on the Bank of Baltimore on 9 May after it suspended payment of specie for all notes over $5. 'Every body was panic struck, and as the butchers and country folks had on Wednesday refused even the 5 Dr notes in Market, each person began to lay in a little stock of silver for the purpose of supplying provisions', Robert Gilmor wrote, before learning that the New York banks had stopped specie payment and that credit had been suspended everywhere. On 12 May the Express mail brought the news to Baltimore of a similar stoppage in Philadelphia by the Bank of the United States in which Louisa held funds. Emily and McTavish suffered as customers of the Bank of Baltimore and the whole family feared its assets were becoming worthless.

It was impossible to send remittances to the sisters in England as not a bill of exchange was to be had. Furthermore, the family's local bankers, William Brown & Sons, were unable to help. 'Brown has long refused to draw, being heavily involved in the state of things in England, which threatened the stability of his house', Gilmor explained. 'It is said they must lose heavily by failures & protested bills, a million at least I fear.' While the three Brown banks in America were under pressure, they were well able to survive.[10]

The same was not true of the Liverpool bank, William & James Brown & Co, where the sisters received their American remittances. In spite of possessing ample capital, the panic and delay in remittances, which by now had slowed to a trickle, wrought havoc to the firm. On 1 June the Bank of England refused to help the 'three Ws' again. 'The last ten days have been like a horrid dream! All the Ws are gone and with them many others, indeed as far as respects the American houses, one looks about to see who is left standing, not who has fallen, the list is a brief one now', James Morrison wrote to his US agent on 9 June. His firm only survived after the Bank was willing to lend £325,000 on security. Browns also had to appeal to the Bank to support them and for a much larger sum. As they were able to show that they were good for a surplus of $2 million with guarantors and collateral security, the Bank had no hesitation in advancing them £1.95 million. When the news reached Liverpool, cotton advanced in price and the town was illuminated in celebration – and relief. The worst of the banking crisis was over in England; Browns was able to repay the advance in full six months later and the sisters finally received their delayed funds from Baltimore. Bess, however, was unable to sell some of her Baltimore property to raise the £4,000 sum required as her contribution to the revised marriage settlement trust. This was held in abeyance in the hope that prices might rise sufficiently to make a sale worthwhile.[11]

The gloomy economic climate was brightened for Marianne by an improvement in Wellesley's straightened finances. This was instigated by the directors of the East India Company, of all unlikely people, but Wellesley was the author, literally, of his own good fortune. In the course of leading a retired life – Marianne could only interrupt with brief visits – he started to prepare his India dispatches for publication, immersing himself at seventy-five in the selection of papers. His less scholarly brother over at Apsley House was also busy with his dispatches.

Marianne's hopes to reconcile them were so far without success. Richard objected to Arthur's ingratitude while Arthur objected to Richard's personal conduct. According to Littleton, now Lord Hatherton, Wellesley said: 'Arthur has been my evil genius; when I fall he rises, to adorn himself with the plumes which I shed' while the Duke believed that Wellesley would always 'treat him as an inferior' younger brother. Hatherton knew 'there were faults on both sides; the Duke certainly in all matters of power was thoroughly selfish and hard hearted'. It would never be easy for Marianne to coax them together but, in the meantime, she continued to act as a go-between, ensuring they shared the documents in each other's possession, if nothing else.[12]

In 1836 Wellesley produced the first volume of *The Despatches* to wide-spread critical acclaim. Brougham in an article in the *Edinburgh Review* praised 'the consummate ability, the true statesmanlike views' which marked Wellesley's imperial rule. The publication of four more volumes in 1837 'created quite a sensation', capturing a rising interest in British imperial power and increasing public admiration for Wellesley and his work; the five volumes have remained a standard text for students of British Indian history.

Such praise was not lost upon the once mighty East India Company (having lost its monopoly of the India and China trade it was now an Agency). The directors sent the *Despatches* to all employees and set about making amends for the injustice done to Lord Wellesley. That autumn, the court of directors created a trust of £20,000 to alleviate the 'pecuniary diffi-culties, which greatly interrupt his personal comfort in the decline of life'; well aware of his carelessness about money, the court also acted as his trustee and ensured he would receive £3,650 [£276,600] a year. Congratulations poured in, reopening correspondence with many old political colleagues and friends. He was in soaring spirits which pleased Marianne; she would now also be relieved from providing further funds for Hurlingham.[13]

The subject of further funds also engrossed a different court during the summer. The King proposed to celebrate Princess Victoria's eighteenth birthday on 24 May by granting her £10,000 a year entirely free from her mother the Duchess of Kent's control. This did not suit her mother and Sir John Conroy, her ambitious Comptroller, who browbeat the princess into signing a letter accepting the funds but keeping them in her mother's control. The King was furious: 'The real point is the Duchess and king John want money.' The dispute was interrupted by his illness. Lady Holland reported on 16 June that 'the whole public sympathise with the sufferings of the King, and eagerly catch at any glimpse or hope of his amendment'. The Queen, frail and weary from attending to the almost suffocating, asth-matic king, wrote to Marianne asking her to come into waiting again. Before she could do so, the King died early on the morning of 20 June.

Eighteen-year-old Victoria was woken at six o'clock. 'I got out of bed and went into my sitting room (only in my dressing-gown) and *alone*', she recorded in her journal. 'Lord Conyngham (the Lord Chamberlain) then acquainted me that my poor uncle, the King was no more, and consequently that I am Queen.' Little was known of her character or abilities and such was her youth and inexperience that Wellesley was moved to renew his support of Melbourne's government in what was seen as a time of crisis. Marianne's position at court reflected the abrupt change; when she went into waiting shortly afterwards, an afflicted Adelaide was the dowager queen, already shuffled to one side without the trappings of a reigning court. The Victorian age had unexpectedly come upon them all.[14]

Well-housed

There was another change of rule in 1837. President Jackson retired to Tennessee, leaving the United States not so united under his successor Martin Van Buren and vulnerable to financial instability, conflict with Mexico over Texas, and secession according to a gloomy Emily. 'I look forward to the dismemberment of the Union even in my life, they say we will go with the South, and this accounts for the great sympathy with the Americans on the Borders – I hope England will prevent our annexing Texas to the United States', she commented to Louisa. This was a rare outburst for she was no 'lady politician' but, at the age of forty-two, still the model of female domesticity.

Freed from helping her grandfather she had more time to enjoy her younger children Alex and Richard. Carroll was still away at Stonyhurst and May had followed her cousins to Mother Seton's school at Emmitsburg, where all those years ago Louisa had wished to join the Sisters of Charity. Emily was fast becoming the only point of contact for her sisters with home. Although she wrote: 'I never saw Mamma's health better, and Papa is looking young again' both were noticeably frailer. Their father, at seventy-four, suffered from recurring head colds and, in spite of cataract operations, their mother's eyesight was deteriorating to the extent that Emily thought in 'another year she will be quite blind, unless the eye is operated upon – it is quite distressing to see her walking with fear and hesitation, even when I am leading her in a strange place'. Emily increasingly oversaw domestic affairs at the Caton town house in Baltimore, at Brooklandwood and at Carroll House in Annapolis for her as well as at her own two houses.[1]

Housekeeping of any sort was rendered more difficult that wet summer by the torrential rains pouring over Baltimore. The Jones Falls rose twenty feet in July until, on the 14 July, its raging waters destroyed bridges and killed nineteen people. At Caton House, the garden sloped down to the edge of the falls and was left partially under water. The flooding contributed to the McTavish decision to leave their house in Second Street. This part of Baltimore was now a far cry from the genteel, peaceful neighbourhood of Emily's early married life; it was within walking distance of the busy waterfront and, with the enormous expansion of trade and business, it had become a noisy and crowded commercial centre.

The McTavishes joined the migration of wealthier families to northern Baltimore where, in 1810, Colonel Howard had donated a 200-square-foot parcel of his Belvedere plantation for a public building to commemorate George Washington. The 164-feet-high marble column was not completed until 1829 when a statue of Washington was placed on the top; it was the first public monument erected in his honour, earning Baltimore the title 'Monumental City'. After Howard's death in 1827, the surrounding land was divided into building lots to form four squares with the monument at the centre. One of the earliest purchasers was Mary Carroll Caton who used her father's gift of US Bank shares to buy a site in East Mount Vernon Place in 1836 and build three substantial three-storey houses as an investment and, if desired, future homes for her three elder daughters, should they return to Maryland. The following year, the McTavishes decided to move to this charming, still rural, neighbourhood, fast becoming a fashionable residential district (it is still known as Mount Vernon in the present day). They settled into a large solid house in nearby Cathedral Street (it survives as number 800).[2]

In London, Marianne was to find herself unexpectedly well-housed. Queen Victoria made no political changes on her accession, so that Melbourne remained in office, but she moved from Kensington into Buckingham Palace, which had never before been used as a royal residence. Queen Adelaide then moved from Clarence House into nearby Marlborough House, long kept for her as a dower house. Marianne also moved – from the Clarendon Hotel to an apartment at St James's Palace, accepting her royal mistress's thoughtful offer. She told her husband about the affecting reception of Queen Victoria at her first levee, where 3,000 people kissed her hand, at a Drawing Room and when she prorogued Parliament. 'I am glad she was so gracious to you', he replied on 29 July from Hurlingham House.

He was also being noticeably more gracious since the court of directors' *amende honorable*, though he continued to devote himself not to Marianne but to the proof sheets of his latest Latin verses, writing: '[I]f I am to be disturbed here, I shall quit this place (which I like very much) immediately.' He was, nonetheless, sincerely attached to her – but only on his terms. As she was either with Queen Adelaide, who now required fewer ladies in attendance but for longer periods, or on visits to Bess and Louisa, she had little cause to disturb him, though he was altogether easier whenever she did see him.

The improvement in his humour suggested that she might at last be able to end the estrangement between him and the Duke. She still saw more

Kissing hands at Victoria's first Drawing Room in 1837. Engraving after A. E. Chalon. Marianne described 'the affecting reception' of the young queen to Lord Wellesley.

of the Duke than of her husband and she took the opportunity of bringing about their reconciliation while staying at Marlborough House during the late spring of 1838. She had to be careful and first overcome the difficulty of *amour-propre*, of which brother was to be understood by the other to have opened the dialogue. This she managed by talking to the Duke first and indicating that Lord Wellesley would like to see him again, and to let her know about it when he next called; he did the following day, saying he was happy to meet Wellesley. Marianne wasted no time in conveying this message to her husband. 'You would have been amazed to hear the manner in which he spoke of you – he was *proud* of belonging to *you* &c &c he went through *many* Subjects, all of which you will be surprised how they have been invented', she reported before telling him that the Duke wished to call upon him the next day or two. Marianne also told Wellesley that there had clearly been 'some terrible mischief maker busy' to prevent friendship between them. She couched her letter in a way that would appeal to his esteem, only allowing herself to add at the end: 'but I am *sure Peace* with him is the wisest thing.'

Wellesley signified his agreement and a relieved Marianne arranged for the Duke to call upon him at Hurlingham. The two elderly brothers met privately on 15 May and, without further ado or apologies, enjoyed each other's company for the first time in a decade. The duke told Lady Salisbury, a confidante who saw more of him after Harriet Arbuthnot's death from cholera in 1834, how 'Lord Wellesley had sent him a message, thro Lady Wellesley; in consequence he rode immediately down to Fulham. There was no *explanation*, but the two brothers met most cordially.' To Marianne, however, the Duke showed more emotion; he was 'much affected and evidently highly pleased' at seeing his elder brother. He told her that Wellesley was 'the most brilliant and wonderful Person in the world' and the most eloquent – praise she knew her husband would enjoy hearing. Wellesley told her that nothing could have been more pleasing than their interview. 'I could not resist thanking him for his kindness, which I could not do without great emotion; he was also much affected & very kind.' Her own view of these proceedings was to thank God that they were now on good terms, 'and that nothing will ever change it'. She also basked in Wellesley's praises. 'The beautiful Manner in which you have expressed your affection, and good opinion has touched me deeply', she replied. 'I trust you will always have the same kindness toward me.'[3]

Louisa had long hoped that Car might be noticed in some official way. She had been urging Marianne to intimate to the Duchess of Kent that Car would like to have some place in Princess Victoria's establishment. 'Unless you speak in time, every place will be promised.' She reiterated her favourite Franklin saying, 'When you wish to *be well served, serve yourself*' and continued: 'Now dear Sister mind what I say on this subject & let me know.' Events had overtaken her plan and Victoria had immediately separated herself from her mother's influence. Car did not support Melbourne nor did he have any patronage at his disposal to attract even a minor appointment.[4]

His advancement received a sudden fillip on 10 July 1838, when his father was unexpectedly taken ill and died. The announcement of his death included the information that Car and Louisa had been with him. 'It is *false* in the papers to assert the Marq & Marchioness were by his bedside offering their consolation. They were at the Clarendon Hotel. When the Marq did arrive after a note & two messengers had been despatched, the poor Duke had been dead above an hower', Ralph Sneyd's agent indignantly wrote to him on 19 July. Wishing to preserve the dignity of the family in public, Louisa had dictated the paragraph to Sir Henry Halford for insertion in the newspapers.

'I hope *Their Graces* are recovering from their recent affliction. Pray present my kindest respects & condolence on this sad misfortune', was how Lord Wellesley expressed his view of the Duke of Leeds's death. It was not so easy to remain-light hearted after the reading of the will on 18 July. Car inherited all the entailed property, that is, all the landed estates in Yorkshire and Cornwall, but 'not one Shilling more'. Everything else, including all the family portraits and historical papers, the racing stud and the house in St James's Square, went to Car's brother-in-law, Sackville Lane Fox. The property, fixtures and fittings and effects at Hornby were left to trustees for immediate sale, the proceeds to be held for the Lane Fox children in addition to specific bequests. The sixth duke had left his parliamentary robes to Car, presumably because Lane Fox was not entitled to wear ducal ones.

Car was speechless and Louisa shocked. Car had long suspected 'the underhand intention' of other family members, but never imagined that, after his sister's early death, his father would favour Lane Fox to such an extent. Wellesley spluttered indignantly, 'It is unjust, undignified & cruel' and advised Car, as he continued to be called, to dismiss all the late duke's legal advisers and prosecute the executors. This is, indeed, what happened after Car learned that, in a late codicil, the sixth duke had directed his executors to offer all the Hornby effects to him first at 20 per cent less than valuation but much of which they seemed intent upon allowing Lane Fox to sell at full price. Car was thereafter embroiled in litigation for many years.[5]

Louisa was, at last, able to visit Hornby Castle, the family seat barred to her for ten years. She journeyed there with Car and his mother. As she drove along the winding lanes approaching the estate, the turreted towers and battlements of the ancient castle stood proud in the distance. Hornby commands magnificent views; first over the small valleys lying green amidst the Bedale hills and stretching away towards Wensleydale; then southwards down to the wide vales of Mowbray and York dotted with fields and villages; and northwards where the country rolls over to Catterick. The park encloses 800 acres of wooded land through which rivers and streams flowed. The main gateway under which Louisa drove faces due south and dates from about 1230. Hornby was exactly as many Americans would imagine an English castle to be – a vast, romantic, mysterious building, redolent of medieval history with its private chapel, maze of corridors and numerous apartments, their thick walls covered with tapestries and 'rich in works of art'.

It was hard for Louisa to savour this long-awaited moment when the enormous castle was full of valuers taking inventories, workmen dismantling effects, servants removing everything down to the sponge trays and tin cans. The contents of Hornby, every item from large ormolu bookcases to the warming pans, not to mention nearly 100 quilts and counterpanes including 'one old covering from the Marquis's Bedchamber', were to be

sold at Bedale. In the Yorkshire Archaeological Society lies an auction catalogue of 1843 closely annotated with prices and buyers' names by Louisa,
who wrote on the first page '*c* against each article come back!'

The sixth duke's executors instructed their solicitors to write to the
Dowager Duchess Charlotte advising that they were unable to permit her
to retain so great a quantity of furniture as she claimed for her new residence under the will and would file a Bill of Complaint immediately. She
might have been trying to help Car and Louisa by keeping as much as she
could at Hornby, even though she was supposed to move into a separate
house. Louisa could not be doing with the English aristocracy's habit of
turning out widows from the family home and, with Car's approval, she
invited Duchess Charlotte to live with them for as long as she pleased,
which made them all happy. Louisa planned to make Hornby a home for
all the Osborne family, although first there was the difficulty of the Lane
Foxes to overcome.

Also crowding through the castle were the solicitors' clerks and servants
of Sackville Lane Fox, whose only interest was the sale of his inheritance
so as to pay off creditors and fund his extravagance. The sixth duke might
have wished to spite his son but he had handed over the Leeds family
heritage to a wastrel who would bring unhappiness to his four children,
flee abroad to escape creditors, court judgments and imprisonment, and
make Louisa and Car's lives miserable. The four children were quite another
matter and welcomed at Hornby where they could see their grandmother
and grow up sure of Louisa's 'unvarying kindness', as one of them said, and
of Car's guidance over the ensuing years.[6]

Car now had a seat in the House of Lords and he was a rich landowner,
commanding a rental income of over £50,000 [£4.9 million] a year and
managing his estates with an army of tenants, estate officers and workers.
Louisa assumed the role of mistress of a large country house, one she had
only just stepped into at Lainston before it was taken from her all those
years ago. Hornby was a vast mansion but the duties of a chatelaine were
essentially the same. She was soon learning from her mother-in-law about
the large number of servants and the tenants and people who lived in the
surrounding estate villages.

She and Car had built their marriage into a genuine partnership, one
that did not change with his dukedom. He consulted her about the direction of his extensive estates and she oversaw them whenever he was away.
'I often heard my mother say [how] devoted the Duchess was to the Duke,'
recollected Margaret Fenton, 'studied his interests in every way & was most
careful in all household matters.' When, at Mar Lodge, he expressed an
interest in eating a hash made of venison, a dish unfamiliar to their French
chef, Louisa persuaded Mrs Fenton, a Highland woman but not then a

cook, to prepare it. Louisa afterwards told her 'with much pleasure that the Duke was highly pleased with it & never tasted anything better in his life'. From then on Mrs Fenton combined the posts of Highland cook and stocking-knitter to His Grace; he provided the game and Louisa the finest wools. Descriptions of Louisa as 'haughty' and 'stately' are wide of the mark for she was never one to stand on ceremony and did not change when she became a duchess. Christian Watt, whom Louisa employed as a maid in London and Scotland and found work for with the Jeromes (parents of the future Jennie Churchill) in New York, was a fisher girl from Buchan. 'The first time I had ever seen maids bow to their mistress was in London – I thought they were going to do a "strip the willow"', she wrote in her memoirs. 'The Duchess of Leeds was an American and did not ask us to bow.'[7]

That autumn the sisters were impatient for news from home assuring them of nineteen-year-old Carroll McTavish's safe arrival after finishing his studies at Stonyhurst and in Paris. 'The letter from McTavish is as late as the 13 of August, and no Carroll. I own I am very uneasy about him', Marianne admitted that September. She had taken Bates's advice and booked him passage on one of the new packet ships of the Black Ball line, which made regular transatlantic crossings from Liverpool. She would not hear of his safe arrival for another six weeks. Carroll was 'always either on his horse or driving about visiting persons endeared to him from infancy' and in good health, Mary Carroll Caton told Wellesley. After nine years' absence, Emily and McTavish wanted to keep their son at home for at least six months before they would even contemplate releasing him to follow a career.

Mary Carroll Caton amused Wellesley by telling him about Berkeley Springs in the mountains of western Virginia. If he could have been transported there for forty-eight hours 'what a horrible purgatory it would have been'. What with the thermometer registering above a 100°, 'tough Beef & Mouton for our food – all boiled in the same Cauldron; we dined in a room twelve feet high about six hundred persons, altogether so detestable that I preferred remaining in my cabin without dinner, as we had no vegetables and the dessert was sour trifle and blackberry tarts!' The only similarities with Ballston Springs were the 'nauseous' water they had to drink and the elite society happy to suffer such privations for health. Emily and her mother met Van Buren and other Cabinet members, who mixed with the crowd and dined upon tough beef like everybody else. When a friend offered Van Buren a silver fork 'he was too republican to accept it' though 'with all his urbanity of manner & meeting with the people, no one could forget from his dignified conduct that he was *"the President"*', exclaimed Mary.[8]

In the meantime, Marianne returned from staying with the Staffords to find her husband installed in a new mansion in Knightsbridge, then a tranquil village outside London. 'Thank God we have got a creditable shelter for a year!' he had written. 'Down was able to settle for Lord Listowel's House (Kingston House) this morning . . . This relieves me from great trouble.' He found everything very comfortable. 'The House & Place are delightful; but there is a sad smell from the Kitchen.' This must have been sorted out for he was soon telling her: 'I like my new residence *more than we must mention*; otherwise we shall lose it. I have been upstairs & I think your apartment beautiful.' Kingston House, built in 1757, was set in grounds of about seventeen acres and boasted a seventy-five-foot-long conservatory and its own private carriage entrance to Hyde Park (the house was demolished in 1937). It was the first house they shared since Dublin but whenever he became irascible and difficult, Marianne could escape to St James's Palace or rooms at Marlborough House with the understanding dowager queen.[9]

Louisa then became severely ill in November, it was thought with rheumatic fever, and Car 'was thrown into the greatest agitation' before her strong constitution started to pull her through. As soon as she was well enough to leave her bedchamber in January, her thoughts turned to her Braemar church. Although by no means her first charitable venture, nor indeed the last, the building of this church encapsulates her approach to all these projects. She was never one merely to dabble in the role of a 'Lady Bountiful', confining herself to visiting the sick and poor cottagers and attending fêtes, though she was always 'most kind to the priests & the poor people, & gave generous donations to all charities'. She was much more interested in project management and was a marvellous enabler, galvanising people to support and raise funds for her special charities, often in the face of opposition. When told a bazaar must fail, she retorted, 'If people are *so desponding* nothing would ever succeed.' She had worse to contend with during the building of a new large chapel and conversion of the old one into a school at Braemar. Although she had done all the difficult work, from negotiating with the Fife Estate trustees and getting them to donate the timber to raising the funds and employing an architect and a schoolmaster, the local bishop had refused to write two simple letters, one confirming the building work and the other authorising the collection of donations, and had done his best to scupper a project he believed would fail. Louisa went ahead anyway and raised £350. The bishop buckled, and acceded to her requests.[10]

On 18 March 1839, Louisa could assure him, 'I am nearly as strong as I was before my illness, though not able to dine at the Palace today with the Duke [Car], as there is too much standing which I feel unequal to.' She had not forgotten Braemar, even Lionel de Rothschild 'kindly offered to collect for me in the city'. Her departure for the North was delayed after her elder sister developed a chest infection. Marianne had to miss a family wedding in April when Wellington's son Douro married Lady Elizabeth Hay, a marriage that Louisa had helped to promote. Marianne was prevented from presenting the bride at the June Drawing Room, but the Duke would not trust anyone else when it came to choosing his new daughter-in-law's dress. He sent over the family diamonds for Marianne to select but, as she told Lucretia Bates and Harriet Paige when they called the following day, he had not grasped the time necessary for such endeavours. Her dressmaker Mrs Murray was occupied from early in the morning, until the hour for going to court, in sewing on the diamonds of the bodice alone. Marianne remained a celebrity for Americans and Harriet Paige could see why. She was 'still a superb woman and although thin and pallid by illness, possesses the remains of great beauty and charm of manner' added to which she was 'intelligent and gentle'.[11]

Louisa was by then preparing for Mar Lodge and the end of her Scottish project. On 17 September she attended the consecration of the new chapel. The bishop reserved his last words for her, urging everyone 'to retain till death a grateful remembrance of the munificence of her Grace the Duchess of Leeds who had exerted herself with untiring zeal to erect a temple worthy of the ancient faith'. Car's negative views on building Catholic chapels did not prevent his fulfilling Louisa's wish for a private chapel of her own. It was much easier to deal with the Leeds Estates steward and workmen. The estimate given was not exceeded and the work speedily completed. The whole chapel cost Car £137–7s 6d [£10,000] and Louisa some expense in furnishing and plate as well as the stipend for the Revd Mr Clifford (Catholic priests were not then called 'Father'), her resident chaplain. It was with some satisfaction that she urged her sisters to come to stay: 'you must come to us on a visit – after which we go to Paris if Bess is there.'

Each of the three sisters would now be settled in a grand house. Bess was already on her way back to live with Plantagenet at Cossey Hall; economising had worked. Time had not, however, softened her step-children's antipathy, and Stafford's gifts of jewellery had not improved matters. 'My dearest Wife,' he had to write from Vichy, 'for fear there should arise any dispute about the Diamonds after my decease, I think it right to declare in writing that I have given them to you in full possession to do what you please with them.' Although his first wife's jewellery had already been distributed, some of his children thought that a second wife should give way to them when it came to the Stafford jewellery and made diffi-culties over settling Bess's jointure. The problem was finally resolved in the autumn once the Staffords and his heir Henry Jerningham were together at Cossey.[12]

'To be together'

The American bank failures had continued after the panic of 1837 and swept away the reconstituted Bank of the United States which suspended specie payments in October 1839 and tried to stay afloat by raising a loan in London with the help of Barings. Louisa had retained a large shareholding, which only the previous year had elicited Emily's ringing endorsement: 'how fortunate you were to keep your money in' for, with shares at $12 each, 'it is very high and safe, Biddle is a clever fellow'. His cleverness could not save his bank, which suspended trading early in 1841. 'What a set of swindlers the Directors must be', Bates wrote to Ward and no doubt Louisa agreed. She was so occupied with Hornby and Mar Lodge affairs that she had not given her customary close attention to business matters and was caught out. The most she could hope to recoup was about a dollar and a half per share. 'I am sorry that the Duchess of Leeds has so large a share in the wreck, but I cannot gather for her ... any hope that the loss will diminish in the future', Joseph Ingersoll, a Philadelphian friend and lawyer, condoled with Emily.[1]

The wreck looked as if it would engulf the whole country; between 1841 and 1842 eight American states were either unable to pay the next dividends on their loans and defaulted or just repudiated the debt altogether. Among the outraged investors were the sisters, all of whom held stock in two of the defaulting states, the Maryland 6 and 5 pr Cts and the Pennsylvania 5 pr Cts. Bess had even patriotically increased their holdings, though now under the name of Lord Stafford, when Barings sold £700,000 of Maryland's securities. 'I feel ashamed of my country,' Bates confessed, writing in despair to Ward, 'there never was a Country so disgraced in point of Credit as the United States of America.'[2]

Anglo-American relations inevitably deteriorated, especially after British pressure on the federal government to assume the obligations of the defaulting states failed. Although American residents encountered hostility, the sisters were protected by their social position and British titles and did not suffer the ignominy of being cut; others, like financier and future philanthropist George Peabody, were even blackballed in clubs. The controversy raged in the American and British press after Sydney Smith's petition to Congress appeared in American newspapers and the British *Morning Chronicle*. Smith was himself a Pennsylvania investor and railed against the fraud committed by the richest state in the Union, 'I cannot shut my eyes to enormous dishonesty', declaring that American stocks were now 'in the ghettoes of finance'.

The Rothschilds were of the same opinion. When agents of the US Treasury dared to try to raise a new loan from European investors in 1842, they were cold-shouldered. 'You may tell your government', commanded James de Rothschild, 'that you have seen the man who is at the head of the finances of Europe, and that he has told you that they cannot borrow a dollar, not a dollar.' All was not lost for the sisters, however, as dividends would be resumed by Pennsylvania in 1845 and Maryland shortly there-after; 'of all the embarrassed States, Maryland has undergone greater self denial to effect the recovery of her position than any other state, and her efforts have been crowned with success', was how one English investment guide later assured its investors, which was quite enough to make the patriotic hearts of the sisterhood swell with pride.[3]

Although it was a long time since Joseph Ingersoll had seen 'any of the four charming sisters' he begged Emily to allow him 'to believe that you are all as handsome, and as enchanting as you were formerly'. She was about to find out for herself. During a long spell at home, her son Carroll had prevaricated over settling on a career. Emily had once hoped he would make himself a man of business but banking was no longer such an attract-ive prospect. McTavish, anyway, considered a diplomatic career far more suitable for a gentleman and feasible through the Wellesleys. At some point in 1840 it was settled that Carroll would return to London. After Wellesley pursued the matter through Lord Palmerston, an unpaid attaché's post was found for Carroll at Constantinople. The ensuing turn of events is difficult to follow given the dearth of letters between the sisters.

In July, Louisa exclaimed with excitement to Marianne: 'We must arrange all so as to be together.' All four sisters were going to meet in London – they would be reunited after almost twenty-four years – brave Emily with 'a horror of the sea' and of leaving home, was coming to see them – oh, what heaven to be together – she would embrace them once more – meet their husbands – stay at Kingston House, at Hornby and at Cossey – they would coo over her children – and never was such an event more happily anticipated by them all.

Emily brought May, aged fourteen, to meet her godmother and from the first it is clear that Marianne was to have charge of this 'dear Child' who quickly became the centre of her life. Petite with dark hair and 'liquid blue eyes', May bore more of a resemblance in her face to Marianne and in her figure to Louisa than to her mother. Louisa always said that whereas Marianne 'had the most beautiful face, and Bess the kindest heart, she herself had the best figure'. May promised to be a great beauty. Her mother wanted her to complete her education in England and, after much consultation between the sisters, they chose to send her to New Hall, one of the oldest Catholic girls' schools in England.[4]

A year later, Marianne was at Kingston House, savouring the last month of Emily's visit. They were waiting for McTavish's arrival in England so that he could pass some time with May before she went to school, and also comfort Emily. During her long visit to England her nine-year-old youngest son Richard died on 20 March 1841. McTavish had the agonising task of breaking the news, probably first to her sisters to try to prepare her for what she called 'my overwhelming affliction'. Richard was not buried in the McTavish family plot at Greenmount Cemetery in Baltimore but in some other place sacred to Emily, where in her will she desired to be buried with him, probably the little Folly chapel. She started on her desolate journey home with McTavish in September, leaving all her surviving children behind: Alex having followed his elder brother to Stonyhurst.[5]

Lord Wellesley, though, was in a celebratory mood. The court of directors unanimously voted to commission a statue of him to be placed in the general courtroom of India house 'as a public, conspicuous, and permanent mark of the admiration and gratitude of the East India Company'. Wellesley's published acceptance was pronounced by the Duke as 'inimitable. Nobody but yourself could write such a letter at these times.' These two old gentlemen positively enjoyed honouring each other; Wellington sent Wellesley congratulations on the anniversary of the fall of Seringapatam in May just as Wellesley returned them to Wellington on the anniversary of Waterloo in June.[6]

Wellesley at seventy-eight was sitting for his statue, honoured but at an age that, he admitted to Marianne, brought him now nothing but sadness: '"Tis but the funeral of the former year" says Pope very truly.' He thanked his God for the use of all his faculties, a resource that shed balm over increasing infirmities of body. 'My dearest Wife – I am still very ill and I fear I shall never recover', went one of many such notes. He died on 26 September 1842 after three days' illness, 'without pain or even struggle'. Louisa was at Mar Lodge and offered to come south immediately. She placed Hornby at Marianne's disposal as she might find it preferable to Cossey, which was always full of people. Louisa was terrified that the bailiffs would pounce on Marianne at Kingston House. 'I dread to hear of a seizure from [Lord Wellesley's] creditors – during your stay in the house,' she wrote on 30 October, 'no time should be lost . . . Dismiss soon as possible all servts but 2 persons – all gardeners but *one* – this can be done! All Horses etc', she frantically instructed. Finally, she urged Marianne to '*Beware of expense* – Downes will want you to keep up the establishment for some weeks – *do not*'. Louisa reflected that, without Wellesley's calls upon her, Marianne would be able to travel north more frequently, ending her letter with 'Adieu my precious Sister, *now* we shall see more of each other – as I trust you will be a great deal with us – God bless & preserve thee precious one.'[7]

She was right to be concerned about creditors. Marianne asked Lord Maryborough, now head of the family, to be with her when the will was opened and read. They learnt that Wellesley had died worth 'positively worse than nothing', Maryborough reported, and the arrears to be collected, amounting to about £2,500 [£192,000], would scarcely cover his debts and funeral expenses. Marianne would receive not a farthing. Wellesley's legacies, including £1,000 to Downe (his major-domo who had several times saved him from utter 'Ruin'), were 'mere waste Paper – not a Shilling for any of these purposes will be forthcoming'. This was true – 'There was not enough to pay the legacies, & the personal effects were sold by auction', states the donor of Wellesley's papers to the British Library. Marianne, nevertheless, 'behaved most beautifully'. A widow facing such ruin would have been forgiven for having hysterics.[8]

Marianne had known that Wellesley had very little, if not quite *so* little. She had never relied upon him for money, rather the reverse. It was, nonetheless, a sobering thought that, without an independent fortune, she would, indeed, have faced destitution. A more pressing difficulty concerned his funeral and burial. Richard Wellesley had always carried an inflated sense of his own worth; he continued to believe that he should have been rewarded with a dukedom though how he was to support such a station had never occurred to him. In the same manner, he told Marianne that he could only consider a public funeral and a place in Westminster Abbey as sufficient reward for his great services to the country.

She felt that it was her duty at least to pass on his wishes and so turned to her dearest duke for advice. Neither was under any illusions as to Wellesley's character and, Marianne wrote, 'The Grave now casts a veil over all his weaknesses, which injured no one but himself, and has not left him a spot he could call his own wherein to lay his remains.' It was conveniently discovered that Wellesley had a second choice up his sleeve, namely at Eton College, and he had gone so far as to give the Provost a Latin epitaph for himself, which Arthur later had placed in his memory over the inner archway of the North Transept. Richard Wellesley was buried in the Eton Antechapel on 8 October. Wellington, who 'had previously shown much feeling, being pale thoughtful and depressed', became excited about the hour's delay and, as Hatherton recorded, told the undertaker, 'Had you informed *me* that the funeral would not take place till eleven I could have been doing *other* THINGS!' Wellesley would have been amused; in letters to Marianne he often called Arthur 'Much Ado'.[9]

This could have aptly described Louisa who was already advising Marianne about a petition. Although she was in comfortable circumstances, not quite as reduced as the 'sorry pittance' Lady Holland thought, her income from Maryland had been significantly reduced owing to lower rents and the fall in the stock market. 'There never was a truer saying strike whilst the Iron is Hot,' Louisa urged her, and 'no time should be lost in getting every thing that can be got both from the India House and from her Majesty!' As Louisa pointed out, 'All will be soon forgotten of poor Ld Wellesley by Court, & India Co. Let your friends, therefore lose no time.' She thought the Duke 'might get you a Pension from Govt' but Marianne must act immediately.

The Duke helped her draft a petition for a pension which she submitted to the Queen through the Prime Minister Sir Robert Peel on 29 November. The matter was complicated by the East India interest in a pension of £3,000 a year payable to her upon Wellesley's death but which he had borrowed against and allowed the insurance payments on his life to fall due. The Duke entered into lengthy consultations on her behalf, telling her on 4 February 1843, '[y]ou may rely upon it; that no time shall be lost by me'.

They had loved each other for twenty-seven years and only now were they both free to marry. The Duke, deaf and often lonely, was increasingly susceptible to infatuations with young women. He struck up a bizarre friendship with the beautiful Miss Jenkins, a religious fanatic who wanted to save his soul, and then in 1839 with the young banking heiress Angela Burdett Coutts, who became besotted and would later propose – the seventy-eight-year-old duke gracefully refusing. Marianne preferred to keep to the more tranquil arrangement of their *amitié amoureuse*. Eventually, with his help she received a pension on the Civil List that, taken together with her private income and court salary, afforded her greater financial security in her widowhood than Wellesley had ever provided in her marriage. Moreover, through Queen Adelaide's good offices seven years later, the then Prime Minister Lord John Russell would offer Marianne apartments at Hampton Court Palace, which later became her chief home.[10]

She and Bess were together during another of their father's financial crises. They immediately alerted Louisa, who replied from the Netherlands in great haste, 'Poor Papa, I am very unhappy about him – I will try to save his property – at all events I will speak to the Duke [of W.] I will mortgage my Carrollton Manor & Mountains – I shall write to my Agent Mr Humphreys next post to see what he can do.' She would get $40,000 together – 'I will see when I come to London if there is any thing to be got from the Duke.' With time so short, Louisa instructed her sisters to 'write Em what I have done'.

It is unclear why their mother was not involved; perhaps her large fortune had been so carefully put out of their father's reach that funds could only be drawn upon through the courts or perhaps her daughters tried to keep it from her. Louisa was annoyed that Emily wasted valuable time writing to them when the quickest solution was for her to raise the money and pay the £8,000 [£668,500] debt at home first and save Papa's property, not wait for their money. She should be doing this as his daughter, 'or else, in justice, she has no right to any share of it – nor *shall she have* if I have anything to do with it', Louisa declared to Marianne and Bess. 'I have no idea of making a sacrifice – by which she is to benefit, unless she also will help especially when she has the means.' Emily, though rich, was exceedingly tight with money, always saying how little she could afford this or that.

Yet the sisters' love always overcame any differences of opinion. Thus Louisa could berate Emily in one letter but in the next say 'I approve of all Emily has done'. By the autumn of 1842, Louisa reported she had sent the money in the usual way through Messrs Brown to their grandfather's trustees to '*act* as they think *best*' with Emily to pay their father's debts. The sisters agreed with Louisa's insistence upon one point: Emily was 'not to let it get into Papa's hands on any account'. Emily, in turn, urged her adviser, 'Lest I should not see you tonight, I beg you to secure the money before Papa can get hold of it.' It was a precautionary measure they had learned to adopt many years ago.[11]

Money was also on Bess's mind. Marriage and her father's dire straits had by no means diminished her interest in having a spec or two and, in the 1840s, few lady speculators or investors could resist the lure of the railways. The sisters had kept their early shares and were ready to enter the market again. Although railway shares had been selling at a discount to their issue price in early 1840, after Prince Albert persuaded Queen Victoria to make her first railway trip from Slough to Paddington in 1842 the publicity produced a second and greater surge of interest. Railway shares, it was said, would remain 'safe in midst of panic'. It was certainly easy to find out about them; the public was bombarded with publications, such as *The Railway Investment Guide: How to Make Money by Railway Shares* (1845), and periodicals and newspapers stoked the general enthusiasm. Where in the early 1840s three railway journals sufficed, during 1845 alone over twenty new railway papers appeared. *The Railway Bell and London Family Newspaper*, for instance, pandered to a female readership with railway share lists jostling for space with 'Fashions for the Week' and 'Costumes for the Fair Sex'. Moreover, nothing could be simpler than buying railway shares – just a small deposit of 5 per cent paid on each one and further payments or calls made on the remainder when 'called-up' – as the whole country discovered during the ensuing 'Railway Mania'.[12]

With the forty-four companies promoting railways in 1844 having increased to 270 in 1846, there was clearly no shortage of lines to choose from and, as share prices increased 167 per cent between 1840 and 1845, no shortage of investors. The man who whipped up the greatest frenzy for railway shares was George Hudson the 'Railway King', who said he wanted to make 'all t'railways cum t'York' which, if he succeeded, would be a great boon for Louisa and Car. After opening the York & North Midland line and then extending his railway system to Birmingham, Bristol, London and Scotland he wielded an extraordinary influence: when he became chairman of the failing Eastern Counties Railway in the summer of 1845, its shares soared. 'In the journals of the day, men read of [Hudson's] wonderful doings', recalled John Francis in 1850. 'The press recorded his whereabouts; the draughtsmen pencilled his features . . . Peers flattered the dispenser of scrip, and peeresses fawned on the allotter of premiums.'[13]

Louisa was unlikely to fawn but she was certainly one of the many peeresses who were interested in the profits of his shares. As a large Yorkshire landowner, Car was inevitably concerned with the location of railway tracks and the rise in value of land next to any proposed lines. Louisa corresponded with their legal adviser about Hudson's York to Sheffield railway line, which ran on some Kiveton land. She and Car were also involved in a petition to re-route a proposed branch line from crossing part of the park at Hornby, which she insisted 'was unthinkable', no matter what vast sum of compensation was on offer. Their attitude differed considerably from other landowners who used legislative influence in Parliament to gain exorbitant compensation for lines across their property; according to *Fraser's Magazine*, 'hundreds of thousands have been paid in supposed injury, which could not as injury have been estimated at more than a few thousands'.[14]

In addition, Louisa invested in railway companies, such as the London & Yorkshire Railway, which formed part of the Great Northern Railway; in Hudson's York & North Midland Railway and his York, Newcastle & Berwick Railway, which would make the journey to Mar Lodge shorter. She was a long-term investor rather than a speculator, and the distinction between them was still important in the mid-1840s as Charlotte Brontë made clear when discussing the Brontë sisters' investment in the York North Midland: 'as we have abstained from all gambling, all "mere" speculative buying-in & selling-out, we have got on very decently.' The attraction for everyone, of course, was the money to be made; as Charlotte Brontë told her publisher, from an original price of £50, shares in the York & North Midland rose to £120 and paid a dividend of 10 per cent. It is hardly surprising that prospective lines had only to advertise in the press to be inundated with applications for shares. Scotland was just as caught up in the railway euphoria. 'From Edinburgh to Inverness, the . . . country is an asylum of railway lunatics', the poet Wordsworth noted.[15]

Spain and France were not far behind as Bess discovered when she wanted to have a spec in their railway shares. 'You really must have been bitten by a mad stock broker, for your speculative propensities seem to develop more & more as you proceed', declared Edward Jerningham, manager of the West End branch of the London Joint Stock Bank [LJSB] in Pall Mall and Lord Stafford's nephew. She had written to him about shares in the proposed Madrid & Valencia Railway of which a friend of Stafford's was listed as a director. Sir Henry [illegible surname], it transpired, was quite unaware of this and told Jerningham he had not even seen a prospectus. This was by no means unusual. Railway promoters often used the names of distinguished men, and offered them free shares, to act as 'decoy ducks' on a provisional committee to entice potential investors, who assumed their presence guaranteed the integrity of the company. This was rarely the case and Bess quickly abstained from the spec.[16]

Instead, she successfully embarked upon specs in French railways, partly because she knew the country and its financial markets, and partly because of her excellent contacts. While living in Paris after her marriage she had come to know Stafford's niece and her husband Edward Blount, whose bank Laffitte, Blount et Cie, looked after Stafford's banking affairs. Blount was also an early promoter of railways in France. He won the bid for the line from Paris to Rouen, the Chemin de fer de l'Ouest, of which he was chairman and Baron James de Rothschild was among the directors. It was comparatively easy for the Staffords to obtain shares in this line, which opened in May 1843 and prospered from the outset.

By this time a railway craze had Paris in its grip. 'The business with the rail road is rather tedious and troublesome. The French Gentlemen are careful with their benefits', Hannah de Rothschild warned her son Lionel that May about the bidding for the concession for a line from Paris to the Belgium border, which was the subject of bitter competition; Rothschilds and a consortium that included Barings were amongst the unsuccessful bidders. However, Baron James de Rothschild, who had first taken on a railway venture in 1837, already had another line up his sleeve, the Paris – Lille – Brussels service of the Compagnie du Chemin de Fer du Nord (the Northern Railway). Although Bess's account with Rothschild's in London held nearly £1,450 in December 1844, she preferred to use funds from the LJSB borrowed against securities they already held for her, though Edward Jerningham advised her that 'it will be better not to make any mention of the French Railway shares you intend purchasing' to the cautious directors. He assured her the shares would 'infallibly be at a premium of 4 or 5 per cent very soon after they are issued', and on 6 December Blount bought 150 shares from Rothschilds for her.[17]

When the subscription opened in 1845 some 20,000 stockholders virtually trampled over one another to gain some shares. The *haute banque*, Neuflize, huffily commented that Rothschilds 'place shares with their friends and a few privileged firms, among which we are not numbered', and the baron was courted shamelessly for shares 'not only by deputies and public officials but also by ladies of rank', as one deputy observed. The author Balzac was delirious about finally obtaining a few shares: 'I've got fifteen shares of the Chemin de Fer du Nord – it's gained 400 francs, and it's expected to gain 1,500.' That Bess did extremely well with this spec is evident from Bates's reaction to taking the shares at £12 and selling them at £20: 'I hope it is not wicked to make money so fast, I settle the account with my conscience in the belief that a share is really worth £40.'[18]

Although Bess and Louisa were informed investors, Samuel Smiles declared that most people knew nothing about railway finance in Britain 'but hungering and thirsting after premiums, rushed eagerly into the vortex of speculation ... "Shares! Shares!" became the general cry.' The fraudulent supplied all manner of fictitious schemes and fake accounting to whet the gullible public appetite. In September 1845 over 450 new schemes were registered in a glut of over-speculation.

In October a small rise in interest rates triggered a panic, with people rushing to sell shares to meet calls on other shares. The Brontës lost much of the inherited money they had invested in Hudson's line as shares plummeted from a high of £120 down to £20 'and it is doubtful whether any dividend will be declared this half-year', Charlotte Brontë confessed to her publisher, who advised her to place any future earnings in the safe Funds. They were not alone. As Francis wrote, 'no other panic was ever so fatal to the middle class. It reached every hearth, it saddened every heart in the metropolis. Entire families were ruined.' As always there were winners and losers. Bess sold out of her French spec at the top of the market but she and Marianne kept the London & Birmingham shares as an investment, just as Louisa kept her railway shares, with one exception. This was the York & North Midland, which she sold at a loss after the dividends were cut and criticisms of Hudson's probity became more overt. Eventually, investigations into his railway companies revealed the corruption engendered by the Railway Mania and, in particular, his embezzlement. The sisters remained investors as they could afford to meet the calls, even when prices were depressed, and the lines they invested in were established, dividend-paying railways, which as one City historian states, would achieve over time 'an almost Consol-like status'.[19]

*

A debutante in the 1840s. May McTavish would have worn a similar ball gown during her first London season.

Marianne had left the railway business to her sisters as she was enjoyably occupied with her lovely niece. After May left New Hall in 1843, a phalanx of dancing masters and piano teachers, dressmakers and glove makers descended upon Kingston House. Amid silks and muslins, flounced petti-coats and silk stockings, ribbons and flowers and the smallest of blush roses, Marianne selected and May was fitted with a new wardrobe for her debut in 1844. Being much praised for her beauty and delightful singing voice, she was judged among the successes of the Season. 'The persons most admired yesterday were Lady Ormonde, Lady C Villiers, and an American girl, a niece of Lady Wellesley's, Miss Macvigor [sic]', Lady Holland noted in April.

In July Marianne and May went to stay with Louisa who took them in September to the Caledonian Perth Meeting, where, she said, 'all the aristocracy of Scotland' gathered for four days of 'horse racing – balls – and the theatre'. This was swiftly followed by the main social event in Scotland, the Northern Meeting at Inverness in October. It was at a Northern Meeting that, at the age of seventeen, Carroll had fallen in love with Isabella Jerningham, much to his aunts' tender amusement.[20]

During the winter of 1845, the year of the 'railway mania', Marianne took May to Paris on a long visit to see Carroll, who was still waiting for a diplomatic promotion. Louisa had tried to obtain a paid attaché position for him in 1841 from her friend Lord Aberdeen, then the Foreign Secretary. As Louisa explained, although she could get Wellesley or the Duke of Wellington to make the application, 'I prefer writing myself & making my own request, which I hope you will grant.' The note of his reply was subsequently heavily crossed out by the Foreign Office, though Louisa understood that he promised to help. In the meantime, once Marianne's brother-in-law Lord Cowley was again British Ambassador in Paris, she arranged for Carroll to be sent there in 1842 as an unpaid attaché.[21]

While there, May attracted the attentions of one of the embassy attachés, Harry Howard, 'reckoned uncommonly good-looking' by Parisian society and a friend of Carroll's. The Honourable Henry Howard was the youngest son of the Earl of Carlisle and an experienced attaché, having been at the embassy with his uncle and aunt Granville in 1838. The following year Harriet Granville had told her sister Georgiana Carlisle that 'we all get fonder of him every day'. By the spring of 1845, Harry was so smitten with

"ARABELLA MARIA. "Only to think, Julia dear, that our Mothers wore such ridiculous fashions as these!"
BOTH. "Ha! ha! ha! ha!"

'Victorian debutantes mock their Regency mammas' clothes'. Anonymous caricature of the difference in fashions between Marianne's debut and that of her niece May.

May that he followed her back to England. Some time at the end of April, he proposed and was accepted. Marianne gave her consent whereupon Harry, 'much in love', travelled to Castle Howard to ask his father's permission to wed, which he received.

Emily and McTavish were delighted only because May was so happy and Marianne approved of the match; they realised that, like her aunts, she would probably never return home. Her grandmother was with Emily when the news came. Mary Carroll Caton was now seventy-five and almost completely blind. She had been feeling low but the announcement quite raised her spirits, to the extent that a Woodville cousin wrote that May's marriage 'has absorbed everything, and she talks incessantly about it, her memory is very bad and not having occupation, dreams many things, relates them as facts which Emily rolls up her eyes and shakes her head at when she returns to Brookland[wood]'.[22]

In England the Duke congratulated Marianne upon the marriage. 'The family are the first in this country – and I am happy to learn they approve of and [illegible] the Marriage', he wrote on 22 April 1845. May might have been forgiven for feeling some apprehension at the thought of passing muster with the *grandes dames* of English society. Harry's sister, Harriet, Duchess of Sutherland, had not known her before 'except thinking her face very pretty & her manner very lively', but after Marianne and May dined at Stafford House, she decided that May's eyes 'have a charming expression of intelligence & fondness for him – the complexion is brilliant & transparent . . . but it is not a perfect face – tho a very attractive one'. Gossip was already circulating about May – 'the world's thoughts have not been kind about her' – but the Duchess took comfort in May's being half-American as American girls 'make excellent wives', she told Ralph Sneyd. As for the latest story that, after they first met, May had said 'Goodbye, Harriet' to her formidable future sister-in-law, 'it was all quite untrue', declared the Duchess.

The marriage was held on 31 May 1845 at St George's, Hanover Square, followed by a Catholic ceremony conducted by Louisa's chaplain and then a wedding breakfast given by the Duke at Apsley House. After a few days, the couple travelled to Castle Howard, where May met Harry's parents for the first time. She was full of cold and rather nervous. Georgiana Carlisle waited until she had recovered before writing to assure Marianne of their high opinion of May. 'Lord Carlisle has been very much pleased with her – She comes in at his tea-time like a bright vision to charm and enliven him.' Georgiana Carlisle understood how anxious Marianne was, 'it must have been a great trial to her to leave your maternal roof and tender care that she pays with so much affection'.[23]

*

May's departure left a void in Marianne's life that was made worse by sad news from home. Unbeknown to the sisters, while they gathered in London for a family wedding, their father was taken ill at Caton House. He died there on 19 May. The funeral was held two days later, and he was buried in Greenmount Cemetery. To the last he was optimistic about an improvement in his fortunes though, as Louisa would say, 'the ways & means' escaped him. He had never managed to clear his large debt of $100,000 to Olivers, despite a 'most decided mania for land speculation', and numerous speculations in coal and mines. This did not prevent him, shortly before his death, from urging their mother to make arrangements to enable him to raise money on Brooklandwood and Caton House, which she circumvented only by confining her interest to a mere life estate with powers to her trustees.

Caton died insolvent, leaving a mere $2,762, which was swallowed up in fees for pending High Court cases against him and a payment insufficient to clear his Neilson debt. Yet he appears to have inspired little acrimony in the community, being remembered for his polished manner and benevolent disposition. He also forged ahead with schemes to develop land owned by his wife and daughters; he built the towns of Catonsville which today is a flourishing suburb of Baltimore. And in the south-eastern part of Steuben County in upstate New York, near the Genesee River, lies a town, a quiet, conservative, friendly place named Caton.[24]

After his death, Mary sold the Brooklandwood plantation to the Brown banking family. She was now almost blind and old age and physical decrepitude assuaged her previous desire for travel. She did not long survive Caton, dying the following year. Her four daughters were deeply distressed, however much her death was expected. For the eldest three, her abiding interest in their doings and chit-chat about all things American had made their exile more bearable but they at least could lean on each other in shared grief; for Emily, it was a terrible strangeness to endure life without her.

Their mother had always been quite candid about her will, telling John Latrobe on one occasion: 'I wish all my daughters to know exactly the state of things at home as my intentions towards them are just.' And so they were. She left a personal fortune of £186,000 [£13.4 million] and a landed estate held in trust, including Carroll House and farm, Caton House, Catonsville, Carrollton, various town houses and lots in Baltimore, and large tracts in Maryland, Pennsylvania and West Virginia; over 200 pages in a foolscap ledger contain descriptions and maps of the real estate. Despite the size and complexity of her property, the will was short and straightforward. She left everything, including all investments and funds, in trust for her four daughters to be divided equally between them as if they were

femes soles and Emily was appointed the executrix. Realising the impracti-
cality of including her three eldest daughters in the bequest of her pews
and personal effects, she left these by codicil in trust to her land agent
Stimpson for the sole, separate use of Emily. [25]

Despite this, the legal settlement proved troublesome. Their mother had
given her trustees powers so as to avoid the difficulties incurred by three
of her daughters being absent and three of them being married. Under
Maryland law, married women could not make deeds of land unless their
husbands joined in the execution of them and they could not execute a
power of attorney even with the co-operation of their husbands. Thus,
unless they filed a bill in the Maryland courts for a decree of equity making
all of them, including their husbands, interested parties, Marianne as a
widow was the only one of the sisters who could legally claim or divide
any of the property.

On Josiah Pennington's advice, Emily asked her sisters to give the trustees
power of attorney to act for them. Bess refused to give her consent. She
already disliked the way the law treated married women but the added
injury of being expected to give trustees unlimited powers to sell and divide
her share of the property incensed her. She became convinced that
Pennington, like so many other lawyers and agents of the day, was not to
be trusted and would take advantage of them as women prevented from
protecting their American estate by being absentee owners and their status
as British subjects.

Marianne and Louisa got round this by persuading her to let Emily act
for them and appoint the lawyers. Bess worried that Emily was 'so *confiding*
that she is no protection' against the 'slippery people' who would try to get
hold of their land. Bess consulted an old family friend, David Hoffman,
then in London, telling him 'I remember riding on your shoulder when I
was a child, & I am now throwing the burden of myself upon you again',
but he agreed with Marianne's opinion that Pennington was an upright fair
man who had merited the confidence of their mother. Bess declared she
would keep control of her inheritance by finding her own lawyer. After she
did, it was Emily's turn to dig in her heels and insist that her trustee *alone*
would divide the estate; to which Bess predictably pronounced: 'To this I
will not consent.'

Such tribulations beset heiresses who would act independently. With
Bess indignant about the very real risk of female exploitation by American
lawyers, and Emily prevaricating and sorely tired dealing with at least six
advisers, it took Marianne's mediation to smooth their ruffled feathers. She
asked Hoffman to review the case, and retained lawyers to settle the will.
She and Bess got James Buchanan (then an American minister) to select
a reputable agent for their Pennsylvania lands. Emily capitulated and agreed

to the partition although it would be some years before their mother's estate was settled.[26]

Throughout the legal rumpus, the sisters' personal as opposed to business relations – for they often differentiated themselves between the two in their letters: 'This little letter is *all about business*' or 'Today I write only on business' – remained unimpaired. And they had such need of one another over the coming months as they tried to come to terms with the saddest of family news. Early in 1848, reports arrived that May Howard was very unwell and asking for Marianne, who immediately set off for Paris. It seems that May was having a breakdown, as letters refer to 'the delicate mental health of Mrs Howard' and Bess confessed to a friend, 'I am so *utterly miserable* at the state of poor Mrs Howard's mind.' May had been married and living in Paris for nearly three years. McTavish, fortunately, was in Britain and quickly joined Marianne at his daughter's bedside.

It was not the happiest of visits. Marianne found herself in the middle of a revolution in February. 'I do not like the state of things,' she admitted to Richard Rush, then in Paris. She was alone as Harry had taken May to convalesce at Vichy and McTavish had sailed for New York. Did Rush think the fighting over 'and one may remain quietly in Paris or if I would be better to go away', she asked. There were demonstrations near the rue de Rivoli where she was staying and the barricades were going up. It was the beginning of the revolt that overthrew Louis-Philippe, who fled with his family to England on 2 March, and that later installed Napoleon's nephew Prince Louis-Napoleon Bonaparte as President of the French Republic. Marianne had by then left for England. As the year wore on, though, the effect of revolutions elsewhere in Europe, recession in Britain and America and fears about Chartist riots made no country seem safe. Louisa's reiterated invitation to the remote Highlands seemed positively enticing.[27]

'I shall be so delighted to have you here, & hope you will stay a long time,' wrote a thrilled Louisa to her elder sisters. She was sure that the refreshing Scottish mountain air would cure Marianne's asthma and that was enough to persuade Bess for once to overcome her aversion to the everlasting rain, mist and cold of the Highlands. Others thought with delight of life at Mar Lodge. After receiving 'a capital account of your gaieties at Mar and of your brilliant Season' for sport, the diplomat James Hudson had written to Louisa from Rio in 1847, 'I need not say how truly my heart was with you all and how I longed for a peep of Your "Gracie" on your Pony – The Duke with his Rifle, and the "General" with his "excellent Highlanders" around him . . .'

Despite the weather it was not such a penance to stay at Mar Lodge. Louisa and Car loved being there. Louisa ensured that the house was warm, comfortable and welcoming for their large house parties. She had the house painted and papered, deer larders redone, peat sheds repaired, bedrooms arranged off a passage and new water closets installed for every bedroom – and that was just the schedule for one year alone. Her enthusiasm for all things Scottish extended to interior decoration and every room was furnished with plaids. Her mother-in-law sent samples of the family Dunblane plaid for them to choose one for the family and one for their piper Millar and his son's dress. The house was on the banks of the Dee and in 1848 they built a new bridge across the river to replace the stone one carried away in the floods, the 'Muckle Spate', of 1829. The Leedses named it in honour of an expected guest that year, the Victoria bridge.[28]

Queen Victoria began her love affair with the Highlands in 1842 when she paid her first visit to Scotland. After her second she wrote in her journal: 'The English coast appeared terribly flat. Lord Aberdeen was quite touched when I told him I was so attached to the dear, dear Highlands and missed the fine hills so much.' When she and Prince Albert decided to find a home there, their doctor recommended Deeside for its healthy climate. Lord Aberdeen had stayed at Mar Lodge and suggested the royal couple take nearby Balmoral Castle. They arrived there on 8 September and were delighted by the view of the Dee winding through the glen and the beautiful wooded hills. 'It was so calm, so solitary, it did one good as one gazed around', the Queen wrote. 'All seemed to breathe freedom and peace, and to make one forget the world and its sad turmoils.'

'Her Majesty is particularly charmed with the mountain scenery around Mar Lodge and the Linn of Dee', reported the *Aberdeen Journal* on 22 September of one royal expedition. 'On their return the Royal party visited the Duke and Duchess of Leeds at Mar Lodge.' Louisa and Car were soon dining at Balmoral and were entertaining the Queen and Prince Albert at Mar. The Leedses always attended the Braemar Gathering and this year was busier than ever. Car and his men attired in Dunblane tartan with General Sir Alexander Duff and his men marched to Braemar to receive the Queen. At the ball afterwards, Louisa was chaperoning Lora Lane Fox the Queen of the ball who presented a silver brooch to the best out of the eight Highlanders who danced at Queen Victoria's request.

The next year Car and Duff and their men greeted the Queen on her arrival and Louisa and the Duff ladies 'came up to the carriage' to welcome her return to Balmoral. By then Prince Albert had determined to buy the estate and started negotiations with the Fife trustees; he or his advisers did not have the benefit of Louisa's honed lobbying skills, however, and it would take over three years before the price of 30,000 guineas could be agreed and the Queen could lead a 'simple' life in her own Highland home.[29]

Louisa, having passed most of her adult life in high society, knew better than to presume that even as a republican duchess in the Highlands she was on an equal footing with Majesty. This was not so clear to some of the American ladies who now came to Britain. The new American Minister's wife was Katherine Bigelow Lawrence whose husband founded the Lowell textile mills. She came from a distinguished Boston family and Herman Melville told a surprised Nathaniel Hawthorne how she wrote to the Queen begging to present Mrs Peabody to her. 'I may assure your Majesty in requesting this favour that I am doing what is with me an unusual thing, for in Boston the Lawrences are more in the habit of conferring than requesting a favour.'[30]

By November 1849, however, the sisters' thoughts were concentrated on events in Paris. May was very ill. 'I do not know when poor Emily is coming to the Country, I will let you know in time', Louisa scribbled to her sisters from Mar Lodge. But whether Emily and Marianne were in time to see their precious May again is unrecorded. She died in Paris on 21 February aged only twenty-four. Even in that era of frequent early deaths, to lose a child was the most tragic of events. Emily was always self-contained about heartache but, having already lost one of her children, she must have suffered torment over May. Yet there seemed to be an emotional as well as geographic distance between them, perhaps the only way Emily could cope with the years of separation.

Marianne had long been wrapped up in May's well-being. Her death was a terrible shock, and she aged with grief. McTavish, who had seen May more frequently than Emily, was openly heartbroken. Harry Howard had been posted to Lisbon and promoted to Secretary of the British Legation in 1849. He lived until 1879 but never married again. McTavish refused to let May be interred at Castle Howard and he and Emily took her body back with them to Maryland.[31]

37

'The desolate state of age'

The four sisters were now at a stage when deaths came with great regularity. 'It is the way of the World and gives occasion for Reflection', the Duke wrote after attending yet another funeral, that of Arbuthnot in 1850. The following year, Stafford at the grand age of eighty died of 'decay of nature'. His family never had anything to fear about Bess being grasping. She wanted the estates to remain with the family and arranged everything with her stepson Henry Stafford. She received an annuity of £800 for life and moved permanently into Hampton Court Palace to live with Marianne, contenting herself with regular visits to Cossey.[1]

In Maryland, Emily was writing a letter of business to Louisa when she broke off to say that she was worried about McTavish who was ill – 'first it was thought Typhoid, then Gastric – now an intermittent' for which he was taking quinine. Mac remained in bed for over six weeks with a chill and fever from which he never recovered, dying on 21 June 1852. Emily's reaction was to move out of Carrollton Hall and to economise. McTavish had calculated he was worth about $30,000 exclusive of his Canadian estate but his losses in the crash of 1848 meant that his estate would not produce half that sum. Other debts came to light when Emily as executrix was settling his estate. It was fortunate that, like Marianne and Bess, she had not been reliant upon her husband for income.[2]

She did, however, have the support of her eldest son. Carroll had been unable to secure a diplomatic post after Paris and had turned to politics instead. He had been elected MP for Dundalk in Ireland in the August 1847 election but the opposition then petitioned to unseat him, a frequent procedure in Irish elections. His opponents were able to bribe enough witnesses to speak against him and in 1848, shortly after May's death, Carroll lost his seat. The experience discouraged him from a political career and he resolved to return home. Emily handed Carrollton Hall over to him and lived in her Cathedral Street town house where she continued to plead poverty though Louisa knew that of the four, she and Emily were the richest.

Marianne suffered greatly from asthma that year and was increasingly confined to her rooms. Wellington too suffered that year, from age, from

deafness and from falling asleep everywhere. His slight frame seemed
shrunken, his stoop more pronounced, and he was inclined to totter as he
walked. But walk he did and unaided – woe betide anyone who tried to
help him mount his horse or remove his boots, as the painter Weigall
discovered when he was sharply rebuffed. The Duke's handwriting had
become illegible, one of his last surviving notes to Marianne is a spider's
scrawl, written at midnight on 14 February to say he had just then received
her note, 'I have certainly intended to go to see her and I will carry the
intention into execution' and the rest tails off into a jumble of squiggles.[3]

He was eighty-three and everyone, the whole country, assumed he would
live for ever. He still slept on his army camp-bed, only 2 feet 9 inches wide;
when asked how he managed to sleep in such a narrow bed he replied,
'When it's time to turn over it's time to turn out.' The bed was afterwards
given to Marianne and made its way, perhaps with Alex McTavish, to
Maryland. But on the morning of 14 September the Duke was woken in
it for the last time. He suffered several fits and, after seeing the apothecary, became unconscious; in the afternoon he was lifted into his favourite
wing chair where, with his younger son Charles and daughter-in-law Sophia
beside him, and watched by his devoted servants and the doctors, he died.[4]

'The greatest man that England ever knew is no more', was how Prince
Albert's secretary broke the news to the royal family at Balmoral. Victoria's
cry echoed the public reaction: 'one cannot think of this country without
the Duke, our immortal hero' as it did Louisa's at Mar Lodge. It was impossible to realise that he was gone, he had been like a father to her for thirty-six
years, her oldest English friend, and a link with so much past happiness.[5]

As the Queen decided to postpone the public funeral until after Parliament
met, it was not until 10 November that the coffin arrived to lie in state at
Chelsea Hospital. His sons had wished for a private funeral and the ensuing
havoc in the Hall did little to change their feelings. Douro declared it 'a
really disgusting affair, seven people they say were killed by the crowd today'.
Lady Palmerston thought it 'so unnatural and so grating to one's feeling to
make a festival of a funeral!' Car attended the state funeral at St Paul's
Cathedral on 18 November. Marianne, joined by Louisa and Bess, watched
from the windows of Apsley House as the large procession started off from
Grosvenor Place and passed before them en route to St Paul's. Marianne,
usually so composed, wept openly for her dearest Duke. He had loved her
and been a devoted friend; there had been other loves but, in the words of
his biographer Elizabeth Longford, 'she was the love of his life' and he always
wore a miniature of her. When he died, it was found with him still.[6]

If he had become shrunken with age, she presented the reverse. She suffered
from dropsy, the name given to congestive heart failure characterised by
fluid retention and swelling. In spite of undergoing 'tapping', which

consisted of agonising operations to cut away her stretched flesh and remove the accumulating fluid, her once ethereal body and beautiful oval face were swollen almost beyond recognition. Her asthma attacks intensified and she had to forgo drives as she could hardly move about in her chamber. She never complained about the pain but then Bess always said, 'Beloved Mary lives more in Heaven than on earth.'[7]

It was remarkable that she had lived to be sixty-four *and* she retained her dark hair and eyesight. Bess needed spectacles, ordering a new pair that year 'of blue steel frames and finest Brazilian pebbles', and obtained through Marianne's apothecary Mr Peregrine the receipt for hair dye made from walnuts, which 'had the advantage over the nitrate of Silver dye that it does not injure the texture of the hair, or produce different shades of colour'.[8]

Marianne's malady was incurable; water was accumulating on her chest, which threatened suffocation. In desperation she tried one more tapping operation on 12 December. It left her in severe agony. Louisa nursed her 'with the utmost tenderness & skill', according to Bess, but inflammation set in. Marianne knew she was dying and sent for her household to wish them goodbye and ask them to pray for her.

> Henny came last broken-hearted. Her ladyship took her hand & said 'Goodbye Henny dear you shall not want, you shall be taken care of.' Poor Henny could only say 'Thank you my Lady.' The Bishop of Southwark Dr Grant as well as several priests were with her at the last. Walstan her attendant [her butler] a fine handsome man who had been many years with her, was there too,

Margaret Fenton recollected. Marianne died a little before eight o'clock on the evening of 16 December 1853. 'You will pity me when I tell you, that the charm of my life, the tenderest of sisters, my comfort, my joy is taken from me', Bess cried to Lady Westmeath two days later. 'I cannot tell you how desolate I feel.'[9]

She and Louisa travelled with Marianne's body to Cossey where they were received by Dr Husenbeth, the Stafford chaplain, at the chapel door at about six. Bess described to Emily how the coffin was covered with a crimson velvet pall and the coronet 'she wore so meekly' placed in the centre upon a velvet cushion. 'I have a childish horror of the black plumes & was pleased to see they were not used', she admitted. The pall was the Stafford one '& Henry requested me to allow it to be put over her dear remains, as suitable to her rank – nothing could exceed his kindness & . . . his gentle sympathy'. The coffin lay surrounded by candles and guarded by watchmen overnight in the family chapel. The next day, after Mass and the funeral service 'her dear body was lowered into the vault to remain as she wished with that of my beloved husband', and where Bess would one day lie by their side. 'Oh the beloved the precious one!' she cried to Emily, 'it was the most afflicting day I ever spent.'

Marianne had been for her sisters 'a perfect Being' and, as Bess said, they ached for her ever afterwards. For the greater part of Bess's life, Marianne had been the centre of her existence. Without her, Bess felt just half a person, racked with grief and headaches, living in the shadows and waiting to die. She clung to Louisa at Hornby and, whenever the Leedses were in Scotland, ventured to the Clarendon, telling Emily Westmeath, 'I have formed no plans for myself except not to go into housekeeping, I could not endure being alone.' She had a certain amount of business to conduct as the executrix of Marianne's English will and fortunately Carroll was the executor of the more complicated American one; apart from some specific bequests, all the rest of Marianne's land, rents and stock were divided equally amongst her sisters with reversion to Carroll. Carroll House was bequeathed to its tenants, the Redemptionist Fathers; a plaque still commemorates the sisters' gift.[10]

Carroll had married General Winfield Scott's daughter Ella and it was cheering to hear not only that he was 'very happily married & very much attached to his wife' but also that Emily would be a grandmother. Emily was delighted, telling 'dearest Lou' on 31 October that 'Carroll will have a large family – he has really married a gem – for her qualities are *sterling* – & she is beautiful – I trust I shall be of use to her as far as faith goes this winter [Ella was not a Catholic] – I never saw such perfect happiness as reigns between those two young people'.[11]

Louisa buried her grief in occupation. Car was Crown Ranger of Swaledale in the North Riding and liked to hunt there in the winter when he and Louisa stayed in one of his hunting boxes, an old lodge up the dale from Gunnerside. Louisa set about buying two acres of land at Thistlebout, near Gunnerside, where she financed the building of another plain Gothic church with a separate presbytery. 'I most cordially welcome establishing so great and good a work of charity in my District', John Briggs, Bishop of York hastened to assure the abbess of the Sisters of the Assumption in Paris about another plan of 'the good and charitable Duchess' to endow an orphanage run by three of the order's nuns near Richmond, North Yorkshire. Louisa's agent Peter Maxwell had purchased about four acres of land with a house, to which she later added several adjoining fields, for which she furnished the necessary funds from her own private fortune.[12]

Louisa was contributing to the wave of religious orders of women flooding Britain: in 1850 there were over fifty religious orders conducting schools for girls. The quiet style of British Catholics also underwent considerable change. The atmosphere of general belief depicted by Newman: 'An old fashioned house of gloomy appearance, closed in with high walls, and with an iron gate, and yews, and the report attaching to it that "Roman Catholics" lived there; but who they were, or what they did or what was meant by calling them Roman Catholics no one could tell – though it had an unpleasant sound, and told of form and superstition', was giving way. Cathedrals and churches were being built everywhere; St George's Cathedral in Southwark, built by Pugin, was completed in 1848. Pope Pius IX in 1850 re-established the Catholic hierarchy in Britain, which had been extinct since the reign of Elizabeth I, creating Catholic dioceses and appointing English Catholic bishops. Publicity attached to prominent converts, such as Newman and Manning, seemed to symbolise the advance of Catholicism from disillusionment with the established Church. Added to which was the huge increase in the Catholic population through the mass immigration of Irish Catholics fleeing the famine of the 1840s. 'Something very strange is passing over this land, by the very surprise, by the very commotion, which it excites', proclaimed Newman in his most famous sermon, preached in 1852. 'It is the coming in of a Second Spring; it is a restoration in the moral world.' Louisa and Bess were at the forefront of this. In 1855, Bess supported the foundation of Mount St Bernard, the first Cistercian house to be built in England since the Reformation, in the vanguard of a monastic revival in England. She gave a house and three acres of land near the abbey as well as some money to help.[13]

Bess might say 'I only wish I was as pious as Emily & had her vocation for a conventual life' but lonely as she was, she was not yet ready to retreat. Emily made the move and entered the Convent of the Sisters of Mercy in Houston Street, New York City. She wondered how she could have endured the world so long, telling Bess how she liked to go out to nurse the sick whatever their disease. Although she was 'perfectly happy' in the convent, she ended up admitting, 'I am too old to transplant' and decided to return to Baltimore. She was not renouncing the conventual life, though, merely transferring from one house to another and, in this case, to her own one: Caton House. She had inherited it but never lived there and when Alex married a Maryland girl, Ellen Gilmor, in 1856, they did not consider down-town Baltimore a suitable neighbourhood and lived instead in Mount Vernon. Although Emily's father would have forbidden his home becoming a convent, she gave the property to the Sisters of Mercy, after which it was known as (and continues to be) the Carroll Mansion. She also bought another house in Baltimore, Willowbrook, and gave it to the Sisters of the House of the Good Shepherd along with her only known portrait, which can still be seen at the Convent today.[14]

Long-standing associations with a different loved house were severed when Car determined not to renew the lease on Mar Lodge. He had been unhappy about the stalking for some time. Despite his maintaining keepers and a large staff of forest rangers at great expense to preserve the seclusion of the glens, his forests were crawling with noisy parties of people. The reason was not difficult to fathom: Queen Victoria. Ever since her arrival at Balmoral, hordes of the curious had descended upon the district where, Car explained, 'under the excuse of seeking views, enumeralizing or botanising, every hill and glen of Mar Forest is over run by intruders' who not only laughed at the keepers but also frightened the deer until they disappeared, leaving Car with very poor stalking. Although Car and Louisa had loved being there, Mar Lodge was no longer the tranquil place they remembered.

'The Duke has purchased a very large Estate in Scotland called Applecross' for £135,000, Bess affirmed in October. Consisting of 144,000 acres of mountains, woodlands, freshwater lochs and Upper Loch Torridon in Wester Ross, it was about as remote as it was possible to be. Amidst this wilderness there was only a small shooting lodge so that Louisa was soon involved with improvements again, no easy task when transporting Mar estate workers and supplies to Lochcarron, the largest township on the estate, was always troublesome, if not impossible during the winter.[15]

In 1859, she was alone with Bess at Hornby, her mother-in-law having died in 1856, when she received an urgent summons from London on 1 May. Car needed her. She and Bess arrived to find him suffering from diphtheria and 'between life and death'. He was exceedingly ill during the night and the next day asked his London parson to call in the evening to give him Holy Communion. In the meantime the Catholic Bishop of Beverley visited. Death was on Car's mind and he said he would be happy to have the ministrations of Dr Manning or Mr Oakley 'as they had been Protestants'.

Although Louisa kept reiterating that Car must be kept quiet, the constant interruptions of doctors, nurses, priests and parsons together with the family cannot have helped. As Car worsened, new medical advice was sought. The parson arrived to find Car claiming he was 'a shade better'. Later that evening, Bishop Briggs and Dr Manning found Car sitting up in an easy chair with Louisa near him. Car grasped the bishop's hand and said he would like to make his confession. He was in the middle of it when the surgeon came in and said the doctors were anxious to operate. Car was then conditionally baptised and received absolution 'with marked devotion and fervour'. It seemed to all present a deathbed conversion.

After the operation Car had a better night but Louisa's hopes were dashed by the afternoon. She had made him promise always to wear a medal of 'Our Lady' which she believed had saved him from death after a hunting accident. As he lay dying that afternoon he tried to comfort his miserable shocked wife and 'held out his hand to her with the little medal in his palm and said "Lou, I promised I would always wear this – see what it has done for me'" but it could not save him now. He died at half past four on that May afternoon. Louisa took him for burial with full ducal honours to the Leeds family vault at All Hallows Church, Harthill in Yorkshire and then returned to Hornby, alone.[16]

Being five years' older than Car she always thought she would die before him. She felt a terrible numbness grip her at this 'dreadful bereavement' and she was 'so very miserable'. She could not hide away as there was so much business to attend to, estates to run and discussions with Car's cousin, now eighth Duke of Leeds. Car had left her a handsome jointure of £6,000 [£0.5 million] a year, Hornby for life and an allowance to cover its running expenses and the wages of staff, a further £5,000 payable immediately, and another annuity of £1,500 from his Post Office revenues as well as the charge of his heirlooms.

On his death the Dukedom and all the entailed estates passed to the eighth duke; the Conyers barony now devolved upon the Lane Foxes. In addition to numerous other legacies, he left £25,000 [£1.9 million] in trust, with Louisa as the trustee, to provide an annuity of £500 for his natural daughter Fanny Roth, born in Whitechapel in 1823, long before he married Louisa. Her existence confirms Louisa's inability to have children, probably caused by the lethal doses of mercury prescribed in her youth. Whether Car's recognition of his daughter extended beyond the annuity or how much Louisa knew about her were not disclosed.[17]

During their remaining years, the sisters plodded wearily through old age. Louisa found it did not become any easier with time to live without Car. 'I feel very miserable and cannot reconcile myself to this afflicting life', she admitted the following March. Bess was visibly failing with severe attacks of heart trouble and Louisa took her to St Leonards-on-Sea, then a fashionable resort on the south coast near Hastings. They found the sea air restorative and settled there, though Louisa paid regular visits to Hornby. They made a new friend in Mother Cornelia Connelly, founder of the Society of the Holy Child Jesus for the education of Catholic girls, whose convent was nearby. She was a fellow American, who knew aunt Harper and was an unexpected link with home during the Civil War. Louisa donated 150 acres of her Pennsylvania lands to establish the first American branch of the society at Towanda in 1862. Her plan to start a school in Baltimore had been derailed by the outbreak of the war, Bishop Kendrick of Baltimore explaining that 'the city and neighborhood and State are overrun with U.S. soldiery, and cannon is implanted in our very midst'.[18]

Bess, now a frail seventy-two, was unable to muster the enthusiasm always kindled in Louisa by new projects. A haemorrhage combined with heart failure carried her swiftly into death on 29 October. Louisa, in great misery, took Bess's body to Cossey for the funeral on 5 November. After the service and tribute for Bess's 'remarkable humility and charity', Louisa came from the family pew down the chapel and laid some simple garden flowers upon Bess's coffin. Then she flung herself onto it, sobbing audibly for her darling Bess. And she afterwards cried, 'I am alone and desolate upon the earth.'[19]

Emily, separated by an ocean and the deprivations of living in a border state during the war, felt cut off from Louisa and equally desolate. She had been wretched when, some years before, Alex suffered a breakdown and returned from hospital in a poor state. 'My aunt Ellen had a tough time', Ellen Gilmor Buchanan remembered and the marriage did not survive the turbulent collapse in his mental health. Fearful of the effect upon their only child Francis Osborne McTavish, always known as Frank, Ellen took him with her to live with her father Robert Gilmor. When Alex was certified insane, she proceeded with a legal separation. Alex survived his aunt Stafford by only six months, dying from paralysis in June 1863.

Emily was now sixty-eight. She had lived to see Carroll and Ella's happy ménage at Carrollton Hall and the birth of five McTavish grandchildren. President Buchanan considered that, despite the 'romantic and interesting lives of her sisters, she perhaps led the happiest' as the only one to have a family; this was said, however, before she had buried three of her children. She died after a lingering illness in 1867. Her funeral was by far the simplest of the sisters as she asked to be buried in the plain black coffin with iron handles of the poor, and for no funeral service to be preached. She died a rich woman, leaving a large landed estate and, like her two elder sisters, made many large charitable donations of land and annuities. As her chief heir, Carroll inherited Carrollton Hall with the extra sixty acres she had purchased 'under a sacred promise to my grandfather', and most of her houses, land and personal effects, though her jewellery and silver went to his children. She did not forget Alex's family, giving Ellen an annuity and Frank a one-fifth share of her land, as well as an annuity. She also left him $20,000 on condition he had already 'bona fide, entered as a partner into some firm or house engaged in commercial business, and not otherwise'.[20]

Still, Louisa lived on. She was nearly seventy, getting 'old, red-faced and dowdyish', according to Moran, who remembered her from younger days. She had moved with her servants and chef into a suite of apartments adjoining the community wing of St Leonard's Convent. Sister Ignatia Bridges recorded how Louisa came 'finding her little cloister ready and the large parlour' downstairs to entertain visitors and henceforth called the Duchess's Parlour. Nevertheless, without her sisters she knew what she could only describe as 'a terrible loneliness'.

The Old Archbishop's Palace at Mayfield purchased by Louisa for Mother Cornelia Connelly. It is now part of St Leonards-Mayfield School for Girls.

She tried to become a postulant but Mother Connelly was certain that such an existence would prove too austere. Louisa could only see this as a challenge: she sold her horses and carriage and gave the proceeds to the poor, thereafter taking a hired cab. Determined to show that she could perfectly well follow the hours of the Community, she ordered her lady's maid to waken her at 5 a.m. to allow time for her bath and toilette before Community Mass at seven o'clock. Mother Connelly remained unimpressed, however, and so, for the second time, Louisa was unable to become a nun.[21]

She was able, though, to see through one last great project. The plight of the orphaned, destitute children of Catholic Irish immigrants was heart-rending and there was still no universal provision for either education or religious instruction. Louisa founded two orphanages, the Holy Trinity for Boys at Mayfield and the Mark Cross Female Orphanage at Rotherfield, where she also built a chapel. She drew up the rules for both orphanages and checked all expenditure, sometimes with comic results; used to house-keeping on a large scale, she ordered a ton of spice so that 'the Duchess's cloves' were still flavouring apple pies forty years later. She also paid £5,250 for an estate at Mayfield that included the ruins of the Archbishop's Palace which she presented to Mother Connelly's religious order. On 19 November 1863 the first Mass was celebrated there since 1543. Building work began the following year and the school is better known today as St Leonards-Mayfield School with its own Leeds House.[22]

As the chatelaine of Hornby, living almost half the year there, Louisa welcomed the eighth duke, a widower, and his eight children to the castle, becoming especially fond of his heir Lord Carmarthen. She thoughtfully started the legal process of handing the heirloom jewels over to George and his wife Fanny Carmarthen. She had made a list of them in a tiny Florentine notebook after Car bought them from Lane Fox and they were reset at Rundell & Bridge. It was a serious collection of fine diamonds with some rubies, amethysts and pearls; the diamonds included a long necklace set with forty-two 'brilliants', a pair of bracelets to wear over gloves, a pair of 'tops & drops' as long earrings were called, and a tiara of sixteen acorns and forty-four leaves. It pleased Louisa that, in her lifetime, another Lady Carmarthen had the pleasure of wearing them.

She also made George Carmarthen her chief heir, settling land around Hornby she had purchased, and she passed other heirlooms, such as the silver and plate, directly to him and also included a large collection of items she had taken to the convent, such as a lovely travelling case of silver cutlery complete with innumerable candlesticks with branches and six pairs of nutcrackers. Finding herself short of a dozen small silver-handled knives, Louisa asked Leeds to send her some non-heirloom ones without the Leeds crest. He was unable to oblige as 'all the knives are so old and worn that I don't think there are a dozen on which the crest or coronet is distinguishable'.[23]

In the autumn of 1868 she made a final American will (there were many versions of the English one) settling the proceeds of all her American property in trust for George Carmarthen, telling the eighth duke on 20 November, 'it is a pleasure to feel that I shall have thus been able to add in the best and most permanent manner over £100,000 [£6.7million] to the Family Estate'. She also made a substantial provision for Carmarthen's heir Lord Danby, aged eleven, who told her, 'Papa has just told me of a very kind letter you have written to him about me, I dare say I shall understand it better when I am older but I can understand it well enough now to be very pleased and think it very kind of you. I will always remember you . . .'[24]

There were no other family members left to remember her in England and in the USA only one survived of her generation, Emily Harper, who lived until 1892. Cousin Charles Carroll died the month after Bess, having compensated for the other stripling branches of the family by having ten children; he left his eldest son, Charles Carroll VI, in possession of the Carroll estates. The sixth generation of Carrolls of Doughoregan's sturdy main branch would spread its roots throughout the aristocratic families of Maryland, England and Europe. Distance had prevented Louisa from knowing this generation of Carrolls. She had been deeply grieved to learn of Carroll McTavish's untimely death in 1868 from the consumption, so prevalent in his father's family; he left Ella and their children a considerable fortune but Louisa never knew them.

At eighty, another attack of pain and fever left her helpless. The doctor thought something was preying on her mind. Whatever it was, past being able to command or confess, Louisa took it with her when she died on 8 April 1874. It was not until 17 April, that Louisa's executors and trustees gathered in the private chapel at St Leonard's for her first, Catholic funeral. The bishops of Southwark and Clifton, their trains held by four little boys from Holy Trinity Orphanage, processed along the nave followed by the priests and chaplains officiating at the High Mass. Early that afternoon her coffin was drawn by carriage to Hastings Station and conveyed by train to London. From there it was taken by the Manchester, Sheffield & Lincoln Railway to Kiveton Park where Leeds estates workmen carried her coffin, surrounded by mourners led by the eighth duke and George Carmarthen, across the fields to the ancient red sandstone family church in Harthill village. At the door of All Hallows, the Revd George Hudson received the coffin for her second, Protestant funeral. After the final blessing, Louisa's body was carried to the family vault and laid to rest beside her precious Car for eternity.[25]

The death of the last of 'the Three American Graces whose beauty and charms were famous' was widely reported in the papers although in *The New York Times* she was 'the philanthropic Duchess of Leeds'. She endowed both the Duchess of Leeds Foundation and the Assumption Fund, which enabled the educational work she began to continue. The eighth duke and Carmarthen erected in the Leeds chapel a stained-glass triptych in her memory. 'This is a beautiful window,' observed *The Yorkshire Gazetteer*, 'the colours are lovely and clear.' It was, however, soon obstructed by a new organ, just as the sisters' fame was quickly obscured by a new band of 'transatlantic invaders'. Two days after Louisa's funeral Jennie Jerome married Lord Randolph Churchill, an event publicised as the first great Anglo-American union. In 1876 Consuelo Yznaga was fêted as the first American to marry a duke's heir, though the Duke of Manchester deplored 'a little American savage' entering his family. The invasion of the 'dollar princesses' was, nevertheless, well under way in life and literature. Edith Wharton's *Fast and Loose* (1876/7) and *The Buccaneers* (1933/38) depict the social adventures of American heiresses who marry English aristocrats. By 1887 Oscar Wilde was writing that American women 'adore titles and are a permanent blow to Republican principles'. Yet, despite their British marriages, the Caton sisters remained true republicans and proud heiresses of the American Revolution.[26]

Acknowledgements

Throughout the writing of this book I have been sustained and delighted by the encouragement and numerous kindnesses offered by very many friends and informed people in America, Britain and Ireland.

My thanks go to all the families associated with the Caton sisters for their interest and assistance. I am also most grateful to Lord and Lady Douro for allowing me to consult and use the Wellington family's personal papers at Stratfield Saye. I would like to thank the Duke of Wellington; the Hon. Georgina Stonor for sharing her extensive knowledge of the first Duke's papers and for all her help; Victoria Crake and Kate Jenkins for their time and help with documents and pictures in the house; and Josephine Oxley, Curator, at Apsley House and the staff and former Curators there. For his extensive help and family stories, I especially thank John Hervey-Bathurst. My thanks also go to him and Caroline for their hospitality; to Lady Camilla Osborne, whose father was the last Duke of Leeds, for the lovely drawings of Hornby and showing me her family letters; to Bernard Cawley and the Trustees of the Duchess of Leeds Foundation for the loan of material; to Sr Helen Forshaw for sending me documents; to Sr Clare Veronica for sharing her research on Louisa so generously; to Dr Walter Ormerod for lending me letters; and to those who wish to remain anonymous.

I have also made use of material elsewhere and gratefully acknowledge the gracious permission of Her Majesty Queen Elizabeth II for letters from the Royal Archives; the Duke of Beaufort for letters in the Badminton Muniments; the Reverend Michael Clifton for documents at Southwark Diocesan Archives; the Marquess of Salisbury for papers at Hatfield House; and my thanks go to all the other owners and copyright holders who have kindly granted permission to quote from unpublished material or to reproduce illustrations.

I am hugely indebted to all the archivists and librarians who have helped me over the years. I especially want to thank Robert Frost, Senior Librarian and Archivist, Janet Senior and Brenda Telford at the marvellous Yorkshire Archaeological Society for the time and care they devoted to me on my

Acknowledgements 341

numerous visits; my thanks also go to Dr C M Woolgar and his team at The Hartley Institute, the University of Southampton; Dr Norma Aubertin-Potter, Librarian, All Soul's, Oxford; Robin Harcourt Williams at Hatfield; Christine Hiskey at Holkham Archives and Margaret Richards at Badminton.

For help in reconstructing the sisters' financial world, I should like to thank Lionel de Rothschild; David Kynaston; John Orbell and Jane Waller, formerly at The Baring Archive and Moira Lovegrove, current archivist; Melanie Aspey at The Rothschild Archive, and especially for sharing her ideas about women's influence; Barbra Raperto, who helped me at Hoare's Bank, Karen Sampson at Lloyd's TSB Group Archives, Philip Winterbottom of the Royal Bank of Scotland Group Archives; and the archivists at HSBC Group Archives. I am, as ever, indebted to the staffs at the London Library, the Kensington Central Library, especially Natasha Boland for her patience with inter-library loans, and the British Library.

I have many Americans to thank for boundless help with research material, information and hospitality, so characteristic of their generosity of spirit to a visitor. For the Caton sisters' Maryland world I have benefitted hugely from the expertise and friendship of Ann Van Devanter Townsend, who also allowed me to quote from her invaluable catalogue *Anywhere So Long as There Be Freedom*. I would also like to thank Professor Catherine Clinton; Tom De Rosa; Charlotte Ponticelli; and Judy Rousuck for ideas and support. I have, however, had to write this book independently of the principal researcher in the field.

The Maryland Historical Society was an invaluable resource and I am particularly grateful for the help of Dr Mary Jeske, Editor of the Carroll Papers, Francis O'Neal, Librarian, Heather Haggstrom, Curator of Pictures, and Jennifer Ferretti. I thank Robert Barnes and Rob Schoeberlein for timely assistance at the Maryland State Archives, Annapolis. As I do Emily Rafferty at the Baltimore Museum of Art; Paula Hankins at the Carroll Mansion Museum; Jean Walsh, Catonsville Historical Society; Sarah Cash, Curator American Art at the Corcoran Gallery of Art; Brian Lang at Dunbarton House; Nicholas B. Scheetz, Manuscripts Librarian, Georgetown University; Catherine Arthur, Curator of the Homewood Museum and the late Helen Ollerenshaw; the perceptive reference librarians of the Manuscript Reading Room, the Library of Congress; Elizabeth Schaaf, Archivist at the Peabody Institute; Pat Lynagh, Librarian, Archives of Art, Smithsonian Institution; Tom and Ann Reid, St Paul's School, Brooklandwood; Sister Susan and Sister Mary Regina of the Sisters of the Good Shepherd, Baltimore.

I should like to thank David Benson, Jef McAllister and Melanie Aspey for reading chapters and offering pertinent suggestions. Ann Bishop; Tom Boyce, who showed me round Aras an Uachterain; and Nicholas Fitzherbert;

Dr Alan Michette and Richard Michette FBDO; and Ned Tozer who have given invaluable assistance.

I am very grateful to the trustees of the Royal Literary Fund for their generous help.

Heartfelt thanks for research go to Edmund Gordon, Harriet Marlow and Annabel Riggs; and to Lucy Malcolm at Georgetown and Casey Olivarius-McAllister at Yale. My daughter Katie Wake has been a model researcher and helped me think more clearly about American history through her own scholarhip and knowledge.

I have learnt a great deal from my editor Jenny Uglow and I am so grateful to her and my agent Deborah Rogers for their moral support and continuing faith in the book. Thanks also to Alison Samuel, Parisa Ebrahimi, Michael Salu, and all the team at Chatto, to Jenny Overton for copy-editing and Sandra Oakins for the maps.

Special thanks for encouragement and help go to Nazie Batmangelidj; David and Elizabeth Benson; Pamela and Jeremy Bryson; Robert and Bambina Carnwath; Janet and James Greenfield; Penny Hammar; Elizabeth Malcolm; Belinda Mitchell-Innes; Mike and Muriel Riggs; Elizabeth de Rothschild; Guy and Joan Thomas; Fiona and Johnny Torrens-Spence; Margaret Turner; Renee Waterman; David Waterman; Rosie and the late Charles Wynne Finch; and to Louise Williams who generously provided writing space. My mother Olive Williams and my mother-in-law Olwyn Wake have always given unfailing support. I owe an immense debt to Sandra Thomas, Fiona Torrens-Spence and Mia Stewart Wilson who have been the best of informed research friends and given me help in countless ways. And, as always, particular thanks to William, wise and wonderful throughout, and to Katie and David, the new historians of the family, for putting up with my absorption in the sisters' lives with good humour and patience.

Notes

This book is based on unpublished letters and papers, mainly from six collections: the Charles Carroll of Carrollton Papers, the Robert Goodloe Harper Papers, and the Betsy Patterson Bonaparte Papers in the Maryland Historical Society, Baltimore; the Osborne family, Dukes of Leeds Papers in the Yorkshire Archaeological Society, Leeds, and the British Library; and the Wellesley family, Dukes of Wellington at Stratfield Saye, at the Hartley Institute, University of Southampton and at the British Library. I have also found the sisters' letters as well as the diaries, letters and papers of those who knew them in many archives, libraries and private collections throughout North America, Great Britain and Ireland.

All letters listed in the Notes are in the Carroll and Harper Papers at the Maryland Historical Society unless otherwise stated. Where a location is not provided, the letter is in a private collection and seen by the kind courtesy of the owner.

ABBREVIATIONS

The following abbreviations are used in the notes.

Individuals

AW	Arthur, Duke of Wellington
BPB	Betsy Patterson Bonaparte
CCA	Charles Carroll the Squire
CCC	Charles Carroll of Carrolton
CCH	Charles Carroll Jr
CH	Charles Harper
CMT	Carroll McTavish
FBH	Sir Felton Bathurst Hervey, Bt
FL	Francis, Lord Carmarthen, later 7th Duke of Leeds
JMT	John McTavish
KH	Catherine (Kitty) Harper
MBS	Margaret Bayard Smith
MC	Mary Caton
MDH	Mary Diana Harper
NC	Ann (Nancy) Chase
RC	Richard Caton
RGH	Robert Harper

RW   Richard, Marquess Wellesley
WP   William Patterson

Archives, Libraries and Manuscript Collections

BL   British Library, London
DLC   Library of Congress, Washington DC
LAC   Library Archives of Canada, Ottawa
LP   Duke of Leeds Mss
MHS   Maryland Historical Society, Baltimore
MSA   Maryland State Archives, Annapolis
NA   National Archives, Kew
NLI   National Library of Ireland, Dublin
NYHS   New York Historical Society, New York City
NYPL   New York Public Library, New York City
PRONI   Public Record Office of Northern Ireland, Belfast
RA   Royal Archives, Windsor
RWP   Wellesley Papers
WF Mss Wellington Family Mss
W Mss   Wellington Mss

Printed Works

Anywhere Van Devanter, Ann, *Anywhere so long as there be freedom*, catalogue (Baltimore
        Museum of Art, Baltimore) 1975
MHM   *Maryland Historical Magazine*
WDNS   Wellington, *Despatches* (New Series)
WSD   Wellington, *Supplementary Despatches*

PROLOGUE

1   H. Littleton to G. Wellesley, 14 Nov.
    1825, Hatherton Papers; D260 f.62;
    Ly Shelley I, 95; CCC to Marianne,
    16 Oct. 1816, MS 220 J.S. Smith,
    n.d., LP, DD5/V/1/12 Watson, WM
    18
2   Bess to Ly Westmeath, 18 Feb. 1835,
    Baring Archives BB HC l.ll.
3   Waln 80
4   George Washington to Charles
    Carter, 14 Sept. 1790, *Writings*, ed.
    Fitzpatrick 36:114
5   Raikes, *Journal* II:384; CCA to CCC,
    1 June 1772, MS 206

CHAPTER I: A REVOLUTIONARY
HERITAGE

1   Marianne's insurance policy c.1824,
    MS 220 box 15; MC to NC, 15 Oct.
    1821, *passim*, Chase Howe Book MS
    969; M. Fenton to Dr R. Caton, n.d.,
    Ormerod Papers; I am grateful to Dr
    Mary Jeske for confirming the sisters'
    order of birth; Bess to Marianne, n.d.,
    LP, DD5/V/1/5

2   'Genealogy of O Carroll' MS, cited
    Hoffman 37–8
3   K. Rowland I:3–4 Marye, W. B.,
    'Patowmeck Above Ye Inhabitants',
    MHM, vol. XXX no. 1 (March 1935)
    8–9; Hanna I:80–1, 156; Alsop 76
4   Browne VIII:408, 508; CCC to
    Comtesse d'Auzouer, 20 Sept. 1771,
    Letterbook 1770–74, f.13, MHS;
    Hoffman 73, 68, 70
5   Risjord xiii; Eddis, Letter II, 1 Oct.
    1769, 19; Stephens 49 Crawford 255
6   CCC to Marianne, 10 June 1828, MS
    220; CCC to W. Graves, 15 Sept.
    1765, Letterbook 1765–68, f.22, MHS
7   CCC to W. Graves, 16 Jan. 1768,
    Letterbook 1765–68, f.96; CCC to
    W. Graves, ibid 1765–68, ff.99, 115,
    MHS; *Anywhere* 27
8   CCC to Messrs West & Hodson, 26
    Oct. 1771, 21 Sept. 1772, 1 March
    1773, Arents Collection 50767, NYPL;
    CCA to CCC, 1 June 1772, MS 206
9   Eddis, Letter VIII, 2 Nov. 1771, 106;
    Anywhere 6; Diary of Washington,
    Vol III 1771; G. Washington, Ledgers
    1750–84, Ledger 'A' f.345

10 Marianne to Ld Lansdowne, 31 Aug. 1826, Moore, *Journal*, III:958; the Revd Constantine Pise, cited K. Rowland I:344

11 CCA to CCC, 14 July 1760; MS 206

12 see Skaggs 341–9; CCC to CCA, 3 Apr. 1773, MS 206; Risjord 88

13 Eddis, Letter XVII, 28 May 1774, 159; CCC to CCA, 7, 9, 12 Sept. 1774, MS 206; Cresswell 21

14 Isaacson 313; CCC to Marianne, 1829, MS 220

15 CCA to CCC, 17 May 1775, MS 206; CCC to CCA, 12, 15 March 1776, MS 206; CCA to CCC, 30 March 1781, MS 206

16 CCC to CCA, 23 March 1776, MS 206; CCC to W. Graves, 15 Aug. 1774, Letterbook 1770–74, f.30; Royall cited Semmes 216; CCC to MC, 13 May 1814, MS 220

17 Norton 156; Edenton Petition, 15 Oct. 1774, printed in *Morning Chronicle*, 31 Jan. 1775; CCC to CCA, 15 March 1776, MS 206; Norton 178–9; S. Smith to Otho H. Williams, 5 July 1780, O. H. Williams MS 908; Anna Rawle to Rebecca Shoemaker, 30 June 1780, Rawle-Shoemaker Papers; J. Hanson to CCC, 7 Aug. 1780, MS 206; Norton 187–8

18 Bryan 248

19 The presence of the family at Carroll House is inferred from Lafayette's reception there; Lafayette's Encampment, March to April 1781, the Historical Marker Database www.hmdb.org; Norris 178; *Atlantic Monthly*, Nov. 1890, 651 cited Norris 184

20 Wood 85, 54

CHAPTER 2: MISS CARROLL'S CHOICE

1 John Carroll to Anthony Carroll, 23 Sept. 1784, LP DD5/XI/V/5; H. Ogle to John Thomas, n.d. 1782, Pennington Collection, cited Mason 287

2 M. Dulany to Walter Dulany, 23 April 1783, Francis Sims McGrath, 'A Letter to Eileen', MHM, vol. XXIV, no. 4 (Dec. 1929) 317

3 Fitzpatrick 26, 136–7; Wills, 3–16; *Anywhere* 127; Edgar 276

4 Howard Jones 242; Wecter 199, 205, 61

5 *Anywhere* 213

6 Lewis, Jan, 'The Republican Wife: Virtue and Seduction in the Early Republic', *W&M Quarterly*, Third Series, vol. XLIV (Oct. 1987) 694; CCC to MC, 18 Apr. 1796, MS 220; CCC to CCA, 19 Feb. 1763, MS 431

7 *Williamson's Advertiser*, cited Gomer Williams 300–1; Thomas C. Deye to CCC cited Keidel 4; CCC to Daniel Carroll, 13 March 1787, MS 431; *Maryland Journal*, 30 Nov. 1787, 2

8 *Anywhere* 55–7; Carroll Financial Papers 1792–1832, Carroll Family Papers, DLC; MC to KH, 25 July 1819, MS 431; MC to NC, 20 July 1823, Chase Home Book, MS 969

CHAPTER 3: PLANTATION GIRLS

1 Charles Bagot to John Sneyd, 12 June 1816, Canning 2:21; CCC to CCH, 7 July 1800, 14 Feb. 1801, MS 203

2 Davis 211; Mary Bagot journal, 18 March 1816, Levens MSS; Keith Thomas 282–3; Kalm, 15 Sept. 1748, 415; Hughes 137

3 Katharine Jones 2; Lane-Poole 329; Addington 55; MC to NC, 20 July 1823, Chase Home Book MS 969

4 Hodgson I:327; Harriet W. Jones, 'A Childhood at Clynmalira', MHM, vol. 51, no. 2 (June 1956) 101–2; CCA to CCC, 23 June 1772, MS 206; CCC to W. Graves, 15 Sept. 1765, Letterbook 1765–68, f.23; CCC to CCH, 18 Sept. 1797, MS 203

5 Bess to Marianne, n.d., LP, DD5/11/V/5; Ellen H. Smith 305

6 Kennedy 82–3; Quincy 265

7 Lane-Poole 328; H. Gilpin, 'A Glimpse of Baltimore Society', MHM, Vol. 69 no. 3 (1974) 266–8

8 Addington 56; MC to NC, 20 July 1811, Chase Home Book, MS 969; CH to his parents, 9 Aug. 1822, MS 431; *Anywhere* 57; Gilpin, *op. cit.*

9 CCC to W. Graves, 17 March 1772, Letterbook, MS 206; Brown Jr 89; F. Trollope 188; Louisa to sisters, n.d. LP DD5/V/13

10 Grattan II:149; Harriet Jones 119–20; Hoffman 241; C. J. Latrobe 38; Hodgson 327; CCC to CCH, 17 July 1808, MS 203

11 *Anywhere* 136–7; Gordon Wood,

'The Ghost of Monticello' in Lewis and Onuf eds. Sally Hemmings and Tobias Jefferson 2r; Cicely Cawthon, Georgia Narratives, supp. series I, vol. 3, pt. I, 185, cited Fox-Genovese 154; Calhoun, 2:281; H. Benton, Georgia Narratives, supp. series I, vol. 3, pt. I, 46, cited Fox-Genovese 155.

12   Resahe Calvert 137; CCA to CCC, 15 Sept. 1771, MS 206; J. King to F. King, 6 Oct. 1858, Thomas B. King Papers, University of North Carolina, Chapel Hill, NC; Eleanor Baker journal, 1848, 16 cited Fox-Genovese 133; Fanny Kemble, *Residence*, 22

13   Muhlenfield 16; K. Jones 57; Fanny Kemble, journal, vol. 2, 1832–3, MS 843, DLC; Fanny Kemble, *Residence*, 11; Addington 56

14   Woloch 184; Blassingame 94; Kulikoff 179–82, 184, 189

15   CCA to CCC, 23 Nov. 1772, MS 206; CCC to CCH, 1 Feb. 1808, MS 203; Hoffman 258

16   Thomas Day, *A Fragment of an original letter on the Slavery of the Negroes*, cited P. Rowland 85; K. Rowland, I:143; Carpenter, 355; T. Jefferson to D. Holmes, 22 Apr. 1820, in *Works of Jefferson* XII:159

CHAPTER 4: FRENCH INFLUENCES

1   *Maryland Gazette*, 11 July 1763; *Maryland Journal*, 12 July 1793; Walter C. Hartridge, 'The Refugees from the Island of St Domingo', MHM vol. 96, no. 4, Winter 2002, 475

2   Eric Williams 237, 238, 246; CO 245/10, 6 & 122; Roscoe 16; Geggus 1

3   Hazen 81–2, 109; Journal of William Macleay, 232 cited K. Rowland I:168; CCC to T. Jefferson, 10 Apr. 1791, cited K. Rowland I:171–2

4   B. Hall 2:394; Browne 27–9; Cassell 42–3; Melville Du Bourg 1:38

5   Wright and Tinling eds. 12; Papenfuse 156; Hartridge 477; *Baltimore Daily Advertiser*, 18 July, 2 Aug. 1793; *Maryland Journal* 24 July 1793; Melville 39; Hartridge 489 f. 73; *Anywhere* 92–3

6   K Rowland I:317–18

7   CCC to J. Johnson, 8 Oct. 1794 cited

K. Rowland I:200; Trappes-Lomax 60

8   Bryan 300

9   St Jean de Crèvecoeur 57; Childs 104; Van Wyck Brooks 15

10   Breck 113–14; Wecter 62, 306; Childs 29

11   Liston, Letter XXII, 28 Sept. 1798, 619–20; CCC to CCH, 8 July 1800, MS 203; Liston, Letter XXXI, 3 Jan. 1800, 628–9; Scharf 287

CHAPTER 5: REPUBLICAN GIRLS

1   Thornton 113; Olivers to J. Craig, 8 Jan. & 9 March 1800, ORB, 3, 477–8, 523–4, to Kirwans, 24 Feb. 1800, ORB 3, 504–5, 30 Apr. 1800, ORB 4, 9–10, to H. de Butts, 16 July 1800, ORB 4, 24–5, to J. Craig, 6 Aug. 1800, ORB 4, 36, Robert Oliver Papers, MS 626.1, MHS

2   CCC to CCH, 23 Oct. 1800, MS 203; Jefferson to John Wise, 12 Feb. 1798, cited Ellis 186; *Connecticut Courant*, 20 Sept. 1800, cited Allgor 14; CCC to CCH, 12 March 1807, MS 203

3   R. Caton, 'A Brief Statement of Facts', 1832, 48, Ormerod papers; Olivers to Kirwans, 30 Feb. & 16 Apr. 1802, ORB, 4, 353–4, 366–7, Robert Oliver Papers, MHS; Keidel 8; CCC to RGH, 5 Dec. 1801, MS 431

4   Brady 12; CCC to RGH, 14 Dec. 1802, MS 1225; CCC to CCH, 29 Aug. 1803, MS 203; CCC to RGH, 7 Jan. 1803, MS 431

5   CCC to Emily, 2 March 1803, MS 220; Bess to RGH, 16 June 1818, MS 431

6   Journal of Sally Ripley cited Kerber 221; Austen, *Northanger Abbey*, 99

7   Norton 272–3; Kelley, 67; Rudolph, 59; Donovan, 'The Caton Sisters', 296; CCC to Marianne, 2 Feb. 1803, MS 220; Milton, *Paradise Lost*, bk IV, 846–8

8   'Excerpts from the Papers of Dr Benjamin Rush', *Pennsylvania Magazine of History and Biography*, vol. XXIX (1905) 21; 'Alphonzo's Address to the Ladies', *American Magazine*, vol. I (March 1788), 246; Lewis, 'The Republican Wife', 700; 'Female Economy', *Ladies' Literary Cabinet*, New York (8 July 1820) 67 cited Lewis 702; 'Female Influence',

NY Magazine (May 1795) 305, cited Kerber 230

9 'The Gossip', no. XXVII, *Boston Weekly Magazine* (28 May 1803) 125, cited Lewis, 'The Republican Wife', 702; CCC to Marianne, 6 Aug. 1804, 2 Feb. 1803, MS 220

10 'Asthma in History', Wellcome Institute, www.wellcome.ac.uk; *cf.* Painter for Proust's asthma, 12; Addington 103 n. 82; Edgeworth, *Letters* 486–7; Van Wyck Brooks 44–6

11 CCC to Bess, 22 May 1817, MS 220; Emily to RGH, 2 Sept., 17 Dec. 1816, MS 431; CCC to MC, 28 Jan. 1798, MS 220; CCC to RGH, 7 Feb., 2 July 1805, MS 1225

12 CCC to RGH, 28 June 1805, MS 431; CCC to Louisa, 19 Sept. 1803, MS 220; *Anywhere* 299; CCC to MC, 28 Jan. 1798, MS 220; CCC to Louisa 19 Sept., *op. cit.*

13 CCC to MC, 28 Jan. 1798, *op. cit.*; CCC to Emily, 2 March 1802, MS 220

14 RC to RGH, 18 Feb. 1815, MS 431

15 D. Thomas, I:221–23; R. E. Lewis 285

16 RC, Sale notice, *Federal Gazette and Baltimore Daily Advertiser*, 15 Dec. 1812; Gilmor 341–2; Harriet Jones 120–1

17 Louisa to Marianne, n.d., LP, DDV/11/5/13; Bayard 40; Stockett 65

CHAPTER 6: A PATTERSON CONNECTION

1 CCC to Marianne, 21 Aug. 1804, MS 220

2 Henry Adams I:92; McMaster II:543–4

3 Howard Jones 263; Low, 'Of Muslins & Merveilleuses' 8–9, 38, 33; Howard Jones 263; Low, *op. cit.* 56, 59, 39

4 William Patterson's Will and Testament, MS 145, MHS; Sergeant 69, 76; Bp John Carroll to his sisters, 1803, cited Shea 511; Macartney and Dorrance 20; Lester 32–3; cited Henry C. Adams, *History*, 2:368–9; Merry to George Hammond, 7 Dec. 1803, cited Adams, *History*, 2:372; Pichon to Talleyrand, 5 Feb. 1804 2:368–9; Robert Davis Jr 338; Lester

38–9

5 Sergeant 84; CCC to CCH, 14 Feb. 1804, MS 203; Catharine Mitchell to her sister, 2 Jan. 1811, Catharine Mitchell Papers, DLC MS 34819–1; Hunt 46; Sarah Gales Seaton cited Wharton, *Salons* 204; Baldwin 345; Marianne to BPB, 15 Nov., 18 Dec. 1815, MS 220

6 Napoleon to M. Decrès, 20 Apr. 1804, cited Bonaparte 25–7;

7 BPB's Notebooks, 6 Apr. 1805, BPB MS 142; *Correspondance de Napoléon*, 1, X, 357; Napoleon to Madame Mère, 22 April 1805 cited Sergeant 94; BPB's Notebooks, 9 Apr. 1805, MS 142; Dorothy M. Quynn & Frank F. Wright Jr, 'Jerome and Betsy Cross the Atlantic', MHM, (vol. 40, no. 3 (1953) 209

8 Saffell 185; Quynn & Wright 212; *The Times*, 21 May 1805; Napoleon to Jerome Bonaparte, June 1805 cited Sergeant 102; Quynn & Wright, ibid 212; Sergeant 98–100 Jerome B to BPB, Oct. 1805, Liverpool Papers Add. MS 38,241 ff.204, 241

9 BPB to Ly Morgan, 14 March 1849, Morgan MS 10, 417

10 Saffell 127; KH to RGH, 28 Jan. 1806, MS 431; Bp Carroll to James Barry, 8 Apr. 1806, cited Melville, *John Carroll* 263

CHAPTER 7: DEBUTANTES

1 Glenbervie 2:227; Eliza Godefroy to Ebenezer Jackson, 27 Nov. 1836, cited Quynn 15; CCC to Bess, 22 May 1817, MS 220; Bp Carroll to Joanna Barry, 16 June 1806, John Carroll, 1:57

2 Rosalie Calvert 196; Bess to CCC, n.d., MS 220

3 Davidson 6–7, 10, 16; Eliza Anderson (Godefroy) to BPB, 4, 8 June 1808, BPB MS 142, Eliza Godefroy on Bess, cited Quynn 15

4 KH to RGH, 7 Mar. 1809, MS 431; MC to RGH, 18 Sept. 1816, MS 431

5 Melville, *Du Bourg* I:164; White 210

6 Du Bourg to RGH, 8 Apr. 1809, MS 431; Bp Carroll to his sisters, 20 Apr. 1809, Archives of Georgetown University, Shea Transcripts 31–3

7 Bp Carroll, ibid.; CCC to CCH, 12

Feb. 1808, MS 203; Du Bourg to RGH, *op. cit.*; Bp Carroll to his sisters, 18 Aug. 1809, op. cit; E. Seton to Juliana Scott, 9 March 1811, cited Code 210–11; Melville, *Du Bourg* I:240

CHAPTER 8: IN WASHINGTON CITY

1 Emily to RGH, 19 March 1810, MS 431; Bess and KH to RGH, 23 Jan. 1812, 24 Jan. 1816, MS 431; BPB 126
2 Wharton, *Social Life* 58–9; Addington 20–1; Wharton 60; E. Mattoon to T. D. Wright, 2 March 1800, Dwight-Howard Papers, cited Allgor 4–5; Wharton 161
3 Anthony 94; Margaret B. Smith [MBS] to Jane B. Kirkpatrick, 13 March 1814, MBS Papers, DLC
4 F. Jackson to his mother, 7 Oct. 1809, George Jackson I:20; Wharton, *Social Life* 38–9; Crawford 192; Wharton ibid 117; Rosalie Calvert 224
5 Hunt 75
6 Rosalie Calvert 125. This and the next four paragraphs draw heavily on Catherine Allgor's account in *Parlour Politics*; Wharton, *Social Life* 144, 149
7 Foster 84–5; Mary Latrobe to Juliana Miller, 12 Feb. 1812, Latrobe Family Papers, MS 523, Box 4 f.35, MHS; KH to RGH, 20 Feb. 1804, 27 Feb. 1814, MS 431
8 MC to NC, 20 July 1811, Chase Home Book, MS 969, MHS

CHAPTER 9: THE WAR OF 1812

1 RC to RGH, 23 Feb. 1812, MS 431
2 Andrew Jackson, *Correspondence* 1:221; A. J. Foster, Journal, 17 June-12 July 1812, Foster Papers MSS 21139 DLC; Willson, *Relations* 92–3
3 Latimer 152; Little 194; *Lancaster Journal*, 31 July 1812; Cassell, *Riot* 241–2, 254–6
4 CCC to Col. John E. Howard, 1 Aug. 1812, MS 216; CCC to CCH, 5 Aug. 1812, MS 203
5 Elizabeth Seton to J. Scott, 30 May 1810, cited Code 199; Low, 'Youth of 1812' 173–4
6 CCC to CCH, 31 Oct. 1812, MS 203; K. Rowland I:291; CCC to CCH, 1 Nov. 1812, MS 203

7 Crawford 191–2
8 Wharton, *Social Life* 96–7
9 Dolley Madison to Lucy P. W. Todd, 23 Aug. 1814, Dolley Madison Digital Edition, cited Allgor, *Perfect Union* 312–13; Anthony 225, Allgor, *Perfect Union* 313 and see also Paul Jennings's account, www.whitehouse history.org
10 M. Hunter, 'The Burning of Washington', *New York Historical Society Bulletin* 8 (Oct. 1925) 82; MBS 109
11 CCC to Governor Winder of Maryland, 14 Sept. 1814, MHM, vol. XXIV, no. 3 (Sept. 1939) 244
12 Hunt 1–3, 7; Hurd, 54–5; Ellet 93
13 Wharton, *Social Life* 179; Robert F. McNamara, 'In Search of the Carrolls of Belle Vue', MHM, vol. 80 no. 1 (Spring 1985) 101, 103
14 Capel 81; BPB to Marianne, 7 Nov. 1815, BPB MS 142; BPB to WP, 14 Aug. 1814, *Letters* 42; Crawford 278
15 Marianne to BPB, 15 July & 18 Dec. 1815, MS 220; WP to BPB, 16 Nov. 1815, BPB 58; BPB to WP, 2 Sept. 1815, *Letters* 56; Marianne to BPB, 16 Dec. 1815, BPB MS 142;
16 Marianne to BPB, 15 Nov. 1815, BPB MS 142; BPB to Marianne, 7 Nov. 1815, MHM, vol. XX, no. 2 (June 1925) 124; Marianne to BPB, 18 Dec. 1815, BPB MS 142; BPB to WP, 2 Sept. 1815, *Letters* 55–6

CHAPTER 10: EMILY'S CANADIAN ADVENTURE

1 KH to RGH, 27 June 1815, MS 431
2 Brooks 49, 52 Van Wyck
3 Melville, *John Carroll* 204; Ap Carroll to Bp Plessis, 9 July 1815, *Records of the American Catholic Historical Society of Philadelphia*, vol. XVIII (Oct. 1907) 304–5; Sandham 99
4 Peter Newman 2:7; RC to RGH, 30 Aug. 1815, MS 431
5 CCC to MC, 19 May 1815, MS 202; Bowne 128; Bess to Marianne, 16 Aug. n.d.; Bowne 128; MDH to RGH, 30 Aug. 1815, MS 430; RC to RGH *op. cit.*; Bowne 41; RC to RGH *op. cit.*
6 RC to RGH, 19 Feb. 1816, MS 431
7 Carrolls of Belle Vue 101; RC to RGH, 8 March 1816, MS 431

8   Emily to RGH, 6 & 12 March 1816,
    MS 431
9   RC to RGH, 20 March 1816, MS
    431; RGH to MDH, 12 Aug. 1816,
    MS 430
10 Hook 145–6
11 Lawson 143; Adam 448–9
12 Johnson, *Western Islands* 80, 73;
    Hunter 38; Boswell, *Tour to the
    Hebrides* 327, 345–6
13 Whyte I:129–30, 143–4; Peter
    Newman II:10, xix; Simon
    McTavish, Will, 1802 NA PROB
14 Peter Newman II:4, 3, 35; Hunter
    159, 161
15 Peter Newman I:99, 106; JMT to
    George Jackson, n.d., Jackson MSS
    FO 353/91; Peter Newman II:7–8

CHAPTER 11: FAMILY TROUBLES

1   Louisa to Emily, 9 Nov. 1818, MS
    220
2   CCC to CCH, 7 June 1801, MS
    203; Marianne to RGH, 22 Dec.
    1818, MS 431; KH to RGH, c. 1803,
    MS 431
3   Gurn 184; Arthur and Kelly 3; Tripp
    10–11; author's notes
4   KH to RGH, 20 Feb. 1814, RC to
    RGH, 22 Feb. 1816, Emily to RGH,
    12, 19 March 1816, MS 431
5   CCC to Col. John E. Howard, 21
    Feb. 1814, CCC to RGH, June 1816,
    MS 431; M. Fenton to Dr R. Caton,
    3 July 1908, Ormerod Papers
6   CCC to CCH, 29 Jan. 1811, MS 203;
    CCC to RGH, 7 Feb. 1805, KH to
    RGH, 8 Feb. 1811, RGH to CCC,
    25 Jan. 1807, MS 431; Rosalie S.
    Calvert to her father, 10 June 1814
    Rosalie Calvert 267
7   Bess to David Hoffman, n.d. 1846,
    MS 1229; Emily to CMT, 23 May
    1831, LP DD5/11/II/1; RGH to
    Louisa, 14 Nov. 1817, MS 431; CCC
    to MC, 12 June 1814, MS 216

CHAPTER 12: 'MAD ABOUT
EUROPE'

1   CCC to MC, 12 June 1814, MS 216;
    MC to BPB, 30 June 1816, MS 142
2   Edward Patterson to BPB, 6 March
    1816, 15 Dec. 1815, MS 142
3   Emily to RGH, 12 March 1816, MS

431; RGH draft to Marianne, 20 Dec.
1833 & to Louisa, 14 Nov. 1817, MS
220; Robert Patterson to RGH, 11
March 1816, MS 431; Eliza Godefroy
to BPB, 27 March 1816, MS 142
4   Thomas H. Hubbard to Phoebe G.
    Hubbard, 30 Nov. 1817, DLC;
    Marianne to BPB, 18 Dec. 1815,
    MS 142
5   Green 67, 77, 80; Crowninshield 35
6   MBS 134; Rosalie Calvert 336; Mary
    Bagot's journal, 19 Dec. 1816, Mary
    Bagot 45
7   Marianne to BPB, 18 Dec. 1815, MS
    142; Emily to RGH, 19 March 1816,
    MS 431
8   C. Bagot to Ld Binning, 6 May
    1816, cited Canning II:16; Mary
    Bagot's journal, 27 March 1816,
    Mary Bagot 36
9   Emily to RGH, *op. cit.*; Anon., *Letters
    from Albion* 1:89
10 C. Bagot to Ld Binning, 24 Oct.
    1816, cited Canning II:33; Harriet
    Granville, Self, 20; Cloake 287;
    Harriet Granville, Letters, 46
11 Mary Bagot's journal, *op. cit.* 36;
    Mary Bagot to Ralph Sneyd, 11 Aug.
    1816, Sneyd MSS SC3/95; Malcolm-
    Smith 66
12 Crowninshield 66
13 Dolley Madison to Hannah Gallatin,
    20 Apr. 1816, Gallatin MSS Box 77
    # 43, NYHS; CCC to MC, 26 Apr.
    1816, MS 216
14 Emily to RGH, 12 March 1816, MS
    431; BPB to Marianne 16 Mar. 1816,
    MS 142

CHAPTER 13: IN LONDON SOCIETY

1   Jane Austen to (James) Edward
    Austen, 7 July 1816, *Letters*, 457–9
2   Pss Lieven to Pr. Metternich, 2 July
    1824, *Private Letters*, 262
3   Hudson II:38; V. Murray 82; Howitt
    I:110
4   Bess to KH, 25 June 1818, MS 431;
    Rush 118; Bovill 77; Simond 30
5   Louisa's notebooks, LP DD5/11/V/37;
    Rush 29
6   Bess to RGH, 7 July 1818, MS
    431
7   RC to RGH, 22 July 1816, MS 431;
    V. Murray 20; Downing 550;
    Hawthorne 607; Charles Bagot to

Louisa Sneyd, 5 May 1817, Sneyd
MSS SC1/15

8 Simond 29; Catherine Wellesley-
Pole to Mary Bagot, no. 8, 2 July
1816, Levens MSS

9 C. Percy to Ralph Sneyd, 18 May
1816, Sneyd MSS SC11/255;
Gronow 43; Ly Louisa Hardy to
Louisa Lloyd, Sir Eliab Harvey
Papers, D/Dgu/Z2; Gronow op. cit.;
Prince Pückler-Muskau 39

10 Chorley et al.18; Ticknor 1:54

11 Ly Williams Wynn 191; Ly Shelley
1:95; Bess to Emily, 16 July 1816, MS
431

12 Ly Shelley 1:67; Berry 3:16; Rogers
217

13 Richard Wellesley to Edward
Wellesley, 3 Oct. 1842, Carver MSS;
Iris Butler 24; Longford, 1:123

14 Bess to Emily, 16 July 1816, MS 431;
Ly Shelley 1:68–9; Iain Pears, 'The
Gentleman and the Hero:
Wellington and Napoleon in the
Nineteenth Century' in Roy Porter,
ed., Myths of the English, 1992,
217–18, 227

15 Bess to CCC, n.d. Aug. 1816, CCC
to Bess, 22 May 1817, MS 220; W.
Wellesley-Pole to C. Bagot, 5, 7
July 1816 cited Canning 2:31;
Pückler-Muskau 135; Ly Shelley
2:33

16 RGH to MDH, 22 Oct. 1816, MS
430; Bess to KH, 25 June 1818, Emily
to RGH, 2 Sept. 1816, MS 431

17 Simond 31; Ly Shelley 2:12; Louisa
to MC, n.d. July 1816 LP
DD5/11/V/13; Emily to RGH op. cit.;
Erickson 51

18 CCC to Marianne, 16 Oct. 1816, MS
220

CHAPTER 14: ANGLO-AMERICAN
DIFFERENCES

1 Warner 100; Warren 1:439–41; Van
Wyck Brooks 154

2 Irving Sketch Book 66; J. Q. Adams
to Robert Walsh, 10 July 1821,
Adams Family Papers, vol. CXLVII
cited Perkins 174

3 Marianne to BPB, 10 Oct. 1816, MS
142; The Times, 20 Apr. 1817; Robert
Southey to W. S. Landor, 7 May
1819, Letters 3:134; Quarterly Review,

no. 20 (Jan. 1814) 524; Paul
Langford, 'Manners and Character
in Anglo-American Perceptions
1750–1850' in Levanthal &
Quinault, eds, 77; Perkins 184

4 C. Bagot to John Sneyd, 12 June
1816, cited Canning 2:23; Bess to
RGH, n.d. c. 1818, MS 431

5 Lieven, Private Letters, 39; J. Morier
to Sir Harford Jones, 10 March, 27
June 1810, Kentchurch Court Papers
9574, 9576, NLW; Ly Morgan,
Passages 37

6 Semmes 216–17; E. Littleton's diary,
22 July 1836, Hatherton Papers D260

7 Bryant 164; Simond 351; Morning
Chronicle, 3 July 1816

8 Lamb 6:578; Thackeray, Vanity Fair
212; Lees-Milne 18; V. Murray 79

9 Bryant 366; Buckingham, Regency,
2:165–6; Villiers 313

10 Bess to MDH, 25 Oct. 1816, MS 430;
MC to RGH, 13 Sept. 1816, MS 431;
CCC to Marianne, 16 Oct. 1816, MS
216

11 Adams, John Q., Memoirs 2:410

12 RGH to MDH, 16 Oct. 1816,
Marianne to MDH, 30 Aug. 1816,
MS 430; Spiller 286; Marianne to
BPB, n.d. July 1816, MS 142

13 Searle 17–18; Austen, n.d. 1816,
Letters 462; Alderson 55; Schopenhauer 105, 118

14 Henry Wellesley to Charles Vaughan
[CRV], 12 July 1816, Vaughan MSS
C127/5; Mary Frampton 288; CCC
to Bess, 22 Oct. 1816, MS 216;
Pakenham 90

15 BPB to John S. Smith, 22 Aug. 1816,
MS 142; Mary Berry 3:100; Ly Morgan
cited G. Brooks 149; Marianne to
BPB, 2 Aug. 1816, MS 142

16 Coke I:207–10, 190, 248–9; Bovill
81; Coke I:314

17 Bess to MDH, 25 Oct. 1816, MS 430;
Coke 2:155; Spencer-Stanhope 2:30–1

18 Marianne to BPB, 10 Oct. 1816, MS
142; W. H. Lyttelton to C. Bagot, 30
Dec. 1816, Canning 2:39; Coke
1:311–12

CHAPTER 15: 'WE ARE ALL FOR
AMERICANS VERY WELL'

1 RC to RGH, 1 July 1816, MS 431;
CCC to CCH, 12 Aug. 1816, MS

203; Emily to RGH, 2 Sept. 1816, MS 431

2 RGH to MDH, 2 March 1817, MS 430; Emily to RGH, 22 May 1817, MS 220; Campbell 2, 243–41

3 Merck x; P. Newman 2:137; Ld Selkirk to Ly Selkirk, n.d., Selkirk Papers vol. A27, 425, LAC, and see Sia Bumsted, 'Lady Selkirk and the Fur Trade' in *Manitoba History*, no. 3 (Autumn/Winter 1999–2000); Peter Newman 2:146–8; Morton 541–2

4 P. Newman 2:179; Emily to RGH, 2 Sept. 1817, MS 431

5 Bess to MDH, 25 Oct. 1816, MS 430; J. Q. Adams, *Memoirs* 2:469

6 Stirling, *Coke* 220; C. Percy to R. Sneyd, 18 Dec. 1816, Sneyd MSS SC11/268; T. Coke to Bess & Marianne, *passim*, 13 Nov. and 1 Dec. 1816, LP DD5/11/V/3

7 Bess to RGH, 17 Dec. 1816, MS 431

8 De Boigne 2:248; Ly Palmerston 95; Lieven, *Private Letters* 11; Bess to RGH, 17 Dec. 1816 & to Emily, cited Emily to RGH, 24 March 1817, MS 431; *Morning Chronicle* 6, 10 Jan. 1817, *The Times*, 10 Jan. 1817

9 Bess to Emily 16 July 1816 & Emily to RGH, 2 Sept. 1816, MS 431; Willard 254; C II to MDH, 19 Sept. 1816, MS 430; Bess to RGH, 17 Dec. 1816, MS 431

CHAPTER 16: DANCING IN PARIS

1 Bess to MDH, 5 March 1817, MS 430 & to RGH, 17 Dec. 1816, MS 431

2 Berry 3:78; Ly Malmesbury to Ld Malmesbury, 21 Sept. & 3 Oct. 1815, Lowry Cole Papers, NA 30/43 ff. 43, 58

3 Delaforce 97; Sir William Fraser 97; Longford *Sword* 37 C. Percy to R. Sneyd, 29 Sept. 1815, Sneyd MSS SC11/240

4 Burnett 199; Paston & Quennell 113–14; Lennox, *Three Years*, 181–3; Longford, *State* 23; Harriet Granville, *Letters* 1: 74, 109; AW to H. Arbuthnot, 20 July 1816, WF

5 Ly Shelley 1:107; Sultana 45

6 CCC to Bess, 22 May 1817, MS 220; Hill 230

7 Louisa to KH, 15 June 1816, and Bess

to KH, 4 May 1816, MS 431

8 Fremantle 3:385; Spencer-Stanhope 1:329–30; Mansel 47

9 FBH to Louisa Lloyd, 2 Jan. 1817, Sir Eliab Harvey MSS D/DGu/C6/1/14; AW to Ly Georgy Lennox, 15 Jan. 1817, De Ros Papers, MIC 573/23/36/13; Ly Shelley 1:106, 70

10 Spencer-Stanhope 1:344; Mansel 15

11 AW to Ly Georgy Lennox, 1 Feb. 1817, De Ros Papers, MIC 573/23/36/14; Bess to Emily, 2 Feb. 1817, MS 220; Ld C. Fitzroy to Louisa Lloyd, 25 Feb. 1816, Sir Eliab Harvey MSS D/DGu/C6/1/8

12 Spencer-Stanhope 1:343; C. Percy to R. Sneyd, n.d. Feb. 1816, Sneyd MSS SC11/269

13 Lowry Cole 187; AW to Ly Georgy Lennox, 17 Nov. 1817 & 15 Dec. 1816, De Ros Papers, MIC 573/23/36/9, 11

14 Albemarle 2:232; Capel 134, 155–7; Marianne to Ld Albemarle cited Albemarle 2:232

15 Ly Burghersh 17

CHAPTER 17: LOUISA IN LOVE

1 Bess to MC, 5 March 1817 & CCC to Bess, 22 May 1817, MS 220

2 William Fremantle [WHF] to Admiral Fremantle, 12 May 1817, Fremantle MSS D/FR/31/2/15 Selina Fremantle's diary Selina Fremantle to WHF, n.d., D/FR/50/1/17; Louisa to Emily, 9 Nov. 1817, MS 220

3 Selina Fremantle, n.d., 14 & diary, 24 May 1809; Buckingham, *Regency* 1:85, 134–5

4 FBH to CCC, n.d. 1817, copy, LP DD5/II/11; Longford, *Sword*, 479, 481

5 MC to MDH, 24 March 1817 MS 430

6 AW to Ly Georgy Lennox, 8 March 1817, De Ros Papers, MIC 573/23/36/15; AW to Mary Bagot cited Canning 2:42

7 Bess to CCC, 5 March 1817 & CCC to Bess, 22 May 1817, MS 220

8 Selina Fremantle's diary, 22, 26, 29, 30 March 1817; WHF to Admiral Fremantle, 4 May 1817, Fremantle MSS D/FR/31/2/14

9 Stuart 195; Alberts 437; see, for

example, the *Star*, 27 March 1817, cited Perkins 177, 185

10   Willis 3:467–8; Preston 30; Sack 109–110; Ly Carysfort to her daughter, March 1812, Proby MSS; *Courier*, 30 March, 8, 24 Apr. 1812 Selina Hervey to WHF, July 1797, Fremantle MSS D/FR/50/1/55; WHF to Admiral Fremantle, 26 Oct., 1819, Fremantle MSS, D/FR/31/2/52 & 12 May 1817 *op. cit.*

11   Selina Fremantle's diary, 21 Apr. 1817

12   John Q. Adams, *Memoirs* 3:507–8; *Morning Chronicle*, 25 Apr. 1817

13   John Sneyd to C. Bagot, 23 May 1817, Canning 2:48; Ly Williams Wynn 201

CHAPTER 18: MARIANNE AND THE DUKE

1   C. Percy to Ralph Sneyd, n.d. 1817, Sneyd MSS SC11/269

2   Longford, *State*, opp. 76; *Any-where*145; 'Private correspondence', WFM f.158; Selina Fremantle's diary, 16 June 1817

3   Ly Burghersh 17; Glenbervie 2:227; Hon. Ms Calvert, 279–80

4   Eliza Godefroy to BPB, 27 March 1816, Edward Patterson to BPB, 21 March 1816, Eliza Godefroy to BPB, *op. cit.* & 10 May 1816, EP to BPB, 25 Sept. 1816, MS 142; BPB *Letters*, 474

5   BPB, *Letters* 162, 131; Ly Morgan to BPB, 26 May 1817, Lady Morgan MSS; Lennox 1:289–91. Gallatin scholars have verified that one other scintillating source, *The Diary of James Gallatin* ed. Count Gallatin 1914, is completely fraudulent, see Raymond Walters Jr, 'The James Gallatin Diary: A Fraud?', *The American Historical Review*, vol. 62 (4) 1956/57 878–85

6   Marianne to RGH, 26 Aug. 1817, MS 431; Longford, *State* 46

7   Iris Butler 497; Arbuthnot 1:168; Longford, *Sword* 122; Arbuthnot 1:169

8   WHF to Admiral Fremantle, 19 June 1817, Fremantle MSS D/FR/31/2/16

9   Longford, *State* 45; AW to FBH, 4 July 1817, & FBH to AW, 5 July 1817,

LP DD5/II/14; Louisa to RGH, 28 June & RGH to Louisa, 14 Nov. 1817, MS 431; AW to FBH, *op. cit.*

10   AW to FBH, 25 July 1817, LP DD5/II/14; Louisa to RGH, *op. cit.*; AW to Mary Bagot, 14 Dec. 1817 cited Canning 2:63

11   Louisa to RGH *op. cit.*; Marianne to RGH, 26 Aug. 1817, MS 431

12   Marianne to RGH, 19 Nov. 1817, MS 431

13   MC to RGH, 6 Jan. 1818, Louisa to RGH, 25 Sept. 1817, MS 431; Ann Spear to BPB, 7 Apr. 1817, MS 142; Robert Patterson to WP reported by Louisa to RGH *op. cit.*; CCC to Bess, 22 May 1817, MS 220; Louisa to KH, 19 June & MC to KH, 16 Aug. 1818, MS 431; Louisa to MC, 26 Feb. 1819, MS 220

14   Marianne to RGH, 4 Dec. 1818, MS 431; C. Percy to R. Sneyd, Sneyd MSS SC12/5; Bess to RGH, 17 Dec. 1818, MS 431; Ly William Russell to Mary Berry, 22 March 1818, cited Russell 41

CHAPTER 19: EMILY'S RETURN

1   Hodgson 1:368; Emily to KH, 2 Sept. 1817, MS 431

2   RGH to MDH, 25 Jan. & MC to MDH, 24 March 1817, MS 430

3   Emily to RGH, 22 May 1817, MS 431; RGH to MDH *op. cit.*; Emily to RGH, 24 March 1817, MS 431

4   Emily to RGH, 24 Mar, 22 May 1817, MS 431

5   Emily to RGH, 24 March *op. cit.*; P. Newman 1:181; Emily to RGH, 22 May *op. cit.*

6   Emily to CCC, 29 July 1817, MS 220; RGH to MDH, 14 Nov. & Marianne to MDH, 1 Dec. 1817, MS 430; CCC to Harriet Carroll, 21 Feb. 1818, MS 216

CHAPTER 20: UNFULFILLED HOPES

1   Marianne to KH, 19 June 1818, MS 431

2   MC to Bess & Bess to KH, 9 July 1818, & MC to KH, 9 June & 16 Aug. 1818, MS 431

3   MC to RGH, 20 Feb. & to KH, 10 & 15 June 1818, MS 431

4　CCHarper to RGH, 18 Nov., MC to KH, 16 Aug. & Bess to RGH, 6 Sept. 1818, MS 431

5　RGH to RC, 27 Sept. 1818, MC to KH, 15 Aug, & Marianne to RGH, 22 Dec. 1818, MS 431

6　Such as MC to Marianne, Bess & Louisa, 8 July 1829, LP DD5/II/25; MC to KH, 15 June 1818, MS 431

7　MC to KH, 10 June 1818, MS 431

8　Bess to KH, 7 July, Louisa to KH, 25 June, Bess to KH, 19 June 1818, MS 431

9　CCC to Bess, 22 May 1818, MS 220

10　Louisa to KH, 19 June 1818, MS 431; Creevey I:278–9

11　Marianne to RGH, 22 Dec., RGH to RC, 27 Sept. 1818, MC to KH 27 Jan. 1819, MS 431; Wharton 149

12　Selina Fremantle's diary, 9 Jan. 1819; Louisa to KH, 20 Jan. 1819, MS 431

13　Bess to RGH, 1 Feb., Louisa to KH, 11, 16 May, Bess to KH, 4 May 1819, MS 431

14　Selina Fremantle's diary, 4 June 1819; Louisa to RGH, 25 June 1819, 18 Sept. 1818, Bess to KH, 2 March 1819, MS 431

CHAPTER 21: 'PLUNGED IN SORROW'

1　Marianne to RGH, 22 Dec. 1818, MC to RGH & KH, 2 Dec. 1818, MC to KH, 3 May 1819, MS 431

2　John Q. Adams, *Memoirs* 4:382; Cary A. Smith to Peggy Nicholas, 18 June 1819, Wilson Cary Nicholas Papers; MC to RGH, 2 Dec. 1818 & to KH, 2 Jan. 1819, MS 431

3　Louisa to RGH, 16 May, & MC to KH, 2 June, Louisa to KH, 6 July 1819, MS 431; CCC to MC, 19 July 1819, MS 220

4　Louisa to KH, 5 June 1819, MS 431; Irving 'Sketch Book' 75–6

5　Derry 139–41; *The Times*, 19 Aug. 1819; Longford, *State*, 62; Bess to KH, 4 May 1819, MS 431 & *cf* Ly Shelley 2:7–11

6　Buckingham, *The Regency*, 344–5; Selina Fremantle's diary, 17 Sept. 1819

7　Selina Fremantle's diary, 19, 20 Sept. 1819; WHF to Admiral Fremantle, 26 Oct. 1819, D/FR/31/2/52; Selina

Fremantle's diary, 24 Sept. 1918; E. Seton to J. Scott, 18 Apr. 1820, Seton, letters, 284; Selina Fremantle's diary, 25 Sept. 1819

8　WHF to Admiral Fremantle, 26 Oct. 1819, *op. cit.*; Selina Fremantle's diary, 2 Oct. 1819; CC Harper to his parents, 8 Dec. 1819, & Bess to KH, 19 June 1818, MS 431

9　C. Percy to R. Sneyd, Sneyd MSS SC 12/29; Gen. J. Devereux to RGH, 26 Oct. 1819 & Bess to RGH, 8 Jan. 1819, MS 431; WHF to Admiral Fremantle, 26 Oct. 1819, *op. cit.*; Bess to RGH, 8 Jan. 1819, *op. cit.*

10　Ibid; E. J. Lloyd to Louisa, 9 March 1823, LP DD5/11/II/7; WHF to Admiral Fremantle, 26 Oct. 1819, *op. cit.*; Selina Fremantle's diary, 3 Feb. 1820

11　Ilchester, 343; AW to Marianne, 27 Feb. 1820, WF; Gleig 292; AW to Marianne, *op. cit.*

12　Bess to Emily, n.d. *c.* June 1820, LP DD5/11/II/14; CCC to RGH, 22 Apr. 1820, MS 1225; CC Harper to RGH, 8 June 1820, MS 431

13　Bess to RGH, 21 June 1821, MS 431

14　Lieven, *Private Letters* 12, 18; Bess to RGH, 21 June, *op. cit.*

15　Bess to RGH, 27 Oct. 1821, MS 431

16　MC to NC, 15 Oct. 1821, Chase Home Book, MS 969; Ld Wilton to Louisa Lloyd, 20 July 1821, D/DGu/C6/1/23; AW to Pss Lieven, 29 July 1821 cited Arbuthnot 108; Flora Fraser 476

17　MC to NC, *op. cit.*; Villiers 336; Rush 85; MC to NC, *op. cit.*; Emily to RGH, 2 Sept. 1816, MS 431

CHAPTER 22: AFFLICTING CIRCUMSTANCES

1　William McGillivray to John Strachan, 20 July 1821, Strachan Papers, Archives of Ontario; Irving, *Astoria* 1:22–3

2　CCC to RGH, 22 Oct. 1822, MS 1225; RGH to Elizabeth Harper, 3 Nov. 1822, MS 431; Lane-Poole 1:329

3　Will and Estate of Robert Patterson, 'A True and Perfect Inventory', 16 Dec. 1822–12 March 1823, and J. Patterson to Marianne, 19 Dec. 1822, MS 220

4   RGH to Marianne, 7 & 21 Nov. 1822, MS 220; RC to Roger B. Taney, 28 Nov., & R. B. Taney to RC, 5 Dec. 1822, MS 220

5   R. Patterson to RC, 8 Feb. 1821, J. Patterson to Marianne, 9 Dec. 1822, Marianne to J. Patterson, 9 Dec. 1822, R. B. Taney to Marianne, 1 March 1823, MS 220

6   WP to Marianne, 4 Mar, & Marianne to WP, 4 March 1823, & Marianne's note to RGH, n.d. 1823, MS 220; BPB to WP, 12 July 1823, *Letters* 157; BPB's note, 15 Nov. 1835, MS 142; MC to NC, n.d. 1823, Chase Home Book, MS 969

7   MC to NC, 20 July 1823, MS 969; Marianne to WP, 29 March 1824, MS 220

CHAPTER 23: MARIANNE'S RETURN

1   JMT to G. Jackson, 17 May, 12 Apr. 1824, Jackson MSS FO 353/91; MC to NC, 2 July 1824, Chase Home Book MS 969, List of slaves belonging to Emily McTavish, 1832, MS 220

2   JMT to G. Jackson, 9 Aug. 1824, Jackson Papers FO 353/91; Wright 522; Heineman 14; Royall 176

3   *Edinburgh Review*, XXXIII (Jan. 1830) 78-80; *Port Folio*, XXXIII (1819) 495; Adams, *Address*; Perkins 334-5

4   Longford, *State* 86; Col. Greville to Ly C. Greville, n.d., WF; Charles Greville, 18 Sept. 1852, *Memoirs* 6:361-2; Ly C. Greville to C. Greville, n.d., WF; Arbuthnot, *Journal*, 29 Aug. 1822, 1:185; see AW to C. Arbuthnot, 18 May 1820, WF; Abruthnot, *Journal*, 20 Oct. 1825, 1:421

5   Marianne to Mary Butler, 10 Aug. n.d., H. Butler Papers, MS 10304/35/2; 'The Memorial of Lady Hervey', Liverpool Papers, Add. MS 38301 f.193, f.197

6   Marianne to MC, 24 July [1824], LP DD5/11/V/6; Eliza Coke to J. Spencer-Stanhope, 30 & 31 Oct. 1822, Spencer-Stanhope 2:39, 40

7   CCC to Marianne, 18 Nov. 1824, LP DD5/11/IV/3

8   N. P. Dunn, 'An Artist of the Past', *Putnam's Monthly*, vol. 2 (Sept. 1907) 622

9   JMT to G. Jackson, 20 Jan. 1825, Jackson Papers, FO 353/91; Granville, *Letters* 1:323-4

10   Pennington 23-4; W. Irving to W. West, 15 July 1825, W. E. West Papers, AAA Folder Acc no. 57.2, Corcoran Museum of Art

11   JMT to G. Jackson, 13 Jan. 1825, Jackson MSS FO 353/91; CCC to Marianne, 22 Jan. 1825, LP DD5/11/IV/4; JMT to G. Jackson, 6 & 11 Apr. 1825, Jackson MSS FO 353/91; CCC to Bess, 27 Apr. 1825, LP DD5/11/IV/3

12   BPB to WP, 6 May [1824], *Letters* 150; *ibid.*, 11 Dec. [1824], 162; BPB, June 1867, MS 142

CHAPTER 24: HIS DELINQUENCY

1   Hoffman xxvi

2   MC to NC, n.d. Sept. 1825, Chase Home Book MS 969; Binns 1:3; Ly Gower to R. Sneyd, 28 Oct. 1836, Sneyd MSS SC 13/126; Sir Walter Scott to M. Edgeworth, *Letters* IX:190

3   Osborne 1:10; MC to NC, n.d. Aug. 1825, Chase Home Book MS 969

4   Cloncurry 284; Cloake 37

5   Marianne to Col. Merrick Shawe, n.d. [1825], RWP, Add. MS 37315 f.218

6   Marianne to RW, all undated, RWP, Add. MS 37315 f.2801, ff.283-4, f.286, ff.287-9, *ibid.*

7   Bess to W. West, 20 Oct. 1825, W. E. West Papers, AAA; Marianne to RW, n.d., RWP 37315 f.301; JMT to G. Jackson, 13 Nov. 1825, Jackson MSS FO 353/91

8   Marianne to RW, n.d., RWP, Add. Ms 37315 f.291; MC to NC, 20 Dec. 1825, Chase Home Book, MS 969

9   Arbuthnot, *Journal*, 20 Oct. 1825, 1:421

10   Gash 204; Ly Liverpool to Ly Erne, 26 Jan. 1810, cited Ly Wharncliffe 1:171; Harriette Wilson 157-9; AW to W. Wellesley-Pole, 6 Apr. 1810, Webster 30, 31; Ld Galloway to Hon. Arthur Paget, 1 July 1810, Paget 140-3

11 Arbuthnot, *Journal, op. cit.* 421; AW to Marianne, 12 Oct. 1825, WF
12 Marianne to RW, n.d., RWP, Add. MS 37315 f.295; AW to RW, 13 Oct. 1825, RWP, Add. MS 37415 f.78; Marianne to RW, *op. cit.* 37315 f.294
13 Ld Clare to R. Sneyd, 30 Oct. 1825, Sneyd MSS SC5/220; BPB to WP, 23 Jan. 1826, *Letters* 187
14 Iris Butler 23; the following four paragraphs are also drawn from Iris Butler, *The Eldest Brother* 57, 448, 492 *passim*
15 MC to NC, 8 Jan. 1826 & 20 Dec. 1825, Chase Home Book MS 969
16 Marianne to RW, n.d., RWP Add. MS 37315 ff.302–3; 'Marquess Wellesley & Mary Anne Patterson Marriage Agreement' 8 Oct. 1825, VF 47151, MHS
17 RW to George IV, 9 Oct. 1825, RA/GEO/24990–1; Marianne to RW, n.d., RWP Add. MS 37315 f.295; Ld Liverpool to R. Peel, 11 Oct. 1825, Peel Papers 2:378; *Dublin Evening Mail*, 14 Oct. 1825; Ld Liverpool to C. Arbuthnot, 17 Oct. 1825, Arbuthnot Corresp. 81
18 Twiss 2:330; M. K. Bachman, 'Bulwer Lytton's Palham: The Disciplinary Dandy and the Art of Government', *Texas Studies in Literature and Language*, vol. 47, no. 2 (Summer 2005) Parliamentary Papers, 1825, VII:134; Creevey 2:175
19 Cloncurry 328; Ilchester 236
20 Daniel to Mary O'Connell, 18 May 1825, *Correspondence* 3:176; *ibid*, 29 Oct. 1825, 3:193–4
21 Gregory 73–4; H. Goulburn to R. Peel, 2 Oct. 1825, Peel Papers Add. MS 40331 f.184 & *ibid.*, 13 Oct. 1825, f.174; R. Peel to H. Goulburn, 20 Oct. 1825, Add. MS 40331 f.178
22 W. Wellesley-Pole to RW, 14 Oct. 1825, RWP Add. MS 37416 f.183; Jekyll 159; Liverpool to Peel, *op. cit.*; George IV to RW, 20 Oct. 1825, RWP Add. MS 37414 f.50

CHAPTER 25: THE LADY LIEUTENANT

1 H. Goulburn to R. Peel, 16 & 2 Oct. 1825, Peel Papers Add. MS 40331 f.176, f.184
2 MC to NC, 20 Dec. 1825, Chase Home Book MS 969; RW to Archbishop Beresford, 22 & 25 Oct. 1825, PRONI D3279/D/2/2 & 3; *Belfast Newsletter*, 4 Nov. 1825; Marriage certificate, 29 Oct. 1825, LP DD5/11/IV/9
3 Arbuthnot, *Journal* I:423; AW to RP, 3 Nov. 1825, Peel Papers, Add. MS 40331 f.185
4 R. Peel to H. Goulburn, 12 Nov. 1825, Peel Papers, Add. MS 40331 f.187; H. Goulburn to R. Peel, 15 Nov. 1825, Peel Papers, Add. MS 40331 f.211, f.213
5 MC to NC, 20 Dec. 1825, Chase Home Book, MS 969; W. Plunkett to G. Canning, 19 Oct. 1825, Canning Papers, HAR GC 66a; MC to NC, 25 Dec. 1825,; George Montgomery to Ly Elizabeth Herbert, 22 July 1826, Clanwilliam Papers D/3044/G/1/104
6 Ly Morgan to BPB, 13 Jan. 1826, Sydney Lady Morgan Papers; MC to NC, 26 Jan. 1826, Chase Home Book, MS 969; Ly Morgan to BPB, 22 March 1826, *op. cit.*
7 H. Goulburn to R. Peel, 2 Jan. 1826, Peel Papers, Add. MS 40332 f.1; Marianne to AW cited Arbuthnot, *Journal* 2:2; H. Goulburn to R. Peel, *op. cit.*
8 Iris Butler 413, 498; G. Wellesley to R. Wellesley, 10 Oct. 1818, Carver MSS 63; Edward Littleton's diary, 27 July 1819, Hatherton Papers D260; AW to M. Shawe, notes Aug. 1828, WF; Arbuthnot, *Journal* 1:219
9 Arbuthnot, *Journal, c.*11 Jan. 1826, 2:2; Jenkins 143; HG to R. Peel, 27 Jan. 1827, Peel Papers, Add. MS 40332 f.226; R. Peel to Ld Liverpool, 12 July 1826, Liverpool Papers, Add. MS 40305 f.48
10 R. Peel to Julia Peel, 6 Jan. 1826, *Private Letters* 86; R. Peel to H. Goulburn, 6 Jan. 1826, Peel Papers, Add. MS 40332 f.10; AW to R. Peel, 7 Jan. 1826, Goulburn MSS, Surrey History Centre
11 Louisa to Ld Liverpool, 10 Aug. 1826, Liverpool Papers, Add. MS 38475 f.355; Dss of Wellington's journal, 29 Jan. 1811, WF; Ld Liverpool to RW, 19 Aug. 1826, Liverpool Papers, Add. MS 38301

f.65; Farmer 2; R. Wellesley to Henry
Wellesley, n.d., RWP, Add. MS 37315

12   AW to Louisa, 1 Jan. 1826, WF

13   MC to NC, 20 Dec. 1825, *op. cit.*;
Allgor 93, see also *Letters of Sir Walter
Scott*, 29 Nov. [1825], IX:320; CCC
to Marianne, 14 March 1826, LP
DD5/11/V/3; MC to Marianne, 26
Jan. & 16 March 1826, LP
DD5/11/V/25

14   MC to Marianne 16 March, ibid.;
RW to Marianne, 5 Apr. 1827, LP
DD5/11/VII/1; Iris Butler 523–4

15   Louisa to Ld Liverpool, 10 Aug.
1826, Liverpool Papers, Add. MS
38475 ff.352–5

16   AW to M. Shawe, Aug. 1828, WF;
Iris Butler 524; F. Lamb to Ld Fitzroy
Somerset, n.d.[1828], WF; M. Shawe
memo, Aug. 1828, WF; Louisa to Ld
Liverpool, 20 Aug. 1826, *op. cit.*

17   Geoffrey Atwell, 'Wanstead House'
in *Essex Review*, vol. LXIII (1954)
73–8; Longford, *State*:253–4

18   RW to Marianne, 2 Apr. 1827, LP
DD5/11/VII/1; G. Wellesley to R.
Wellesley, 25 Oct. 1827, Carver MSS
63 f.4; Jekyll 170

19   Farington, 8 Apr. 1811, XI:3908; E.
Littleton's diary, Hatherton Papers
D260

20   *Anywhere* 166; CCC to Marianne, 2
Nov. 1827, LP DD5/11/V/33

21   CCC to Marianne, 20 June 1828, MS
220; MC to Marianne, Bess, Louisa,
8 July 1829, LP DD5/11/V/25; CCC
to Marianne, 15 May 1827, LP
DD5/11/V/33; MC to Marianne, 29
July 1831, LP DD5/11/V/ 25; JMT to
G. Jackson, 25 Feb. 1826, Jackson
Papers FO 353/91

CHAPTER 26: UNCERTAIN
FUTURES

1   JMT to George Jackson, 12 Sept.
1825, 22 Oct. & 5 Sept. & 21 Nov.
1826, Jackson Papers FO 353/91

2   CCC to Marianne, 2 Nov. 1827, LP
DD5/11/V/33; *Anywhere* 252; JMT
to G. Jackson, 12 May 1826, Jackson
Papers, FO 353/91

3   *Dictionary of Canadian Biography*
764–5; Denison 1:212; Stanhope
158–9; JMT to G. Jackson, 12 & 20
Jan. 1826, Jackson Papers FO 353/91

4   JMT to G. Jackson, 2 Feb. 1826, *op.
cit.*; Emily Eden to Ld Clarendon,
Clarendon 2:232

5   JMT to G. Jackson, 12 Aug. 1826, 3
Apr. & 6 July 1827, Jackson Papers
FO 353/91

6   CCC to Marianne, 3 Dec. 1827, LP
DD5/11/IV/3

7   CCC to Marianne, 13 Dec. 1825, LP
DD5/11/IV/3

8   *Dublin Evening Mail*, 20 Feb. 1826

9   Marianne to G. Canning, 4 May
1827, G. Canning to Marianne, 6
May 1827, G. Canning to RW, 27
June 1827, Canning Papers
HAR/GC 66a

10   Marianne to R. Wellesley, 18 July 1827,
Carver MSS 63; CCC to Marianne,
27 Feb. 1828, LP DD5/11/IV/9

CHAPTER 27: PERPLEXING POSI-
TIONS: MARIANNE

1   Marianne to R. Wellesley, 18 July
[1827], Carver MSS 63; Marianne to
JMT, 5 July 1827, Jackson Papers FO
353/91; JMT to R. Colt, 26 July &
21 Aug. 1827, MS 202; Marianne to
R. Wellesley, *op. cit.*

2   H. Addington to Charles Vaughan,
14 Jan. 1828, Charles R. Vaughan
Papers, C4/4; Arbuthnot, *Journal*
2:137; W. Holmes, MP cited
Arbuthnot, *Journal* 2:148; *Letters* of
George IV, no. 1436, 3:346;
Arbuthnot *Journal* 2:150

3   M. Prendergast to RW, n.d., RWP
Add. MS 37310 f.268

4   AW to R. Peel, 1 Jan. 1828, *Private
Letters* 26; AW to H. Arbuthnot, 29
Dec. 1827, WF

5   AW to Marianne, 4 & 6 Jan. 1828,
LP DD5/11/V/21; see also Longford,
State 148; ibid 146; Marianne to Jane
Wellesley, n.d., Carver MSS 63

6   Longford, *State* 147; AW to R. Peel,
9 Jan. 1828, WDNS IV:184;
Arbuthnot, *Correspondence* 100

7   Marianne to R. Wellesley, Tues
[1828], Carver MSS 63;
Memoranda, Aug. 1827, RWP Add.
MS 37297 f.371; H. Addington to
C. Vaughan, 14 Jan. 1828, C. R.
Vaughan Papers C4/4; R. Wellesley
to Marianne, 7 Jan. 1828, RWP
Add. MS 37316 f.4

8 Marianne to R. Wellesley, Sunday [Jan. 1828], Carver MSS 63

9 R Wellesley to Marianne, 7 Jan. 1828, *op. cit.*; RW to Marianne, 26 Jan. 1828, LP DD5/VII/2; AW to RW, 3 Feb. 1828, RWP, Add. MS 37415 f.89; Marianne to Jane Wellesley, Wed [1828], Carver MSS 63

10 Fox, *Journal*, 8 March 1824, 274; R. Wellesley to Marianne, 5 Jan. 1828 *op. cit.*

11 Hyacinthe Littleton to R. Wellesley, 1 May 1828, Carver MSS 62

12 Ly Holland, 17 Apr. 1828, 81; CCC to Marianne, 10 June 1828, MS 220; R. Wellesley to RW, 15 June 1828, RWP, Add. MS 37316 f.289; *Hansard*, vol. XIX, 10 June 1828, 1286–7; Arbuthnot, *Journal* 2:198

13 R. Wellesley to Hy Littleton, 7 Nov. 1828, Carver MSS 36/2; Iris Butler 533; Jekyll 240

14 MC to Marianne, 27 July 1831, LP DD5/11/V/25; CCC to Marianne, 13 March 1829, LP DD5/11/IV/3

15 MC to Marianne, *op. cit.*; Ray 50; Thackeray, *Letters* 2:511; Ray 63; HMC, Dropmore Papers, IV:474; WSD VII:279

16 M. Shawe to AW, 10 Aug. 1828, WF; 'Substance of a letter from the Duke of Wellington to Lt Col Shawe relative to Mr Johnston', Aug. 1828, WF

17 M. Shawe to AW, 17 & 29 Sept., 29 Oct. 1828, WF

CHAPTER 28: PERPLEXING POSITIONS: LOUISA

1 CCC to Louisa, 11 June 1828, LP DD5/11/IV/3; WHF to 6th Duke of Leeds, 25 Apr. 1828, Fremantle MSS D/FR/49/3/20

2 FL's diary, 1823, LP DD5/11/III/14

3 Woodham-Smith 8–9; Ly C. Greville to Ly Charles Bentinck, n.d. [1828], Carver MSS 63

4 Ly Bute to R. Sneyd, 10 Dec. 1824 & 14 Nov. 1826, Sneyd MSS SC4/93, SC4/1826; R. Sneyd to Ly Bute, 27 Feb. 1827, *ibid.*, SC4/182

5 Bakewell 10–12

6 C. Bagot to R. Sneyd, 21 Nov. 1822, Sneyd MSS SC3/47; Ly Bute to R.

Sneyd, *op. cit.*; Harriet Granville to D of Devonshire, 22 June 1829, *Letters*, 2:42

7 RW to Marianne, 4 Apr. 1828, LP DD5/11/VII/3; Norman 19, 21; M. Trappes-Lomax 76; CCC to Marianne, 22 July 1817, MS 220; Louisa to RW, n.d. [Apr. 1828], RWP, Add. MS 37310 f.294

8 Selina Fremantle's diary, 10 Apr. 1828; Ld Conyngham to WHF, 12 Apr. 1828, Fremantle MSS D/FR/4/9/35; Louisa to RW & Marianne *op. cit.*

9 RW to Marianne, 24 Apr. 1828, LP DD5/11/VII/2; Selina Fremantle's diary, 24 Apr. 1828

10 Ly Holland 82; H. Addington to C. Vaughan, 23 Apr. 1828, C. R. Vaughan Papers C4/7

11 CCC to Marianne, 16 May 1828, LP DD5/11/V/33; MC to Mrs Carroll, 28 June 1828, Hoffman & Darcy eds. microfilm reel 16, n.2707

12 G. B. Wharton to FL, 31 March–2 Apr., LP DD5/11/III/19 & 3 June 1829, LP DD5/11/V/29; c.f. FL letters in 1830s DD5/11/V/29 *passim*; FL to W. Stephens & Stephens to FL, 15 March 1820, LP DD5/11/III/19

13 C. Percy to R. Sneyd, 18 Oct. 1819, Sneyd MSS SC 12/29; MC to 'all 3', 29 March 1831, DD5/11/V/25

14 Sir C. Campbell to Dss of Wellington, 1 Apr. 1829, WF; Longford, *State* 195

15 Ld Wharncliffe to FL, 19 July 1830, Louisa's 'Paper of estimates made by Ld Carmarthen', 27 Aug, FL to Ld Wharncliffe, 25 Sept., Ld Wharncliffe to FL, 2 Oct., FL to Ld Wharncliffe, 13 Oct., Ld Wharncliffe to FL, 19 Oct., FL to 6th D. of Leeds, 16 Oct., 6th D. of Leeds to FL, 9 Nov. 1830, LP DD5/11/V/29

16 Ly Holland 82; Ly Bedingfeld to Marianne, n.d. [1831], LP DD5/11/V/5

17 Louisa to Marianne & Bess, n.d. [1831], LP DD5/11/V/13

CHAPTER 29: PETTICOAT POLITICS

1 MBS to Jane B. Kirkpatrick, 29 Aug. 1831, MBS Papers, DLC; Allgor 237; Harry L. Watson 91; CCC to A. de

Tocqueville, 5 Nov. 1831, Non-Alphabetical Notebooks 2 & 3, in *Journey*

2 Allgor 237; MBS to J. B. Kirkpatrick, 11 March 1831, cited Allgor 201–2

3 Louis McLane to James Bayard, 19 Feb. 1829, Bayard Papers, DLC; Marszalek, 'Margaret Eaton, The Politics of Gender', ed. Morrison, *Antebellum America* 204, 205; John Q. Adams, *Memoirs* 8:185–6

4 Allgor 205

5 Wallace 30–1, 33–6; Emily to Marianne, 18 March [1831], LP DD5/11/V/25

6 Emily to CMT, 19 Dec. 1834, LP DD5/11/II/2 & 24 Dec. 1929, LP DD5/11/V/14

7 MC to CMT, 23 Apr. 1830, LP DD5/11/IV/2; JMT to CMT, 27 Oct. 1831, LP DD5/11/II/2; Emily to CMT, 4 Nov. & 19 Sept. 1831, LP DD5/11/II/2; MC to CMT, *op. cit.*

8 RW to Marianne, 24 June 1830, LP DD5/11/IV/6

9 Frampton 343; Ld Broughton 4:33; Eden 198

10 Arbuthnot, *Journal* 2:367, 368; RW to Marianne, 2 July 1830, LP DD5/11/VII/4

11 RW to Marianne, 5 July 1830, LP DD5/11/VII/4; Marianne to RW, 5 July 1830, RWP Add. MSS 37316 f9

12 Greville 2:4; Longford, *State* :213; Frampton 366–7

13 Buckingham, *The Regency* 1:39; Leconfield 176; Fitzgerald 2:224–5; Buckingham *op. cit.*; Frampton 371

14 Creevey 2:217; Q. Adelaide to Marianne 3 Oct. n.d., LP DD5/11/II/6; RW to Marianne, n.d. note, LP DD5/11/VII/9

15 RW to Marianne, n.d. note, *op. cit.*; Erskine 23–4; Raikes, 6 Jan. 1833, 1:135–6

16 Ly Wharncliffe 2:171

17 Trollope 263; Creevey 2:217, 248; RW to Marianne, n.d. note, LP DD5/11VII/10

18 MC to daughters, 29 March 1831, LP DD5/11/V/25

19 Emily to Louisa, n.d. 1831, LP DD5/11/II/7; Marszalek, *Petticoat* 124; Benjamin Crowninshield to

Gen. Dearborn, 4 Jan. 1831, Crowninshield Papers, DLC

CHAPTER 30: THE REFORM BILL

1 Butler, *Reform* 58; Flick 17–18; Buckingham, *The Regency* 1:25; Longford 215

2 Hilton 416; Hobsbawm & Rude 15; see Mitford, *Our Village* for the best contemporary account of rural terror, 2:287–91

3 Gordon 104; Greville (Reeve ed.) 2:59–60, 73

4 Lawrance 175; Jaggard 171

5 Le Marchant's diary, Aspinall 298, 310; MC to Marianne, 19–22 March 1831, LP DD5/11/V/25; Creevey 1:225

6 Greville (Reeve) 2:95–6, 228, 235–8 for examples of Ly Lyndhurst's, Ly Harrowby's and Ly Cowper's influence

7 Herries to Ld Ellenborough, 11 Apr. 1831, Aspinall 75; M. Edgeworth to Mrs Edgeworth, 14 March 1831, *Letters* 487

8 XXVII. Memorandum by C. R. Vaughan, 1832, see 'The Papers of Sir Charles Vaughan 1825–1835', ed. John A. Doyle *The American Historical Review*, vol.7, no.3 (Apr. 1902) 530–3

9 *Morning Herald*, 1 Apr. 1831; Ld Grey to Ly Grey cited Butler *Reform* 209–10; *The Times* 9 Apr. & 1 Oct. 1831; Doran 37; clipping n.d. [1831] LP DD5/11/IV/3

10 Broughton 4:138; Brougham 4:107

11 RW to Marianne, 25 Apr. 1831, LP DD5/11/VII/7; AW to H. Arbuthnot, 2 May 1831, WF

12 RW to Marianne, 16 July 1831 LP DD5/11/VII/7; JMT to CMT, 27 Oct. 1831, LP DD5/11/II/2, Marianne to Jane Wellesley, 11 Sept. 1831, Carver MSS 63; Leconfield 198; CCC to Marianne, 12 Sept. 1830, MS 431; RW to Marianne, Friday [1831], LP DD5/11/VII/7

13 James Stuart-Wortley to Ly Wharncliffe, 18 Sept. 1831, Wharncliffe 2:84; AW to Ly Shelley, 24 Sept. & 1 Oct. 1831, Shelley 2:209; RW to Marianne, Saturday [1831], LP DD5/11/VII/7

14 Leconfield 209; *Hansard* 7, 5 Oct. 1831, PD7: 1308; Leconfield 132; Ld Ellenborough's diary, 6 Oct. 1831, Aspinall 142 f3; Ly Holland to Henry Fox, 11 Oct. 1831, Ly Holland 121

15 Bess to Louisa, n.d. [1831] LP DD5/11/IV/7; Leconfield 213; Butler *Reform*, 285, 292, 297

16 Ld Grey's account to Ld Holland, 12 Oct. 1831 Holland 65–6; Ld Grey to William IV, 10 Oct. 1831, see Grey, *Correspondence* 2:372

17 Queen Adelaide's diary, 10 Oct. 1831, transcript, RA Add. 21/7a; cited Ziegler 199; William IV to Ld Grey, Grey, *Correspondence* 1:291

18 Marianne to Louisa, n.d. [1831], LP DD5/11/V/3; Jerningham 376; Queen Adelaide's diary, Oct. 1831, *op. cit.*; Ld Howe to AW, n.d. [24 May 1831], WDNS VII:443

19 Ld Ellenborough's diary, 11 Apr. 1831, Aspinall 76; Dino 1:65; E. Littleton's diary, 20 Nov. 1831, Hatherton MSS D260; Marianne to Louisa, LP DD5/11/VII/21

20 Ld Holland's diary, 14 Oct. 1831, Holland 69; Marianne to Louisa, *op. cit.*; see also the anon. pamphlet *A Secret History of the late Petticoat Plot Against the Liberties of the People by an Officer of Her Majesty's Household* (1832)

21 Leconfield 217; Ld Holland's diary, 20 Oct. 1831, Holland 71; Ly Holland to Henry Fox, 21 Oct. 1831, Ly Holland 123

22 *Morning Chronicle*, 23 Oct. 1831; E. Littleton's diary, 1 Nov. 1831, Hatherton MSS D260; Le Marchant's diary, January 1832, Aspinall 152

23 E. Littleton's diary, 9 Apr. 1832, Aspinall 221; William IV to Ld Grey, Grey, *Correspondence* 2:232; Creevey 2:244

24 Louisa & Car to Marianne, 12 May 1832, LP DD5/11/V/3; Creevey 2:294; Le Marchant's diary, May 1832 Aspinall 258–9

25 Butler *Reform* 394; E. Littleton's diary, 14 May 1832, Aspinall 253; Greville 2:326; RW to Marianne, n.d. [May 1832], LP DD5/11/vii/11

26 Bess to MC, 20 June 1832, MS 220

CHAPTER 31 THE LAST SIGNER

1 Emily to CMT, 19 Sept. 1831, LP DD5/11/II/2; Emily to Louisa, 18 Jan. 1837, LP DD5/11/V/1

2 Hone 1:67; *Baltimore Evening Sun*, 17 Sept. 1990; Macready 1:322; R. Gilmor Jr 'The Diary of Robert Gilmor Jr', 28 Jan. 1827, MHM, vol. XVII, no. 3 (Sept. 1922) 253

3 Margaret Hall 158, 162; CCC to CMT, 18 June 1830, LP DD5/11/II/5

4 RW to CMT, 23 Aug. 1830, LP DD5/11/V/14; JMT to CMT, 28 May 1830, LP DD5/11/V/14

5 Emily to CMT, 24 Dec. 1829, *ibid.*; H. Addington to C. Vaughan, 2 Nov. 1827, Charles Vaughan Papers C4/4

6 Emily to CMT, 23 May 1832 & 4 Nov. 1831, LP DD5/11/II/2; Deposition of Rev. John Chanche, Perine Papers MS 645; Ellen H. Smith 310

7 Diary of Rev. Louis Deluol, 14 Nov. 1832, and I am grateful to Louis Collins of the Carroll Mansion Museum for sending me this; CCC to Marianne, 4 July 1829, LP DD5/11/V/33

8 Hoffman 389; Arfwedson 1:299; *Niles' Weekly Register*, July 1820, cited *Baltimore Evening Sun op. cit.*

9 Rev. Deluol's diary, 17 Nov. 1832, *op. cit.*; Emily to CMT, 23 May 1832, LP DD5/11/II/2

10 J. White to D. Perine, 19 Nov. 1832, cited Perine 'Proceedings on the application for the original will of Charles Carroll of Carrollton', 5 Dec. 1832, f.9, MS 645, box 13; Baltimore County Inventories DMP no. 42, MSA 1833–4; Robert Oliver, Administrator Pendente of Charles Carroll of Carrollton deceased, 'Special Inventory in the City and County of Baltimore', Carroll Family Papers, DLC

11 CCC's Will and codicils, Perine Papers MS 645

12 RW to Marianne, n.d. [1832], LP DD5/11/VII/25; Deposition of Rev. Chanche in Charles Carroll *et al.* vs Emily McTavish, Perine Papers MS 645; Emily to CMT, n.d., LP DD5/11/II/2

13 JMT to CMT, 26 Apr. 1835, LP DD5/11/V/2; Emily to Emily Harper, 29 July 1831, Carroll Family Papers,

DLC; Emily to CMT, 19 Dec. 1831, LP *op. cit.*; John Latrobe, Scrapbook, 'The Breaking the Entail on Doughoregan Manor', Latrobe Family Papers, MS 532, MHS; Emily to D. Perine, n.d. 1840, Perine Papers, MS 645

14 'Faith at Folly Quarter: The Manor House', www.companions ofstanthony.com; Bills and accounts for the building of Emily's mansion at Folly Quarter, 1830–2, Perine Papers MS 645; Warfield 509–16

15 Charles to Emily Harper, 26 Oct. 1835, MS 431; see also Ellen H. Smith's note about 'the jealousies that love of money' bred among the McTavish and Harper branches, in her *Charles Carroll of Carrollton* 304 f.29; Depositions in Charles Carroll *et al., op. cit.*

CHAPTER 32: A LONGED-FOR REUNION

1 RW to Marianne, 13 Aug. 1833, LP DD5/11/VII/14; Ld Holland diary, Holland 243; Queen Adelaide to Marianne, 11 Sept. 1833, RWP, Add. MS 37414

2 Greville, 16 Sept. 1833, 2:415; RW to Marianne, 2 Oct. 1833, *op. cit.*; Ly Shelley 2:249; RW to Marianne, *op. cit.*

3 Greville, 14 Nov. 1833, 2:420; cf E. Littleton's diary, 28 Aug. 1833, Aspinall 318–19; RW to Marianne, 20 Sept. 1832, LP DD5/11/VII/11; Ly Wharncliffe 2:197

4 Marianne to RC, 12 July 1834, & RC to Marianne, 25 Aug. 1834, MS 220; Emily to Anne Woodville, 16 Nov. 1834, Woodville Butler Papers, MS 1264

5 MC to Anne Woodville, n.d. 1834, *op. cit.*

6 MC to CMT, 2 Nov. 1834, LP DD5/11/V/2; MC to Bess, 10 Feb. 1831, LP DD5/11/V/25; MC to Emily, 3 Nov. 1834, LP DD5/11/V/2

7 MC to Marianne, 19 Oct. 1834, LP DD5/11/V/25; JMT to CMT, 20 Dec. 1834, LP DD5/11/V/2; MC to CMT, 28 Nov. 1834, LP DD5/11/V/2

8 Iris Butler 551; RW to Marianne, n.d. 1835, LP DD5/11/VII/16

9 MC to NC, 30 March 1835, Chase Home Book, MS 969; Marianne to RW, n.d. 1834, RWP Add. MS 37310; Marianne to CMT, 21 June 1834, LP DD5/11/V/2

10 MC to Anne Woodville, *op. cit.*; MC to NC, n.d. 1834, Chase Home Book MS 969

CHAPTER 33: LADY SPECULATORS

1 CCC to Bess, 6 Nov. 1826 & 30 Aug. 1828, LP DD5/11/V/3

2 *Anywhere* 52–5

3 Sakolski 30; Chevalier 305

4 Hannah to Lionel & Mayer Rothschild, 13 Nov. 1846, RFam C/1/103 RAL

5 Dickson 268; Chancellor 78–80, 89

6 Mortimer 28; *Annual Register*, 1824

7 Alexander Baring *c.*1825, cited Chancellor 109–10; Arbuthnot *Journal* 1:382

8 David R. Green & Alastair Owens, 'Gentlewomanly Capitalism? Spinsters, widows, and wealth holding in England and Wales, *c.*1800–1860', *Economic History Review*, vol. LVI, no. 3 (2003) 524–5

9 Disraeli, *Endymion*, Chapter XCVI 499; see also Copeland for 'a blessed competence', 23–33; Louisa to Marianne, 28 July 1836, LP DD5/V/13; Thackeray. *Vanity Fair* 87; Lady Hervey, Ledger 58 f.195, 1819, & Mary Anne Patterson, Ledger 88 f.432, 1824, Hoares; Cecil Roth, 'Lady Montefiore's Honeymoon', ed. Lucian Wolf, *Essays in Jewish History* (1934), 243–4

10 Ly Holland to H. Fox, 4 March [1834], 145; Bess to Bates, 10 Oct. 1833, Baring Archives (BB) HC 1.11

11 Carl to Charlotte de Rothschild, March 1839, cited Melanie Aspey, 'Si constante et si sûre': testimonies of Rothschild friendships', The Rothschild Archive, 2005–6, 50

12 Bess to Ly Westmeath, 14 Oct. n.d., HHP; e.g. *The Times*, 2 Apr. 1832

13 J. K. Rutterford & J. Maltby, '"The Nesting Instinct": women and investment risk in a historical context', *Accounting History* (Aug. 2007) 10; Bess to J. Bates, n.d. [1835], BB HC1.11

14 Bess to Lucretia Bates, 1 Apr. 1830, BB HC1.11

15 Chancellor 101; Martineau 1:357; Rush cited Kynaston 1:63; Canning, Address on the King's Message to Portugal', *Hansard*, 12 Dec. 1826, XVI, 390–8; Arbuthnot, *Journal* 1:382; CCC to Marianne, 15 May 1827, MS 220

16 CCC to Bess, 26 Feb. 1828, MS 220; Louisa's ledger, 58 Hoares *passim*; Alex Baring, 'Address to a Latin America bondholders' meeting' 1828, cited Dawson 193

17 Martineau 1:352; Disraeli, *Vivian Grey* 117; Byron, *Don Juan* canto XI verse V

18 Bess to Ly Westmeath & Ly Westmeath to J. Bates, 18 Feb. 1835, BB HC1.11

19 Ziegler, 123; Moran 2:1331

20 CCC to CCH, n.d. 1807, MS 203; Munroe 281–2

21 Emily Eden, 19 Oct. 1829, *Letters* 189; T. W. Ward's diary, 30 Aug. 1841, cited Ziegler 124

22 Bess to J. Bates, n.d. and 2 Feb. and 30 Dec. [1835], BB HC1.11

23 Morier Evans, *The City*, 189–90; Pückler-Muskau 3:45, 59; Gaskell 345 6; Rush 77; Edgeworth 538

24 Schlesinger 219; 'Dividend Day', *All the Year Round*, 11 Nov. 1893, 462–3

25 Bess to J. Bates, n.d. [1832], BB HC1.11; Fox 133; Stone 297; *Westmeath* v *Westmeath*, 1826; Bess to J. Bates *op. cit.*

26 Ziegler 48; Kynaston 1:30

27 Stone 333–4; Anglesey 206; Greville 1:239, 242, 312; clerk Downing St to AW, 17 Apr. 1838, Westmeath MSS HHP

28 Bess to J. Bates, n.d., f BB to Ly Westmeath, 12 Dec. 1832, BB 3 f.280 C8; Clinton 147, I am most grateful to Professor Catherine Clinton for this reference; Bess to J. Bates, 8 Nov. 1832, BB HC1.11; BB to Bess, 12 Dec. 1832, LB3 f.283 & BB to Ly Westmeath, 8–12 Dec. 1832, LB3 f.280, 281, BB

29 Chapman 40; Richard Davis 33; Gray & Aspey 9–11, 20; Hannah Rothschild [HR] to Anthony Rothschild, 1 Aug. 1831, RFam

C/1/133 and HR to Nathan Rothschild [NMR], Tues. c.Sept. 1830, RFam C/1/70, RAL

30 HR to Louisa, 24 Sept. [1830], RFam C/1/80, RAL; Louisa to Marianne & Bess, n.d. 1832, LP DD5/11/V/13

31 Richard Davis 26; NMR will 1836, RAL 000/111; HR to NMR, n.d. [1831] RFam C/1/125, RAL

32 HR to Anthony Rothschild, 11 Aug. 1831, RFam C/1/131, RAL; Louisa's a/c stock ledgers 92f 447, 448 f215, Hoares

33 HR to NMR, 5 Sept. 1831, RFam C/1/136 & n.d. 1831, RFam C/1/129, RAL

34 HR to NMR, 5 Sept. 1831 *op. cit.* & Tues. Sept. n.d., RFam C/1/70, RAL; Bess to J. Bates, 1 Oct. 1833, BB HC1.11

35 Morier Evans, *Fortunes*, 155–65; Raikes 1:275; Bess to J. Bates, n.d. [1834], & Ly Westmeath to J. Bates, 18 Feb. 1835, BB HC1.11; Francis 312–13

36 Kynaston 1:100; Thornbury I:128; J. Bates, 31 May 1835, BB DEP 74; Ziegler 139–40; see E. Penn, 'The Spanish Agents', *The Rothschild Archives Review of the Year* (1999 2000) 15; Bess to J. Bates, n.d. c. 1834 & c.1835, BB HC1.11

37 Bess to W. West, 16 Sept. 1835 & 17 Nov. 1834/4, West Papers 3094; Glyn cited Kynaston 1:103; Wake 149; Louisa's a/c ledger 97 f 447, Hoares; Arbuthnot, *Journal op. cit.*; Stoves 14–16; Chancellor 24–5

38 BPB to Ly Morgan, 14 March 1849, BPB Papers MS 142; WP will 2 July 1835, Vertical File MHS; A. Spear to BPB, c. Feb. 1827, MS 142

39 M. Freeman, R. Pearson & J. Taylor, 'A Doe in the City', *Accounting, Business & Financial History*, vol. 16, no. 2 (July 2006) 265–7; Lisa W. Waciega, 'A "Man of Business": The Widow of Means in Southeastern Pennsylvia 1750–1850', *W & M Quarterly*, Third Series, vol. XLIV (Jan. 1987) 53–4

40 Marianne to W. West, 14 Sept., 2 Aug. 1834 & Bess to West, 12 Sept. 1834, n.d., 16 March 1835, n.d., West Papers 3094; JMT to Louisa *et al.*, 15 July 1835, MS 220

CHAPTER 34:   PLANTAGENET

1 RW to Marianne, Tues nd., 1836, LP DD5/11/VII/25

2 Indentures, Mq of Carmarthen and Ly Hervey, 13–14 Apr. 1834, DLF, box 4; Louisa to Bess, 1 May 1836, LP DD5/11/V/13; Draft Marriage Settlement, Rt Hon. Lord Stafford and Miss Caton, 7 May 1836, LP DD5/11/V/38; Louisa to Marianne & Bess, 26 Aug. & 1 May 1836, LP DD5/11/V/13

3 Cuthbert Fitzherbert, 'Notes on the Jerningham Family' 1–3 Fitzherbert Papers; *Gentleman's Magazine*, July–Dec. 1832, 645; Jerningham 1:184

4 Gordon to MC, Apr. 1836, LP DD5/11/V/25; E. Godefroy to BPB, 8 June 1815, BPB MS 142; Jerningham 1:358; *Gentleman's Magazine*, Nov. 1851, 540; Mr White's statement of Cossey Expenditure, LP DD5/11/III/10; Jerningham 1:95, 167

5 MC to NC, 25 June, 21 [July?] 1836, Chase Home Book, MS 969; Bess to RW, 5 June [1836], RWP Add. MS 37416 ff.300, 301

6 Louisa to Marianne, 28 July 1836, LP DD5/11/V/13; Mortgages Bond Debts Schedule to the Trust Deed of 14 Oct. 1835 for Ld Stafford, LP DD5/11/II/7

7 MC to NC, 21 July 1836, *op. cit.*; M. Fenton to Dr RC, 3 July 1908, Ormerod Papers; Louisa to Marianne & Bess, 5 Sept. 1836, LP DD5/11/V/13

8 Sallie Stevenson to Emily Rutherford, 12 Dec 1836, 14 & 22 Apr. 1837, Stevenson, 50, 53

9 HR to Meyer de Rothschild, 11 Oct. 1836, Rosebery Papers, transcript RAL; J. Bates, journal, 13 Nov. 1836, BB; Kynaston 1:107–8; J. Bates to J. Morrison, 21 May 1837, cited Kynaston 1:109

10 R. Gilmor to Charles Harper, 12 May 1837, Gilmor MSS, MHS

11 Morrison cited Kynaston 1:110; Aytoun Ellis, 49–50; Ld Stafford to E. Jerningham, memo re Bess settlement, 1837, LP DD5/11/V/13

12 E. Littleton's diary, *c.* Jan. 1836, 5 Jan. 1835, 13 March 1837, Hatherton Papers D260

13 *Edinburgh Review*, vol. LXIII (July 1838) 537–59; Iris Butler, 558; Wellesley, *The Wellesley Papers* 2:330–1, 326

14 Ly Holland to Henry Fox, 16 June 1837, 165; Longford, *Victoria* 57; RW to Ld Melbourne, 21 June 1837, RWP Add. MS 37312

CHAPTER 35:   WELL-HOUSED

1 Emily to Louisa, 11 Jan. 1837, LP DD5/11/V/1

2 Stockett 187–8; Rice 59–50; Douglas H. Gordon, 'An Essay on the Three Graces' Baltimore Houses', MHM, vol. 65, no. 3 (1970) 296–300

3 RW to Marianne n.d., LP DD5/11/VII/18 & DD5/11/VII/19; Marianne to RW, n.d. [1838], RWP Add. MS 37316 ff. 272–4; Ly Salisbury's diary, 16 May 1838, HHP; AW to RW, 20 May 1838, (no. 72) WF; RW to Marianne, 1838, LP DD5/11/VII/19; Marianne to RW, n.d., RWP Add. MS 37416 f.426, 427; AW to Marianne, 24 May 1838, RWP Add. MS 37415 f.99

4 Louisa to Marianne, 1 May 1836, LP DD5/11/V/13

5 P. Cherry to R. Sneyd, 19 July 1838, Sneyd MSS S.2874; RW to Marianne, n.d. [1838], LP DD5/11/VII/10; Extract of the Will of the Late George Duke of Leeds, LP DD5/11/II/7; RW to Marianne, n.d., *op. cit.*

6 Sale catalogue of Hornby Castle, 1843, LP DD5/11/IV/9; Messrs Raymond & Rackham to Dow. Dss Charlotte, 6 March 1839, LP DD5/11/V/29; Charles Lane Fox to FL, 6 May 1846, LP DD5/11/V/18

7 M. Fenton, Memoirs, 3 July 1908, Ormerod Papers; Watt 44–5

8 Marianne to RW, Sept. 1838, LP DD5/11/V/18; MC to RW, n.d., LP DD5/11/VII/16

9 RW to Marianne, 1838, LP DD5/11/VII/12

10 Marianne to Rev. Walter Lovi, 11 Dec 1838, BL 6/223/12, SA Papers; Louisa to Rev. Charles Fraser, 1834, BL6 85/17, & Louisa corr. with Rev. Walter Lovi, 11 May 1836 to 1839, & Louisa to Bishop Kyle, 17 May

1836 to March 1839, PL3/282/2, SA Papers

11 Louisa to Bp Kyle, 17 March 1839, SA Papers; Harriet W. Paige, June 1839, 55–6

12 Bp Kyle's Address at Braemar Church, 17 May 1839, SA Papers; Clerk of Works' estimate for Hornby Chapel, LP DD5/11/V/7; Louisa to Marianne, n.d., LP DD5/11/VI/5; Ld Stafford to Bess, 20 Aug. 1839, DLF Papers, box 4

CHAPTER 36: 'TO BE TOGETHER'

1 Emily to Louisa, n.d., LP DD5/11/V/29; J. Bates to T. Ward, 9 Feb. 1841, Ziegler 152; S. J. Ingersoll to Emily, 7 Jan. 1852, LP DD5/11/V/31

2 Morier Evans, *Fortune's Epitome* 234,253; J. Bates to T. Ward, 3 Nov. 1841, Ziegler 152–3

3 Ziegler 153; Sydney Smith to Ly Grey, 9 Sept. 1842, *Letters* 765; Jenks 105; Morier Evans, *Fortune's Epitome* 237

4 Ingersoll, *op. cit.*; Louisa to Marianne, 16 July 1841, LP DD5/11/V/5; Marie Thérèse 337

5 Emily to RW, March 1841, LP DD5/11/V/17

6 Wellesley, *The Wellesley Papers* 2:385; Iris Butler 568; Severn 516

7 RW to Marianne, 20 June 1838, LP DD5/11/VII/20 & n.d., LP DD5/11/VI/19; A. Montgomery to Ld Maryborough, 27 Sept. 1842, Badminton MSS FmO1/11/5–9; Louisa to Marianne, 30 Sept. 1842, LP DD5/11/V/13

8 Ld Maryborough to Ly Anne C. Smith, 28 Sept. 1842, Badminton MSS FmO1/11/5–9; Ernest Law, annotation, RWP Add. MS 37416 f.371

9 Marianne to AW, 29 Sept. 1842, Case E, WF; E. Littleton's diary, 8 Oct. 1842, Hatherton MSS D260

10 Ly Holland to H Fox, 12 Oct. 1842, Ly Holland 203; Louisa to Marianne, 30 Sept, *op. cit.*; AW to Marianne, 2, 4 Feb. 1843, RWP Add. MS 37415 ff.160, 161

11 Louisa to Marianne & Bess, 4 July 1842 & 30 Sept. 1842, LP

DD5/11/V/13; Emily to D Perine, n.d. 1842, Perine Papers MS 645

12 Chancellor 125; Francis 2:139; Preda 211, 212; *The Railway Bell and London Family Newspaper*, 3 Jan. 1846 cited Sarah Hudson, 'Attitudes to Investment Risk among West Midland Canal and Railway Company Investors 1760–1850', Doctoral Dissertation, University of Warwick, 2001; Robb 39

13 Preda 208; Chancellor 185, 138; Francis 2:218–19

14 G. Wharton to Louisa, 3 March 1847, Wharton to FL, 9 Oct. 1844, LP DD5/11/I/5; E. B. Denison, 'Railways part I', *Fraser's Magazine*, 39 (June 1849) 615

15 Louisa's a/c ledgers, 58, 61 Hoares *passim*; Brontë, *Letters* 1:390, 2:264; Ransom 83

16 Edward Jerningham to Bess, 23 Sept. 1845, LP DD5/11/III/10; Robb 37

17 HR to Lionel de Rothschild, 4 May 1843, RFam c/1/30 RAL; Muhlstein 111; Edward Jerningham to Bess, 3 Dec 1844, LP DD5/11/III/10

18 Muhlstein 112, 113; Bates to Ward, 29 Oct. 1845, Ziegler 141

19 Robb 40; Brontë, *Letters* 2:264; Francis 2:195; Kynaston 1:153

20 Ly Holland to H. Fox, n.d. Apr. 1844, 214; Louisa to Marianne, Sept. 1844, LP DD5/11/V/3

21 Louisa to Ld Aberdeen, 1841 & 7 May 1843, Aberdeen Papers Add. MS 43237 ff.216, 24

22 Ly Granville, *Letters* 2:297; Harriet, Dss of Sutherland to R. Sneyd, 12 May 1845, Sneyd MSS SC13/142; Elizabeth Woodville to Rev. E. Butler, 13 Aug. 1845, Woodville Butler Papers MS 1465

23 AW to Marianne, 22 Apr. 1845, RWP Add. MS 37415 f.162; Harriet, Dss of Sutherland to R. Sneyd, *op. cit.*; Ly Carlisle to Marianne, n.d. 1845, LP DD5/11/IV/25

24 Louisa to Marianne & Bess, 4 July 1842, LP DD5/11/VII/3; Registry of Administrations in Baltimore County, May 28 1845; R. Caton's 1st & 2nd Administrations, MSA; J. Jackson, 'Catonsville's God-Father', *The Meteor* June 1845

25 MC to J. Latrobe, 5 Aug. 1834,

Ormerod Papers; Mary Caton's last will, 13 June 1845; Real Estate Book, Division of the Estate of Mary Caton, MS 1541

26 J. Pennington to Marianne, Bess & Louisa, 26 Nov. 1846, 26 Feb. 1847, MS 1229; Bess to David Hoffman, 9 Dec 1846, n.d. 1847 & 17 Feb. 1848, Hoffman Papers, MS 1229; Buchanan to Bess, 13 Sept. 1853, LP DD5/11/III/23; Bess to J. Buchanan, 18 Oct. 1855, 10 Dec 1853, James Buchanan Papers, HSP

27 Louisa to Emily, 23 Jan. 1856, MS 216; Bess to Mrs Hoffman, Thurs. [1847/8], MS 1229; Marianne to R. Rush, 22 Feb. 1848, Richard Rush Papers 0079/32, PUL

28 Louisa to Marianne & Bess, n.d., [1847], & J. Hudson to Louisa, 1 Jan. 1847, LP DD5/11/1/5; excerpt A. Inkson McConnochie, 'The Royal Dee', 1898, 31, Mar Lodge Folder, SA

29 Queen Victoria's Highland Journal [QVHJ], 2 Oct. 1847 & 8 Sept. 1848, 47, 60; Aberdeen Journal, 22, 27 Sept. 1848; QVHJ, 15 Aug. 1849, 68

30 Herman Melville's Journals, c.1849, Notes of refs. 23-11-12, 281

31 Louisa to Marianne and Bess, 23 Nov. 1839, LP DD5/11/V/6; W. Stephens to Marianne, 31 Dec 1848, LP DD5/11/V/21

CHAPTER 37: 'THE DESOLATE STAGE OF AGE'

1 AW to Ly Salisbury, 6 Aug. 1850, cited Longford, State:378; Ld Stafford's will, 20 May 1850, trust settlements, DLF Papers, box 4

2 Emily to Louisa, 17 April 1852, LP DD5/11/1/15; John McTavish will, copy, LP DD5/11/1/18; George H. Hysley to H. Ammon, Montreal, 29 Nov. 1848, Vertical File 'Mactavish' MHS

3 Hibbert 395; AW to Marianne, 14 Feb. 1852, LP DDV/11/VI/5

4 Longford, State, :399–400; Anywhere 164

5 RA, Queen Victoria's Journal, cited Woodham-Smith 397; Hibbert 397; Ly Burghersh 303–5

6 Healey 113; Airlie 2:148; Emily to

Louisa, n.d., 1852, LP DD5/11/V/13; the beliefs of Ly Longford & the D. of Wellington, the Hon. Georgina Stonor and Ann Townsend expressed to the author. The Duke also apparently kept a miniature of Marianne inside the Breuget watch he always wore.

7 Bess to Ly Westmeath, Friday [1853], HHP

8 Bess note re specs c.1852, LP DD5/11/V/6; M. Peregrine to Bess, 26 Nov. 1852, LP DD5/11/V/14;

9 M. Fenton, Memoirs, Feb. 1908, Ormerod Papers; Bess to Ly Westmeath, 18 Dec 1853, HHP

10 Bess to Emily, 26 Dec 1853, MS 220; Bess to Ly Westmeath, 6 Feb. 1854, HHP Marianne's will and probate, PROPB 11; her UK estate was valued at £5,600, NA/IR/26/206

11 Emily to Louisa, 31 Oct. 1854, LP DD5/11/V/1

12 Sr Clare Veronica, 'St Mary's Gunnerside, A Lost R C Church of the Nineteenth Century', SA Papers; C. Blount to FL, 30 Nov. 1857, LP DD5/11/V/19; John, Bp Briggs to Rev. Mother, 4 Jan. 1850, & to Louisa, 6 June 1850, SA Papers

13 Norman 182–3; J. H. Newman 200; Gwynn 134; J. H. Newman, op. cit., 195–6; Anselm Baker, Book of Benefactors, Mount St Bernard donations, SA

14 Bess to Ly Westmeath, 6 Feb. 1854, HHP; Emily to D. Perine, 30 March 1854, MS 645; Catholic Review, 17 March 1972, Baltimore Sun, 15 March 1872

15 FL to Wharton, Memorial for the Opinion of Counsel, 2 Sept. 1850, LP DD5/11/I/3; Bess to Ly .Westmeath, 14 Oct. 1854, HHP

16 Differing accounts of Car's conversion appear in The Times, 6, 10, 18, 20 May 1859, and The Tablet, 4 May 1859; see also under SRCD, Positio: Documentary Study for the Canonization Process of Cornelia Connolly, vol. III, chap. XIX, references, n25, 1421, for Car's being received into the Church by the Rev Henry Manning

17 Louisa to Bp Kyle, 23 Aug. 1859, PL 3/622/7, SA Papers; Wills of 7th

18 Duke of Leeds and probate duty, 4
May 1859, PROPB 11; probate duty,
4 May 1859, NA IR 26/2181 f 647;
Declaration as to Birth of Fanny
Roth, 23 May 1876, Deed of trust
and Annuity papers, DLF box 4

18 Louisa to Dr Kyle, 3 March 1860; PL
3/652/11, SA Papers; C. Connolly to
Louisa, 5 March 1861, HCJ/R
D29:30; Louisa to the Superior of the
Jesuit Fathers, 26 Nov. 1862; Ap
Kendrick to Cornelia Connelly, 3
July 1861, HCJ/R D29:52; see
Positio, vol. II chap. XII. 569–607

19 *The Tablet*, 15 Nov. 1862; *The
Catholic Mirror*, 27 Dec 1862; Louisa
to Emily, n.d., MS 220; Bess left an
estate valued at £18,000 in 1862, NA
IR 26/2348

20 Elinor Buchanan Smith, 'The Gilmor
Family', Gilmor family file, Case A,
Diehlman collections, MHS;
Anywhere 230; Emily MacTavish's
last will and testament, 12 June 1863,
and three codicils, two letters of
wishes, inventories of her estate, petitions etc., Donohue Rare Book
Room, University of San Francisco

21 Moran 2:1093; Sr Ignatia Bridges,
diary, Nov. & 17 Dec. 1862, see
SRCD, Positio vol. XX, notes
D66:5096,; Mother Marie Thérèse
206–7; Positio, vol. II, chap. XX:358

22 Positio XIII:618–24; Marie Thérèse
232, 207; Louisa to Bp Grant, 4 Oct.

1863, Letters Box, SRCD Archives;
Positio, vol. II, chap. XIII: 649 citing
Annals D69:143–5; St Leonards-
Mayfield School, History

23 'List of Family Jewels', & Louisa's
Florentine notebook no. 8, & Bond
of Indemnity to Jewels 1863–8, DLF,
box 4; Louisa to 8th Duke of Leeds,
20 Nov. 1873, & Louisa notes n.d.,
1873, DLF box 4

24 George Ld Carmarthen & Ld Danby
to Louisa, 24 Nov. 1873, DLF, box
4; Louisa's American and British
wills, 1 Dec 1863, 17 Nov. 1866, 6
Dec 1866, 20 Feb. 1867, 6 Aug. 1872,
10 July 1873 & 19 Nov. 1873, DLF,
box 4; her whole estate was valued
at over £1m., Louisa C Dow. Duchess
of Leeds Estate Duty, NA IR 26/2848

25 C. Connolly to Mother Tracey, 10
Apr. 1874, HCJ/R D32:23032; *The
Tablet*, 25 Apr. 1874; *The Hastings &
St Leonards News*, 17 Apr. 1874; *The
Times*, 20 July 1874

26 *The New York Times*, 23 June 1895;
The Yorkshire Gazetteer, Addenda
XVIII:292; Brandon 6; Richard
Davis, W. "'We Are All Americans
Now!"Anglo-American Marriages
in the Later Nineteenth Century',
*Proceedings of the American Philo-
sophical Society*, vol.125, no.1
(March 1991) 144–5; O. Wilde,
'The American Invasion' in *The
Court and Society Review* (1887)

Select Bibliography

MANUSCRIPT SOURCES

England

All Souls College, Oxford
Charles R. Vaughan Papers, the Codrington Library, C4/4

British Library, London [BL]
Aberdeen Papers, Add. MS 43242
Liverpool Papers, Add. MS 38241, 38301, 38475, 40305
Peel Papers, Add. MS 40331, 40332, 40519
Wellesley Papers, Add. MS 37305, 37310, 37311, 37315, 37316, 37415, 37416

Buckinghamshire County Record Office, Aylesbury
Fremantle MSS, D/FR/31

Essex County Record Office, Chelmsford
Family Papers of Sir Eliab Harvey, D/DGu

City of London
The Baring Archive [BB]
The Rothschild Archive [RAL]
C. Hoare & Co. Archives [Hoares] in Fleet Street
HSBC Bank Group Archives (now in Canary Wharf)
Lloyds TSB Group Archives

Hampshire County Record Office, Winchester [HCRO]
Hervey Bathurst Papers, 193M85
Earls of Malmesbury Papers, 9M73

Hartley Institute, University of Southampton
Carver MSS 63
Wellington Papers

Keele University Library, Keele
Sneyd MSS

National Archives, Kew [NA]
Jackson Papers, FO 353/91
Lowry-Cole Papers, PRO 30/43
IR 26, 27: Estate Duty registers
PROB 11: Wills

Southwark Roman Catholic Diocesan Archives, Southwark [SRCD]
Thomas Grant, Bishop of Southwark, Papers
Positio: Documentary Study for the Canonization Process of Cornelia Connelly, 3v

Staffordshire County Record Office
Hatherton Papers, D260

Survey History Centre
Goulburn Papers, 304

The Royal Archives, Windsor [RA]
Lord Wellesley Papers, RA/GEO

West Yorkshire Archives Services, Leeds [WYAS]
Canning Papers Harewood House, HAR/GC

Yorkshire Archaeological Society, Leeds
Duke of Leeds Papers, DD5

The Irish Republic and Northern Ireland
National Library of Ireland, Dublin [NLI]
Sydney, Lady Morgan Papers, MS 10,417

Trinity College Dublin MSS Library, Dublin [TCD]
H. Butler Papers, MS 10304

Public Record Office of Northern Ireland [PRONI]
Beresford Papers, D/3279/D/2
Clanwilliam Papers, D/3044/G/1
De Ros Papers, D638 & MIC 573
Foster Papers, D3618

Wales
National Library of Wales [NLW]
Kentchurch Court Papers

Canada
Library Archives of Canada [LAC]
Selkirk Papers, Addendum vol. A27

Archives of Ontario, Toronto
Strachan Papers

United States
Archives of Georgetown University
Bishop John Carroll Papers, Shea transcripts 31–3

Historical Society of Pennsylvania, Philadelphia [HSP]
James Buchanan Papers
Etting Collection
Rawle Family Papers, 536

Library of Congress, Washington DC [DLC]
James A. Bayard Papers
Carroll Family Papers 1776–1837
Mary Caton Real Estate Record Book, MSS 1541
Benjamin Crowninshield Papers

Sir Augustus Foster Papers, MSS 21139
Thomas H. Hubbard Papers
Fanny Kemble Collection, MS 843
Catharine Mitchell Papers, MS 34819–1
Margaret Bayard Smith Papers, MS 40436
Samuel Smith Family Papers, MS 40469

Library of Virginia, Richmond
Wilson Cary Nicholas Papers, accession no. 24693

Maryland Historical Society,Baltimore [MHS]
Charles Carroll of Carrollton Papers, MS 203, MS 220, MS 1225, MS 216
The Charles Carroll of Carrollton Family Papers, A Microfilm Edition eds. R. Hoffman
    & E. S. Darcy, 41 reels (Annapolis, MD 1985)
Chase Home Book, MS 969
Robert Goodloe Harper Papers, MS 431
Mary D. Harper Papers MS 430
Charles C. Harper Letterbook MS 1029
Hoffman Papers, MS 1229
Howard-Gilmor Papers, MS 2619
Keidel Papers, MS 504.1
Latrobe Family Papers, MS 523
Robert Oliver Papers, MS 626.1
Elizabeth (Betsy) Patterson Bonaparte Papers, MS 142
William Patterson Papers, MS 145
Perine Papers, MS 645
Otto Holland Williams Papers, MS 908
Woodville Butler Papers, MS 1264

Maryland State Archives, Annapolis [MSA]
Baltimore County & City Register of Wills
Ridout Papers, MSA 373

New York Historical Society [NYHS]
Gallatin Papers

New York Public Library [NYPL]
Arents Collection, Ms 50767

Princeton University Library, Princeton [PUL]
Richard Rush Papers MS 0079

Smithsonian Institution, Washington DC
William E. West Papers, Archives of American Art [West]

PRIVATE COLLECTIONS
Badminton MSS, Papers of the Duke of Beaufort
Duchess of Leeds Foundation for Boys and Girls, Enfield [DLF]
Levens MSS, Levens Hall
Ormerod Papers
Proby MSS, Elton Hall
Sisters of the Assumption Papers, Kensington [SAA]
Society of the Holy Child Jesus Provincial Archives, Mayfield [HCJ/M]
Society of the Holy Child Jesus Archives, Rosemount, PA [HCJ/R]
Duke of Wellington Papers, Stratfield Saye [WF]
Westmeath MSS, Hatfield House Papers [HHP]

PRINTED SOURCES
Place of publication for all published material is London, unless otherwise stated

Historical Manuscripts Commission [HMC]
XIII Report *Manuscripts of J.B. Fortescue, Esq. preserved at Dropmore*, vols I-X, 1925

Newspapers and Periodicals
Aberdeen Journal
Baltimore Daily Advertiser
Baltimore Evening Sun
Baltimore Sun
Belfast Newsletter
Catholic Review
Courier
Dublin Evening Mail
Edinburgh Review
Federal Republican
Fraser's Magazine
Gentleman's Magazine
Maryland Gazette
Maryland Historical Magazine [MHM]
Maryland Journal
Morning Chronicle
Morning Herald
New York Times
Niles' Weekly Register
Quarterly Review
Portfolio
The Catholic Mirror
The Meteor
The Tablet
The Times
William & Mary Quarterly

Parliamentary Papers
Hansard's Parliamentary Debates

Books
Adam, Frank, *The Clans, Septs and Regiments of the Scottish Highlands*, 1970 edn.
Adams, Henry B., *History of the United States during the Administrations of Thomas Jefferson*, (Boston, MA) 9v 1889–91
Adams, John Q., *An Address Delivered . . . on the Fourth of July, 1821*, (Washington) 1821
Adams, John Q., *Memoirs of John Quincy Adams*, ed. C. F. Adams, (Philadelphia, PA) 12v 1857–77
Addington, Henry U., 'Youthful America, Selections from Henry Unwin Addington's Residence in the United States of America', ed. Bradford Perkins, *University of California Publications in History*, (Berkeley, CA) vol. 65 1960
Airlie, Mabell, Countess of, *Lady Palmerston and Her Times*, 2v 1922
Albemarle, Earl of, *Fifty Years of My Life*, 2v 1876
Alberts, Robert C., *The Life and Times of William Bingham 1752–1804*, (Boston, MA) 1969
Alderson, Frederick, *The Inland Resorts and Spas of Britain*, (Newton Abbot) 1973
Allgor, Catherine, *Parlor Politics*, (Charlottesville, Va) 2000
Allgor, Catherine, *A Perfect Union* (New York) 2006
Alsop, George, *A Character of the Province of Maryland,1666*, rev. edn. (Ohio)1902
Anglesey, Marquess of, *One-Leg, The Life and Letters of Henry Paget, First Marquess of Anglesey 1768–1854*, 1961

Anon., *Letters from Albion to a Friend on the Continent*, 2v 1814

Anthony, Carl S., *First Ladies: The Saga of the Presidents' Wives and their Power 1790–1981*, (New York) 1990

Anywhere So Long As There Be Freedom, exhibition and cat. by Ann Van Devanter (Baltimore Museum of Art, Baltimore, MD) 1975

Arbuthnot Charles 'The Correspondence of Charles Arbuthnot', Royal Historical Society, Camden Third Series vol LXV (1944)

Arbuthnot, Harriet, *The Journal of Mrs Arbuthnot 1820–1832*, ed. F. Bamford and 7th Duke of Wellington, 2v 1950

Arfwedson, C. F., *The United States and Canada in 1832,1833 and 1834*, 2v 1834

Arthur, Catherine Rogers & Cindy Kelly, *Homewood House*, (Johns Hopkins University Press, Baltimore, MD) 2004

Ashton, John, *Social England under the Regency*, 2v 1899

Aspinall, A. ed. *Three Early Nineteenth Century Diaries*, 1952 [Denis Le Marchant; Lord Ellenborough; Edward Littleton]

Austen, Jane, *Jane Austen's Letters*, ed. R. W. Chapman, (Oxford) 2v 1952

Austen, Jane, *Northanger Abbey*, (Penguin, Harmondsworth) 1995

Bagot, Mary, 'Exile in Yankeeland: the Journal of Mary Bagot', ed. David Hosford, *Records of the Columbia Historical Society of Washington D.C.* vol. 51, 1951–2

Bakewell, M. and M., *Augusta Leigh* (Pimlico), 2002

Baldwin, S. B., *Life and Letters of Simeon Baldwin*, (New Haven, CT) 1919

Bayard, Ferdinand, *Travels of a Frenchman in Maryland and Virginia*, ed. Ben C. McCary (Ann Arbor, MI) 1950

Berry, Mary, *Journal and Correspondence of Miss Berry 1783–1852*, ed. Ly Theresa Lewis 3v 1865

Binns, Jonathan, *The Miseries and Beauties of Ireland*, 2v 1837

Blassingame, John, *The Slave Community* (NY) 1972

Bohner, Charles H. *John Pendleton Kennedy*, (Baltimore, MD) 1961

Bonaparte, Elizabeth P. [BPB], *The Life and Letters of Madame Bonaparte* [cited as *Letters*], ed. Eugene L. Didier 1879

Boswell, James, *The Journal of a Tour to the Hebrides with Samuel Johnson LL.D* (1785), ed. R. A. Chapman (Oxford) 1984

Bovill, E. W., *English Country Life 1780–1830*, (Oxford) 1963

Bowne, Eliza Southgate, *A Girl's Life Eighty Years Ago*, 1888

Brady, Patricia ed., *George Washington's Beautiful Nelly: the letters of Eleanor Parke Custis Lewis to Elizabeth Bordley Gibson 1794–1851*, (Columbia, SC) 1991

Brandon, Ruth, *The Dollar Princesses*, 1986

Breck, Samuel, *Reminiscences*, (Philadelphia, PA) 1862

Brontë, Charlotte, *The Letters of Charlotte Brontë*, ed. Margaret Smith, (Oxford) 3v 1995

Brooks, Geraldine, *Dames and Daughters of the Young Republic*, (NY) 1901

Brooks, V. Wyck, *The World of Washington Irving*, (NY) 1944

Brougham, Henry, Lord, *Works of Henry Lord Brougham*, v3–5 'Statesmen' 1872–3

Broughton, John Cam Hobhouse, Lord, *Recollections of a Long Life*, ed. Lady Dorchester, 6v 1909–11

Brown Jr, Marvin, *Baroness von Riedesel and the American Revolution*, (Chapel Hill, NC) 1965

Browne, Gary L., *Baltimore in the Nation*, (Chapel Hill, NC) 1980

Browne, William H. *et.al.* eds., *Archives of Maryland* vi (Baltimore) 1883

Bryan, Helen, *Martha Washington*, (New York) 2002

Bryant, Sir Arthur, *The Age of Elegance, 1812–1822*, 1955

Buckingham, 2nd Duke of, *Memoirs of the Court of England during the Regency 1811–1820*, 2v 1856

Buckingham, 2nd Duke of, *Memoirs of the Courts and Cabinets of William IV and Queen Victoria*, 1861

Burghersh, Priscilla, *The Correspondence of Lady Burghersh with the Duke of Wellington*, ed. Lady Rose Weigall 1903

Burnett, T. A. J., *The Rise and Fall of a Regency Dandy*, 1981
Butler, Iris, *The Eldest Brother*, 1973
Butler, J. R. M., *The Passing of the Great Reform Bill*, 1914
Calhoun, Arthur W., *A Social History of the American Family*, (Cleveland, OH) 2v 1918
Calvert, the Hon. Mrs, *An Irish Beauty of the Regency*, ed. Mrs Warrenne Blake 1911
Calvert, Rosalie Stier, *Mistress of Riversdale, the Plantation Letters of Rosalie S. Calvert 1795–1821*, ed. Margaret L. Callcott (Johns Hopkins Univ. Press, Baltimore, MD) 1991
Campbell, Rev. Robert, *History of St Gabriel's Church*, (Montreal) 1887
Canning, *George Canning and His Friends*, ed. Josceline Bagot, 2v 1909
Capel, Caroline, *The Capel Letters 1814–1817*, ed. the Marquess of Anglesey 1955
Carpenter, J. C., 'Doughoregen Manor' in *Appleton's Journal*, vol. XII no. 287, 19 July 1874
Carroll, John, *The John Carroll Papers*, ed. Thomas O'Brien Hanley, (University of Notre Dame Press, Notre Dame, IN) 2v 1926
Carrolls of Belle Vue, 'In Search of the Carrolls of Belle Vue', Robert F. McNamara, MHM vol. 5 no.1 (Spring 1985)
Cassell, Frank A., *Merchant Congressman in a Young Republic*, (Univ. of Wisconsin) 1972
Cassell, Frank A. 'The Great Baltimore Riot of 1812', MHM vol 70 (–1975) Fall
Chancellor, Edward, *Devil Take the Hindmost: A History of Financial Speculation*, 1999
Chapman, Stanley, *The Rise of Merchant Banking*, 1984
Chevalier, Michael, *Society, Manners and Politics in the United States, Being a Series of Letters on North America*, (Boston) MA 1839
Childs, Frances S., *French Refugee Life in the United States 1790–1800*, 1940
Chorley, Henry F. et al., *Personal Reminiscences*, ed. R. H. Stoddard 1875
Clarendon, George, 4th Earl of, *Life and Letters of George William 4th Earl of Clarendon*, ed. Sir Herbert Maxwell, 2v 1913
Clinton, Catherine, *Fanny Kemble's Civil Wars*, 2000
Cloake, Margaret M., ed., *A Persian at the Court of King George 1809–10*, 1988
Cloncurry, Baron, *Personal Recollections of the Life and Times of Valentine Lord Cloncurry* (Dublin) 1849
Coke, Thomas, *Coke of Norfolk and His Friends*, ed. A. M. W. Stirling, 2v 1908
Copeland, Edward, *Women Writing About Money*, (Cambridge) 1995
Crawford, Mary C., *Romantic Days in the Early Republic*, 1913
Creevey, Thomas, *The Creevey Papers*, 2v ed. Sir Herbert Maxwell 1904
Cresson, W. P., *James Monroe*, (Chapel Hill, NC) 1946
Cresswell, N., *The Journal of Nicholas Cresswell*, (Northwood, MA) 1924
Crowninshield, Mary B., *Letters of Mary Boardman Crowninshield 1815–16*, ed. Frances Boardman Crowninshield (Cambridge, MA) 1935
Davidson, Carolina V., 'Maximilien and Eliza Godefroy', MHM, vol. XXIX (March 1934)
Davis, R. B. ed., *Jeffersonian America: Notes on the United States of America by Augustus Foster*, (San Marino, CA) 1954
Davis, Richard, *The English Rothschilds*, 1983
Davis, Robert Jr, 'Pell-Mell: Jeffersonian Etiquette and Protocol' in *The New American Nation*, ed. Peter S. Onuf 1991
Dawson, Frank G., *The First Latin American Debt Crisis*, (Yale Univ. Press, New Haven, CT) 1990
de Boigne, Adele, *Mémoires de la Comtesse de Boigne*, ed. M. C. Nicoullard, 3v 1907–8
Denison, Merrill, *Canada's First Bank, a History of the Bank of Montreal*, (Toronto) 2v 1966
Derry, John, *Politics in the Age of Fox, Pitt and Liverpool*, 2001
de Tocqueville, Alexis, *Journey to America*, trans. G Lawrence, ed. J. P. Mayer 1959
Dickson, P. G. M., *The Financial Revolution in England: A Study in the Development of Public Credit 1688–1756*, 1967

Didier, Eugene cf. Bonaparte

Dino, Duchess of, *Memoirs of the Duchesse de Dino*, 3v 1909

Disraeli, Benjamin, *Endymion*, 1880

Disraeli, Benjamin, *Vivian Grey*, 1859

Donovan, Grace E., 'An American Catholic in Victorian England: Louisa Duchess of Leeds, and the Carroll Family Benefice', MHM, vol. 84 (Fall 1989)

Donovan, Grace E., 'The Caton Sisters: The Carrolls of Carrollton Two Generations Later', *The US Catholic Historian*, vol. 5, nos. 3 & 4 (1986)

Doran, Dr, *Memoir of Queen Adelaide*, 1861

Eddis, William, *Letters from America, historical and descriptive, 1769–1777*, 1792

Eden, Emily, *Miss Eden's Letters*, ed. Violet Dickinson 1919

Edgar, Mathilda, Lady, *A Colonial Governor in Maryland*, 1912

Edgecumbe, Richard, ed., *The Diary of Frances, Lady Shelley 1787–1873*, 2v 1912

Edgeworth, Maria, *Letters from England 1813–1844*, ed. Christina Colvin (Oxford) 1971

Ellenborough, Lord, see Aspinall

Ellet, Elizabeth, *The Court Circles of the Republic*, (Hartford, CT) 1869

Ellis, Aytoun, *Heirs of Adventure: The Story of Brown Shipley & Co 1810–1860*, 1960

Ellis, Joseph J., *Founding Brothers*, (NY) 2002

Erickson, Carolly, *Our Tempestuous Day*, 1996

Erskine, Mrs Stuart, *Twenty Years at Court*, 1916

Farington, Joseph, *The Diary of Joseph Farington*, ed. Kathryn Cave, (Yale Univ. Press, New Haven, CT) 19v 1878–84

Farmer, Hugh, *A Regency Elopement*, 1969

Fitzgerald, Percy, *The Life and Times of William IV*, 2v 1884

Fitzpatrick, John C., ed., *The Writings of George Washington*, (Washington, DC) 39v, 1931–9

Flick, Carlos, *The Birmingham Political Union and the Movements for Reform in Britain 1830–1839*, (Hamden, CT) 1978

Foster, Augustus, *Jeffersonian America: Notes on the United States of America*, ed. R. B. Davis (San Marino, CA) 1974

Fox, Henry, *Journal of the Hon. Henry Edward Fox, 4th and last Lord Holland, 1818–1830*, ed. Lord Ilchester 1923

Fox-Genovese, Elizabeth, *Within the Plantation Household*, (Chapel Hill, NC) 1986

Frampton, Mary, *The Journal of Mary Frampton*, ed. Harriet G. Mundy 1885

Francis, John, *Chronicles and Characters of the Stock Exchange*, 2v 1855

Fraser, Flora, *The Unruly Queen*, 1997

Fraser, Sir William, *Words on Wellington*, 1899

Fremantle, Anne, ed., *The Wynne Diaries 1789–1820*, (Oxford) 3v 1935–40

Gash, N., *Lord Liverpool*, 1984

Gaskell, Elizabeth, *The Life of Charlotte Brontë* (Penguin, Harmondsworth) 1975

Geggus, David, *Slavery, War and Revolution*, (Oxford) 1982

George IV, *The Letters of George IV*, ed. A. Aspinall, (Cambridge) 3v 1938

Gilmor Jr, Robert, 'Diary of Robert Gilmor Jr', MHM, vol. XVII, nos. 3 & 4 (Sept., Dec 1922)

Gilpin, Henry, 'A Glimpse of Baltimore Society', MHM, vol. 69, no. 3 (1974)

Gleig, G. R., *The Life of Arthur Duke of Wellington*, 1904

Glenbervie, Lord, *The Diaries of Sylvester Douglas (Lord Glenbervie)*, ed. Francis Bickley 2v 1928

Gordon, Sir Arthur, *The Earl of Aberdeen*, 1893

Granville, Harriet, *A Second Self, The Letters of Harriet Granville 1810–45*, ed. Virginia Surtees (Salisbury, Wilts) 1991

Granville, Harriet, *The Letters of Harriet, Countess of Granville 1810–1845* [cited as Granville, *Letters*], ed. the Hon. F. Leveson Gower, 2v 1894

Grattan, T. C., *Civilized America*, 2v 1859

Gray, Victor & Melanie Aspey, *The Life and Times of N. M. Rothschild 1777–1836*, priv. pr. 1998

Green, Constance M., *Washington, a History of the Capital 1800–1950*, (Princeton, NJ) 1962

Gregory, Lady ed., *Mr Gregory's Letter-Box*, (Gerrards Court) 1961

Greville, Charles, *The Greville Memoirs 1817–1860*, eds L. Strachey & R. Fulford 8v 1938 & ed. Henry Reeve, 3v 1888

Grey, Earl, *The Correspondence of Charles 2nd Earl Grey with William IV and Sir Herbert Taylor*, ed. Henry 3rd Earl Grey, 2v 1867

Gronow, R. H., *The Reminiscences and Recollections of Captain Gronow*, 1964

Gurn, Joseph, *Charles Carroll of Carrollton 1737–1832*, (New York) 1932

Gwynn, Denis, *The Second Spring, A Study of the Catholic Revival in England*, 1942

Hall, Basil, *Travels in North America*, 2v 1828

Hall, Margaret, *The Aristocratic Journey, being the Outspoken Letters of Mrs Basil Hall*, ed. Una Pope-Hennessy (New York) 1931

Hanna, Charles A., *The Wilderness Trail*, (Baltimore, MD) 2v 1911

Hartridge, Walter C., 'The Refugees from the Island of St Domingo in Maryland.' MHM vol 96 no 4 (Winter 2002)

Hawthorne, Nathaniel, *The English Note-Books*, ed. R Stewart (New York) 1941

Hazen, C.D., *Contemporary Opinion of the French Revolution*, (Baltimore) 1897

Healey, Edna, *Lady Unknown:The Life and Times of Angela Burdett-Coutts*, 1978

Heineman, Helen, *Restless Angels*, (Ohio) 1983

Henry, Nancy, '"Ladies Do It?": Victorian Women Investors in Fact and Fiction', in Francis O'Gorman, ed., *Victorian Literature and Finance*, 2007

Hibbert, Christopher, *Wellington, A Personal History*, 1997

Hill, Constance, *Maria Edgeworth and Her Circle*, 1910

Hilton, Boyd, *A Mad Bad & Dangerous People*, (Oxford) 2006

Historical Marker Database, www.hmdb.org

Hobsbawm, E. J. & George Rude, *Captain Swing*, 1969

Hodgson, Adam, *Letters from North America*, 2v 1824

Hoffman, Ronald, *Princes of Ireland, Planters of Maryland*, (Chapel Hill, NC) 2000

Hoffman, Ronald & Albert, Peter J., *Women in the Age of the American Revolution*, (Charlottesville, VA) 1989

Holland, Lady, *Lady Holland to her Son*, ed. Earl of Ilchester 1946

Holland, Lord, *The Holland House Diaries*, ed. A. D. Kreigel 1975

Hone, Philip, *The Diary of Philip Hone*, ed. B. Tuckerman, (New York) 2v 1889

Hook, Andrew, *Scotland and America: a Study of Cultural Relations 1750–1835*, (Glasgow) 1975

Howe, M. A. De Wolfe, ed., *The Articulate Sisters*, (Cambridge, MA) 1946

Howitt, William, *The Rural Life of England*, 2v 1829

Hudson, Marianne, *Almack's*, 3v 1826

Hughes, Robert, *American Visions*, 1997

Hunt, Gaillard, *The First Hundred Years of Washington Society*, (New York) 1906

Hunter, James, *A Dance Called America*, (Edinburgh) 1994

Hurd, Charles, *Washington Cavalcade*, (New York) 1948

Ilchester, the Earl of, *The Home of the Hollands 1650–1820*, 1937

Isaacson, Walter, *Benjamin Franklin: An American Life*, (New York) 2003

Irving, Washington, *Astoria, or an Enterprise beyond the Rocky Mountains*, 3v 1836

Irving, Washington, *The Sketch Book of Geoffrey Crayon*, (New York) 1849

Jackson, Andrew, *The Correspondence of Andrew Jackson*, ed. J. S. Bassett, (Washington, DC) 7v 1926–35

Jackson, D. & Twobig, D., eds., *The Diaries of George Washington 1748–1799* (Charlottesville, VA) 6 vols 1976–79, see American Memory Collections, www.memory.loc.gov

Jackson, George, *The Bath Archives*, ed. Ly Jackson, 2v 1873

Jaggard, Edwin, *Cornwall Politics in the Age of Reform*, (Suffolk) 1999

James, C. L. R., *The Black Jacobins*, 1938

Jefferson, Thomas, *The Works of Thomas Jefferson*, ed. Paul L. Ford (New York) 1905

Jekyll, Joseph, *Correspondence of Mr Jekyll with his sister-in-law Lady G Sloane Stanley 1818–1838*, ed. Hon. Algernon Bourke 1894
Jenkins, Brian, *Henry Goulburn*, (Liverpool) 1996
Jenks, Leland, *The Migration of British Capital 1875*, 1927
Jerningham, Lady, *The Jerningham Letters*, ed. Egerton Castle, 2v 1896
Johnson, Dr Samuel, *A Journey to the Western Islands of Scotland* [1775], ed. R. W. Chapman (Oxford) 1984
Jones, Harriet Winchester, 'A Childhood at Clynmalira' in MHM, vol. 51 no. 2 (June 1956)
Jones, Howard M., *America and French Culture 1750–1848*, (Chapel Hill, NC) 1927
Jones, Katharine M., *The Plantation South*, (New York) 1957
Kalm, Pehr, *Travels into North America*, 1749
Keidel, George C., *The Catonsville Lutheran Church*, (Washington DC) 1919 priv. pr.
Kelley, Mary, *Learning to Stand and Speak: Women, Education and Public Life in America's Republic*, (Chapel Hill, N.C.) 2006
Kemble, Frances Anne, *A Residence on a Georgian Plantation in 1838–1839*, ed. John A. Scott (Univ of Georgia Press, Athens, Georgia) 1984
Kennedy, John Pendleton, *At Home and Abroad*, (Baltimore, MD) 1872
Kerber, Linda K., *Women of the Republic*, (Chapel Hill, NC) 1997
Kulikoff, Allan, 'The Beginnings of the Afro-American Family in Maryland' in *Law, Society and Politics in Early Maryland*, eds Aubrey C. Land, Lois C. Green and Edward C. Papenfuse (Baltimore, MD) 1977
Kynaston, David, *The City of London*, 4v 1994–2001
Lamb, Charles and Mary Lamb, *The Works of Charles and Mary Lamb*, ed. E. V. Lucas 12 v 1905
Lane-Poole, S., *The Life of Rt Hon. Stratford Canning, Viscount Stratford de Redcliffe*, 2v 1883
Latimer, Jon, *1812 War with America* (Belknap Press of Harvard Univ. Press, Cambridge, MA) 2007
Latrobe, Charles J, *The Rambler in North America* (1835)
Lawrance, W .T., *Parliamentary Representation of Cornwall*, (Truro) 1925
Lawson, Alan B., *A Country Called Stratherrick*, (Inverness) 1987
Leconfield, Maud, Lady, *Three Howard Sisters*, 1955
Lees-Milne, James, *The Bachelor Duke*, 1991
Le Marchent, Denis, see Aspinall
Lennox, Lord William, *Fifty Years of Biographical Reminiscences*, 2v 1863
Lennox, Lord William, *Three Years with the Duke of Wellington in Private Life* (1853)
Leonard, Lewis A., *The Life of Charles Carroll of Carrollton*, (New York) 1918
Lester, Malcolm, *Anthony Merry Redivivus*, (Charlottesville, VA) 1978
Leventhal, Fred M. & Roland Quinault, eds, *Anglo-American Attitudes*, (Aldershot) 2000
Lewis, Jan, 'The Republican Wife', *William & Mary Quarterly*, 3rd Series vol. XLIV (Oct, 1987)
Lewis, Robert E. 'Brooklandwood, Baltimore County', MHM, vol. XLIII, no. 4 (Dec. 1948)
Lieven, Princess, *The Private Letters of Princess Lieven to Prince Metternich 1820–1826*, ed. Peter Quennell 1937
Liston, Henrietta, 'A Diplomat's Wife in Philadelphia: Letters of Henrietta Liston, 1796–1800', ed. Bradford Perkins in *William & Mary Quarterly*, 3rd Series, vol. II, issue 4 (Oct. 1954)
Little, George, *Life on the Ocean; or, Twenty Years at Sea*, (Boston, MA) 1843
Littleton, Edward, Baron Hatherton, see Aspinall
Lloyd, Alan, *The Scorching of Washington*, 1975
Longford, Elizabeth, *Victoria R.I.*, 1998
Longford, Elizabeth, *Wellington: Years of the Sword*, 1969
Longford, Elizabeth, *Wellington: Pillar of State*, 1972

Low, Betty-Bright P., 'Of Muslins & Merveilleuses', *Winterthur Portfolio* 9 (1974)
Low, Betty-Bright P., 'The Youth of 1812', *Winterthur Portfolio* 11 (1976)
Lowry Cole, Galbraith, *Memoirs of Sir Galbraith Lowry Cole*, eds Maud Cole & Stephen Gwynn 1934
Macartney, Clarence E. and Gordon Dorrance, *The Bonapartes in America*, (Philadelphia, PA) 1939
Macready, William Charles, *Macready's Reminiscences*, ed. Sir F. Pollock Bt 2v 1875
Malcolm-Smith, E. F., *The Life of Stratfield Canning*, 1933
Mansel, Philip, *Paris Between Empires 1814–1852*, 2001
Marie Thérèse, Mother, *Cornelia Connelly, A Study in Fidelity*, 1961
Marszalek, John F., *The Petticoat Affair: Manners, Mutiny and Sex in Andrew Jackson's White House*. (Louisiana State University Press) 1999
Marszalek, John F., 'Margaret Eaton, The Politics of Gender' in Michael Morrison, ed., *The Human Condition in Antebellum America*, (Washington, DC) 2000
Martineau, Harriet, *The History of England during the Thirty Years' Peace*, 2v 1848
Mason, Sally, 'Mama, Rachel, and Molly', in R. Hoffman & P. J. Albert eds, *Women in the Age of the Revolution*, (Charlottesville, VA) 1989
McCullough, David, *John Adams*, 2001
McMaster, John B., *A History of the People of the United States*, 2v 1886
Melville, Annabelle M., *John Carroll of Baltimore*, (New York) 1955
Melville, Annabelle M., *Louis William Du Bourg*, (Chicago) 2v 1986
Merck F., ed. *Fur Trade and Empire* (Harvard Univ. Press) 1931
Mitford, M. R., *Our Village*, 2v 1839
Moore, Thomas, *The Journal of Thomas Moore*, ed. Wilfred S. Dowden (NJ) 1986
Moran, B., *The Journal of Benjamin Moran*, eds S. A. Wallace & F. E. Gillespie, (Chicago) 2v 1848–9
Morgan, Sydney, Ly, *Passages from my Autobiography*, 1859
Morier Evans, David, *Fortune's Epitome of the Stocks and Public Funds*, 1850
Morier Evans, David, *The City; or The Physiology of London Business*, 1845
Mortimer, Thomas, *Every Man His Own Broker; or, A Guide to Exchange-Alley*, 1761
Morton, A. S., *A History of the Canadian West to 1870*, (Toronto UP) 1973
Muhlenfield, Elizabeth, *Mary Boykin Chesnut, A Biography*, (Louisiana State Univ. Press) 1981
Muhlstein, Anka, *Baron James: The Rise of the French Rothschilds*, 1983
Munroe, John, *Louis McLane, Federalist and Jacksonian*, (New Brunswick, NJ) 1973
Murray, Elizabeth H., *One Hundred Years Ago*, (Washington DC) 1895
Murray, Venetia, *High Society in the Regency Period 1788–1830*, (Penguin) 1999
Newman, John Henry, *Sermons Preached on Various Occasions*, 1857
Newman, Peter C, *Caesars of the Wilderness*, (New York) 2v 1987
Norgate, T. B., *The History of Costessey*, priv. pr. 1972
Norman, Edward, *The English Catholic Church in the Nineteenth Century*, (Oxford) 1984
Norris, Walter B., *Annapolis: its colonial and naval story*, (New York) 1925
Norton, Mary Beth, *Liberty's Daughters*, (Boston, MA) 1980
O'Connell, Daniel, *The Correspondence of Daniel O'Connell*, ed. Maurice O'Connell, (Dublin) 8v 1972–80
Officer, Lawrence H., www.measuringworth.com
O'Gorman, Francis, ed., *Victorian Literature and Finance*, 2007
Osborne, Lady, *Memorials of the Life and Character of Lady Osborne*, ed. Catherine Bernal-Osborne, (Dublin) 2v 1870
Paget, Sir Arthur, *The Paget Brothers 1790–1840*, ed. Lord Hylton 1918
Paige, Harriet White, *Diary of Harriet White Paige*, ed. Edward Gray (Boston MA) 1917
Pakenham, Simona, *Cheltenham A Biography*, 1971
Palmerston, Emily, Viscountess, *The Letters of Lady Palmerston*, ed. Tresham Lever 1957
Papenfuse, Edward, *In Pursuit of Profit*, (Johns Hopkins Univ. Press, Baltimore, MD) 1975
Paston, G. & Peter Quennell, *To Lord Byron*, 1959

Peel, Sir Robert, *The Private Letters of Sir Robert Peel*, ed. George Peel 1920

Pennington, Estill C., 'William E West 1788–1857, Kentucky Painter', exhibition and cat. (National Portrait Gallery, Washington, DC.) 1985

Perkins, Bradford, *Castlereagh and Adams, England and the United States 1812–1823*, (Univ. of California Press, Berkeley and Los Angeles) 1964

Preda, Alex, 'The Rise of the Popular Investor: Financial Knowledge and Investing in England and France, 1840–1880', *The Sociological Quarterly*, vol. 42 no. 2

Preston, William C., *The Reminiscences of William C. Preston*, ed. M. C. Yarborough (Chapel Hill, NC) 1993

Pückler-Muskau, Prince, *Pückler's Progress: The Adventures of Prince Pückler-Muskau in England, Wales and Ireland as Told in Letters to his Former Wife*, 1987

Quincy, Josiah, *Figures of the Past From the Leaves of Old Journals*, (Boston, MA) 1883

Quynn, Dorothy M., 'Maximilien and Eliza Godefroy', MHM, vol. 52 no. 1 (1957)

Quynn, Dorothy M. and Frank F. Wright Jr, 'Jerome and Betsy Cross the Atlantic', MHM, vol. 4 n. 3 (1953)

Raikes, Thomas, *A Portion of the Journal kept by T. Raikes, Esq.*, 2v 1856

Ransom, P. J., *The Victorian Railway and How It Evolved*, 1990

Ray, Gordon N., *The Buried Life*, 1961

Redemptorist a Father, *History of the Redemptorists at Annapolis from 1853–1903*, (Annapolis) 2009

Rice, Laura, *Maryland History in Prints 1743–1900* (Maryland Historical Society) 2002

Risjord, Norman K., *Builders of Annapolis* (Baltimore, MD) 1997

Robb, George, *White Collar Crime in Modern England*, (Cambridge) 1992

Robin, Abbé, *New Travels through North-America* (Philadelphia) 1784

Rogers, Samuel, *Recollections*, 1859

Roscoe, W., *An Inquiry into the Insurrection of the Negroes on the Isle of St Domingo*, 1792

Rowland, Kate Mason, *The Life of Charles Carroll of Carrollton 1737–1832, with His Correspondence and Public Papers*, (New York) 2v 1898

Rowland, Peter, *The Life and Times of Thomas Day 1748–1789*, (Lewiston, New York) 1996

Royall, Anne (A Traveller), *Sketches of History, Life and Manners* (priv. pr.) 1826

Rudolph, Friederick, ed., *Essays in Education in the Early Republic* (Cambridge, MA) 1965

Rush, Richard, *Residence at the Court of London*, ed. Benjamin Rush 1872

Russell, Ld William, *Lord William Russell and His Wife*, ed. Georgiana Blakiston 1972

Sack, James J., *The Grenvillites 1801–29*, (Urbana, IL) 1979

Saffell, William T. R., *The Bonaparte-Patterson Marriage in 1803*, (Philadelphia, PA) 1873

Saint Jean de Crèvecoeur, J. A., *Letters from an American Farmer*, 1912

Sakolski, A. M., *The Great American Land Bubble*, (New York) 1932

Sandham, Alfred, *Ville Marie, or Sketches of Montreal*, 1870

Scharf, J., *Chronicles of Baltimore*, (Baltimore, MD) 1874

Schlesinger, Max, *Sauntering in and about London*, 1853

Schopenhauer, Johanna, *A Lady Travels: journeys in England and Scotland from the diaries of Johanna Schopenhauer*, eds R. Michaelis-Jena & W. Merson 1988

Scott, Sir Walter, *The Letters of Sir Walter Scott*, ed. Sir Herbert Grierson 12v 1932–7

Searle, Muriel, *Spas and Watering Places*, (Tunbridge Wells) 1977

Semmes, John E., *John H. B. Latrobe and His Times, 1803–1891*, (Baltimore, MD) 1917

Sergeant, Philip W., *The Burlesque Napoleon*, 1905

Seton, Elizabeth, *Letters of Mother Seton to Mrs Juliana Scott*, ed. Joseph B. Code (New York) 1960

Severn, John, *Architects of Empire, The Duke of Wellington and His Brothers* (University of Oklahoma Press, Norman, OK) 2007

Shea, John G., *The Life and Times of the Most Revd John Carroll, Bishop and Archbishop of Baltimore . . .* (Baltimore, MD) 1888

Shelley, Frances, *The Diary of Frances Lady Shelley*, ed. Richard Edgecumbe, 2v 1912
Simond, Louis, *An American in Regency England*, 1968
Skaggs, David C., 'Editorial Policies of the *Maryland Gazette*, 1765–1783', *Maryland Historical Magazine*, vol. 59 (1964)
Smith, Ellen Hart, *Charles Carroll of Carrollton*, (Cambridge, MA) 1942
Smith, Margaret Bayard [cited as MBS], *The First Forty Years of Washington Society*, ed. G. Hunt 1906
Smith, Paul H. *et al.* eds, *Letters of Delegates to Congress, 1774–1789*, vol. I–VIII (Washington, DC) 1976–81
Smith, Sydney, *Letters of Sydney Smith*, ed. C. Nowell Smith (Oxford) 1953
Southey, Robert, *Selections from the Letters of R. Southey*, ed. John W. Warter, 1856
Spencer-Stanhope, Elizabeth, *The Letter Bag of Lady Elizabeth Spencer-Stanhope*, ed. A. M. W. Stirling, 2v 1913
Spiller, Robert E., *The American in England*, (New York) 1926
Stanhope, Philip Henry, 5th Earl, *Notes of Conversations with the Duke of Wellington 1831–51*, (Oxford) repr. 1947
Stevens, William O., *Annapolis*, (New York) 1937
Stevenson, Sallie, *Victoria, Albert & Mrs Stevenson*, ed. E. Boykin 1957
Stirling, A. M. W., *A Painter of Dreams, and Other Biographical Studies*, 1916
Stirling, A. M. W., *Coke of Norfolk and His Friends*, 1908
Stockett, Letitia, *Baltimore, A Not Too Serious History*, (Baltimore, MD) 1928, 1997 edn.
Stone, Lawrence, *Broken Lives*, (Oxford) 1993
Stoves, John F., *A History of the Baltimore & Ohio Railroad*, (Baltimore, MD) 1995
Stuart, Dorothy M., *Dearest Bess: The Life and Times of Lady Elizabeth Foster afterwards Duchess of Devonshire*, 1955
Sultana, Donald, *From Abbotsford to Paris and Back: Sir Walter Scott's Journey of 1815*, (Stroud) 1993
Tayloe, Benjamin Ogle, see Watson, Winslow M.
Thackeray, William, *Letters of William Thackeray to Mrs Brookfield*, 2v 1911
Thackeray, William, *Vanity Fair*, (Penguin, Harmondsworth) 1968
Thomas, Dawn F., *The Green Spring Valley, Its History and Heritage*, (Baltimore, MD) 2v 1978
Thomas, Keith, *Man and the Natural World*, (Penguin, Harmondsworth) 1984
Thornbury, W., *Old and New London*, 2v 1878
Thornton, Anna M., 'Diary of Mrs William Thornton 1800–1863' in *Records of the Columbia Historical Society*, Washington DC, 10 (1907)
Ticknor, George, *The Life, Letters and Journals of George Ticknor*, ed. G. S. Hillard, 2v 1876
Trappes-Lomax, M., *Pugin, a Medieval Victorian*, 1932
Trappes-Lomax, Richard, 'Records of the English Canonesses of the Holy Sepulchre at Liege' in *Publications of the Catholic Records Society*, 17 (1915)
Tripp, Susan Gerwe, *Homewood* (Johns Hopkins Univ. Press, Baltimore, MD) nd
Trollope, Frances, *Domestic Life of the Americans* (1974 ed. Folio Society)
Twiss, H., *Life of Lord Chancellor Eldon*, 3v 1844
Villiers, Marjorie, *The Grand Whiggery*, 1939
Wake, Jehanne, *Kleinwort Benson, a History of Two Families in Banking*, (Oxford) 1998
Wallace, W. Stewart, *The Pedlars from Quebec*, (Toronto) 1954
Waln Jr, Robert, *The Hermit in Philadelphia*, (Philadelphia, MA) 1821
Warfield, Joshua D., *Founders of Anne Arundel and Howard Counties* (Baltimore, MD) 1967
Warner, C. D., *Washington Irving* (American Men of Letters Series), 1881
Warren, Charles, *The Supreme Court in United States History*, 2v (Boston) 1922
Washington, George, *Writings*, see Fitzpatrick, ed.
Watson, Harry L., *Liberty and Power: The Politics of Jacksonian America*, (New York) 1990
Watson, Winslow M., *In Memoriam: Benjamin Ogle Tayloe*, (Washington, DC) 1872
Watt, Christian, *The Christian Watt Papers*, ed. David Fraser 1983

Wecter, Dixon, *The Saga of American Society*, (New York) 1937

Wellesley, the Marquess, *The Wellesley Papers; the Life and Correspondence of Richard Colley, Marquess Wellesley 1760–1842*, by the Editor of 'The Windham Papers', 2v 1914

Wellington, Arthur, 1st Duke of, *Supplementary Despatches, Correspondence and Memoranda of Field Marshal Arthur Duke of Wellington 1794–1818* [cited as WSD] ed. his son 15v 1858–72

Wellington, Arthur, 1st Duke of, 'Some Letters of the Duke of Wellington to His Brother', Professor Sir Charles Webster, Camden Miscellany vol. XVIII, Third Series vol LXXIX 1948

Wellington, Arthur, 1st Duke of, *Despatches, Correspondence and Memoranda of Arthur Duke of Wellington (New Series) 1819–1832* [cited as WDNS], ed. his son 8v 1867–80

Wharncliffe, Lady, *The First Lady Wharncliffe and Her Family 1779–1856*, eds Caroline Grosvenor & Charles Beilby, Lord Stuart of Wortley, 2v 1927

Wharton, Anne Hollingsworth, *Salons Colonial and Republican*, 1900

Wharton, Anne Hollingsworth, *Social Life in the Early Republic*, 1902

White, Charles I., *The Life of Mrs Eliza A. Seton*, (New York) 1853

Whyte, Donald, *Dictionary of Scottish Emigrants to the USA*, (Baltimore) 2v 1986

Wiencek, Henry, *Virginia and the Capital Region*, (New York) 1998

Willard, Emma, *Journals and Letters from France and Great Britain*, 1833

Williams, Eric, *From Columbus to Castro: a History of the Caribbean*, 1970

Williams, Gomer, *History of the Liverpool Privateers*, 1897

Williams Wynn, Ly, *Correspondence of Charlotte Grenville Lady Williams Wynn*, ed. Rachel Leighton 1920

Willis, Nathanial P., *The Pencillings of the Way*, 3v 1942

Wills, Gary, *Cincinnati, George Washington and the Enlightenment* (New York) 1984

Willson, Beckles, *Friendly Relations*, 1934

Willson, Beckles, *America's Ambassadors to England*, 1938

Wilson, Harriette, *Memoirs*, ed. Lesley Blanck 2003

Woloch, Nancy, *Women and the American Experience*, 1994

Wood, Gordon, 'The Ghost of Manticello' in Jan Lewes and Peter Onuf eds., *Sally Hemings and Thomas Jefferson: History, Memory and Civil Culture* (University of Virginia Press, Va) 1999

Wood, Gordon S., *The American Revolution*, 2005 edn

Woodham-Smith, *Queen Victoria, Her Life and Times*, v.1 1972 [v2 never written]

Woodham-Smith, C., *The Reason Why*, 1953

Wright, Frances [An Englishwoman], *Views of Society and Manners in America*, 1821

Wright, Louis B. and Marion Tingling, eds., *Quebec to Carolina in 1785–6*, (San Marino, CA) 1943

Ziegler, Philip, *The Sixth Great Power, Barings 1762–1929*, 1988

Ziegler, Philip, *William IV*, 1971

Index